THE NEW KINGDOM OF GRANADA

THE
NEW KINGDOM
OF GRANADA

The Making and Unmaking of
Spain's Atlantic Empire

SANTIAGO MUÑOZ-ARBELÁEZ

Duke University Press   *Durham and London*   2025

Project Editor: Michael Trudeau
Designed by David Rainey
Typeset in Portrait Text and Zuumi by Westchester Publishing Services

Library of Congress Cataloging-in-Publication Data
Names: Muñoz Arbeláez, Santiago, author.
Title: The New Kingdom of Granada : the making and unmaking of
Spain's Atlantic empire / Santiago Muñoz-Arbeláez.
Description: Durham : Duke University Press, 2025. | Includes
bibliographical references and index.
Identifiers: LCCN 2024033260 (print)
LCCN 2024033261 (ebook)
ISBN 9781478031840 (paperback)
ISBN 9781478028611 (hardcover)
ISBN 9781478060802 (ebook)
Subjects: LCSH: New Granada. Viceroy. | New Granada. Real Audiencia. |
Indigenous peoples—Colonization—Colombia. | Spain—Territorial
expansion—History. | Spain—Colonies—America. | Spain—Politics and
government—18th century. | Colombia—History—To 1810.
Classification: LCC F2272 .M87 2025 (print) | LCC F2272 (ebook) |
DDC 986.1/0200497—dc23/eng/20250220
LC record available at https://lccn.loc.gov/2024033260
LC ebook record available at https://lccn.loc.gov/2024033261

Cover art: Painted manta. British Museum, Department Africa,
Oceania and the Americas, Am1842,1112.3.

Para María Clara y Alberto

CONTENTS

A NOTE ON TERMINOLOGY

Colonialism partly consists of a flawed vocabulary to speak of non-European societies. The Spanish established a rigid taxonomy that encompassed and simplified Indigenous societies for legal and administrative convenience. All Native societies of the Americas could be called *indios,* a term that re-created medieval imaginaries of the peoples living on the other side of the world, while their leaders were deemed *caciques,* which the Spanish took from the Caribbean and applied indiscriminately to refer to Indigenous authorities throughout the continent. *Indio* was often accompanied by other adjectives, like *amigo* (friend or ally), *caribe* (cannibal, enemy), *de paz* or *de guerra* (of peace or of war, depending on whether they were waging war against the Spanish), *ladino* (meaning "latinized," referring to someone who speaks Spanish), *bozal* (someone who does not speak Spanish), or even *útil* (useful). Those adjectives frequently clarified their relationship to and status vis-à-vis the empire. Some of that blunt colonial vocabulary survives today in terms like *Indians, natives, tribes,* and *chief.*

I use the terms *Indigenous* and *Native* to refer to the many peoples and ethnic groups aboriginal to the Americas. By contrast, *"indio"* refers to the demeaning colonial imaginary and stereotype that pigeonholed Indigenous peoples into a common term and assigned them a legal identity. *Indigenous* and *Native* will be capitalized, just like *Spanish, Iberian,* and *European,* which refer to the peoples aboriginal to Spain, Iberia, and Europe. In translated quotes from primary sources, I keep the original terms in Spanish to refer to Indigenous peoples (often *indio* or *naturales,* along with qualifying adjectives).

I use *New Kingdom of Granada* and *New Kingdom* as synonyms, for convenience; both were common expressions in the sixteenth century. In contrast, I avoid using *New Granada,* which became prevalent in the eighteenth century after the establishment of the Viceroyalty of New Granada (first established in 1717 and then reestablished in 1739).

FIGURE 1.1. The New Kingdom of Granada, sixteenth century. Map by Santiago Muñoz-Arbeláez, based on Herrera Angel, "Poblamiento," 68.

INTRODUCTION

A Kingdom in the Mountains

This book is an ethnography of the building of empire in a place where the odds were stacked against it. In the early sixteenth century, the mountainous landscapes of what is today central Colombia—a remarkably diverse site that extended over three different Andean ranges and was delimited by the Caribbean Sea, the Pacific Ocean, and the rainforests of the Amazon and Orinoco river valleys—were inhabited by myriad ethnic groups with different cultural backgrounds who spoke hundreds of different languages (figure I.1). They were roughly divided between the Muisca peoples of the high plateau of the eastern Andean range, where power was tied to kinship, and the lowlands, occupied by peoples of Carib and other linguistic families, where leadership was gained through strength in battle. After the Spanish invasion in the 1530s, conquistadors named these lands the New Kingdom of Granada—el Nuevo Reino, the New Kingdom.[1] Until then, Indigenous inhabitants had no label to define the area as a whole; rather, they conceived of their identities and territories at smaller geographic and political scales. By introducing this term, officials set out to remake those diverse Indigenous areas into a "kingdom"—a centralized political entity that, paradoxically, did not have a king of its own but was rather an appendage of the Spanish monarchy. In the century that followed, roughly between 1530 and 1630, a range of people from Indigenous, European, and mixed backgrounds designed and co-produced an administrative schema to incorporate that ethnically diverse and politically decentralized network of Indigenous groups into the Hispanic monarchy under a unified political and economic structure. The result was a distinctive political system in the Iberian Atlantic. *The New Kingdom of Granada* is the history of the making of that kingdom, both as a political ideal, one that people could debate, praise, and condemn, and as an infrastructure of governance—a spatial system that regulated the movement of people, information, and things.

The book traces the consolidation of this early modern political system as it strove to transform Indigenous lives and landscapes from the 1530s, when Spaniards first arrived in this area, to 1630, when the kingdom culminated a long-awaited expansion. I argue that after a painstaking, century-long process, an unstable kingdom was woven into the contentious geographies of the northern Andes through the often tense and violent intercultural interaction between peoples of Indigenous and European descent. Between the 1530s and 1550s, imperial officials installed an infrastructure of governance both grounded on and modifying the Muiscas' organizational logic: a system of cities, villages for "indios," and encomiendas—grants of Indigenous labor—that absorbed Indigenous ethnic divisions into the monarchy's institutional framework and installed a system of managing justice through flows of paper in which letters connected vassals to the king.

Santa Fe de Bogotá, the kingdom's capital, was located far from the coast and deep in the eastern mountain range in Muisca territory. Control was much harder to achieve in the lowlands, where emerging Indigenous political projects challenged the kingdom's sovereignty and its capacity to communicate to other imperial centers like Quito, Lima, or Seville. These lands were mastered by peoples like the Pijaos, who developed a thriving anticolonial project in the Magdalena River valley and the central Andean range. By the 1570s, these competing political visions had pushed the kingdom near collapse. Political advocacy at the royal court by Indigenous intellectual and leader Don Diego de la Torre, who personally delivered two maps and a report with advice for good government to King Philip II, paved the way for major reform in the governance structure of the kingdom in the late 1580s, which paradoxically led to further loss of Indigenous autonomy. During a final juncture between 1590 and 1630, newly arrived kingdom officials made the genocide of the Pijaos a governmental priority and envisioned transforming the lowlands into thriving mines by introducing enslaved people from Africa and experimenting with novel techniques to police the most intimate dimensions of Indigenous minds and bodies (their sexuality, customs, and thought), reallocate their homelands as property, and make their labor available for purchase by settlers. By the mid-seventeenth century, the kingdom functioned as a political and economic unit that extended from the highlands to the lowlands.

The New Kingdom of Granada reveals what empire-making looked like in a zone where there were no previous models of political centralization. Much of what we know about the Spanish empire is modeled on the cases of the viceroyalties of New Spain (Mexico) and Peru, where colonial governance and territories built on infrastructures developed by the Mexica and Inca empires, respectively. The officials of the Spanish empire reproduced Indigenous power structures and relied heavily on Nahuatl and Quechua as "general languages," re-creating imperial geographies of power that looked like the preexisting Indigenous empires—often with the same centers and borderlands.[2] In contrast, the New Kingdom was a new scale of governance built on a site of decentralization, where there was no common language or encompassing governance systems, and in a place that crosscuts the spatial categories we have traditionally used to make sense of colonial Latin American history (the Andes, the Caribbean, the Amazon). Colonial officials frequently classified the New Kingdom as the "third" kingdom because, while it trailed the viceroyalties of Mexico and Peru in wealth and importance, they saw potential for great profit in the combination of its highland populations and lowland mines.

The history of this polity poses deep questions about the nature and technologies of early modern Spanish imperial power, about Indigenous participation in and contestation of imperial rule, and about the creation of geographies of rule and dissidence. Throughout the book, I lay out the techniques of Spanish imperial power and the ways in which Indigenous peoples participated in, disrupted, and negotiated the making of the kingdom. I reveal what it meant for many Indigenous people to suddenly become the vassals of a king who lived across the Atlantic—whom they heard about but never really met—and I study their appeals for freedom and justice, as well as how they intervened in politics, even disputing the very nature of imperial rule.

Colonizing Downhill

From its inception, the New Kingdom had a specific geographic projection, with its epicenters of power up in the cold highlands of the Andes, aiming to spread downward into the hot lowlands, especially into the Magdalena River valley. In an equatorial region, with wet and dry seasons rather than a four-season cycle, altitude created notable geographic contrasts.[3] Societies with different forms of social, economic, and political organization inhabited the cold highlands of the Andes and the warm river valleys and coastlands. A people who called each other Muiscas (meaning "people") inhabited the high plateau of the eastern range of the Andes, making it the most densely settled area. They were organized politically in cacicazgos (chiefdoms) and had an active industry of producing cotton textiles, salt, ceramics, and objects worked in gold, as well as agricultural products like maize and tubers.[4] Peoples from the Carib linguistic family, like the Panches, Muzos, Coyaimas, and many others, lived in the neighboring Magdalena River valley and the central Andean range. They produced cotton and gold, among other products, which they traded with the peoples of the highlands for textiles and salt. These groups had a flexible understanding of politics, as individual leaders often gained followers through success in war and prophetic messages.[5] Despite their differences and clashes, the peoples of the highlands and lowlands kept close economic ties, but they did so without a centralizing power and in a very diverse cultural and ethnic landscape, to the extent that some anthropologists and archaeologists believe their organizational logic was designed to prevent the concentration of power and development of state structures.[6]

Throughout the sixteenth and seventeenth centuries, the empire's officials used a lexicon of heat to describe the kingdom. They called the highland plateaus of the eastern mountain range tierra fría, or cold land, while they referred to the lowland, inter-Andean river valleys as tierra caliente, or hot land. The officials conceptualized the highlands and lowlands as separate worlds. The earliest definition of the kingdom came in the first account of the conquest. It stated: "The New Kingdom is all flat land closed in by peaks and mountains and by a nation of indios called Panches, who eat human flesh, different from those of the New Kingdom who do not, and their lands are different because those of the Panches are hot and the New Kingdom is cold or at least temperate."[7] For the earliest conquistadors, the kingdom consisted of the cold areas occupied by the Muisca, surrounded by peoples they could not control. For centuries, settlers and officials complained that the Spanish empire in the northern Andes looked like a cold island, a kingdom in the mountains encircled by Indigenous rebels and insurmountable geographic obstacles. Juan de Castellanos, the author of the longest poem ever written in the Spanish language, an elegy for conquistadors, wrote that the kingdom was like a "cloister," a "box surrounded and defended by a rugged terrain."[8] In the mid-sixteenth century, a Spanish settler added that the problem was not only geographic but also ethnographic: the "kingdom [is] enclosed in the mountains by warlike natural indios."[9]

The political backbone of the kingdom was the Audiencia of Santa Fe, a judicial tribunal in charge of government and representing the Spanish king's authority, which gave the kingdom an amorphous, irregular geographic character. The audiencia was installed in 1547 in Bogotá, the political heart of the cipa, the highest level of Muisca authority. During the entire sixteenth century, Indigenous peoples called the audiencia magistrates cipas, revealing the overlap of Indigenous and European politics. While the Iberian Peninsula was divided into sixteen kingdoms, principalities, and manors, the Crown expected the audiencia to govern a territory four times the size of the entire Peninsula, spanning some of the planet's most diverse environmental regions. The audiencia combined two different jurisdictions: the smaller governorship of the New Kingdom of Granada and the broader district of the court, which included three governorships (Santa Marta, Popayán, and the New Kingdom of Granada) and four bishoprics (Quito, Santa Fe, Santa Marta, and Popayán). In this sense, the New Kingdom was not the audiencia's sole district but rather a compact governorship within the audiencia's broader jurisdiction. However, the audiencia was responsible for the administration of the governorship of the New Kingdom of Granada and oversaw the surrounding governorships.[10]

The dense Muisca settlements of the cold plateaus—with predominantly textile and agrarian economies—contrasted with the hot river valleys, which were rich in gold and silver but whose peoples were deemed backward. If cold was a synonym for the kingdom and the setting of the empire's headquarters, hot implied the unruly—the kingdom's opposite, a land of behetría. *Behetría* was a derogatory term used to describe the attitudes of those peoples who, rather than blindly following a lord or cacique, only accepted temporary rulers. In the first dictionary of the Spanish language, Sebastián de Covarrubias devoted an entire page to the concept, using a series of historical examples to illustrate it. He explained that in old Castile, some towns had the odd custom of changing rulers as they pleased until 1309, when King Alonso XI revoked those liberties and started collecting royal tributes. Covarrubias assured readers that history proved that the freedom to pick and change lords brought confusion and chaos to government. Although some had argued that the term *behetría* had its origins in Arabic and Hebrew, Covarrubias pondered whether the concept had derived from the old Castilian term *herria*, which meant "confusion," "mess," and "mixture."[11] Behetría meant the absence of unquestioned compliance with rules and authorities. The imperial officials often used the term to describe lowland peoples. According to them, the peoples of the hot lands had "no lords or caciques" and they "obeyed nobody."[12] The officials also referred to them as bárbaros, peoples who did not know any form of authority.[13] In the hot lands, imperial dreams and metaphors were inverted. Hot became synonymous with places where Native sovereignties emerged to challenge imperial rule and where European empires acted from a position of weakness and fear.

With its headquarters high in the eastern Andean range, far away from the ports of the Caribbean and the Pacific, the audiencia depended on internal transportation arteries that ran through rivers and crossed mountains, deserts, and rainforests to reach other imperial centers in the Indies and the Iberian Peninsula. The Magdalena River endured for centuries as the kingdom's primary artery to ports in the Caribbean Sea. Every single letter, decree, or piece of cargo that reached the heights of the audiencia moved upriver by human force, then traveled on the backs of Indigenous cargueros (porters). The boga system, in which people of Indigenous and African descent propelled these boats upriver, was a painful, muscular means of labor extraction. Indigenous Atlantic traveler Don Diego de la Torre wrote in the 1580s that this system had consumed all Indigenous peoples of the Magdalena River Valley. During the sixteenth century, the roads were usually inadequate for horses to traverse. Instead, travelers walked or, more often, rode on the shoulders of Indigenous cargueros.

Perched on the plateaus of the eastern Andean range, the kingdom was weakest along its avenues of communication. As a cold island that thrived in the heights of the Andes, its capacity to enforce its power diminished precipitously along the winding, precarious paths that connected the audiencia not only to Seville and Madrid but also to Popayán, Quito, and Lima. Throughout the sixteenth century, imperial officials wrote that the Magdalena River was plagued by Indigenous bandits who stole merchandise from travelers. The hazardous path to Peru that crossed the central range, the most irregular in its topography, was often called the "impenetrable mountain": it had steep drops, snowy peaks, and the highest precipices of the three ranges (figure I.2). There, Spaniards risked not only having their merchandise stolen but also being taken captive by the powerful Pijaos.

This topography of rule of a colonial administrative center unable to climb down the mountains was atypical in relation to other imperial spaces. Legal historian Lauren Benton has shown that early modern empires did not cover space evenly but rather spread their tentacles irregularly across oceans, rivers, islands, jungles, hills, and mountains. These polities were porous, uneven, and "stitched together out of pieces." Benton argues that while rivers and sea lanes created corridors that connected commercial networks, the verticality of hills and mountains interrupted circulation, causing early modern agents of empire to see them as "legally archaic places, and as zones of primitive sovereignty."[14] The idea of mountains as places of limited state rule has

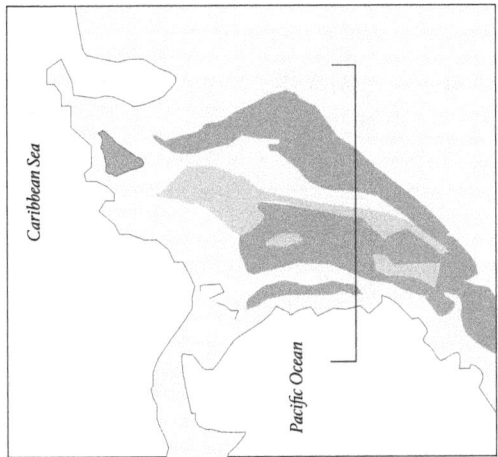

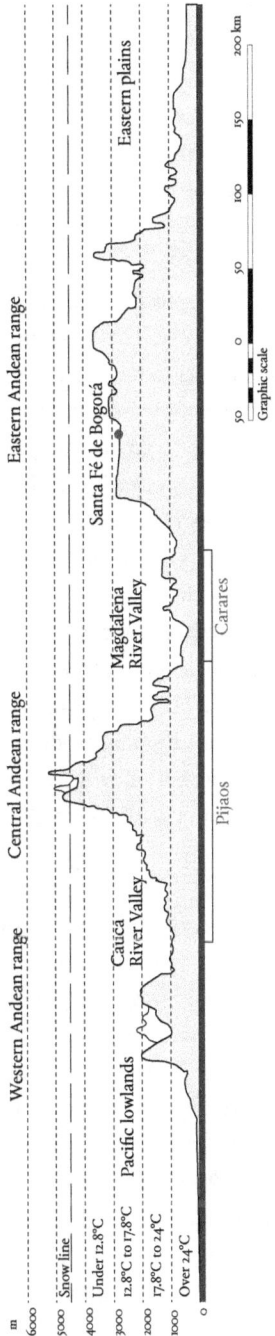

FIGURE 1.2. Profile of altitude and topography of the three northern Andean ranges, sixteenth century. Map by Santiago Muñoz-Arbeláez, based on Guhl, *Colombia*, 67.

a long historiographic tradition, from historian Fernand Braudel, who famously argued that the sixteenth-century Mediterranean civilizations were the product of cities in lowland plains and deemed the "currents of civilization" unable to climb hills of only a few hundred meters of altitude, to social theorist James C. Scott, who argued that the hills and mountains of Southeast Asia were lands of possibility, zones of refuge for people seeking to escape the pressures of the lowland agrarian states. While Braudel posited mountains were archaic, remnants of the past, and obstacles to civilization, Scott argued they were the product of the political choices of escapees and that the history of the mountains was "the history of deliberate and reactive statelessness."[15] In Peru, the Spanish empire inherited from the Incas a vertical form of organization based on kin communities that spread themselves across different layers of the Andean mountain.[16] In contrast, the New Kingdom was neither a remnant of the past, a zone of statelessness, nor a vertical empire with ancient roots, but rather an outpost of the early modern Spanish empire enclosed in the cold plateaus of the Andes, and it struggled to colonize its way down. The European settlers who lived in the kingdom felt isolated and enclosed. They were encircled by Indigenous rebels who inverted power relations, rebuffed imperial aspirations, and constantly seized the corridors that linked the kingdom to Peru, to the Caribbean, and, ultimately, to the Iberian Peninsula. This book examines how this entity of governance, entrapped in the Andean highlands, deployed institutions, practices, and technologies to colonize its way down, carving out a distinctive political space in the global constellation of the Spanish empire.

The New Kingdom of Granada and Spanish Colonialism

By examining the making of this unusual geographic formation, *The New Kingdom of Granada* joins a robust historiography that asks how colonial spaces were imagined, governed, and contested in everyday practice in the New World during the early modern period. Historians of early modern Iberian empires have revealed the polycentric and multidirectional flow of imperial power that gave rise to diverse geographies, spreading from the Americas into the Atlantic and Pacific Oceans.[17] The Spanish called its overseas possessions "the Indies"—a complex concept that included Asia and the Americas and that early modern Spanish authors imagined as a continuous space.[18] This encompassing terrain broke down into smaller areas delineating coherent, if not self-contained, geographic zones. The viceroyalties of Peru and New Spain were centers of power in their own right, built on the ruins of the Inca and Mexica empires, respectively, with access to the rich silver mines of

Potosí and Zacatecas and configuring large continental areas that largely reproduced the territories of pre-Hispanic empires. In fact, from the sixteenth to the nineteenth century most of Spanish South America fell into one large spatial system—extending from Ecuador to Chile and Argentina—that essentially replicated the Tawantinsuyu (the Inca empire). This "Andean economic space," as Carlos Sempat Assadourian called it, depended politically on the Viceroyalty of Peru and was full of internal regional markets that revolved around the silver production of Potosí in a way that connected the textile production of Quito and the mule-herding of Argentina into a large geographic ensemble.[19]

Within the Spanish empire's geographic expanse, the Spanish Caribbean formed an aqueous space of connection and circulation relying on port cities that to a large extent were operated by people of African descent, where Spanish fleets would cyclically pick up mining yields from the Americas and ship them to Iberia, fending off pirates and advances from rival empires.[20] The Pacific offered access to another global market, especially after the founding of Manila in 1571, when, through a fleet departing from Acapulco, China became the main consumer of South American silver to support its silver-based tributary system. Other places, like Guatemala, Northern New Spain, Venezuela, the Amazon, and Rio de la Plata, perceived as "distant" from decision-making entities and with numerous sovereign Indigenous peoples repelling Spanish governance, were more obviously marginal to imperial rule.[21]

The New Kingdom was a peculiar formation within the Iberian Atlantic and Pacific—it fell out of the orbit of these large geopolitical spaces. It was not a complete backwater or periphery like Rio de la Plata or Guatemala, but it lacked the opulence of Peru and New Spain and the centrality of the Caribbean. It was not part of the continental economic system structured around Potosí, nor did it respond to any viceroyalty; instead it reported directly to the king's advisory council for the governance of its overseas territories, the Council of the Indies. Despite having some sugar plantation areas, it did not develop a plantation economy like Brazil or other Caribbean areas. Instead, it had its own mining centers, textile complexes, and agrarian economies linked to the Iberian Peninsula; its own centers and margins, its own political and economic space.[22] This does not mean that it was isolated or disconnected from global networks. On the contrary, the precious stones and metals extracted there ended up halfway across the globe: emeralds in Middle Eastern courts, silver in China, and gold in Europe, just as Chinese silks were present even in remote Indigenous chapels.[23]

Historians have overlooked the novelty, fragility, and sheer contingency of this political formation. Long trapped in a conceptual scheme that viewed power as emanating in one direction from one strong, despotic monarchical center in Spain to its margins, peripheries, or fringes, historians have taken the existence of colonial territories for granted. While historians interested in the making of territories often seek answers in imperial treaties and decrees, it was people on the ground, often fighting for rights or seeking new opportunities, who appealed to different imperial frameworks and established commercial routes, who brought these imaginary lines to life and defined their contours, or made them collapse; peoples of all backgrounds, acting against the backdrop of enduring Indigenous territories and infrastructure.[24] Historian Marta Herrera Angel, one of the only scholars to consider the origins of colonial borders and territories in the New Kingdom of Granada, argued that the Spanish empire adopted many pre-Hispanic ethnic territorial contours at a smaller, regional scale. For Herrera Angel, the territorial divisions that demarcated the imperial provinces almost invariably could be traced back to the precolonial period.[25] Building on Herrera Angel's work, this book examines how the New Kingdom came together as a new political configuration, tying these many Indigenous territories into a new scale of governance.

In this sense, I examine the process of creating a distinct spatial system that, in contrast to Peru or Mexico, was built not on the ruins of an Indigenous empire but in a decentralized Indigenous area where there were no dominant languages like Quechua or Nahuatl, nor any centralized institutions of governance. This intermediate, transitional area was an experimental formation that came to be through the quotidian encounters and collisions between people of different backgrounds who were suddenly forced to exist alongside each other.[26] Though they had unequal access to power, Indigenous people, Africans, and Europeans all shaped the kingdom, but it was not what any specific group of actors intended it to be. Examining the process of making and unmaking this geographic ensemble—how it was built, negotiated, and contested—sheds light on what people understood imperial power to be and how they engaged with it. It invites us to reflect on the meaning of Spanish colonialism.

What is an empire and how does it work? Considering this question means wading through a sea of flawed concepts and reconciling diverging historiographic traditions. Historian Tamar Herzog has shown that our conceptual vocabulary is built on a series of dichotomies that explain the emergence of the modern state by detaching politics from society. But nineteenth-century models of the "state" and its "bureaucracy" as a rational and impersonal organization of government are too narrow to account for a time in which "there was no true distinction between a state and a society as we imagine it today."[27] This has led scholars to acknowledge that the language of modern colonialism, structured around an opposition between a powerful metropole and a series of colonies exploited for its profit, cannot be uncritically applied to the early modern Spanish empire, which was composed of different kingdoms attached to a composite monarchy that ruled them according to their own legal traditions.[28]

As a result, scholars have presented conflicting images of Iberian imperial politics: at once a baroque world of politics meant to provide justice, evoking complex rituals that enacted the king's presence throughout the globe, and a robust knowledge-producing enterprise that pioneered in natural history, cosmography, and navigation, ultimately contributing to the sixteenth-century empirical revolution.[29] Though both approaches have furthered our understanding of the early modern Spanish empire, they also have potentially problematic implications—namely, that by focusing on the specificity of baroque politics we fail to see its similarities to modern colonialism or that by stressing its modern elements we neglect the uniqueness of this imperial project.

By examining the making of a "kingdom"—a concept that has fallen out of use in our modern political vocabularies—amid the irregular topographies of the northern Andes, this book merges these two, apparently contradictory approaches: it reveals the rituals of monarchical politics in the New World and how the monarchy deployed a system to govern Indigenous lives and landscapes, as well as how Indigenous peoples contested it from within and without. The kingdom was, in a way, an image, an idea, and a concept.[30] It was a way of seeing, depicting, classifying, and identifying others. The term *kingdom* was rooted in an early modern Christian tradition of how to rule and build polities. In fact, officials, friars, and bishops of the New Kingdom of Granada evoked the idea of building a kingdom using a lexicon of domestication.

Quite literally, Spaniards perceived the building of the kingdom as an act of taming beasts. They spoke of empire-building as making a spiritual garden blossom amid the diabolic wilderness. They described themselves as ministers who needed to tame the wild and as gardeners who struggled to remove the weeds from the hearts and minds of the "indios."[31] They saw themselves as shepherds who had to correctly guide flocks of Native peoples to calm and peaceful meadows, to be organized in villages like sheep in corrals. Under the same logic, they described the peoples in the hot lands as fierce, untamed beasts; they saw them more as wolves than sheep, more as weeds than crops, more as predators than prey. When an animal or group of animals escaped from the corral and roamed freely, they were called cimarrones or maroons, the same term that came to be used to talk about former enslaved or Indigenous people who fled the villages in search of new opportunities and possibilities. Other idioms used to classify bodies and organize the social worlds of the kingdom, like *mestizo*, *mulato*, and *zambo*—and even *raza* (race)—also emerged from those applied to the animal world.

The term used to describe the process of confining Native peoples into villages, *reducir*, had a double meaning: it meant to simplify diversity and "to order" or "to bring to reason."[32] Catholicism and its invented Roman classical tradition provided a universal order, a framework to organize societies. Everything that did not fit this mold was thought to be chaotic, hellish, and in need of correction. Hence, building a kingdom meant giving order to that which they believed had none. It meant dissecting and restructuring Indigenous languages using Latin as a universal language, making Indigenous peoples live in monogamous families, and replacing Indigenous rituals with Catholic practices. *Reducir* was the verb that alluded to creating the kingdom. It meant, to paraphrase Bruno Latour, to "keep the social flat," to eliminate diversity and shape all forms of existence into a single mold.[33] From this point of view, the landscapes and peoples of the New World were chaotic and ungodly adversaries to be tamed and conquered, and empire-building meant remaking these different peoples so they would live a "life in good order" (vida en policía)—an urban and civic life according to Catholic precepts.

The early modern Iberian lexicon of empire-making, like that of many modern states, was built on metaphors of pastoralism and gardening, in which natural chaos was domesticated by institutional order.[34] Thus, to see the kingdom as an idea or an illusion, as Philip Abrams would put it, is to miss more than half the picture—the half in which the basic, pastoral image of social relations gave way to an infrastructure of governance that aimed to regulate people's thoughts and actions, how they defined property, and where they were required to work. This infrastructure was largely a spatial system, consisting of fixed nodes on the landscape intended to control the flows of people, things, and information, ultimately allowing for the establishment of a relatively coherent structure of governance that provided a platform for different ideas of the kingdom to be displayed and discussed, while also installing a series of routines and instruments of rule.

Indigenous politics were central to the making and unmaking of the kingdom. Yet in the New Kingdom they do not easily conform to the categories scholars have proposed for other areas. For instance, historians of the new conquest have emphasized that the fall of the Mexica empire in Mesoamerica was also the work of Indigenous allies of Spaniards, like the Tlaxcalans, who saw the Aztecs as a foreign power and held the prestigious position of "indios conquistadores" after the conquest.[35] Historians of borderlands and Indigenous politics in North America have challenged traditional models of colonialism to reveal the many situations in which power fluctuated in a sort of middle ground between Europeans and Native groups, or where Indigenous people were firmly in control, even establishing full-blown empires.[36] Scholars of maroon societies have revealed the political ambitions of the communities of African and Indigenous escapees, who imagined new futures at the margins of colonial control.[37] Indigenous politics in the Northern Andes were equally radical and creative, developing full-fledged anticolonial projects, as in the case of the Pijaos (chapter 4), or battling with paper weapons in the halls of the king's court in Madrid, as in the case of Don Diego de la Torre (chapters 5 and 6).

I aim to historize Indigenous engagements with empire, inquiring about the meaning of colonialism and anticolonialism, but I am cautious not to paper over the kingdom's colonial violence, project illusions of success, or assimilate its power dynamics into categories developed for other areas. As we will see, by the early seventeenth century Torre's litigation had given way to a new model of economic governance that significantly diminished Indigenous autonomy, and the anticolonial Pijao project was squashed by a genocidal campaign spearheaded by the audiencia president. These projects did not lead to Indigenous control; rather, they had bitter consequences for all. But the fact that colonialism was harsh should not stop us from acknowledging the many ways in which Indigenous peoples conceived of politics and confronted colonialism.

Africans and their descendants, too, played an increasingly important role in the making of the kingdom. They arrived with the first conquistadors, lived in rural and urban settings, learned Indigenous languages, served as interpreters and encomienda managers, and worked as healers, miners, and peasants, among many other occupations, thus leaving imprints on every aspect of the kingdom.[38] To put it in historians' common parlance, the sixteenth-century New Kingdom of Granada was not a slave society—a society in which slaves are the main demographic force and slavery is the main system of distributing labor—but a society with slaves, profoundly influenced by the presence of enslaved peoples from Africa and of African descent.[39] Some regions strongly connected to the New Kingdom were in fact slave societies, like Cartagena de Indias, South America's main slave trading post in the seventeenth century, or the governorship of Popayán, later in the eighteenth century.[40] However, given the predominance of Indigenous politics in shaping the New Kingdom, my focus here is primarily on Indigenous engagement with the empire.

The early history of the New Kingdom of Granada was one of expansion and consolidation. Between 1530 and 1620, the kingdom emerged as a new social ensemble that forced people to define their identities in preestablished molds—as indios, mestizos, negros, or españoles—then delineated the obligations and privileges of each type of vassal, to finally enforce them by law. The subjects of the empire had to reimagine themselves and redefine their lifestyles within the tropes used by others to name them. As a category of being defined by the Spanish, "indios," in particular, were forced to adapt to legal, political, and economic regimes that conceptualized them as "miserables"—wretched people who could not rule themselves, like minors or disabled persons. The only alternative to a subjugated existence was to take up arms against the largest empire of the time. The results were violent: Native peoples faced one of the highest mortality rates in human history and confronted the expropriation of their lands and installation of compulsory labor systems. In spite of this, the kingdom's history was not only one of exploitation and cultural loss. It was also a story of contestation, participation, and transformation, one in which Indigenous peoples—both rebels and vassals of the empire—envisioned, intervened in, and transformed the meaning of the empire. In this scenario, the kingdom was both an idealized image of politics, one that people used to make claims and to seek redress for hardships, and the institutional matrix that placed them under unfavorable, violent, and coercive conditions in the first place.

In essence, the imperial institutions devised to police Indigenous intimate spaces, social lives, and thought consolidated an administrative rationale and infrastructure that triggered dispossession, economic encroachment, and genocide. In this sense, the history of the kingdom intersects in many ways with that of modern colonialism. That the kingdom's ultimate goal was to provide justice should not eclipse the fact that what it offered was a kind of imperial justice that aimed to remake Indigenous peoples according to its own notions of virtue and economic needs. In this way, it was a colonial venture.

But even if the history of the kingdom is one of expansion, we cannot lose sight of the fragility and complexities of the historical processes that led to this outcome. A coordinated rebellion of Native peoples or Iberians—even of the audiencia's own magistrates—was always a possibility, hovering on the horizon of functionaries' expectations. The whole system was often on the verge of collapse, and we cannot neglect these uncertainties of empire. One of the principal aims of this book is to restore contingency to the making of the New Kingdom of Granada as a political unit: a kingdom that was a kind of fabric in a continuous process of creation, destruction, and re-creation; a pliable blanket, with its gaps and holes, that expected to blend into the topography of the northern Andes; a human product, woven together by the circulation of objects and by the action of an eclectic cast of people of Indigenous, African, and European descent who sought to build, reform, or destroy the kingdom.

An Ethnography of History

A historical approach to the making of a kingdom over the course of a century—a problem of broad temporal and spatial scale—inevitably requires an eclectic methodological and narrative strategy. Rather than providing a static theoretical framework for empire-building that divides and gives pre-eminence to realms such as economics, culture, or politics, I have sought to create a layered approach to the different human experiences involved in the definition of the empire. Instead of discrete realms, I have tried to evoke the messy bundles of empire, in which economics and politics are entangled with cultural and social arrangements.

Through this approach, the empire acquires concrete shapes and meanings. We see empire in the tribute collector, in the newly built villages for Indigenous vassals, in the cows and sheep roaming in their fields, and in the efforts to translate Catholic concepts into Indigenous languages. Indigenous people, people of African descent, and Europeans appeared in the tribunal's courts to fight passionately for and against the kingdom, advocate for its transformation, or debate whether it had gone awry, and if it was legitimate or not. Native people, mestizos, and Africans played central roles in the transatlantic bureaucracy, as scribes, caciques, interpreters, and soldiers. To address the tangible faces of empire, I have chosen to focus on the histories of specific people and objects—an imperial official, an Indigenous intellectual, Indigenous textiles, a map of the Bogotá savannah or the Magdalena River. Each of these has a particular story to tell about the kingdom, showing the plurality of voices that participated in its making. The focus on biographies and objects reveals the kingdom as a process, as a product of history made by people in their everyday lives as they dealt with things like building a home, choosing clothes to wear, paying taxes, and keeping records.

A diverse group of vassals and officials, including Indigenous interpreters, scribes, and intellectuals, built the kingdom's infrastructure through apparently simple acts like numbering, listing, drawing, and mapping—what I call "textual technologies." Through the marks they made with ink on paper, officials and vassals incorporated the kingdom into their visual regimes, using familiar codes and conventions. These depictions implied a theory of politics. They rendered the kingdom visible by defining how societies should be organized and what people—their bodies, families, beliefs, and homes—should look like. On paper, officials and vassals of the monarchy could draw, describe, name, measure, and organize the kingdom. Indigenous people and people of African descent often wrote letters and outlined maps appealing to monarchical justice and their own (often contradictory) notions of vassalage and freedom, or found a way to express their discontent precisely by interrupting paper flows and channels of communication.[41]

Historians have called attention to the constraining logics of document production, collection, and storage that underlie the building and maintenance of archives, showing at once the limitations of written sources and the inherent violence of their creation. Spanish archives are full of stereotypical, archetypical figures like "indios" and "caribes" (cannibals), who in these simplistic terms existed only in the imagination of imperial officials and settlers. Even when they took care in describing, explaining, and recording Indigenous practices, officials and settlers accommodated those practices in their own categories and reproduced their own biases. Inversely, when Indigenous people of the New Kingdom of Granada left written records in colonial archives, they were usually addressing colonial magistrates or officials, often through the mediation of translators and scribes, and crafted their words for their audience, tailoring their message to what they thought colonial authorities expected to hear.[42] In other words, when you read historical archives you get not hard facts but rather a series of stories indicative of how people strove to narrate their lives and the lives of others, how they tried to make sense of complex and fluid realities. For this reason, a big part of what was happening fell out of the formulaic narratives preserved in the archive, remaining unretrievable for us today.[43]

Informed by these debates, *The New Kingdom of Granada* aims to offer an ethnographic approach to history, reconstructing different visions of colonialism as inscribed in archival texts and images. It interrogates disjointed, fragmented, incomplete documents incorporated into colonial archives as a way to understand what people of multiple backgrounds thought they were up to; what they considered just and unjust, moral and immoral; what they imagined their range of possibilities to be; and how their interpretations informed their actions. The book draws from a corpus of more than seven hundred archival documents, including correspondence, visitation reports, judicial records, maps, land titles, and accounting and legal books kept in archives and research libraries in Colombia, Spain, the United Kingdom, and the United States. I pay special attention to how the kingdom was sketched from contested visual regimes in maps, drawings, manuscripts, and prints.[44] Rather than taking these sources as neutral representations of the social and natural worlds of sixteenth- and seventeenth-century South America, I document the diverging ways in which Indigenous peoples and Europeans depicted and iterated the kingdom. I take these gestures and inscriptions as performative, as instruments for the consolidation and negotiation of power. Through these renderings they were not merely depicting an existing entity but producing the kingdom itself.

The greatest challenge has been to uncover Indigenous politics, with its nuances, ambitions, and motivations, from records created by imperial agents who did not realize the full scope and scale of Indigenous peoples' actions, but rather underestimated them and pigeonholed them in conceptual straitjackets. Inspired by experimental methodologies that aim to advance a series of speculative arguments based on meticulous reading of colonial archives, such as Saidiya Hartman's "critical fabulation"—"playing with and rearranging the basic elements of the story . . . [and] re-presenting the sequence of events in divergent stories and from contested points of view"—I reread archival evidence through a deeply contextualized approach that draws on archaeology, material culture, and ethnography, situating colonial archives in a larger spectrum of evidence to shake the contours of what was possible and envision new possibilities. Hartman deploys critical fabulation to get to a level of individual experience—what a murdered Black teenage girl's experience of slavery might have been like and how it destabilizes historical narratives.[45] I use it as a means to uncover political practice: to reconstruct the political notions that inspired some of the most important political movements of the New Kingdom in the sixteenth century, but which have seldom been recognized as such—like the Carib anticolonial project of the Pijaos or the events surrounding Don Diego de la Torre's quest for freedom. Through this interpretive method, I reveal how Indigenous peoples' frameworks for political action and economic interaction shaped the kingdom, making it a truly transcultural assemblage.

The book is divided into three parts and eight chapters, organized in chronological order from the conquest in the 1530s to the moment in the 1620s in which the kingdom took its first recognizable shape. The first part examines the setup of the kingdom's institutions between the 1530s and 1550s. Chapter 1 reframes the "conquest" as a structural interaction between the cold lands and the hot lands that resulted from the Spanish effort to transform Indigenous commercial networks into a centralized polity, rather than a short phase of military expansion. The second chapter examines the creation of the audiencia—a royal judicial tribunal that enacted the presence of the king—through the disillusionment of Tomás López Medel, a humanist-turned-bureaucrat who initially was firmly convinced of the empire's benefits for Indigenous peoples but whose convictions were shaken when faced with the on-the-ground realities of the empire. Chapter 3 examines the creation of an imperial economy based on Indigenous textiles, which emerged as the main good for tribute and one of the primary engines of the kingdom's economy.

Part II explores two different Indigenous political projects that deploy radically different notions of freedom and reactions to the kingdom from the 1550s to 1580s and beyond. Chapter 4 examines the history of the Pijao peoples, who formed a multiethnic Indigenous coalition that destroyed the kingdom's infrastructure and offered a viable alternative to the kingdom, growing exponentially during the second half of the sixteenth century. In contrast, chapters 5 and 6 consider the history of Indigenous intellectual Don Diego de la Torre, a Muisca cacique who visited Philip II and offered advice regarding the good government of the New Kingdom of Granada, based on his readings of the empire's legal frameworks. While Pijao anticolonialism threatened to destroy the kingdom, Torre's legalism culminated in the replacement of all the audiencia magistrates and laid the groundwork for a new phase of reform that gained predominance at the turn of the seventeenth century.

Part III explores transformations in governance that took place between 1590 and 1630. These reforms installed a new system to dispossess Indigenous peoples of their homelands, assign those lands to European settlers, and forcibly distribute the Native peoples' wage labor—an early example of the enclosure of the commons that had lasting implications for Indigenous lives and landscapes (chapter 7). Chapter 8 examines the efforts to transform the hot lands into wealthy mines by waging a genocidal war against the Pijaos and importing Indigenous laborers from the cold lands and enslaved people from the African continent. These measures in many ways culminated a century-long process of establishing the kingdom, giving it an orientation and a recognizable shape, if not a completely coherent and hegemonic dominance. In the centuries that followed, new efforts to centralize the diverse landscapes and peoples of the northern Andes would ensue. The epilogue frames the history of the kingdom in subsequent projects of centralization during the eighteenth and nineteenth centuries, revealing the long-standing tensions between topography and centralizing schemes in the northern Andes and arguing that the active engagement of Indigenous peoples with the kingdom has been obscured by the constraining republican narratives of the past.

This book explores the creation of an abstract entity (a "kingdom") that had concrete implications in people's lives. The history of this kingdom is a broader meditation on how political entities—empires, states, monarchies—work. It is an inquiry into their ethereal existence. They live in our imaginations, but they also establish strict procedural manuals and routines that endow them with an objective quality. They promote beliefs that privilege some over others, unleash violence, establish tacit agreements regarding how people should live their lives, channel their most innate desires, and model their interactions with one another. These abstract entities develop mechanisms that encroach on people's lives, sometimes silently, sometimes loudly and dramatically. Some people are integral participants in these imagined polities and some are partially included, while many others are excluded and outlawed.

In this way, this book is a history of politics in its broadest sense. I follow common practice among historians of monarchical politics, who have sought to disentangle our understanding of early modern politics from our conceptual vocabularies for modern states. But I differ in my conviction that, in their rawest form, modern and early modern forms of political practice have common threads. When viewed from the perspective of Indigenous peoples—who were subjected to the consolidation of new tributary economies and to systems that allocated and claimed property, rights, legal responsibilities, and values—the kingdom shares some characteristics of modern colonialism and states. To shed light on these commonalities, we need not impose our contemporary vocabulary or project back the functioning of the modern state. But I do propose we focus on how empire-builders solved concrete problems, like surveying, classifying, taxing populations, or consolidating jurisdictions and bounding territories, in order to reveal the basic structure of the empire, its very fabric.

PART I   PRODUCING INDIOS

On a bitter day in 1540, the bodies of between three and four hundred Indigenous people hung in the central square of the city of Tunja. It all started when some Spaniards noticed a series of odd behaviors among Indigenous people in the region. Antonio Cardoso was near Tunja, recruiting soldiers to fight against rebels of Tinjacá, when he overheard two Muisca men whispering. Cardoso played dumb but sent a young interpreter of the Muisca language to talk to the two men. His subterfuge unveiled a secret plan to kill the Spaniards of the cities of Tunja, Santa Fe, and Vélez. The Muisca conspirators had established separate appointments to meet their Spanish encomenderos (masters) at their residences one night in Tunja. Once they were face-to-face with their encomenderos, each one would slay his encomendero in the intimacy of his own home. It was a bold plan that aimed to put an end to Spanish colonialism, which was then a very recent phenomenon. In the four years since Spaniards first arrived in the Andean highlands, the Muisca peoples' world had changed dramatically: their communities were now expected to obey and serve Spanish encomenderos and reject their own beliefs. Their radical plan was an attempt to eradicate the foreigners and regain their ordinary lives.[1]

Cardoso returned to the city to inform Hernán Pérez de Quesada, interim governor of the kingdom, but Pérez de Quesada had learned about the rebellion on his own, when he was near the city of Santa Fe de Bogotá, and was preparing to retaliate. The result was a violent, performative massacre: Pérez de Quesada and his men encircled the Native conspirators as they entered the city, took them to the main square, and hanged them symbolically in the city's most notorious landmark, the central plaza. Juan Izquierdo calculated that seven or eight caciques and three to four hundred commoners died that day, while García de Malvaceda believed the death toll was well over four hundred men. The display of brutality aimed to suffocate any illusions of freedom and to instill fear in those who desired a way out of the kingdom. It was a statement to prove there was no going back. When asked by the authorities if he thought the reaction was excessive, Antonio Cardoso posited that Pérez de Quesada had served God and the king with his deeds. Had he not, the Muisca conspirators might have succeeded, exterminating the settlers and erasing the kingdom.[2]

Indeed, the kingdom was under constant, imminent threat. This was only one of at least fifteen uprisings that took place in the Andean highlands between 1539 and 1549, fourteen of which took place between 1539 and 1543.[3] Indigenous resistance came in all shapes and colors. The Indigenous people of Tinjacá were in full-fledged rebellion during this period. Saboyá, Saquencipa, and several other caciques had fled to the forests and hills, leaving traps and poisoned arrows hidden along the road, hoping to harm the newcomers. An Indigenous man named Tisquisoche had killed his Spanish encomendero.[4] Many of those efforts were largely individual and revealed the fragmented political landscape left by the deaths of the most prestigious preconquest Indigenous leaders.

The last Muisca ruler—named Sagipa and identified in the Indigenous political lexicon as the cipa, the highest level of authority—died after he was tortured by the conquistadors. They claimed that Sagipa concealed a huge treasure of gold that had belonged to the previous ruler of Bogotá, and which the conquistadors claimed was theirs by right of conquest. In a scene mimicking Pizarro's seizure of Atahualpa five years earlier, Jiménez de Quesada and his men took Sagipa captive and requested that he fill an entire hut (bohío) with gold before they would free him. The conquistadors had heard and read about Cortés and Pizarro, and modeled their actions on that example. In a sense, the conquest consisted of a series of images and practices that reproduced themselves, as conquistadors rehearsed and repeated common tropes. It was a scripted conquest that, nevertheless, could yield unexpected results.[5] Sagipa, ordered to fill a hut with gold to save his life, instead filled it with figures made from bones, feathers, and seashells—all of them extremely valuable items from distant and exotic regions, crafted by Indigenous artisans and brought together by Indigenous traders. The circulation of material objects like these stitched together the rugged geography of South America's northern end. Not only were they a testament to these lively Indigenous networks, but they were also some of the most valuable objects of distinction anyone could own.

Yet conquistadors did not interpret it that way: they wanted gold and silver. Feeling duped, Jiménez de Quesada initiated a sham lawsuit against Sagipa for hiding the treasure. He named his brother, Hernán Pérez de Quesada—who would lead the Tunja massacre a few years later—to be Sagipa's attorney and defender. When confronted, Sagipa pled for his life and claimed that "he valued those items as gold itself."[6] During the trial, Sagipa was brutally tortured. They disjointed his limbs by pulling him with ropes and cut the soles of his feet open before burning them. He died a few days later.

A brutal world emerged from such encounters between Indigenous peoples and Europeans. Scholars have already remarked on the centrality of justice procedures to imperial politics—even if sometimes sham, as the trial against Sagipa, legal formality was a pillar of Spanish power. But the promise of wealth and the meticulous display of violence also shaped the kingdom's institutions and the status of Indigenous peoples in it—a problem of imperial scale as the Spanish monarchy turned global. In fact, the killing of Sagipa occurred simultaneously with a cross-Atlantic debate that scrutinized Indigenous emotions and bodies to cope with questions about their humanity.[7] Theologians and scholars asked whether "indios" were the embodiment of Aristotle's category of natural slaves or whether they could be considered fully human, capable of rational thought. Imperial officials transformed these abstractions into legislation, officially defining what it meant to be an "indio" in the global Spanish empire and assigning "indios" a special legal status as members of the empire.[8] "Indios" were conceptualized as "miserables," wretched people who needed to be protected and instructed in the holy faith and, in exchange, were required to pay "tribute" to both their encomenderos and the king. Officials laid out a new institutional architecture to convert the kingdom's Native inhabitants into tribute-paying, Catholic vassals of the king. They created narratives about how Native peoples should live their lives, design their spaces, worship, have sex, and die, and then designed routines of surveillance to make sure they adopted these behaviors. Native peoples were not left at the margins of the empire, nor did they passively accept these strictures. On the contrary, they reshaped nascent imperial institutions through their daily actions. Indigenous people were active litigants, petitioners, and even lawmakers.

The muddled, violent encounters between Spanish and Native peoples resulted in the creation of a political system that in discourse promoted itself as warrantor of justice and protector of "indios"—a motto at odds with the realities of colonialism and the desire for wealth extraction. The result was a complex, contradictory governing scheme and economic system suspended between different forms of social organization and regimes of value. Part I examines the conquest and the creation of the kingdom's administrative architecture. I consider the installation of institutions, routines, and instruments of rule that defined the legal condition of "indios" as members of the Spanish empire and the obligations they had vis-à-vis the imperial administration between 1530 and 1560. The first chapter describes how the initial confrontations between Indigenous peoples and Europeans set the foundation for the kingdom, with its divisions between cold lands and hot lands. Chapter 2 focuses on the creation of the audiencia through the story of Tomás López Medel, an imperial official educated in a humanist university in Spain who carried out some of the most important policies of the sixteenth century, shedding light on what colonialism meant to its practitioners. Chapter 3 considers the establishment of the tax system in Indigenous textiles and how these goods were repurposed to become a platform for negotiations and disputes over the meaning of colonialism. Overall, part I shows the functioning of an infrastructure of governance that largely reproduced Indigenous spatial organization, was primarily oriented to provide justice, and was built around economic circulation of Indigenous objects.

1

LABYRINTHS OF CONQUEST

In the late 1530s, three Spanish expeditions crossed paths by chance at about 2,590 meters (8,500 feet) in the Andean mountain chains. It was an unusual site for such an encounter. Among the decorated palisades, agricultural terraces, and ceremonial pathways of the local Indigenous settlement marched three groups of European soldiers in search of social status and wealth. The first expedition, led by Gonzalo Jiménez de Quesada, came from the coastal settlements of what the Spanish called Tierra Firme (mainland), looking for an alternative route to Peru. The second came from the region they called Venezuela, where a conquering expedition financed by German bankers and authorized by a special permit for conquest from emperor Charles V had heard of the wealthy Native peoples of the highlands. The last group came from the south, led by Sebastián de Belalcázar. Its members had decided to try their luck northward after participating in Pizarro's seizure of the Inca empire and hearing news of a rich area to the north called Cundinamarca.

Each of these itineraries was inspired by words uttered by Indigenous peoples—usually in violent cross-cultural conversations—onto which the invaders projected their desires and expectations. In the early sixteenth century, the boundaries separating reality and fiction were blurry. Two decades before the three expeditions met in the mountains, Hernán Cortés had seized Tenochtitlan, the world's third-largest metropolis and seat of one of the greatest empires of the era. Half a decade before, Francisco Pizarro had captured Atahualpa, the ruler of another great empire unknown to Europeans at the time. From the conquistadors' point of view, anything was possible. The possibility of finding a golden city in the middle of the jungle, like the famous El Dorado, or of encountering lost civilizations was not beyond hope. These illusions were embedded in a way of thinking about Indigenous landscapes and empire that motivated men to venture into the unknown, terra incognita.

The three expeditions hoped to find a water passage from the Atlantic to the "South Sea" (the Pacific Ocean), a land route to Peru, and an access point to the golden veins they thought lay beneath the earth near the Equator. Instead, in the mountains they encountered a people so numerous they called them Moscas—a term specialists later identified as "Muisca," which meant "the people" but sounded like the Spanish word for flies (moscas). From then on, the Spanish often used the term in this second sense as well, since "there was an infinity of indios" in the mountains.[1] The expeditions' leaders struggled in this new area, located at the nexus of the Andes, the Caribbean Sea, the Pacific Ocean, and the Orinoco River. It was promising and deceptive at once. In 1562, Jiménez de Quesada expressed confidently that Cortés and Pizarro "did not discover or settle better or richer provinces than I, even if [the lands they conquered] were larger."[2] The comparison to Mexico and Peru loomed large in the minds of the conquistadors, and they had high hopes about what would come. This chapter examines the collision of Indigenous and European worlds and how those early encounters paved the way for the establishment of a kingdom settled high in the Andes Mountains, a kingdom that viewed the lowlands as a wealthy, if hermetic, land of promise.

Encounters between Indigenous peoples and invaders were multiple and complex, yet for a long time historical narratives flattened them into stories of brave European conquistadors who quickly dominated sizeable Indigenous forces due to their military and biological superiority.[3] These scholars presented Indigenous people as unable to cope with cultural difference, arguing that the Spanish rapidly stripped them of their beliefs and turned them into Catholic subjects.[4] In their eyes, the conquest paved the way for European dominance: a twenty-year phase followed by a stable, centuries-long peace that historians call the pax Hispanica. In more recent decades, historians of

Mesoamerica have debunked this narrative and shown the messiness of encounters between Indigenous peoples and Europeans, as well as their plural outcomes.[5] They have revealed the crucial participation of go-betweens who mediated between Europeans and Native peoples. They have shown that conquest was rarely a polarized clash between two discrete and stable groups—Europeans and "indios"—and have demonstrated that, in many places, the "conquest" featured Europeans entering contentious Indigenous worlds, rather than Europeans running roughshod over Native worlds. In some cases, Native peoples saw themselves as conquistadors who fought alongside the Spanish and, from the sixteenth to eighteenth centuries, reclaimed a privileged political position as special vassals of the king.[6] In others, what Europeans saw as a cataclysmic "conquest" seldom marked a cleavage in Indigenous accounts.[7] In yet other instances, Indigenous peoples reinvented themselves by incorporating horses and firearms into their political, economic, and military life and became conquerors who built empires in their own right.[8]

As in Mesoamerica, on the South American mainland the "conquest" was not a brief moment that gave way to colonization. Conquest was more than military invasion. It involved a series of encounters and clashes in which different peoples tried to make sense of each other. It was a chaotic and plural set of experiences that transformed an Indigenous landscape into a kingdom of the global Spanish monarchy. It entailed a series of rituals, practices, and methods that translated the peoples and landscapes of the New World into members of the empire. It was a "bureaucratic conquest" that required a series of strategies to absorb varied Indigenous worlds into the legal forms of the Spanish empire. In that sense, the conquest was an unfinished process, one that no one could fully grasp at the time. No one could truly envision the South American mainland's place vis-à-vis a Catholic monarchy that ruled from across the Atlantic.

The bureaucratic routines of conquest and violence were intimately connected. The kingdom fed on violence and conquest. Agents of the empire employed violence to crush the utopias of Indigenous peoples and of Spaniards who imagined themselves breaking loose from the empire. In the following pages I will argue that, rather than a discrete stage, the conquest was the condition of existence of the kingdom proper. Only through recurrent military aggression and expropriation would the kingdom survive and grow over the next century. Moreover, that aggression created a durable pattern of interaction between the cold highlands of the Andes and the hot lowlands of the Magdalena River valley.

A Trail of Salt: From the Caribbean to the Andes

It was salt, its forms and characteristics, that led Gonzalo Jiménez de Quesada and the members of his expedition toward the northern Andean highlands. Jiménez left the coastal city of Santa Marta on April 5, 1536, for the vast and largely unknown interior of the continent with six hundred soldiers on foot, one hundred horsemen, and three ships on the large waterway they knew as Rio Grande de la Magdalena, or the Magdalena River. By March 1537, only two-thirds of the troops were still alive. After one year of trouble-ridden journeys through tropical forests, Jiménez happened upon an unexpected flow of salt along the Magdalena River. Throughout the voyage, the explorers had observed how salt was made from seawater in coastal areas and taken by river to be traded in the interior. This salt was in loose grains, and the farther they got from the coast, the scarcer and more expensive it became. As the journey progressed, the Europeans noted that salt became so expensive that only Indigenous elites could secure it, while commoners "made their own salt out of human urine or palm powder."[9]

But in a settlement in the north Andean foothills, which the soldiers identified as Tora, they encountered a new kind of salt. This salt was made into cakes that resembled sugar loaves (pilones de azúcar), and the farther they went into the interior, the cheaper it became. The men realized that if loose salt traveled upriver from the coast, salt cakes must have come down from the mountains. Based on the characteristics and routes of the salt cakes, Jiménez and his captains speculated about the complexity of a society that could produce such a commodity for long-distance trade. They decided to abandon their original route along the Magdalena River and sent the ships back to Santa Marta. They would now follow the salt into the mountains.[10]

The salt road brought the travelers to new landscapes and placed them in contact with new peoples, both of which contrasted in many ways with the Caribbean worlds they had left behind. In the highlands, they came across a series of human settlements spread over the plateaus of the eastern mountain ranges of the northernmost region of South America. These groups were unlike any others they had met during their journey. During the eleven months between their departure from the coast and their arrival in the highland Indigenous settlement they renamed La Grita on March 9, 1537, Quesada's men had left no stone unturned in their frenetic search for gold. During those months, the expedition's scribes recorded taking a total of 149 pesos and six tomines of gold from the Indigenous peoples of the Caribbean coast. But on that single day in La Grita, on March 9, the bounty increased to 1,173 pesos of fine gold and 73 pesos of low-quality gold.[11] In other words, they stole eight times more gold in one day than they had acquired in almost a year.

Everything about the mountain people seemed different to the newcomers. Spaniards had developed criteria to observe and classify other peoples and cultures according to their degrees of social control and political authority—a distinction grounded in classical and medieval philosophy. Thus, Spaniards assessed civility according to the acceptance of authority. They observed, understood, and represented other societies from that standpoint. It was a framework that served as an implicit ethnography, to use Stuart B. Schwartz's term—a selective understanding of self and other, and the traits that gave peoples those identities.[12] The salt-producing Native peoples of the highlands were well dressed, were shamed by nudity, did not eat human flesh, and had severe penalties for crimes. In addition to cutting off the hands, noses, and ears of criminals, they employed symbolic punishments, such as ripping off their clothes or cutting their hair. They respected their lords so much that they did not make eye contact with them. The Spanish read these traits as evidence of a higher degree of civility; they took them to mean that Native peoples of the highlands might be relatively organized and capable of reasoning. Based on these readings, they assessed that the peoples of the highlands had a moderate level of civilization.[13] At that point, Jiménez de Quesada's quest for Peru—the initial objective of the expedition—was over. A new outpost of the empire was in the making.

By the time Jimenez's expedition set off for the interior of the continent, the Caribbean mainland had already felt the heavy imprint of colonialism. It had given rise to a dichotomous classification between what Spaniards deemed to be good, peaceful Indigenous peoples and the "caribes": a mix of different ethnic groups that raided the "good indios," took captives, and ate them.[14] While the "good indios" were vassals of the king, the "caribes" lived against natural law and therefore could be enslaved, according to Spanish law. These statuses emerged from the experiences of people like Juan de la Cosa, the chief pilot of the Spanish monarchy, who had sailed with Amerigo Vespucci to the continental coast in 1499 and authored the first known map that shows the New World as a separate land mass. Cosa and his contemporaries were deeply engaged in slave-raiding campaigns, tomb raiding, and plunder; Gonzalo Fernández de Oviedo thought him part of a breed of explorers who "might be more correctly called alterers and destroyers of the land, since their purpose was not so much to serve God and king as to rob."[15] Still, he probably influenced royal policy, since in 1503, after corresponding with Cosa and others, the queen legally permitted the enslavement of "a certain people called Cannibals."[16]

The early experiences of the Caribbean gave rise to a nascent network of cities established in the Isthmus of Panama between 1510 and 1522, including Santa María de la Antigua del Darién, Nombre de Dios, Panama, Acla, and Natá, which laid bare the shared dynamics of power of early imperial experiments. Settlers established town councils and used the legal stature of municipalities to plead for common interests. In this sense, municipalities served as political instruments to advocate for privileges and distinctions. In the following decades residents of municipalities advocated forcefully for their communities, sending procurators to represent their interests directly to the king, earning the title of city and a coat of arms, and seeking to fend off efforts at imperial control.[17]

New cities also emerged to the east of Santa María de la Antigua. Rodrigo de Bastidas founded Santa Marta in 1526, and Pedro de Heredia founded Cartagena in 1533.[18] The Magdalena River became an administrative boundary for Spanish authorities, though one that did not necessarily coincide with Indigenous territorial demarcations.[19] Both Santa Marta and Cartagena survived economically in their early decades through a practice known as rescate. *Rescate* is a puzzling term that translates as "rescue"; it could be used to refer to the recovery or redemption of something taken by one's enemies. In the Mediterranean, it referred to established forms of trade used to recover enslaved Christians.[20] In the sixteenth-century Caribbean main, however, it was a euphemism for enslavement and the desecration and plunder of tombs and sanctuaries revered by Indigenous peoples. This period had devastating effects on the Indigenous communities of the Caribbean main. In 1568, Melchor Pérez de Arteaga summed up the situation with the phrase "the indios have died out."[21]

March to the Highlands

After Bastidas's death, the Crown granted the governorship of Santa Marta to Pedro Fernández de Lugo, who decided to explore the interior of the continent. The conquistadors had many labels for what they imagined as a land of possibilities. *Tierra firme* meant it was not an island but a vast continental territory. *Castilla del oro* indicated they thought it to be filled with gold. Fernández de Lugo gathered an expedition of fifteen hundred foot soldiers and two hundred horsemen to sail from Spain and the Canary Islands to Santa Marta. That expedition arrived in Santa Marta in 1536 with twelve hundred members. That same year, eight hundred soldiers set off into the continent's interior, commanded by Gonzalo Jiménez de Quesada, hoping to find a continental route, safe from the perils of the sea, to the lands of Tawantinsuyu—the Inca's Realm of the Four Parts, which the Spaniards had begun, misleadingly, to call Peru.[22]

The other two expeditions arrived in the Andes after Gonzalo Jiménez de Quesada. We know much less about them. Nikolaus Federmann came from the northeast, where he heard about a province called Xerira. He explored the region called Cabo de La Vela and then headed south. When he was around Cocuy, a snowy peak north of the plateaus of the northeastern Andean range, a Native person told him about a rich land of people clothed with gold. Federman continued south to climb the eastern Andean range and finally reached Bogotá in early 1539. He considered this land part of the governorship of Venezuela, which Charles V had granted to the Welsers—German bankers who helped make Charles V emperor of the Holy Roman Empire and, in turn, pressured him to allow them to invest in the exploration of the New World.[23] Sebastián de Belalcázar was drawn by accounts of a place called Cundinamarca, which he heard from Native people in Peru. Belalcázar had been among Pizarro's troops when the latter imprisoned Atahualpa, and he headed north in the hopes of finding new kingdoms, in the company of two hundred soldiers and nearly five thousand Native people from Peru—a jaw-dropping number that shows the key role played by Indigenous peoples from Peru in the expansion of the Spanish empire in South America, which still needs to be reckoned with.[24] The crew left Quito in March 1538 and crossed the central Andean range to reach Bogotá in April 1539.

The encounter of the three expeditions led to a juridical battle in Madrid among the governorships of Venezuela, Santa Marta, Cartagena, and Castilla del Oro, all of which claimed the new lands were part of their jurisdictions. In the end, the Council of the Indies accepted the inclusion of the New Kingdom in Santa Marta.[25] Belalcázar became the governor of Popayán, the governorship to the south of the New Kingdom of Granada, which would oscillate between the jurisdictions of the Audiencia of Santa Fe and the Audiencia of Quito. Federman had less luck: while he expected to become governor of Venezuela, Spanish officials accused him of Lutheranism and he spent his final years in a legal battle with the Welsers and the Council of the Indies.

Historian José Ignacio Avellaneda estimates that 483 Europeans arrived in this part of the Andes in those three expeditions. During the 1540s, three more expeditions arrived, adding 400 men, for a total estimate of 933 conquerors.[26] The conquistadors came from middle social groups; there were none who had very high or low social status in Iberia. The fact that people needed to cover their own costs to participate in conquest made it difficult for people of lower socioeconomic status to become involved. Among the conquerors who left traces of their occupations, there were "ten hidalgos, one farmer, nine scribes, thirteen artisans, ten persons in the service of others, ten professionals, eight royal officials and factors, four merchants, and three cases of fairly wealthy persons."[27] These figures broadly coincide with the social makeup of the men who participated in the conquest of Peru.

The conquerors were also fairly literate. While in Spain the literacy rate among men was between 35 to 60 percent, Avellaneda estimates that among the conquerors of the New Kingdom of Granada it was nearly 80 percent, based on the number of conquistadors who could sign their own names. Of course, the fact that men could sign their own name did not necessarily mean they could read and write—in fact, there are only two references to books in the hands of conquerors in the New Kingdom.[28] Furthermore, the surviving evidence may also reflect that illiterate conquistadors from the lowest social tiers and economic capacity left no textual traces. Theirs might be irretrievable voices that left no imprint in the archives. But socioeconomic status did not dictate literacy.[29] For instance, while Jiménez de Quesada and Federman were literate—and wrote and published books—Sebastián de Belalcázar could not write or read.[30]

Entangled Worlds

Following the common saying "all paths lead to Rome," one might think that in the late 1530s, all paths on the South American mainland led to the place the Native peoples of the highlands called Muyquyta and the Spanish transliterated as Bogotá. The fact that the conquistadors reached the plateaus of the eastern range of the Andes from the Caribbean coast (north), Venezuela (east), and Peru (south) illustrates their centrality. The earliest surviving Spanish account, the *Epítome del Nuevo Reino de Granada*, describes the New Kingdom of Granada as a plateau in the highlands about 120 leagues long and 20 or 30 leagues wide (about 300 by 80 kilometers, roughly 185 by 50 miles). It was divided into two "parts or provinces" that were constantly at war with each other. One was named Bogotá, ruled by the cipa, and the other was Tunja, which other chroniclers stated was ruled by the zaque. Both were great lords, and they took the names of their cacicazgos. The author pondered that Bogotá was more powerful than Tunja and estimated that Bogotá could raise an army of sixty thousand men, while Tunja could gather around forty thousand men, though he admitted his estimate was on the low end since other Spaniards calculated the numbers to be much higher. But if Bogotá was more powerful, Tunja was richer, especially in emeralds.[31]

The *Epítome* distinguished the peoples of the cold lands from those of the hot lands by drawing on the gross divide between "good indios" and "caribes." If the peoples of the cold lands were called the Moscas, those of the hot lands

were the Panches: "a people so beast-like that they do not adore or believe anything except their own pleasure and vices . . . and they especially covet eating
human flesh, which is their greatest joy." The Panches of the hot lands were
"more fearsome, they go around naked, and fight with more powerful weapons."[32] Other colonial texts added that the powerful Panches completely encircled the people of the highlands ("una nación de gente que llaman Panches
de la cual está cercada toda la tierra").[33]

The impressions recorded in these early European texts were vulgar sim-
plifications and misrepresentations of the complex Indigenous worlds of the
lowlands and the highlands: they presented these worlds as different in and by
nature. Neither the Native peoples of the highlands nor those of the lowlands
were ethnically homogeneous—they were not determined by their environment, as Spaniards thought—but rather were historical configurations of expanding and contracting webs of human connection and conflict. The peoples
of the highlands were not all part of the same ethnic group, nor did they all fall
under the rule of the cipa of Bogotá and the zaque of Tunja. If we are to believe
chroniclers like Juan Rodríguez Freyle, Pedro Simón, and Lucas Fernández de
Piedrahita, who wrote at different times in the seventeenth century and had different degrees of exposure to Indigenous oral history, the expansion of the cipa
and the zaque began only a few generations before the arrival of the Spaniards,
under the rule of Saguanmachica (cipa) and Michúa (zaque), and entailed a
dual strategy of incorporation that rested on war and extending kin networks.

Saguanmachica and his successors Nemequene and Tisquesusa expanded
the rule of Muyquyta by annexing neighboring cacicazgos, repelling invasions
from the lowlands, disarming rebellions, and fighting the zaque. They operated on a layered system of power built on kin networks that created forms of
Native nobility and governance around matrilineal units called utas and sybin
and were structured around a male leader, the uncle. Conglomerations of these
units created a composite political structure ruled by sihipquas, like Ubaque,
Guatavita, or Fusagasugá. Usually a sihipqua's realm extended over a river valley, and many of these valleys had their own dialects. These were the levels of
authority the cipas were incorporating into their realm of control during the
sixteenth century when the Spanish arrived in their territory. Still, some sections of the eastern plateaus were controlled by autonomous sihipquas. Other
groups from the Chibcha linguistic family also peopled the highlands of the eastern Andean range to the north, which the Spanish called Guanes, Laches, and
Tunebos.[34] They all had their own textile industries and kin-based polities.

The peoples of the lowlands of the Magdalena River valley were not all
Panches, as early Spanish authors depicted them, and they were in their own

process of expansion at the time of the Spanish invasion. The hot lands were peopled by diverse groups that the Spanish later identified as Sutagaos, Colimas, Panches, Muzos, Andaquies, Carares, and others. While these groups did not see themselves as belonging to a common group, many of their languages have since been identified as part of the Carib linguistic family. Their economic activities combined agriculture with mining, and they were dominant in war. These groups were notorious in imperial reports for rejecting rigid social and political hierarchies based on kin, and instead elected leaders based on their display of force or their diffusion of visionary messages.

As three Muzo men put it in 1584 when asked about their precolonial political organization: "They did not pay nor [now] pay tributes to caciques or captains because among them there never were nor did they ever had caciques, natural or foreigners, to whom they were vassals, and if there were some captains it was only during times of war."[35] Even in war, they added, it was a brave man among them who would convene friends for drinks and ask them to join in battle; they joined almost as peers ("casi como compañeros los mandan"), and the instigator's authority did not extend beyond the realm of war ("fuera de la guerra no le obedecían en cosa alguna"). This is a recurrent theme in early Spanish descriptions, which often described the inhabitants of the lowlands as peoples without rulers. In this sense, the language and dynamics of power in the lowlands worked differently than those in the highlands. The lowlands had less stable kin polities, but they had the capacity to form remarkably dynamic and mighty political groupings for certain causes.[36] In fact, at the time of the Spanish invasion some peoples of the lowlands, like the Muzos, were in the middle of a process of expansion toward the highlands.[37]

The conceptual barrier that conquistadors established between hot and cold helped them make sense of ethnic diversity by distorting and simplifying Indigenous societies. It also rendered invisible the complex connections between the Native worlds of the highlands and the lowlands that made the landscapes and peoples of the Andes what they were. Yet the highlands and lowlands were strongly connected worlds, and this is clear in material culture. The bodies of a cipa like Saguanmachica or a sihipqua like Ubaque can easily prove this point: they were adorned with gold jewelry wrought from lowland metals, feathers from the tropical rainforest, textiles woven with lowland cotton, and necklaces made from beads and shells from the Caribbean coastland. Their appearance was itself a testimony to the remarkable connections between highlands and lowlands.[38] These politically and ethnically fragmented landscapes were woven together by the persistent movement of goods. Gold, feathers, ceramics, cotton, coca, shells, salt, and even rocks and clay circulated widely. The items traded across the kingdom included raw materials, tools, food, manufactured goods, and symbolic objects.

Archaeologists disagree about the impact of trade on culture and economy. While some believe trade made highland diets dependent on lowland products—and thus created a series of rather homogeneous cultures in the highlands and the lowlands—others claim that food exchange had minimal impact and that Indigenous societies lacked the infrastructure and instruments, such as money and specialized traders, to move large quantities of food over long distances. The latter group claims instead that trade centered around prestige objects and esoteric goods used by political and religious elites to enact their power and endow themselves with an aura of distinction. Both positions neglect the fact that the highlands relied on trade for the production and consumption of some of their most important and everyday goods—cotton, salt, coca, and gold—but they did so without losing their ethnicities and without political centralization.[39]

The cakes of salt that attracted Quesada to the highlands exemplify these lively transregional networks. Salt production was very important in the highlands, and entire villages were devoted to the manufacture and circulation of salt. It was an ancient trade that goes back over two millennia, although there seemed to be a dramatic increase in salt production around the first century AD. Production was straightforward. Some villages filled ceramic vessels with salty water in highland lakes and heated them until the water completely evaporated. Once the cooking process was done, they would break the ceramic vessels to remove the compact cakes of salt that remained, which were easy to carry to distant regions. With this method, a social unit of seven to thirteen houses (about thirty-five to seventy people) provided enough salt for ten thousand people.[40] With this production capacity, the highlands produced enough salt to meet demand beyond their ethnic boundaries.

As salt streamed down the mountains, other key products came up. Coca leaves, cotton, tobacco, feathers, gold, beads, shells, emeralds, skins, and many other products relevant to the social, cultural, and political life of the highlands traveled there from the lowlands. Many foreign goods were embedded with great cultural significance. Shells, beads, and feathers were deemed valuable as products of distant lands and were charged with ritual, even magical attributes.[41] Even if costly and hard to access, these products left a mark on society as a whole. For instance, some shells from the coastland were so costly that only elites could acquire them, while commoners copied them in ceramic for use in burials.[42]

But trade between the highlands and lowlands was not limited to esoteric goods. Indeed, it included logs for construction and even rocks, which the

Muisca peoples then worked into lithic artifacts.[43] In fact, the long-distance exchange of heavy materials was key to salt production. This scale of salt production involved large quantities of ceramic vessels and wood-fired cooking systems. While archaeologists traditionally deemed ceramic containers too heavy and fragile for transregional trade, recent studies retrieved from salt-production sites in Muisca territory a large quantity of red ceramic shards likely made with material imported from the central Andean range and with motifs similar to those produced in lowland regions from the central Andean range. Even if the Muiscas had their own ceramic tradition, they probably favored this type of vessel for aesthetic and technical reasons: perhaps an admiration of its patterns and designs, or the particular suitableness of this type of clay for cooking salt.[44] Trade created shared iconographic forms that crossed ethnic and linguistic divides.[45] Foreign ceramic vessels were present in small settlements and common households and did not only belong to elites, indicating that this trade may have been driven by commoners.[46]

The movement of material objects across linguistic and ethnic boundaries involved a wide array of peoples sharing ideas, reaching agreements, and developing common terms of exchange. It is difficult to trace the arrangements that allowed goods to move across cultures with only archeological remains and Spanish imperial records for reference. Still, some Spanish observers remarked on how highlanders conducted business in the sixteenth century. In 1560, Tomás López Medel, a Spanish magistrate who traveled extensively across the kingdom, described the Muiscas as "very talented people, all of them are merchants and dealers."[47] The sihipquas held markets every week, which he judged similar to the markets in Spain.

> Great numbers of people come to those markets to buy and sell things for others. They deal in gold. They lack standard weights but do have certain mechanisms to measure and ensure they are not cheated. They usually deal with low-quality gold of different karats.[48]

These markets surface frequently in sixteenth-century documents, though few describe them in detail.[49] López pointed out that salt was "one of the best and major dealings they have." The salt of Bogotá reached every nearby province, including Neiva, Saldaña, Mariquita, and Popayán, and well into the eastern plains— all of which were peopled by different ethnic groups. But the organization of the salt trade did not strike López as dominated by elites. To him, the peoples of the cold lands were skilled merchants who launched their own enterprises as they saw fit. He offered an anecdote that he felt captured the entrepreneurial character of the Muiscas:

We have heard plenty of times of individual indios who leave Santa Fe with a cake of salt on their back, each of them weighing two arrobas, and take it to the market of Tocaima. If he does not find there someone willing to pay what he expects, he continues to Ibagué to sell it. If he is still not satisfied with what he is offered there, he takes it to the mines of Mariquita.[50]

López was impressed by the journey of one such merchant who was able to obtain the hefty sum of two castellanos for a cake of salt, well beyond its price near Bogotá. The anecdote illustrates the functioning of a long-distance, interethnic economic network that operated in the absence of a centralized political system. A commoner could set off to a distant land to sell his products and to get a better price. Indigenous traders overcame linguistic, ethnic, and political barriers to trade.

This type of economic arrangement does not fit the model scholars use to explain Andean economies. John V. Murra argued that the Incas had a large-scale imperial economy that worked in the striking absence of market institutions, money, or merchants. He showed that kin groups spread across the Andean slopes in such a way as to gain access to products from different ecological tiers—a form of spatial organization that he termed verticality. For Murra, verticality was the central principle of the Inca empire's political and economic organization. The Incas sent communities of specialized laborers called mitimaes to different localities to do the work needed by the empire, but did so without money or markets.[51] Murra's model has been critiqued, refined, and nuanced by later researchers, revealing a much more diverse economic system that did include merchants and markets.[52] Despite these findings, the fact that long-distance networks of exchange were tied to the centralized power of the Inca administration remains essential to our understanding of Andean economies.[53]

The Muiscas were Andean peoples who inhabited a plateau, which meant that they did not stretch out across vertical landscapes to control different ecological niches but instead designed alternative strategies to gain access to lowland products. In contrast to the Incas, the economy of the Muisca plateau was driven not by a political entity but rather by a series of different ethnic and political groups interacting with one another and sustaining long-range economic networks that crossed ethnic boundaries and involved many lowland Indigenous groups.[54] This striking articulation between lowland and highland peoples created a polymorphous configuration in which some Chibcha-speaking groups settled the lowlands, while Carib-speaking groups and other groups with traits and organizational patterns resembling those of the lowland groups—like the Pijaos, as I will show in chapter 4—moved into the highlands.

The Spanish lacked a framework to grasp these diverse social worlds and the economic links between them. They misread these dispersed connections by privileging authority and centralization as the main classification criteria, depicting the peoples of the highlands and the lowlands as completely separate entities. The division between the cold lands of the Andes and the hot river valleys of the lowlands became a structuring scheme that guided Spanish imperial policy for centuries, despite the frequent movement of people and goods between these spheres. They categorized Indigenous peoples based on their implicit ethnographies: good "indios" and bad "caribes," cold lands and hot lands. But Indigenous worlds were much more connected, diverse, and complex than the rigid categories Iberians used to pigeonhole them. Notwithstanding, Spanish misnomers served as forms and templates that allowed them to digest diversity, ultimately leading them to develop administrative frameworks to incorporate Indigenous societies into the empire. Institutions like encomiendas and cities served this purpose.

Founding as Translating

On August 12, 1542, eight men—five Indigenous people of the highlands of the New Kingdom of Granada and three Spaniards—gathered together in the recently founded city of Santa Fe de Bogotá for a bureaucratic ritual. Five years had passed since the conquering expedition led by Gonzalo Jiménez de Quesada had first reached the Andes, and four years had passed since they had murdered Sagipa, the cipa (highest Indigenous authority) of the area. On the Spanish side were the scribe Honorato Vicente, local judge Hernán Vanegas, and conquistador Juan de Céspedes. Representing the region's Indigenous groups were five prestigious Native authorities whom the imperial officials, using a mixture of Arawak and Spanish, identified as caciques and captains. Judge Vanegas began the bureaucratic ritual by asking the Native authorities their names and having the scribe annotate them in his book. Their names, in the Indigenous tradition, were complex concepts that described at once a territory, a political formation, and a person. The scribe jotted them down in his books, trying to translate the foreign sounds into the Spanish pronunciation of the Latin alphabet. He recorded them as Ubaque, Quecaçipa, Foca, Yteboye, and Yzaziaga.

With the names in the books, Vanegas took the Indigenous authorities by their hands and in a symbolic gesture handed them to Juan de Céspedes, saying, "In them and with them I give you possession and mastery of all the captains, caciques, and indios" of Ubaque. Céspedes in turn took them by the hand and accepted. To signal possession over the Native peoples of Ubaque, Céspedes stripped the five men of the carefully painted textiles that adorned their bodies and covered them back up again with the same clothes.[55] In other versions of the ceremony, the encomendero would order the Native representatives to rip some grass or herbs from the ground and toss them back down, or make them walk laps as a sign of submission. With this ritual, enacted upon the Native nobility and their textiles, a new institution was coming into existence, one that placed Indigenous peoples and Spaniards under a single system: the encomienda. The symbolic act of stripping Native peoples of their clothing and then re-dressing them meant that Céspedes would now be the encomendero—a type of lord who received a grant of Indigenous labor of the social groups that the five Native authorities belonged to, and was responsible for their evangelization. The point of the ceremony was to convey authority and obedience as the pillar of this new colonial institution.

The encomienda was the first iteration of the early modern Spanish monarchy's project to transform Indigenous peoples into Catholic vassals of the king. From imperial theorists' point of view, this institution benefited all involved. Since the conquest was a private enterprise, the people—mostly men—who engaged in it expected a reward. Some of them gathered soldiers and invested in horses and arms when they embarked on new discoveries. Others had fewer resources but risked war for the possibility of gaining wealth. The encomienda was how the Crown rewarded them. The king awarded former conquistadors— now encomenderos—authority over an Indigenous group, which was obliged to pay them annual tribute. The encomendero was in turn responsible for the "religious instruction" of the Indigenous peoples assigned to them. A fifth of the tribute went to the Crown's treasury. Encomenderos were also expected to maintain horses, arms, and a city residence in order to protect the interests of the monarchy in case of rebellions, foreign invasions, or other possible challenges. After the conquering expeditions invaded the northern Andes in the late 1530s, Jiménez de Quesada dismembered the existing Muisca cacicazgos into 157 encomiendas. In this process, the encomienda reshuffled Indigenous political landscapes. With these grants, the Crown expected to reward particular conquistadors for their role in conquering new peoples and to extend its domain of rule in the New World.[56]

The encomienda sought to transform Indigenous peoples into Catholic subjects while at the same time maintaining local corporate structures as well as the traditional hierarchies, rights, privileges, and customs of the different groups and territories that constituted the monarchy.[57] This approach to colonization was profoundly ambivalent, however, because it meant that the Crown and its agents took an interest in maintaining local economies and polities but not local religious or cultural beliefs, which, in their view, had to be exterminated. Yet the Spanish administration did not attempt to disassemble or eliminate local groups and polities, instead seeking ways to draw them into imperial frameworks. The rights and privileges of Native authorities remained largely unchanged, and agents of the Crown attempted to govern Native communities according to their own traditions and customs. It was an ambiguous system that sought to produce Catholic and tribute-paying vassals while at the same time maintaining local forms of governance.[58] Rather than a centralizing and homogenizing power, the Spanish monarchy is best described as a loose association of polities: a network of institutions that molded themselves to local groups while at the same time imposing on them the cultural and economic burdens of colonialism. As Yanna Yannakakis points out, "As a language of negotiation, costumbre [custom] provided an ideal tool of empire."[59]

Municipalities were another device used to establish control over Indigenous peoples and establish new settler communities as recognized in the Spanish legal system. Two years passed between Jimenez's 1537 arrival in the Andes and the founding of Santa Fe de Bogotá, the first Spanish city in the eastern Andean range, in 1539. Lugo had not authorized Jiménez to found cities, establish permanent settlements, or create new political divisions. But Jiménez did not comply with this limitation.[60] Sebastián de Belalcázar, however, had received authorization from Pizarro to found cities. In fact, he founded four cities in his journey to the north: Quito, Cali, Popayán, and Timaná. It was only seven months after Jiménez, Belalcázar, and Federman arrived in the highlands of the eastern range of the Andes that the three expeditions founded the new city of Santa Fe de Bogotá.[61]

There are more questions than answers regarding the city's founding. The exact date and place of its establishment are unclear. Historian Juan Friede posited that there had been two foundations: one of fact, which entailed the physical occupation of space with the construction of a few huts that took place in August 1538, and another of a juridical nature, carried out on April 27, 1539, that involved creating a cabildo—a municipal council vested with judicial, legislative, and executive functions that consisted of about eleven officials in charge of the city's administration.[62] Friede believed that the place where Jiménez de Quesada established the new city was the palisade of the cipa, the highest Indigenous authority in the plateau.[63] Archaeologist Sylvia Broadbent, in contrast, posited that the conquistadors chose to site the new city in an

Indigenous location known as Teusaquillo, and that the real headquarters of the cipa were located to the south in the region known today as Funza, which was called Bogotá throughout the imperial period.[64] The debate regarding whether the new city had been built on the headquarters of the cipa reveals how new imperial cities mapped onto Indigenous political landscapes. It is also tied to deeper questions about Indigenous naming practices and the nature of political concepts, as well as Muisca forms of spatial organization. In other words, to know whether the city was founded on the headquarters of the cipa, we must comprehend what the headquarters of the cipa might have looked like.

The Muisca peoples called the domains of the cipa Muyquyta, which literally meant a yard or planted field in a savannah but was also a complex concept referring to a political leader (the cipa), a territory, and a political structure.[65] As a political structure, Muyquyta was composed of at least thirteen social units, each of which occupied separate territories and was under a different ruler (in Muisca called sihipquas, and later termed by the Spaniards caciques). As a territory, Muyquyta referred to the terrains occupied by those caciques and their subjects. In both senses, though, the term could be abstracted to refer more generally to the domains of the cipa and the eastern range of the Andes. Muyquyta was not a "city" in the Iberian sense, but a political community divided into different territories and political sections.[66] The Spanish transliterated the term Muyquyta as Bogotá, and included it in the name of the newly founded city, Santa Fe de Bogotá. The seventeenth-century historian Juan Rodríguez Freyle stressed that the new name captured Jiménez de Quesada's association between the northern Andes and the city of Santa Fe in Granada, while also appropriating a Muisca political concept.

The site where Jiménez de Quesada, Belalcázar, and Federman founded the city of Santa Fe de Bogotá was, therefore, not the place where most of the population of Muyquyta lived. According to Indigenous testimonies in the 1540s, however, the site was part of the domain of Muyquyta. Don Gonzalo, an Indigenous man from Bogotá who had served as Jiménez de Quesada's interpreter, claimed that the conquistadors had first established themselves in the "house of Bogotá," a residence of the cipa.[67] The Indigenous people, however, had rebelled twice and burned the houses. For this reason, the conquistadors moved to the site called Teusaquillo, where the new city was founded. Archaeologist Monika Therrien has found evidence of Indigenous occupation of the site of Santa Fe's central plaza dating back to at least AD 300, revealing its deep history. Another historian believes that Teusaquillo, where the plaza of the new city was erected, had previously been the cacique's central palisade and that the central road of the palisade became the royal road of Santa Fe.[68] It is likely, therefore, that the city was built in the ritual and political heart of the cipa, where the cipa and his subjects gathered for political activities, but not where his subjects resided. Whether the new city was exactly located on the palisade of the cipa or not, it took a powerful Indigenous political concept as its name.

Santa Fe de Bogotá became the epicenter of a network of cities. Shortly after its founding, the conquistadores founded Tunja, Pamplona, Vélez, Neiva, Cocuy, Málaga, and Tocaima. They founded twenty-five cities in the kingdom between 1539 and 1576, eight of which were abandoned in the following centuries. Historian Germán Colmenares claims that the foundation of cities and administrative divisions did not have a rationale but followed the erratic ventures of the conquest.[69] However, the logic behind the founding of cities seems clear: the Spanish created most of the new settlements where they identified major cores of Indigenous groups. Bogotá and Tunja were located in the two divisions of Muisca territory, the cipa and the zaque; Pamplona among the Guane; Tocaima among the Panche; Vélez among the Muzo; Cocuy among the Uwa or Tunebo; La Palma among the Colima; and Neiva and Ibagué on Indigenous centers on the border with the Pijaos. In this way, imperial cities were established directly over Indigenous ethnic territories, following their distribution and, in some cases, even their naming patterns. As in the case of Santa Fe de Bogotá, the cities themselves created new political organs of the monarchy, embodied in new spaces, but they did so because of their specific location in a preexisting Indigenous landscape. The multiplicity of ethnic groups, in turn, supported a proliferation of cities uncharacteristic of other parts of the Spanish empire, most of which concentrated around one primary city.[70]

The conquistadors founded the first cities in the cold highlands and then expanded toward the Magdalena River valley and the surrounding ethnic territories. By the late 1540s and early 1550s a shift in the geographical imagination of the kingdom had taken place. In the first decades of the conquest, the conquistadors' income consisted of the spoils of conquest and large reserves of gold they took from the peoples of the highlands. But as time progressed, the conquistadors looked for wealth in precious minerals. The hot lands had the largest deposits of gold and silver, and founding cities there was a way of penetrating Indigenous territories to extract those precious metals. The Spanish created cities like San Sebastián de la Plata and Los Remedios to expand into those mining areas. These new conquering ventures attracted a floating population of poor Spaniards who did not receive encomiendas, as well as many who had fled north after participating in the rebellions of the 1540s in Peru.[71] If initially the expeditions led by Jiménez de Quesada, Belalcázar, and Federman were driven to the cold lands in search of wealth, a decade later the conquistadors projected the same illusions onto the lowlands.

By the 1550s, the organization of the Indigenous peoples of the South American mainland had been adapted and translated into two Iberian concepts: cities and encomiendas. Bureaucratic rituals, such as the allocation of encomiendas and creation of cities, absorbed Indigenous worlds into monarchical legality. The early modern Iberian notion of the city distinguished between the urbs (the physical unit, the built environment) and the civitas (a human association, a community).[72] In this sense, founding a city was more than building houses and designing streets: it meant creating a political community vis-à-vis the monarchy. The city was, therefore, a legal fact that defined who would be considered vecinos (neighbors or citizens) and who would be deemed indios or naturales (Indigenous or Native people). Both were categories of belonging that identified those who could enjoy rights and would be forced to comply with duties.[73] To "found" a city in the heart of an Indigenous territory meant to create a new political community subject to the monarchy and to define which members would enjoy specific rights.

The Spanish presented the founding of cities as creation: a foundational act in which new cities were erected from nothing. In reality, it was a practice of translation and overlap, through which existing Indigenous forms of organization were re-signified into a new bureaucratic structure. The new system of cities was a palimpsest—a manuscript that has been written over—in which Indigenous structures gave shape to imperial administrative structures. Indigenous society, albeit overwritten and subsumed, actualized the landscapes and peoples of the New World. Founding cities was a process of creation only inasmuch as it rendered the landscape visible to the Iberian bureaucracy and gave it a political existence. Indigenous societies, in other words, provided the underlying order for colonialism.

Unending Conquests

The conquest has often been described as an early, twenty-year phase of European occupation. The word *conquest* evokes images of a small group of heavily armed Europeans walking through pristine forests. After their military victory—which was portrayed as relatively easy in the case of the New Kingdom of Granada—things quieted down and gave way to the more stable colonial period. War gave way to mining, political control, and stability—a quiet pax Hispanica, an eventless domination.

This view of the conquest is flawed in several ways. On the one hand, it flattens a complex historical process by excising the mystery, problems, and uncertainty that mark all historical processes. It portrays the conquest as linear and assumes that Native groups were subdued and remained quiet and obedient under Spanish rule. In fact, Indigenous people continually contested the kingdom's sovereignty. The fact that the Spanish Crown did not have a standing military force and that violence was not perpetrated by a centralized, standing army—as would be the case in modern states—should not blind us to the recurrent need for violence to maintain monarchical rule. In order to exist, the kingdom relied on violence. The graphic scenes of the caciques hung in the central square of Tunja or the torture of Sagipa were early examples of an enduring use of violence as a political tool.

In fact, the conquest—its ideas, illusions, and institutions—molded how Europeans understood the kingdom and shaped interactions between the cold lands and hot lands throughout the sixteenth and seventeenth centuries. Initially, the conquistadors saw wealth in the cold lands of the Andes and poverty in the lowlands. After pillaging Indigenous wealth, however, they shifted their dreams of riches to the lowlands. Settlers and officials then envisioned the lowlands as rich sources of gold, populated by fierce "caribes." They launched countless expeditions to the lowlands, searching for golden cities. El Dorado remained a powerful image in their delirious, insatiable thirst for precious metals. It embodied a series of ideas about the hot lands. The eastern plains, in the Orinoco Basin, were renamed the province of El Dorado, and Hernán Pérez de Quesada and Antonio Berrío led ventures to find the treasures they thought were hidden in jungles, valleys, and savannas.[74] In 1624, Antonio de Olalla y Herrera, who had participated in those campaigns, wrote to the king saying that he had heard "news of very wealthy, dressed people; very big provinces of indios."[75] The desire to subdue other peoples and find sources of gold—even rivers or cities of gold—still informed how Europeans thought about their mission in the Indies and the empire itself. It shaped their illusions and expectations, how they thought they could become rich and powerful, and sometimes brought them to death and disaster. Rather than a linear process or a short phase, conquest was an unending labyrinth of violence.

Settlers described the conquest with terms like *exploring, discovering,* and *founding.* It was a form of narrating events that presented the Spanish occupation as a point of departure, rather than a continuum. Following anthropologist Michel-Rolph Trouillot, it could be said that the conquest was also a story.[76] It was a way of remembering the past that established the arrival of the Spaniards as a point of departure. Even today, cities and villages cherish and celebrate their dates of foundation as the moment when their histories began. Yet founding was really a process of absorbing and translating Native realities and economic networks to institutions of the Spanish monarchy. Indigenous cacicazgos, groupings, and political concepts still offered organizing principles. It was a hybrid order that was both Indigenous and European. During the 1530s and 1540s, a new vocabulary of power and hierarchy used terms like *cipa, encomendero, cacique*, and *indio* to describe those overlapping orders. *Cipa* continued to be the term of highest prestige, used to name the most powerful authorities, even the king and the magistrates of the audiencia. Muyquyta/Bogotá was the heart of this kingdom, governed by a town council composed of the most renowned conquistadors, sometimes called cipas. Sihipquas and other Indigenous leaders now reported to encomenderos, and they were now caciques: all flattened into a single level of hierarchy, identified as "nobles of the land" and key figures in the maintenance of the imperial order. The kingdom was a patchwork, sewn from the remnants of previous orders.

In the coming decades, the city of Bogotá would become the setting of a new institution that became the political spine of the kingdom: the audiencia, a royal tribunal of justice that established routines and protocols for the functioning of the new imperial system. The establishment of the audiencia and its instruments of rule are the subject of the next chapter.

A KINGDOM OF PAPER

Around 1570, a fifty-year-old Spanish lawyer named Tomás López Medel drafted a book-length manuscript titled *On the Three Elements*, a summa of the Indies. The summa was a genre that aimed to compile the main traits of a particular topic; it was a philosophical treatise that sought to unveil the composition and nature of a geographical site and its inhabitants. True to its aim, López's treatise offered a description of the Indies organized around the three elements of air, water, and soil—surprisingly, leaving out fire—to explain the societies that had formed in the Indies. López had an eye for detail and used it to describe the natural world. He included careful observations of the skies and winds, hurricanes, lakes, oceans, volcanos, mountains, and climates. He discarded the ideas of the many monsters that common folk in the Iberian Peninsula thought populated the Indies, such as winged dragons, but described in detail the annoyance caused by the near-invisible insects called jejenes that infuriated travelers in the New Kingdom of Granada's hot lands. He quoted his travels, his personal experiences, and even his conversations with prisoners in the Santa Fe de Bogotá jail as his sources of knowledge.[1]

The manuscript was an act of intellectual assimilation, a reflection of López's experience in the Indies that aimed to intervene in Atlantic-wide debates about the morality and legitimacy of the Spanish empire in the New World. His argument was most clearly exposed in the manuscript's final section, which narrated an imaginary trial between the New World and the Old World that he used to assess the outcome of Spain's presence in the New World. The trial reproduced the formalities of Iberian justice, organized as a series of accusations (cargos) and exonerations (descargos), but it was set before God—the ultimate judge. The New World was charged with affronts against natural law. He classified the Native inhabitants of the New World into three categories according to their clothing: those who lived naked, those who lived nearly naked, and those who wore clothing. While he deemed the first group closer to natural men and the last group better suited to live as Christians, he believed that they all lived in sin and would ultimately face divine justice. However, he believed the Old World was responsible for the most serious crimes: "They [the Native inhabitants of the New World] sinned as people distant from God, but they did not know him. . . . We are worse [than the indios], worthy of greater punishment and sentence."[2] In this view, Spaniards had access to the true faith but failed to live up to the divine calling of bringing Native peoples to Christianity. López concluded that if the monarch wished to clear his conscience, he had to reform the Crown's government of the Indies by valuing Catholic education over wealth.

This chapter examines the installation of the Spanish empire's institutions, spatial organization, and administrative routines in the New Kingdom during the 1550s and 1560s, through the lens of Tomás López Medel's writings and records. I ask what one of the empire's firmest believers thought the kingdom should look like and how he came to the dire predicament exposed in the paragraphs above, in which he found Spaniards at fault for creating a cruel, ungodly system of governance.

Tomás López's career took shape amid the intellectual challenges and social transformations that accompanied the Spanish monarchy's expansion in the New World. He was the son of a rural Iberian family, born in 1520 or 1521 in Tendilla, Guadalajara, and received a degree in law from Alcalá de Henares in 1539. In Alcalá, he joined a community of thought that was revisiting classical, medieval, and contemporary authors to envision a universal Catholic monarchy. Alcalá was a newly formed university founded during the Counter-Reformation according to the principles of humanism. The ideas of Erasmus had a special resonance in Alcalá and when Charles V invited Erasmus to give a talk in Spain, he chose Alcalá as the venue.[3] The university had published not only Erasmus's writings but also numerous critical editions or translations of classical humanist writers. It had also been the intellectual home of men like Antonio de Nebrija, the author of the first grammar of the Spanish language (and of any Romance language), who famously wrote, "Language has always been the companion of empire," and Alfonso de Castro, Charles V's confessor and an eclectic thinker who defended the Inquisition, admired Erasmus and humanism, and defended the right of Indigenous peoples to pursue theology and priesthood.[4] It was a creative environment in which post-Tridentine thinkers renovated the precepts of Catholicism in its confrontation against Lutheranism and other heresies, using Thomism, scholastic thought, and humanism, while also pondering the role that the Spanish empire should play in the Indies. With this training, López became part of the professional officials (letrados) formed during Spain's early modern education revolution—to use Richard Kagan's term—and was able to take advantage of the new professional opportunities presented by his education.[5]

In 1549, two decades before writing his summa of the Indies, López ventured to the New World to take part in the expansion of the Spanish monarchy overseas. As an imperial administrator, López had a notable career. He was present at important sites in the definition of empire. His first post in the Indies was as a magistrate in the Audiencia de los Confines in Guatemala in 1550—which had jurisdiction over Yucatán at the time—and he met the Dominicans in Chiapas after Bartolomé de las Casas left his post as bishop to return to Spain. At the time, he was thirty years old and expected to contribute to building a heavenly landscape in the New World. He was convinced of the godly mission of the Spanish empire and was eager to put into practice many of the theoretical discussions he had been exposed to during his studies. López carried out a general visit to Yucatán between 1552 and 1553, where he laid out a plan to gather the Mayas into villages to mold their lives according to Catholic practices and values. According to Inga Clendinnen, López "gave the colonists their most sustained view of the new breed of royal official," who was austere and inflexible; he "had been a reminder of the power and majesty of the imperial government."[6]

In Guatemala he created the post of the "protector of the indios," one that Bartolomé de las Casas and the Dominicans had sought to create since 1517 and which had been excluded from the New Laws. It was an ambitious project: it attempted to establish a position for an official who would, at least in theory, defend and represent Native people in Hispanic courts and advocate for their interests vis-à-vis the imperial administration.[7] While he promoted some protections for Native peoples, López was also skeptical of such measures. From

Mesoamerica, he wrote to the king to express his concern that imperial policies favored Native peoples over Spaniards. He considered this situation unfortunate, since a monarch should not privilege one group of subjects above another.

It is evident that something had radically changed in the two decades between López's work in Mesoamerica and when he wrote his treatise. By that time, his thinking had evolved from seeing imperial policies as unjust toward Spanish settlers to strongly advocating for the defense of Native peoples. It is no coincidence that during the period in between these two experiences, from 1557 to 1562, López participated in some of the New Kingdom of Granada's most important administrative reforms. He was appointed magistrate of the Audiencia of Santa Fe in 1552, but he arrived in Bogotá only in 1557.[8] He served as the most senior audiencia magistrate at a time when there was no active audiencia president. That meant that he was in charge of some of the most pressing administrative tasks, like the visits to Indigenous communities, a central practice of governance in which audiencia magistrates visited, interviewed and counted Indigenous peoples, as I will show below. It was during his time in this corner of the empire that his humanist idealism shattered in the face of the harsh realities of colonialism.

López's illusions and frustrations offer an intimate portrait of the nature of power and governance of the Hispanic monarchy in the Indies and, in particular, in the New Kingdom of Granada. As a humanist scholar who took an active role in empire-building, López was obsessed with law and rituals. He expected the Indies to reflect the majesty and grandeur of the monarchy and strove to align the kingdom to the empire's theoretical claims. For him, the kingdom's moral reasoning was to remake Native peoples according to imperial notions of virtue, spiritual life, and the afterlife. He saw them as people who lived in a "natural" state, who needed to first be taught how to carry out their lives before they could be introduced to the philosophical subtleties of his faith. Armed with this conviction, he strove to produce a governing system that reached the most intimate spheres of Indigenous peoples' lives—to transform their daily existence. The Audiencia of Santa Fe was the entity in charge of governing and keeping track of Indigenous communities. As a magistrate of the audiencia, López employed the empire's paper technologies to bring those ideals into practice and to extend the monarchy's reach into Indigenous peoples' intimate spaces.

López's case illustrates the principles, practices, and instruments of rule deployed by the monarchy to create a Catholic kingdom in the northern Andes in the 1550s and 1560s. Lopez worked to set up a governing system with the broad aims of evangelizing and providing justice. Through this system, Indigenous communities were surveyed and their homelands refashioned to mirror the Renaissance ideals López cherished. Yet the result was more brutal and chaotic than López anticipated. His final evaluation of the kingdom was colored by frustration and disillusionment. He deemed it plagued by ungodly behavior and claimed that it was governed by a dysfunctional royal tribunal that aimed only to extract material wealth. By focusing on López—one of the New Kingdom's framers—I seek to see the empire through its own eyes: its goals, procedures, and outcome.[9] I examine the institutions and paper instruments that allowed the geographic extension of a political system that depended on the personal, highly emotional relationship between the king and his Indigenous and European subjects overseas. López did not challenge the empire's right to rule or to govern Indigenous lives, but he did question the motivation to do so for material gain. His critique of the kingdom's governance shows that by 1560, the kingdom was far from acceptable even for a fervent believer in colonialism: the institutions designed to provide justice left Indigenous peoples at the mercy of economic exploitation and local power factions.

An Audiencia in the Indies

The New Laws of 1542 included a comprehensive set of policies for the government of the Indies.[10] First and foremost, they delineated a geography of governance. The sheer scale of the Indies was daunting in this regard: Spanish officials sought to distribute administrative units in a territory that in size far exceeded the Iberian Peninsula or the monarchy's other possessions, and imperial officials were obliged to draw lines on an imperfect map. To meet that challenge, the Spanish monarchy relied on a series of medieval institutions, forms of governance, and practices, and projected them onto a global empire. The Crown created viceroyalties, audiencias, and governorships—institutions that adapted medieval political practices to the New World. The New Laws decreed the creation of the Viceroyalty of Peru, the Audiencia of Lima, and the Audiencia of Guatemala and Nicaragua (called the Audiencia de los Confines), while eliminating the Audiencia of Panama (which was later revived).

Through this geographical layout and a series of micromanagerial instructions, the Crown aimed to shift power away from local elites, and especially from encomenderos, and concentrate it instead in the hands of imperial officials. For this purpose, they standardized the size and functioning of the Council of the Indies, audiencias, governorships, and town councils, and redefined the royal treasury's procedures. They specified the procedure for embarking on new discoveries and reformed the laws governing work, tribute, and encomiendas in the Indies. In sum, the New Laws intended to draw power away from local elites by standardizing political practice with a clear set of instructions for governing the other shore of the Atlantic.

The New Laws, however, did not introduce government entities in the northern end of South America. This region remained a political vacuum, and settlers routinely decried the problems related to the lack of judicial tribunals in the area. By the 1540s, the distribution of Indigenous cacicazgos to Spanish conquistadors under the encomienda system had generated a divisive and contentious atmosphere among the settlers, many of whom disagreed with the way Gonzalo Jiménez de Quesada had assigned Native communities to conquistadors. They complained that he had granted the most important encomiendas to his friends and kin and that many deserving men who fought and invested in the conquest were left empty-handed. Instead of fixing the problem, the governors who followed Jiménez de Quesada revoked encomiendas from the settlers only to put them under their own names. For instance, Alonso Luis de Lugo, the governor of the kingdom beginning in November 1543, took for himself the encomiendas of men who had played crucial roles in the conquest. By the end of his governorship the kingdom's settlers were restive, and prosecutors and town councils wrote to the king asking for a new mechanism of justice that could settle claims and see to matters of governance.[11] They argued that the distance to the Audiencia of Santo Domingo in the Caribbean, to which they were subordinate, delayed and aggravated problems that required urgent solutions. A new royal tribunal, they argued, would give them autonomy and efficiency to make decisions locally and promptly.[12]

It was in this contentious atmosphere that the Crown decided to establish a new jurisdiction of governance called the Audiencia y Cancillería Real, based in Santa Fe de Bogotá, to fill the void. It is unclear exactly when it was established, but it is likely that the decree creating the audiencia dates from early 1547, and that by 1549 it was already functioning, although the first president would not arrive in Santa Fe de Bogotá until 1564. The development of ecclesiastical jurisdictions came in parallel, as the king appointed high churchmen following the royal patronage (patronazgo real). The first bishop, Juan de los Barrios, arrived in Santa Fe only in 1553, to try to give shape to an incoherent and chaotic evangelization project shaped by a conflict-ridden Dominican order and a scant presence of Franciscans.[13] The region became an ecclesiastical province of its own in 1564, when the archbishopric was established. Like audiencia magistrates, bishops and archbishops were heavily involved in the power networks of Santa Fe.

From the point of view of Madrid, the main goal of the audiencia was to enforce the New Laws. The Crown had been trying to implement this legislation even before it established the audiencia. One of the first actions of Miguel Díez de Armendáriz when appointed governor of the New Kingdom of Granada was to distribute the New Laws. He did so on January 1, 1547 (presumably in the central plaza of Santa Fe), only a couple of months after arriving in the kingdom.[14] Conquistadors and settlers opposed two points of the New Laws: first, that upon an encomendero's death the Crown would take over his encomienda, and second, that those who served as governors or held administrative posts would have their encomiendas revoked. The powerful men of the kingdom did not want to lose their encomiendas, and other settlers, unhappy with the pattern of distribution, were waiting for encomiendas to become available. The New Laws threatened the expectations of both groups. As a result, Bishop Juan de los Barrios, along with many settlers, wrote to the Council of the Indies saying that such measures in an already impoverished land would drive settlers away and leave the kingdom desolate and fragile, impossible to defend should Native peoples take up arms against the king. Amid these adversities, in February 1547 Armendáriz held off enforcing the new legislation, only a month after he first circulated the laws. Settlers' opposition to new instruments of Crown control was clear.

That these were the most contentious points of the New Laws illustrates the issues at the forefront of officials' and settlers' minds, as well as what was at stake in the creation of the audiencia; it reveals the contested visions of this royal tribunal. While the Crown saw the audiencia as a means to enforce the New Laws, thus gaining control over local affairs, settlers simply needed a court that could readily resolve juridical conflicts, not tighter laws governing their behavior and restricting their control over local matters, and they opposed some of the New Laws' most substantive issues in the same letters in which they wrote in favor of the audiencia. This tension would haunt the audiencia throughout the sixteenth century.

That the king opted to create a royal appellate tribunal to oversee the implementation of laws and matters of governance in such a diverse landscape, and indeed in the Indies as a whole, exemplifies the historical tradition that unified politics and the law in medieval and early modern Iberia. From the late medieval period, politics had been tied to the provision of justice. These traditions of governance were heavily anchored in theological reasoning: through creation, God had given a natural order to the world in which different social groups had distinct positions, and the role of the ruler was to support that order and to provide justice to all beings as appropriate to their position in the natural order. The meaning of justice, therefore, was to ensure that everyone got what they "deserved." The king was, above all, a judge: he was responsible for keeping order by mediating between conflicting interests, as inspired by the divine will. Initially, the audiencias were hearings in which the monarch and his councilors first listened as vassals voiced their concerns and then provided justice. As the monarchy expanded from medieval to early modern times, monarchical institutions had to extend the king's presence to vast territories where he could not be physically present. During this transition, the audiencia became a governing entity ruled by high-ranking, highly trained officials called magistrates, who enacted the king's presence and imparted justice in distant lands.[15]

In the sixteenth century, the audiencias were installed in the Indies. The seventeenth-century jurist Juan de Solórzano y Pereira mentioned that the audiencias of the Indies had the same power and authority as those in Spain. Due to the distance and duration of Atlantic crossings, he argued, the tribunals of the Indies supervised matters over which Iberian tribunals had no responsibility, including naming and supervising Crown officials such as corregidores and other local posts. Solórzano y Pereira thanked the king and praised the audiencias as sites where people could find justice for the matters that troubled them. To him, "wherever the kings and princes cannot intervene, rule, or govern the Republic by themselves, there is nothing better to do than to give it to ministers that can, in their name, govern them, protect them, manage them, and distribute justice rightly, cleanly, and in a saintly manner."[16] The audiencia represented an entity of divine justice, in which imperial officials restored the natural Catholic order.

To replicate a hearing with the monarch in the Indies—a moment of interaction between the king and his subjects—required a dual maneuver: to bring the aura of the king's presence to the Indies and to carry the voices of vassals to the king and his officials in Spain. To achieve the first part, the tribunal aimed to replicate the experience of being before the king through mimicry and embodied practice. This involved creating the right setting and following strict protocols on what the audiencia and its officials should look like.[17] As historian Alejandra Osorio has argued, imperial rule took place "through the repetition of a common ceremonial calendar and the forms of ritual ceremonies centered on the king's body," which took form in architectural and urban designs, in churches, palaces, municipal councils, or the urban grid.[18] All of these visible objects, spaces, and rituals enacted the presence of a physically absent king.

The second part of this maneuver entailed translating the experience of hearing into a practice of writing and reading: converting sounds into movable objects. The connections made through writing enabled the empire to operate along its irregular, unstable geographies. Literary critic Ángel Rama has referred to the interdependence between writing and power in Hispanic America using the expression "the lettered city": "a scattering of cities, isolated and practically out of communication with one another," ruled by a plethora of officials, like scribes, notaries, and lawyers, who were "the masters of writing in an illiterate society."[19] This excess of functionaries guarded paper and letters with zeal; they forced Latin American realities into a decontextualized, abstract grid, ultimately installing a new social order through the circulation of paper.

A dot in the middle of the mountains, Santa Fe de Bogotá was one such lettered city—a node in the transatlantic flow of paper. The audiencia participated in a manuscript culture that enabled a personal and emotional connection between the monarch and each of his vassals. Rarely would printed documents—printed in Madrid or other places—take part in this world of letters. In fact, the New Kingdom of Granada did not have a printing press until the eighteenth century. There was, however, a robust infrastructure for producing, copying, and submitting documents, which depended on standardized forms, symbols, and conventions. Royal decrees (cédulas reales) were letters by the king often responding to demands from vassals and signed "I, the King." The petitions authored by vassals highlighted emotions—love, piety, and fidelity toward the king, but also frustration, despair, and suffering—and even spoke of physical interactions between the monarch and the vassals, like kissing the king's feet ("beso a usted los pies").[20] Sometimes they would actually kiss the paper itself, place it on top of their heads, and declare their obedience to the letters before recording the action on paper as evidence of their physical gestures.[21] These vivid, ritualized interactions with paper enacted the king's presence and established an intimate bond between vassals and the monarch despite the physical distance between them.

The audiencia, as a truly scriptural entity, depended on the circulation of paper across these uneven geographies. The Council of the Indies created templates and questionnaires and sent detailed information to officials about what data they needed to collect and how to record it. These guidelines gave imperial authorities a framework to judge whether the information was deemed trustworthy or not. The imperial administration communicated strict protocols for the production, storage, and circulation of documents, while at the same time giving room to local officials, settlers, and Native people to write to convey their perspectives on issues of governance. The audiencia stored mandates from Spain and gathered information about local societies to send to Madrid, together with requests, news, and claims from vassals to the king.

A rare book entitled *Relation of the Provisions and Royal Degrees of His Majesty Kept at the Audiencia of the New Kingdom of Granada* illustrates this point.[22] The book is a compilation of the decrees and instructions that the Council of the Indies issued for the royal tribunal. The Council decreed that the tribunal should consist of a meeting house with royal insignia, a jail, and a gold mint, and in the following decades added 309 rules and procedures that the audiencia had to abide by. The first instructions in the book specified the routines and practices of governance that officials of the royal tribunal should follow to produce, submit, and archive documents as they applied the New Laws as well as other royal mandates. In 1549, the audiencia received an ordinance requiring it to maintain an archive with the relevant royal mandates, as well as magistrates' resolutions and judicial rulings. It instructed the audiencia to be careful with the administration of paper: they were to follow strict guidelines on how to store, exhibit, and circulate paper. Other rules specified the scenarios in which officials could use the royal seal—a means to mark paper with the king's emblem, which had to be employed with the utmost care and strictness, since it enacted the monarch's presence.[23]

That the first decrees in the instruction book for magistrates concerned archiving exemplifies the central place of writing in the functioning of the empire. The book itself, in its materiality, is a testament to the circulation of power in the empire. The handwritten title describes the object as a notebook, and while its pages were also handwritten, it was not a notetaking device. It was an anthology of instructions transcribed and assembled together, to be read and taken as a reference. In addition to the decrees, it included several tables of contents, indexes, and synopses—a series of textual strategies of information management developed in the early modern period to digest the great volume of available information, which allowed notaries, secretaries, and magistrates to find specific content to support decision-making processes. Creating these texts was a highly manual operation involving cutting, pasting, copying, numbering, and indexing, and these processes changed how scholars and officials managed information to produce knowledge in the early modern period.[24]

As a reference book, the *Relation of Provisions* left no space for creativity. The scribe copied the decrees sent by the king and the Council of the Indies, and then the magistrates used those provisions to apply rulings. In its early years, the audiencia received communications from the king stipulating how monasteries should be built, how Indigenous people should be heard in Hispanic courts, and how they should be taught the Spanish language. The book includes guidelines regarding how Spanish homes should be built; how to act if any non-Catholic people like Jews or Moors, who were banned from the Indies, were found there; and how to sell and purchase imperial administrative posts. At first glance, the book gives the impression of an absolutist regime in which politics moved in a linear direction: the king and his councils mandated, the magistrates copied and executed.

Beneath this apparently dull and homogeneous surface, however, were profound layers of history that challenge the linearity of imperial politics. The assortment of decrees reflected the lived experiences and petitions of the diverse members of the empire. Indigenous people, Africans, settlers, clergy, and administrators submitted their claims to the emperor and had their voices heard. For instance, entry number 258 in the book declares that Elvira, a sixty-year-old Native woman from Cuzco, should be allowed to travel to Spain. In the archive in Seville, Elvira's corresponding petition tells her life story, revealing the types of paper interactions with the king that eventually consigned her name to the audiencia's books. She had traveled from Cuzco to Quito and then to Tocaima, where she met and lived with a Spanish man named Juan Diez. They lived together for twelve years and had two daughters, but when Elvira wrote her petition, Diez was planning to travel back to the Iberian Peninsula with their children, leaving her behind. Elvira pled to audiencia official Juan de Penagos to grant her a license to travel with them and asked the vecinos of Tocaima to appear in court to testify that she lived as a Spanish woman ("vive como si fuese mujer española"). To explain to Elvira that only the king could provide such a license, Penagos used the Muisca political concept of "cipa" to refer to the king of Spain. He said "that he could not give that license, that only the great cipa of the Christians that lived in Castile could, but that he would ask the magistrates of Santa Fe to write to the great cipa of the Spaniards so he could give her permission."[25]

That Penagos used the Muisca term *cipa* to explain to a Native woman from Cuzco who presumably spoke Quechua, not Muisca, and lived in the hot lands of the New Kingdom of Granada that the king needed to sign a paper so she could travel with her family to Iberia indicates the many cultural crossings that took place in the practice of politics in the Spanish monarchy. Letters enabled a direct connection between the king and Elvira, albeit through many mediations, including Muisca political concepts and Iberian officials. It was actually very common to refer to the magistrates as cipas and to the tribunal as the Audiencia of Bogotá or the New Kingdom of Bogotá, which appropriated the concept of "Muyquyta."[26] Such appellations made clear how Iberian and Indigenous political concepts merged in Spanish imperial jurisdictions and institutions.

The story behind inscription number 258 in the *Relation of Provisions* reveals the intricate political processes of the Spanish empire. The book was a device, a compilation, an assortment of past lives that informed the expectations and possibilities of those who followed. The monarch's response to their claims, in turn, created precedents and coordinates that guided officials' responses under similar circumstances in the future. The book reveals the intricate paths and collaborative experiences that characterized lawmaking in the Spanish empire. Through the petitioning system, officials transformed vassals' requests into decrees and provisions. Overseas subjects used this petitioning system actively. Rather than an absolutist system created from the top, these legal categories formed through petitions that came from the ground up.[27]

The audiencia's flows of papers created intimate contact between the monarch and his subjects. This connection was possible only through the practice of writing. Paper was the platform on which vassals and officials debated, implemented, and/or rejected the meaning of the empire and its institutions. Paper, in the form of letters and memoriales, was even a means through which Native people presented their own visions of the empire and how it should work. Document production involved objects, spaces, and agents, and included seals, archives, scribes, notaries, translators, copyists, witnesses, and magistrates. As historian Kathryn Burns points out, it would be naive to see archives and the acts of recording, archiving, and retrieval as lineal mechanisms of power directed by an omnipresent state.[28] Indeed, what Rama called the "lettered city" has recently been expanded by Joanne Rappaport and Tom Cummins to render visible a wide range of Indigenous scriptural practices.[29] Indigenous peoples engaged with European forms of writing and navigated imperial landscapes actively and fluently.

The King's Man Arrives

When López first arrived in Santa Fe in 1557, he was thirty-seven years old and had an excellent reputation as an administrator. He was meticulous, sharp, and ambitious, and he expressed a genuine intellectual belief that the empire was necessary for saving the souls of the peoples of the New World. He had already rehearsed in Yucatán and Guatemala many of the policies he implemented in the New Kingdom. But despite his experience, nothing seemed to prepare him for the types of problems and the tense environment he would face during his time as high magistrate of the Audiencia of Santa Fe. In his five years there, López carried out some of the most important tasks the audiencia undertook during that time. He was the audiencia's most senior magistrate before its first president arrived. That meant that he took on some of the audiencia's foundational work: he performed the first general visits of Popayán between 1558 and 1559, and of the New Kingdom between 1559 and 1560, classifying it into regions and subregions, and listing the encomenderos and Native communities assigned to them.[30] López created a general rate for tribute, named a protector of the indios in 1557—only to see the post eliminated a few years later—and carried out the first resettlements starting in 1558.[31]

But productivity was not an indicator of satisfaction. López's impressions are apparent in his first letter to the king after arriving in Santa Fe. There, he emphasized forms and appearances: he complained there was too much velvet used in the carpets and cushions of churches; that the magistrates needed to wear French clothes, for they dressed as soldiers and carried weapons; and that Native peoples lived as they wanted, without much influence from the friars. López grouped these problems into four categories that affected the public customs of the kingdom: attire, food, indecent games, and the Spaniards' example of conduct to Native peoples. His emphasis on forms was structural, rather than superficial. The general subtext was that the Spaniards' bad example was ruining the Indigenous people. López believed that Native peoples needed to learn basic European habits and routines, what was then called "natural law," before learning matters of faith. Evangelization was first a question of customs: Indigenous peoples needed to learn to live a decent and respectful life according to Catholic manners before they would have a chance of understanding the mysteries of the Scriptures.[32] But, in his view, all that could be found in the kingdom was problematic. It was full of troublesome "peruleros"—rebellious Spanish men who had participated in revolts against the Crown in the 1540s and 1550s in Peru and were now in exile in the New Kingdom. They lived freely and recklessly (as vagamundos), had weapons, and were so dangerous that López could only hope for God to send a plague to exterminate them. In the years to come, he wrote, his diagnosis of the kingdom suggested that things would only get worse. Years later, he contrasted Santa Fe to Guatemala, writing: "I blame my bad fortune that brought me from a quiet and peaceful audiencia . . . , to one so troubled and passionate, so inflamed by dirty and evil business."[33]

Examples of these types of conduct are numerous, even among the prestigious magistrates who served as ears for the king. Juan Muñoz de Collantes, the audiencia's accountant in its early years, committed several felonies, fled Santa Fe, and was a fugitive in the late 1550s.[34] Miguel Díez de Armendáriz, who was governor of the New Kingdom after Lugo and first published the New Laws in Santa Fe, was accused of allowing settlers to buy, sell, and trade encomiendas—which the monarch had explicitly prohibited. Perhaps the most serious case that illustrates the uncertainty of communications between the audiencia and Madrid and the hardships that the Council of the Indies and the Crown faced while trying to rule from afar was that of Juan de Montaño, one of the earliest audiencia magistrates. In 1557, some members of the tribunal accused Montaño of plotting a rebellion in alliance with peruleros. Bishop Fray Juan de los Barrios concurred with the accusations and so did the conquistador Juan Tafur, who served as a witness. Montaño was sent to Madrid accused of treason and set to be executed on July 28, 1561, becoming one of only two magistrates of the Indies to be punished by death in the entire history of the Spanish empire.[35] Still, Tomás López, who brought the case to the king, expressed anxiety and caution because of suspicions that Montaño was being framed by a rival audiencia magistrate called Francisco Briceño. No one could be trusted.

Despite its unruliness, the audiencia maintained a surprising stability in the volatile political geographies of the Spanish empire in the Indies, in which the Council of the Indies and the Crown, as well as royal tribunals, visitadores, and even settlers were constantly reconsidering the practicality and effectiveness of existing administrative jurisdictions. Central America offers perhaps the clearest example of the difficulty of establishing appropriate units for the administration of the Indies. The Audiencia of Panama was first created in 1538 and then eliminated in 1542 by the New Laws. This put Central America under the newly created Audiencia de los Confines, the Audiencia of Guatemala and Nicaragua. This tribunal was moved twice—in 1544 and 1548—before it was suppressed in 1563, only to be replaced again by the Audiencia of Panama and refounded. In this context, the continuity of the Audiencia of Santa Fe is remarkable, particularly considering the fragility and inner conflicts of the young tribunal.

At the end of Andrés Díaz Venero de Leyva's tenure as the first president of the audiencia in 1574, most mandates of the New Laws had been ignored. Only two measures had been carried out, and even those remained heavily contested. These were the visita general, the journey of the most senior magistrate of the audiencia to inquire about the conditions of Native communities, and the tasa general, the effort to create a coherent and sustainable tributary system. Tomás López was in charge of both of them.

Gridded Lives

Tomás López Medel, like many Spanish magistrates and priests, believed that Native Americans must be forced to live in quadrilinear towns. Concentrating conquered Indigenous peoples in this way was not simply a means of surveillance or control but also a first step in Christian conversion. The term the Spanish used for this process was *reducir*—roughly meaning "to tame." By the mid-sixteenth century, this process had become a paragon of the Spanish empire. Its conceptual roots lay in the concept of the municipality, which was at the heart of Spanish notions of civility. Peoples that were mobile or unattached to local communities were seen as uncivilized and dangerous, and building settlements was a form of naturalization that compelled vagabonds to build ties to the monarchy by restricting them to fixed settlements.[36] The grid, imagined as the ideal form for a Christian city in a theological tradition stemming from medieval Iberia and building on the layout of military encampments, took root in the New World when the first colonial cities in the Caribbean were designed—such as Santo Domingo (1502) and Santiago de Cuba (1515).[37] In 1503, Queen Isabella herself gave the first instructions to Nicolás de Ovando, governor of Santo Domingo, to resettle Indigenous peoples "so they live like the vecinos [citizens] of our kingdoms [of Castile]." In the following decades, the reducciones became a truly imperial design, structured in a lattice-like form around Christian symbols and political hierarchies.

The grid aimed to bring Indigenous peoples to live under the supervision of friars and imperial officials, in what they called a "life in good order" (vida en policía). These spatial designs aimed to segregate Indigenous peoples in their own settlements, isolating Native peoples from other members of the empire, under a language of protection: officials claimed that separating "indios" from everyone else would shield them from harm and the "bad example" of Spaniards', Africans', or mixed people's reckless behavior. This meant restricting trade and avoiding direct contact between Europeans—especially encomenderos—and Indigenous people. During the sixteenth century, imperial officials carried out massive resettlement projects for Indigenous peoples. In Peru alone more than a thousand towns were created over the course of the century.[38] This spatial framework continued to be the heart of Spanish imperial designs during the seventeenth and eighteenth centuries.[39]

López crafted detailed instructions for Indigenous villages in 1558, building upon the resettlement program he had laid out in Yucatán years earlier.[40] In this design, the plaza (central square) was the town's central axis and always sat at the exact geometric center of the village. The streets extended in every direction from the plaza outward. The church, jail, cabildo, and homes of the cacique and Indigenous nobility enjoyed prestigious locations on the central plaza, while commoners' houses extended toward the margins. López expected these constructions to be large and grandiose (de grandor). Native homes lined the streets in neighborhoods designed to re-create major Indigenous kin divisions, in order to avoid possible confrontations between different factions and to create a sense of belonging among Native people. The villages would ideally gather between one hundred and six hundred people, but no more than eight hundred. López instructed that if a cacicazgo had fewer than one hundred people, it should be combined with another community to make a larger village. If a cacicazgo had more than eight hundred, officials should split it up into two different villages. The villages should be located on plains, near water and wood supplies, and had to be accessible by horse or on foot. Native people were required to maintain the paths and bridges in good condition. The houses were to be as sturdy as possible so that they could last for a long time.

López expected to redraw the landscapes of the Andes by creating fifty-two towns in the Province of Santa Fe and sixty-one towns in the Province of Tunja, for a total of 113 towns in the eastern Andean range alone. He also ordered the construction of many other Indigenous villages, on which little or no documentation survives. In a letter to the king, López reported that he had built villages in many different parts of the kingdom during his visits between 1558 and 1560.[41]

After writing up these general guidelines, López struggled to find an appropriate workflow for a task of this magnitude. He first divided the Province of Santa Fe into districts (partidos). Although this went unspecified in the documents, the partidos roughly coincided with precolonial jurisdictions of midlevel Muisca caciques. Imperial power once again validated and instrumentalized Indigenous political concepts, structures, and divisions. López then chose delegates among the encomenderos of each region to carry out the instructions. It did not take long before the encomenderos expressed their concerns about these measures. The encomenderos of three of the largest Muisca cacicazgos, who oversaw the reducciones, wrote to the audiencia saying they had gathered the caciques to tell them about the great benefits of living in villages. However, the caciques had replied that such a measure would prove difficult, since the commoners would reject their authority if they forced them into the gridded villages. López intervened again in 1560, arguing that the encomenderos "had not done, nor wanted to do" the settlements. In response, he forbade the encomenderos to receive any tribute until the towns were built.[42]

The delays were not caused exclusively by the encomenderos' lack of will. They also resulted from cultural and political problems. The Muiscas' built environment was key to their society and efforts to transform their landscape challenged deep elements of their society and culture.[43] Muisca concepts for the house and for the settlement were tied to broader notions of place, time, and the body, and were central to expressions of identity as well as political organization. This was all the more important in a society organized around matrilineal kin affiliation but avunculocal residential patterns. This meant that offspring belonged to the political unit of the mother's brother; however, they lived in the residence of their father's maternal uncle until they came of

FIGURE 2.1. Village of Paipa, 1602. AGN, Mapoteca 4, 311A.

age. The term *guecha* (literally "man of the house," formed from *gue*, "house," and *cha*, "man") was used to refer to the uncle—the mother's brother—who was the head of the household. The word to designate a stranger, *gueba*, also was formed from *gue*, "house," plus *yba*, "blood." In other words, the house as place and concept helped the Muisca identify those who belonged in their social worlds and those who were outsiders.[44]

One of the Muisca spaces that most intrigued the Spaniards was the cacique's cercado (enclosure or palisade). These ceremonial spaces often were decorated with paintings of different colors and styles on cotton fabric, had wide avenues and plazas used for dances and performances, and were surrounded by wooden logs stacked horizontally. They were built during large, majestic gatherings that united the whole community and involved feasting, singing, and dancing in many types of colorful masks and costumes. The meaningful objects displayed in these ceremonies included feathers, shells, deerskins, and even the heads of jaguars and pumas. An early Spanish observer described the cercados in the following terms: "The forms of their houses and buildings, although they are made of wood and covered with a long straw that is found there, are of the strangest making and manner ever seen, especially those of the caciques and nobles, because they are like fortresses with many fences around them, in the way the Labyrinth of Troy is usually depicted here, [and] the houses have great courtyards with great sculptures and also paintings everywhere in it."[45]

Another significant space was the quca, a building positioned within the cercado where the community trained their political and spiritual leaders. There, trainees were secluded for years, keeping a strict diet and weaving textiles. Their textiles remained inside the quca after their release, adding to its cultural significance. The word quca is closely associated with quyca, which referred to land, region, myth and cosmology, disease, history, and narration. The term's broad semantic field reveals the elaborate connections of Muisca homelands—a deeply meaningful territory—to history-telling, knowledge production and transmission, and leaders' prestige.

These meaningful sites were set in a larger built environment that involved investment of community labor to design spaces for agriculture and fisheries, as well as keeping roads and trade centers. In highly floodable areas, like the Bogotá savannah, developing these spaces required carving ditches to store water and creating raised beds for cultivation and roads.[46] This meant that the spatial distribution between the sihipqua's palisade and the residences of kin units made sense in terms of caring for these larger ecologies. Furthermore, in a complex residential pattern in which kin units were politically affiliated to the mother's brother—whom they considered the guecha—but resided during large stretches of time in the father's lands, the members of a particular community could be widely spread out. While the palisade served as a common space, it was probably not a place for weekly or even monthly gatherings. Nor was it excessively monumental, especially when considered in contrast to urban centers like Tenochtitlan or Cuzco, or even smaller Inca villages with their large storage centers and polished stone architecture.[47] Rather, each community and even each kin unit had its own sacred spots and ritual spaces, crafting a largely decentralized yet interconnected landscape.

Colonial officials deemed these spaces and objects diabolical, since they perpetuated Indigenous cultural practices and rivaled the friars' teachings. Forcing the Muisca to reside in gridded villages was part of a larger war on Indigenous symbolic languages that aimed to erase their forms of cultural expression—an attitude that would continue throughout the sixteenth century. In the first catechism for the evangelization of the Indigenous peoples of the New Kingdom of Granada, dating from 1576, Fray Luis Zapata de Cárdenas wrote that "bodily order" (policía corporal) was the "first step for spirituality," and quoted the scriptures, saying, "I have placed you over peoples and kingdoms, to tear and destroy, to ruin and overthrow, and to build and plant."[48] He meant that planting a Christian landscape first entailed violently destroying sacred Indigenous homelands. Along these lines, in a dismaying account from 1600, Jesuit Alonso de Medrano described how friars compelled the spiritual leaders of Fontibón to tread on their sacred objects, spit on them, curse them, and then burn them.

Through these acts of violence, imperial administrators like López and Zapata expected to install a new social order, dependent on new gender roles and ideas of kin. Feathers, shells, and furs would be replaced by beds, tables, candles, and crosses. Instead of large gatherings under the leadership of the guecha—the mother's brother—embedded in matrilineal kin patterns, in the new villages Native people would live quiet lives centered on nuclear families that reproduced the Christian ideal of the family and would marry under the tutelage of a priest. Children would attend the daily teachings and services run by friars, men would labor to pay tribute and provide for the household, and women would take care of the residence. In this way, Christian piety depended on specific configurations of manhood and womanhood. In fact, the nuclear family established a set of associations and hierarchies with which Christianity (and the empire) would be rendered legible. God was the father, and so was the priest, and so was the encomendero. For the Muiscas, for whom the father was not a particularly important kin figure, this must have been incomprehensible at first.

López envisioned the reducciones as a means for teaching natural law to Indigenous peoples—to instruct them to live their daily lives in Christian ways. He saw them as a stepping-stone toward a massive conversion in the Andes. Such villages were part of a bundle of institutions that sought to insinuate themselves into Native peoples' everyday lives. In reducciones, López expected Native communities to be governed by town councils and to gather around a church.[49] The cacique would apply justice via a jail and stocks (cepo), rather than using traditional Indigenous means. The new spaces would stimulate the senses in different ways, and the new hierarchies of power would be visible and tangible. The sound of the church bell would guide daily rhythms, indicating when to work and when to worship; murmur and chatter would ideally recede before the sound of Christian song and prayer; even the scent of candles would ideally create an appropriate environment for christianization.[50] Furthermore, the grid pattern of the town would provide royal officials with improved access to the villages through well-kept paths and bridges. It would be easier to visit them, observe their customs, rate their tribute, regulate their behavior, and oversee their economic practices.

For many Indigenous peoples, however, the reducciones were ugly, painful, and enraging. They disrupted the values and associations that sustained social life. Barbara Mundy has argued that after the conquest of Tenochtitlan, the city actually started to smell foul, as rotten cadavers and the collapse of the city's infrastructure changed its smellscape.[51] The reducciones in the New Kingdom, too, disrupted Indigenous aesthetics and lifestyles. It is no wonder that they prompted varied reactions from Indigenous peoples. A colonial observer believed that the Muiscas did not like living in villages because they did not want the imperial administration or the Spaniards to learn about their customs.[52] In 1571, for example, an officer reported that the Native peoples of the Province of Santa Fe had been reduced into villages, but reluctantly ("de mala gana"), and at every opportunity they scattered over the landscape and returned to their old ways. In Choachí, the cacique tried to compel Native commoners to live in villages according to López's instructions, but this sparked the rage of the community, and he fled in panic to the nearby settlement of Guasca. When visitador Francisco Briceño passed through Choachí in 1563 he learned that the commoners had burned down the church and elected a new cacique.

Historian Jeremy Mumford argues that the resettlement project carried out by Viceroy Francisco de Toledo in Perú in 1570 aimed not at eliminating Andean customs but at creating a new order of society that would civilize Andeans while building a meticulous ethnography of the Inca past.[53] López's reducciones predated Toledo by over a decade. While López did not admire the Muiscas as Toledo admired—albeit ambivalently—the Inca, López carried out a project of unprecedented scope in the New Kingdom of Granada. The reducciones sought to enforce a system of tight social discipline and to ensure legibility (making it possible for people to be observed, counted, and categorized) in spaces designed according to a neoclassical aesthetic. They dislocated Native communities and reshuffled them into new spaces, forging new relationships and human groupings that, consistent with the rationale of Hispanic colonialism, simultaneously expected to preserve and change Indigenous societies—reproducing political hierarchies but eliminating the cultural systems that had enabled their existence.

The reducciones produced unintended consequences. Gathering Native peoples in villages, with their newly acquired hens, pigs, sheep, and cows, created ideal conditions for plagues. In places like Vélez, the reducciones brought epidemics of smallpox and chickenpox less than a year after people moved into the villages.[54] Despite such dangers, López believed that the villages would benefit Native peoples the most: they opened a path to civilization and a gateway to salvation, in exchange for what he described as a "small material damage." In other words, dramatic demographic collapse was, for him, a small price to pay for eternal salvation. After all, living in their own settlements, they would be far from the misleading example of Spanish society and would be easily accessible for regular visits from imperial officials.

A Personal Visit

The empire's guidelines for governance instructed the audiencia's most senior magistrate to carry out a general inspection of the kingdom each year, which they called the *visita general* (general visit). This was one of the audiencia's main duties and was intended to help officials keep tabs on local conditions. The use of visits in Iberia went back to Alfonso el Sabio's *Siete partidas* (1256–65), the first legal code in a vernacular language.[55] The visitador—a surveyor—was vested with monarchical authority and traveled to sites where the king was not physically present to perform as the living image of the king.[56] In the early modern period, as the monarchy expanded into a global empire, visits became a central practice of governance. Visits thrived as questionnaires also acquired a new predominance in the practice of imperial politics.[57] During the field inspections, magistrates counted and listed local people, noted their names and calculated their ages, identified Native authorities, and described communities' economies, main products, and local settings. They mapped whole societies throughout the world and sent brief and clear summaries to the councils of the king. The paperwork they produced did not merely register something that already existed but also was the first step in creating the types of realities and spatial arrangements prescribed by the Spanish monarchy.[58] In this way, they were templates of practice that, in many ways, profoundly distorted the societies they claimed to represent.

López carried out the first general surveys for the Audiencia of Santa Fe. He departed for a general visit to the governorship of Popayán in 1556, only six months after arriving in Santa Fe. In addition to gathering information about Native peoples and their tributes, he intended to inquire about a rebellion allegedly plotted by Mateo del Saz, Pedro de Mendoza, and Hipólito Villagrán, three peruleros who had been exiled from Peru for taking part in Francisco Hernández Girón's revolt. He also aimed to improve the relationship between Bishop Juan del Valle and the encomenderos, an urgent matter that compelled him to visit first Popayán and then the New Kingdom of Granada. Popayán would fall under the jurisdiction of Quito, but its audiencia was not created until 1563.

Del Valle was a distinguished Popayán bishop who was well known in the New Kingdom for the unorthodox methods he employed to prevent the encomenderos from harming Native communities. He was perhaps the most important supporter of the Dominican scholars who spoke against violence against Indigenous peoples. For instance, he created his own tribute rate for the province of Popayán and threatened to excommunicate encomenderos who did not comply with his requirements. One of his most interesting writings took the form of question and answer. He posed fourteen moral doubts and then offered a response, following a common rhetorical structure at the time—which Las Casas also used in his treatise *Doce dudas*. Del Valle asked, for instance, if the Spanish war on Native peoples had been just and rightful, and he answered that it had been extremely unjust and unfair and that the king was morally obliged to provide restitution.[59] Del Valle's troubled relationship to settlers and imperial institutions revealed the frictions created by contested visions of empire in the sixteenth century. López, with his humanist background, was supposed to ease Juan del Valle's relations with the audiencia and the encomenderos. López claimed to have done everything in his power to restore order through justice procedures, clear tribute rates, and gridded villages with parishes, though the challenges were too structural to be solved by one official.[60]

After Popayán, López turned his attention to the New Kingdom. The audiencia laid out an ambitious agenda for him. He had six tasks as visitador. First was to visit every settlement, count the Native inhabitants, and learn about the quality of the land, local products, and exchange networks, as well as other economic activities such as the payment of tribute. Second was to establish an appropriate rate for tribute, adhering to the firm guidelines of the New Laws. Third was to inquire about the Native peoples' religious training. Fourth was to put an end to forced Indigenous labor in the mines and as porters. Fifth was to gather Indigenous peoples in villages—if they were not already settled as he had instructed some years earlier—create schools, and organize religious doctrine. And sixth was to open or improve the roads and bridges of those villages so they could be accessible by horse or mule. The audiencia expected López to complete this gargantuan operation in only six months—evidence of the audiencia's ignorance regarding the kingdom's size. If gathering Native peoples in villages was a challenging task by itself, this six-part mission seems impossible. To offer a point of comparison, the Spanish monarchy's domains in the Iberian Peninsula were divided into sixteen units of governance that had their own visitadores. The Crown expected Lopez to inspect a territory four times the size of the entire Peninsula, crossing its diverse environmental regions, as the lone visitador. López himself acknowledged that the visit would be an exhausting enterprise, for they would have to journey across swamps, mountains, and deserts.[61]

Like all visitas, López's inspection consisted of a sizeable caravan of colonial functionaries.[62] Although we do not know for sure the full composition of the group, since many tasks went unrecorded, the caravan involved a transcultural network of people with specialized knowledge who fulfilled concrete roles. López, as the most senior magistrate of the audiencia, was in charge of the whole process, accompanied by Bishop Juan de los Barrios. A scribe (escribano) and an interpreter (lengua) were under his leadership. The interpreter translated the magistrate's questions into Indigenous languages and communicated the answer back to López. The scribe was a clerk who adapted the responses into the monarchy's specialized terms, conventions, and legal templates. In some cases, there were two interpreters: one who translated from Spanish to Muisca and another who translated from Muisca to the local Indigenous language. Cooks, guides, and carriers took care of the expedition's logistics. As Raymond Craib has shown for another context, "people experience 'the state' as they experience 'the market' or 'capitalism,' not as a broad abstraction but as a series of manifestations with a very human face: judges, notary publics, police squads, tax collectors."[63] In the early modern Spanish empire, the members of that caravan could well be among the figures through which local Native groups experienced the "empire."

The caravan left first for Tocaima, Mariquita, and Ibagué, then went back to Santa Fe, and finally continued to Tunja, Vélez, and Pamplona. In each of these places the magistrate gathered local caciques and systematically carried out his six tasks. It was a repetitive, reiterative ritual. The expedition crew produced voluminous records from these inspections. They created lists of Indigenous persons, transcriptions of interviews with Native authorities and priests, and inventories of the contents of the churches. When Indigenous residents claimed mistreatment by the encomendero or made any other declaration that pointed to a situation outside the law, more texts were produced. The field inspections were full of mishaps and faced numerous hardships along the way. On many occasions, it was too complicated to get to the settlements, so López cited information from caciques in nearby villages or cities, sometimes even recording the existence, size, and economy of an entire community based on information received from the testimonies of neighboring caciques. The paradox of "visiting" the kingdom without actually arriving in each site shows that visits were primarily epistemological enterprises meant to produce data needed to run imperial institutions, not necessarily field trips to see local villages.

Population counts were an important part of the visitas. The visitador listed the Native people of each encomienda. The lists were structured to reflect Native organization: they started with the cacique's subdivision and continued with the cacicazgos' remaining subdivisions. Each section first listed the names of the Native people of the village, forcing them into a Catholic family framework, beginning by listing the father, then his "wife," and then the children. It would record a European first name for baptized men and women, an Indigenous name, an age, and a colonial label to indicate the person's status vis-à-vis the imperial administration. Since the kingdom's Native peoples did not measure time as Europeans did, ages were more often than not an estimation by the magistrate, the cacique, or some other member of the caravan of inspectors. The colonial labels depended on age and gender: women and children were usually lumped together into a category called "indias y chusma" (Indigenous women and the rest), while old men and disabled people were classified as "reservados" (meaning that they did not pay tribute). These two categories corresponded to the widespread early modern notion of "useless mouths," meaning women, children, and anyone who did not provide military service or pay taxes and was thus deemed expendable. In contrast, men the visitador estimated to be between eighteen and fifty-five years of age were labeled as "useful indios" (indios útiles) and were required to pay tribute. Finally, Native authorities were classified as nobles according to their rank as cacique, capitán, or principal, among other labels and were exempt from tribute.

Population counts were not neutral lists of people; they reflected the principles and practices of imperial governance. As they organized journeys and crafted documents, imperial authorities identified the information they needed and constructed forms and questionnaires that abstracted diverse local arrangements into letters, graphs, and maps. They specified which types of questions were pertinent and which ones were irrelevant or best ignored in the interest of clarity. The most brutal distortions of information resulted from the imposition of a Catholic framework: the lists took the monogamous Catholic family as a given and each entry was organized around a husband, a wife, and their children. As outlined above, the Muiscas maintained a matrilineal kinship system in which the father was less important than the guecha, the mother's brother.[64] Yet the uncle, the head of the household, is not identified on the census. A man's age, however—a piece of information that was completely irrelevant for the Muiscas themselves—was of the utmost importance to the administration, since it defined the labor requirements he owed to the empire.[65] Age defined who was "useful" in the eyes of the administration. In this sense, the social production of knowledge and ignorance is clearly illustrated in the template that determined which information would be recorded about Native peoples.[66]

The lists' categories also revealed the gendered valuation of labor. The system depended completely on the labor of women, who not only provided for the household and cared for children and the elderly but also spun the thread needed to weave the cotton mantles (mantas) used to pay tribute, as we will see in chapter 3. However, this labor was not explicitly recognized, and women were deemed "useless."

The list's distortions in relation to gender and kinship are also visible in the marginalia accompanying the enigmatic entry "indias del servicio" (Indigenous female servants). Noble men among the Muisca could have many wives, a practice that clearly opposed the monogamous ideal of Christian marriage. In some cases, the census recorded many additional entries of women living in the houses of caciques and other Native authorities, and described them as indias del servicio. In these cases, the inspectors wrote in the margin next to the entry the word *ojo*, meaning that the reader should beware. It was a word of caution to note the existence of a non-Catholic kin practice. Inspectors included the same annotation next to the names of people who were unbaptized or those cohabiting without being properly married (amancebados). With this list, the inspectors could identify individuals who were not living as true Christians and work with friars to police their daily activities more closely. It was a means of surveillance and transformation that simplified cultural diversity by reducing it to preexisting Christian forms and templates that were to be applied across the Indies. Native societies were distorted to fit into colonial categories, and then "travelled by paper through bureaucratic pathways of the colonial administration."[67]

Upon finishing the physical journey, this ocean of information needed to be processed before López sent a copy (traslado) to the Council of the Indies, as stipulated in the mandates. After the fieldwork, a new type of work started: a desk job. The scribes and their assistants went through the information to compile, compute, simplify, and calculate, and to produce clean tables that compared the data from different Native settlements. The documents that came out of these journeys were more than just representations of peoples and environments; they were crucial empire-making artifacts that shaped the face of the empire in these zones and created much of the reality imperial officials hoped for. López's visit resulted in a document that synthesized the kingdom. By the end of the process, the copious amounts of information gathered had been digested or reduced to the number of "useful indios," the names of the encomendero and cacique, and the number of mantas and golden pesos paid in tribute. That document was further summarized in a table that enumerated the "useful indios," the tributes they paid, how many were in rebellion, and how many encomiendas had been assigned (table 2.1). At that point, Indigenous societies had been abstracted to their bare minimum expression. They became imperial statistics.

The table summarizing López's visita created something new: a "kingdom" whose population and economy could be measured and governed. The visita officially established that the New Kingdom had 133,590 "indios," distributed among 310 encomenderos, and that the Native inhabitants paid a tribute of 48,052 mantas along with gold, the services of mine laborers, and bushels of cultivated crops. The uncertainty of the visita—a necessarily incomplete, trouble-ridden journey full of hazards and lacunas through a complex map of Indigenous ethnicities—was masked under a veneer of numbers. Regardless of whether the population count was accurate, these numbers determined how much tribute Native peoples would be legally required to pay, and, as a result, how much the encomenderos and the monarchy could receive. The table, therefore, created a kingdom of paper—a productive fiction of a kingdom that would become a template for practice.

The visitas extended the legibility of empire across mountains, valleys, and rivers. They entailed moving inspectors all over the kingdom to record information about Native societies, economies, and territories. Imperial administrators then compiled that information on paper, summarized it in even narrower lists and tables, created numerous copies of these documents, and then shipped all these textual artifacts to administrative centers first in the Audiencia of Santa Fe and then in Spain. By the end of the workflow, the Muiscas, Muzos, Panches, and other Indigenous ethnic groups had been formatted to fit the empire's administrative categories. López's visit records simultaneously inscribed and erased them, submerged them into colonial taxonomies, and flattened them into numbers that could be added, subtracted, multiplied, and classified. They became "indios"—a matter for discussion in the meeting halls of the Council of the Indies, where the advisors to the king could decide on topics directly affecting Indigenous peoples, like taxes, labor demands, evangelization, and linguistic policy. In this sense, López's visit reveals the systematic ignorance, and indeed erasure, of Indigenous knowledge, as well as Native people's submersion into the empire's simplified population categories.

López imposed penalties on encomenderos and strove to align encomiendas with imperial regulations, temporarily alleviating some part of the pressure on Indigenous communities. But at the end of the day, he acknowledged that all of his work would amount to nothing if the visitas did not become routine. The institution was meaningless if the Crown did not send new inspec-

TABLE 2.1 Summary of Tomás López Medel's General Visit

GOVERNORSHIP	Indios	Mantas	Gold (pesos)	Indios in Mines	Cultivated Bushels	Seditious Indios	Encomen-deros
POPAYÁN	65,945	35,313	4,180	6,344	2,469	9,500	245
NEW KINGDOM OF GRANADA	133,590	48,052	26,652	3,052	3,097	5,651	310
SANTA MARTA	2,346	0	0	0	0	0	80
CARTAGENA	7,139	0	0	0	0	0	52
Total	209,020	83,365	30,832	9,396	5,566	15,151	687

Source: Adapted from López Medel, "Visita de 1560."

tors on a regular basis to verify that the visitador's instructions were applied. Without further visitas, the monarchy would have no oversight of Indigenous societies, which could avoid following Catholic guidelines. The Council of the Indies expected the audiencia to carry out visits every year. But the visitas were too challenging and too big an enterprise to be performed so frequently. In fact, visitadores inspected the kingdom's Indigenous villages at intervals of a decade or more, and each inspection had a limited reach.[68] In one of his final reports to the king, López lamented that much of the district of the Audiencia of Santa Fe remained unsurveyed.

A Godless Kingdom

God did not enter there, nor will he enter if they do not open the door.
—TOMÁS LÓPEZ MEDEL, 1561

At the end of his term as magistrate in July 1561, López reflected on his time in the New Kingdom of Granada. Imperial officials like López understood their mission in the Indies as a way of assigning values and hierarchies—defining virtue and civility, right and wrong, good and bad. They set out to fix, organize, and save. López assessed that he had done all he could to "cleanse the kingdom," to create order in it. He had tried to "make the Natives [naturales] Christian, extracting the Devil from among them to bring God instead, and to make civilized beings out of barbarians." But his assessment was dire: "the Natives [naturales] will soon perish." He accepted with regret that tax rates would benefit the Spaniards more than Native peoples. Public life in the kingdom had been "corrupted" and was full of "vices." He advised the Crown to expel most Spaniards—many of whom he described as a "plague"—and bring well-behaved men of God to serve in public posts and to preach.[69]

If López deemed the project of the kingdom a failure, the problem was not a lack of imperial presence. In fact, during the 1550s and 1560s when he was present there, the basic administrative architecture of the kingdom took shape. The audiencia as a government entity and the visita as a practice of governance extended the king's presence to the other side of the Atlantic through paper and writing. Letters were filled with power: phonetic symbols converted sounds and lived landscapes into movable objects and offered ways of organizing knowledge and disposing of people. Imperial sovereignty functioned through the creation of writing networks: cities and Indigenous villages were the new sites of scriptural production, while the visitas were routines of surveillance. Through this structure, functionaries could monitor the intimate lives of the Muiscas and other Indigenous groups to make sure they followed Christian precepts of the family—what officials interpreted to be the most basic tenets of civilized life. As an imperial officer, López set out to affix Indigenous people to a series of overlapping grids: newly delineated streets, population lists, and tax tables. The establishment of gridded Indigenous villages in particular dislocated and rearranged people in the most schematic, programmatic urbanism—the signature of the Spanish empire in the New World. In all its shapes, the grid, as a form of abstraction and distortion, was a frame of reference that not only justified imperial violence but also allowed the empire to function.

That same process of abstraction and inscription offered opportunities for people to make claims and petitions. By appearances, the monarchy was an absolutist regime, but in actuality monarchical politics opened some room for people of all walks of life to participate in imperial governance and lawmaking. The pages of the books of the audiencia and judicial procedures hold traces of the stories of many who expected the magistrates (oidores, "those who listen") to hear and aid them, and so expressed their concerns in writing. Tellingly, in these letters the tribunal and its magistrates were frequently named using the abstract precolonial concept "cipa." As this lexicon of overlapping terms attests, Iberian political institutions operated according to Indigenous understandings of territoriality, politics, and ethnicity, but which remained obscured and silenced behind Spanish words. For example, the Audiencia de Santa Fe de Bogotá was centered in the old palisade of Muyquyta and used its old appellative, but was managed by the new cipas, the king's magistrates. Or take, for instance, the many grid-like Indigenous villages that were built on top of old political groupings and kept their old names. Or the Muisca kinship structure that was forced, uncomfortably, into the limiting logic of the Christian family in the population counts of the visitas. These complex structures—overwritten but not erased—reveal the convoluted construction of colonialism.

López's notion of the kingdom's failure was, rather, a problem of the meaning and aims of colonialism. He saw a contradiction between two sides of colonialism: evangelization, which aimed to offer a path to salvation for Native people through religious conversion, and economics, a means to an end, which frequently was mistaken for the endpoint in itself. In this lay López's frustration with the kingdom: he found that colonists were motivated by the production of revenue, while they cared little about evangelization. He wrote a missive to the king in which—noting the inclusion of fifty thousand pesos he had collected in Popayán during his visita—he remarked: "I found this gold and I assume that most of it comes from the mines, extracted against His Majesty's mandates. I write this so His Majesty does not pretend ignorance and restores it to the Natives [naturales] of those provinces, taking special care in their conversion."[70] He could only report the situation to the king and try to hold the monarch accountable. In advocating for evangelization as the only legitimate motive for empire, López promoted a vision of the New Kingdom that condemned profit as a cause of corruption. This midcentury project of empire will contrast heavily with the last visions of the New Kingdom at the turn of the century, as we will see in the last part of the book.

López took the high moral ground. In condemning economically minded colonial enterprises, he positioned himself as an advocate for Indigenous well-being. Yet López's mentality, attitude, and actions were no less colonialist, acting to the detriment of Indigenous peoples' lifeways—explicitly seeking their subordination and the destruction of kinship networks, built landscapes, and social worlds, ultimately triggering death. For all he thought about the moral compass of the empire and reflected on questions of ethics, justice, and salvation, López was involved in the creation of an inhumane system, one that was despicable in his own eyes. There is no such thing as benign colonialism, and López's "humanism" diminished, infantilized, and stereotyped Indigenous peoples; it imagined them as humans with reduced qualities and capacities, whose religions and cultures needed to be erased and replaced with Christianity.[71]

In 1561, López returned to Spain hopeless, rejected offers to occupy new posts in the Indies, and dedicated himself to writing—avoiding the darker side of the humanism he cherished.[72] He apparently wrote a doctrine to teach Catholicism in the Muisca language, although to date it has not been found. He also wrote his treatise, *De los tres elementos*, building upon his readings, intellectual background, and ample fieldwork in Central and South America.

López's trajectory as an official deeply immersed in humanist thought—a man of letters—provides a glimpse into the meaning of the kingdom. The basic infrastructure of the kingdom was laid out: its landscapes, institutions, and technologies. However, at the end of Venero de Leyva's term as president in 1574, the kingdom was as troubled and unstable as when Tomás López first arrived in Santa Fe. The promise of the audiencia as an entity of justice that would alleviate settlers' problems and apply the New Laws remained unfulfilled. In a kingdom ruled by flowing paper, the letters sent to Madrid conveyed a generalized sense of amorality, chaos, and lawlessness. The plurality of voices became a cacophony. At the same time, an Indigenous sovereignty took over the central Andean range, making communications with Popayán, Quito, and Peru almost impossible. The kingdom's fragile institutional landscapes approached a point of rupture and collapse.

Despite the audiencia's political mess, visits provided useful working data: handy demographic statistics (especially lists of "useful indios") that could be used to calculate the amount of tribute Native people owed to their encomenderos and the Crown. This process entailed developing a common economic framework that could give rise to the kingdom's economy. The development of this tribute system and its central role in the kingdom's economy will be the subject of the next chapter.

3

THE FABRIC OF THE KINGDOM

A thin, delicately woven textile from the Muisca highlands shows a great mastery of cotton fabric and the art of textile painting (figure 3.1). Its designs are composed of a series of panels that alternate human figures with repeating geometric patterns, painted with brown, red, and blue ink. The humans squat with their elbows resting on their knees; large round plumes adorn their heads. Each of the human figures is unique, as are the geometric shapes that stand at their sides. Additional elements—such as a sharp-beaked crested bird head or a long triangular plume-like figure—decorate the borders of the textile. The paintings are part of an elaborate visual language of the northern Andes, manifested in inscriptions on stones, ceramics, and goldwork. Textiles such as this one contain complex mappings of Indigenous societies. Some elements of the drawing mark the individuality of the humans depicted, while other elements may indicate metrics, counting patterns, and forms of quantification. The stories and information contained in this textile remain illegible to us today. The shapes reveal a visual repertoire that we might never be able to read. This chapter examines how treasured textiles like this one came to be at the center

FIGURE 3.1. Painted manta. British Museum, Department Africa, Oceania and the Americas, Am1842,1112.3.

of New Kingdom of Granada's fiscal system and economic organization, channeling the interactions between Indigenous peoples, settlers, and the monarchical administration.

The Spanish introduced the term *mantas* (mantles) to the northern Andes in the first half of the sixteenth century to allude to a variety of textiles woven by the Native peoples of the region. The terms *manta* and *manto* had a rich history on the Iberian Peninsula. They were used to describe the clothing of specific social groups, such as the shawls women wore to cover their heads and faces.[1] In the northern Andes, the term came to be associated with the variety of garments worn by Native men and women of all social levels during both the pre-Hispanic and colonial periods. One of the first Spanish accounts of the conquest described these textiles, saying that the Muiscas wore "black and white mantas and of other different and diverse colors. Some mantas fit tightly and cover them from their chest to their feet and others drop over their shoulders as if they were capes or blankets."[2] The seventeenth-century chronicler Lucas Fernández de Piedrahita distinguished between two types of garments: an interior cotton shirt and an exterior square manta. He added that the most common mantas were white, while the more prestigious ones were painted with brushes and colored in different tones.

Women used three other types of mantas, which Fernández, a mixed-blood chronicler from Peru, identified by their Quechua names: one called chirgate or maure that they wore around their waist; chumbe, a belt that held the chirgate; and líquira, a piece of fabric that hung around the chest and was held in place by a silver or gold pin known as a topo.[3] The topo may have become more popular after the Spanish invasion, as new fashions from Indigenous Peru became available in the New Kingdom. Even though cotton is not easily preserved in humid conditions—which makes the conservation of archaeological vestiges of mantas extremely difficult in this region—the Gold Museum and Costume Museum in Bogotá and the British Museum in London hold pieces that give a sense of mantas' variety and careful construction (figures 3.2–3.5). The fabric remnants showcase the mantas' carefully handcrafted details and artistic composition.

These textiles were called boi in the Muisca language, and they were central to the social, economic, and political lives of many Native communities. There are several archival traces that illuminate the value of mantas as cultural objects among the Native groups of the New Kingdom of Granada in the sixteenth century. Fray Pedro de Aguado, for instance, pointed out that the Catío peoples from the central Andean range "wrote their histories in the hieroglyphics they painted on mantas."[4] A Muisca-Spanish dictionary from 1606 linked memory and textiles by defining memory as a "signal to remember others," and providing an entry (zubasuacac aguene) for a "signal, a garment to remember."[5] Mantas were part of a broader Andean tradition that blended together the acts of weaving, knotting, and painting textiles as forms of recording culturally significant information. Mantas, like the khipus and tapestries of the southern Andes, were forms of writing without words, to use Walter Mignolo and Elizabeth Hill Boone's expression.[6]

Due to their cultural value, the exchange of mantas did not conform to the same patterns as regular commodities. For instance, mantas were among the valuable, inalienable possessions that had to be buried with caciques when they died.[7] In 1569, during an investigation about Indigenous ritual led by the audiencia, a Native witness even explained to colonial officials that one of the reasons some caciques rejected conversion to Christianity and opposed the friars' teachings in the 1560s was to preserve their mantas and other ornaments

FIGURES 3.2–3.5. Mantas. Museo del Oro.

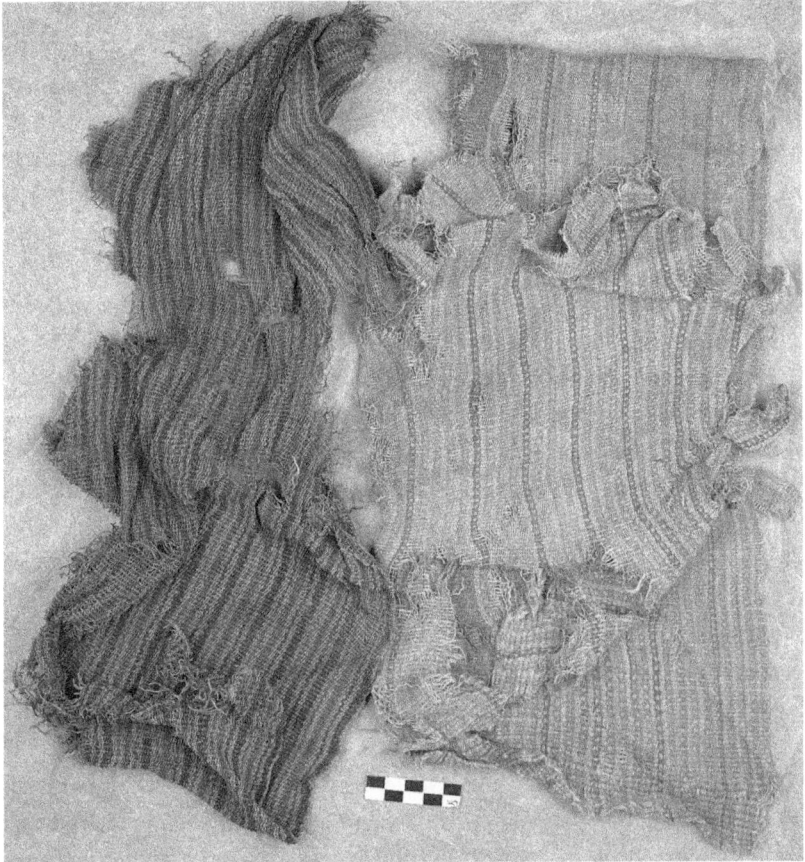

when they died: "They do not want to die as Christians but rather as their ancestors, buried with their gold, and not in churches with just one manta as *chingamanales*."[8] To be buried in a church with one textile meant to die as the least prestigious members of the Native community, what the Muisca called chingamanales. As a consequence, the Muisca caciques tried by any means to be buried according to Native customs. In a few documented cases, when feeling himself close to death, a cacique ordered his subjects to kill a commoner, disguise the commoner as himself, and hand the body over to the Catholic priests. That way the real cacique could be buried in Native ways with his textiles and sacred objects.[9]

While the visual appearance of mantas evokes a precontact Indigenous society, these textiles had a long life and played a key role in the Spanish empire during the sixteenth and seventeenth centuries, although their cultural value shifted during this period. After the conquest, these textiles became the primary good Indigenous peoples paid to the empire as tribute under the encomienda system and remained one of the driving forces of the economy under the Spanish monarchy—much as they had before Spanish rule. In contrast to the textiles' rich meanings for the Muiscas, the Spanish saw mantas as a means of wealth and as an instrument to address the empire's fiscal problems. From the Spanish administrators' perspective, mantas were quantifiable goods, a source of profit. Their language of mantas was associated with words like *tributo* (tribute) and *tasa* (rate)—a language of numbers that created an economic relationship between Native communities and the Spanish empire by conceptualizing mantas primarily as a quantifiable commodity, even a type of currency.

By 1560, in an effort to standardize colonial relations and to expand the administration's reach, magistrate Tomás López set the tribute required of Native peoples of the New Kingdom of Granada to 47,172 mantas per year—double the amount they paid in gold pesos.[10] Some encomenderos, like Diego de Valaderas, received as many as 1,300 mantas every year. It was a robust economy. The encomenderos received an overwhelming number of Native textiles every year. As a result, the mantas' reach extended far beyond Indigenous spheres. Mantas permeated colonial material culture. Encomenderos, merchants, and even Crown officials were challenged by contending with a material object that was foreign to their economic and cultural traditions.

This chapter mines fragmentary colonial records to highlight the centrality of mantas in the kingdom's economy and illustrate how an item produced by Indigenous people for Indigenous people became the heart of the kingdom's fiscal system. I argue that these textiles pieced together an economic system divided between different notions of value that nonetheless fueled the kingdom's economy. I build against the dominant emphasis on precious metals as the basis of the colonial economy, best represented by the following statement by historian Germán Colmenares: "The economy of the territories today comprised by Colombia (then designated New Kingdom and Popayán) was, for more than three centuries, an economy of gold."[11] This iconic statement heralded three decades of scholarship that has described the extraction of metals as the driving force of the New Kingdom's economy: motivating the creation of new cities, directing the flows of commodities, and guiding the establishment of regional systems.[12]

But I would venture to say with just as much certainty that this region's economy in the sixteenth and seventeenth centuries was one of Indigenous textiles, since mantas were at the center of the exchanges that allowed Spaniards to amass gold and silver. It is true that these metals, along with pearls and emeralds, were the main outputs for Spaniards; they were the means the king and his officials used to measure wealth and assess the degree of success or failure of the kingdom's economy, and they were at the center of key global markets including China and Europe. But mantas were the goods that powered the system that circulated metals. If we look at the system not from the perspective of the commodities Spanish settlers and officials coveted but rather through everyday exchanges between Spaniards and Indigenous people, it was the textiles produced by Indigenous artisans that drove the kingdom's economy. Manta production and exchange was a highly decentralized activity that occupied most members of Indigenous households but also guided how they measured success, debated the amount of labor they could reasonably pay their encomenderos, identified what counted as healthy economic interactions, and enunciated expectations regarding a person's suitable place in society. In this way, Indigenous manufacturers, enterprises, and notions of value remained the key drivers of the kingdom's economy.

The transformation of the Indigenous textiles that the Muiscas called boi into the colonial objects known as mantas unfolded parallel to the juridical and economic reinvention of the Muiscas as "indios," a process that aimed to turn them into Catholic, tribute-paying vassals of the Castilian monarchy and which defined their obligations in the new political landscape. Yet the Muiscas were not the only ones who found themselves adapting to new economic circumstances. At the same time, officials of the empire searched for ways to abstract and simplify the great variety of Native textiles into one undifferentiated concept—"mantas"—that could become the basis of a new tribute economy, while encomenderos and other settlers learned to identify the traits and particularities that conferred attractiveness and value on these textiles in the eyes of Native peoples. Muisca mantas soon decorated altars in the empire's newly established churches and confraternities. They reached the homes of Iberian immigrants, either as decorations or incorporated into containers (petacas) or other practical goods of everyday use. In many ways, the movement of Indigenous textiles shaped interactions between Native peoples, settlers, and imperial officials. All these groups' experiences and expectations—how they sought profit, distinction, recognition, and how they carried out daily tasks—were embedded in the fabric of mantas. The diversity of these textiles' forms and meanings signaled the emergence of new patterns of interactions in a transatlantic polity that forcefully brought together peoples from different ethnic backgrounds and with different life stories.

Examining the history of such culturally significant objects as mantas in Spanish colonial documents is often a frustrating experience. Though scribes, chroniclers, and accountants recognized the importance of mantas and frequently mentioned them, few considered writing about them in any significant detail. Fewer still devoted more than a couple of lines to mantas, and none of them described the characteristics, significance, and meaning of mantas to Indigenous peoples. In the imperial archives, mantas appear barely as crude statistics. Though imperial officials seldom left hints regarding the meanings of mantas, they meticulously counted them and recorded the figures. They wrote down how many mantas Native people paid, noted their monetary value, and earmarked how many should be given to encomenderos and the royal treasury. Only scattered traces and isolated quotes can help us make sense of their importance for Native cultures, politics, and economies. Isolated as they are from their symbolic contexts of production, reading the surviving textiles as texts—as encoded cultural scripts—remains out of reach.[13]

We may not be able to read the codes Indigenous painters inscribed on these textiles, but by tracing mantas' circulation throughout their social lives we can read the human relations they facilitated. Following their movement through Indigenous and European spheres it is possible to see how an Indigenous object came to be at the center of the emerging colonial economy, weaving together an economic space that was anchored in precolonial trade networks but now added mining centers and Spanish cities as new nodes and centers. This economic space was the result of the meshing of Indigenous and European economies, and it provided the basic system for relations of production and exchange in the New Kingdom. Through this process, Indigenous textiles condensed the types of transactions available in the new economy, the forms of accessing wealth, and negotiating extraction for both Indigenous and European peoples.

Indigenous Transactions

The production, circulation, and use of textiles was one of the largest and most important economic enterprises in the northern Andean highlands. Textile production involved the efforts of all households and the participation of every member of Indigenous communities. It entailed mobilizing human power, maintaining extensive networks of exchange across natural and ethnic borders, manufacturing tools, and distributing and coordinating tasks and responsibilities among family members. Textile exchange involved a set of dissimilar transactions that occurred in two different realms: within Muisca cacicazgos and in larger trade circuits.[14] Each of these involved different kinds of economic calculation, commensuration standards, modalities of exchange, and forms of consumption. Households participated in extended trade circuits, where textile exchange worked as a straightforward economic transaction that provided access to indispensable products like cotton, gold, and coca. At the level of cacicazgos, however, textiles were embedded in a gift economy crucial to the sihipqua's power, which channeled labor for the construction and maintenance of the community's infrastructure and economic base. The flows of mantas responded to closely monitored social agreements associated with power relations among cacicazgos. As a result of their role at these two levels, cotton cloths pieced together a lively interregional system of exchange and enabled the distribution of labor in Muisca communities. By designing, weaving, and wearing mantas, the Native peoples of the cold lands made status visible: they enacted power and inscribed it on their bodies.

Textile production was a decentralized activity that took place in every household. Archaeologist Ana María Boada has shown that the textile economy was not completely governed by the Native nobility in pre-Hispanic times. Had it been an elite-controlled activity, the archaeological record should reveal fairly standardized and homogeneous equipment for the production of mantas, and the traces of it would be concentrated around elite households. In her excavations in the Muisca site of El Venado (Boyacá), Boada instead found a large variety and diversity of utensils dispersed throughout the settlements, indicating that every household had its own tools. There was a greater number of tools in a specific area of the settlement, which probably marked the residence of the sihipqua (leader or cacique). This area also had a stronger concentration of jars, cups, decorated ceramics, and foreign objects, such as beads and corals, meaning that its occupants accumulated items of prestige and had the infrastructure to host large meals and banquets—an activity that, as we will see, was at the center of textile exchange. Although there was evidence of a more specialized and larger-scale production of textiles—associated with a wealthier household in general—every household of the settlement was involved in textile manufacture.[15]

Production was organized along gendered lines, though it was not a task performed exclusively by women. In the Peruvian Andes, women were the main textile producers, which made them active economic actors, though they seldom enjoyed the wealth they produced.[16] In Peruvian textile traditions, threads were usually dyed in different colors and artists wove them together on looms, creating stylized representations of people, animals, nature, or abstract motifs. In the northern Andes, women had a less prominent role in textile production. Most mantas were in cotton, but other vegetable fibers were used as well. Production consisted of three basic processes: spinning, weaving, and painting. Spinning was by far the most time-consuming. It consisted of taking the raw cotton fiber and twisting it into a very thin cord using spindles. It could take around 160 hours to spin the thread for a single cloth.[17] Women and children were probably in charge of spinning, though on occasion men also spun. Men seem to have done most of the weaving, using looms and other tools made mostly from carved deer bones.[18]

The process of coloring and drawing on textiles was apparently a more controlled activity restricted to elite households. In contrast to Peruvian textiles, northern Andean dyed textiles were usually of a single color, though some surviving fragments show that in some cases threads were combined to form patterns, especially around their borders. The most prestigious textiles were those artists painted using brushes to apply vegetable inks. Among the most widely available colors were red, brown, black, and blue.[19] Only high-status men—such as caciques, painters, and religious leaders—painted them. We have evidence that some specialized manta artists sometimes traveled to different sites to design manta patterns, suggesting that being a manta painter was a prestigious position that could bring mobility.[20]

In order to gain access to raw cotton, households engaged in long-distance exchange networks that spread to the lowlands, where cotton was raised. As mentioned in chapter 1, this was a decentralized trade, not the task of a specialized merchant class or that involved a standardized coin. Rather, it probably occurred at the level of the household. Individuals would carry their finished cloths to exchange them for raw cotton and other lowland products. There were some cyclical markets in different settlements, where these transactions took place. The markets of important political centers like Duitama, Sogamoso, Tunja, and Bogotá had an abundance of goods for sale; others, like Turmequé and Zipaquirá, were known for specialized goods like emeralds and salt.[21] I have also found mention of markets beyond the Muisca territory, in the Magdalena River valley and the central Andean range.[22] Gold dust and gold beads seem to have been used as means of exchange in some transactions—the Muisca word for gold was *nyia*, which also meant "money" (dinero, plata).[23] It is unclear if gold was a universal currency, and it remains unknown to what extent this was a market economy with prices denominated in cash or whether barter predominated in certain spheres of exchange. In interregional markets, though, cloth exchange was possibly thought about in terms of augmenting income. It was a means to access the necessary materials for the household's economy.

At the level of the cacicazgo, cloth exchange worked with a different logic. The responses offered by caciques and commoners to questionnaires in colonial visitations provide brief descriptions of the inner workings of cloth exchange in this realm, indicating that it was tied to Indigenous hierarchies and social organization and that it relied on a conceptual distinction between plain and decorated cloths. For instance, in his 1594 testimony, the Pausaga cacique Antonio Ladigno distinguished between three levels of hierarchy among the Muisca peoples ("indios," or commoners; "captains"; and "caciques") and between three types of textiles (plain mantas; painted mantas, or pintadas; and colored mantas, or coloradas). It is likely that what Ladigno called "painted mantas" were those painted by artists, while the "colored mantas" were probably dyed. Ladigno pointed out that in pre-Hispanic times each captain gave his cacique fifteen to twenty plain mantas per year, while commoners gave the cacique one or two plain mantas, cultivated his lands, and built his houses and palisades. The cacique in return gave one painted manta and one colored manta to the captain, who had given him the plain mantas. The cacique also honored the captains by painting their bodies. To the commoners, he provided food and drinks.[24] The number of textiles gifted was flexible; in their testimonies, captains and commoners mentioned differing amounts of mantas. But all referred to manta exchange as the key instrument for negotiating power and labor in the cacicazgo.

While the cacique—or the scribe who recorded the cacique's testimony—employed the Spanish term *tributo* to describe the exchange of mantas, the context of these exchanges in Native economies was very different from what the word alluded to in an Iberian setting.[25] The cacique's testimony offered a glimpse of a complex system of organizing labor, exchange, and consumption. The cacicazgo's economy depended on the expected and highly standardized exchange of textiles during vivid collective celebrations that involved feasting and drinking, along with music and dance. During these ceremonies, commoners planted the cacique's fields and built his palisades and houses, and in return he hosted a lavish banquet. These events strengthened the cacicazgo's economy; they were performed in a complex language of mantas and materialized in the exchange of expected gifts common in the Andes and other Indigenous societies.[26] During these festive occasions, Indigenous peoples built and repaired infrastructure and devoted time to the community's fields and base—upon their arrival, the Spaniards derided them as "borracheras" (drunken binges) and aimed to eliminate them, as I will show below.

There were many versions of these ceremonies: some were large and majestic with prestigious guests, while others were smaller, devoted to plantations or concrete works. In the Muisca language the words used were *biohote*, "drinking together," and *iebzasqua*, "making a place" (alluding to the fact that they built infrastructure and public works during these events), among other terms. The language used to describe these events built on a series of metaphors related to kinship, bodily parts and functions, and power.[27] The most thorough description of this kind of ceremony in colonial documents is of an event that took place in Ubaque in 1563.[28] It was a truly grandiose occasion, with some ten thousand guests, by some accounts, in which people danced, chanted, and played instruments wearing symbolic costumes of jaguars, pumas, and bears as they processed down a long road at the entrance of Ubaque's palisade. Ubaque prepared special buildings for the event, along with feathered items, food, and accommodations for visitors. The cacique's ability to attract and accommodate many guests reinforced the cacique's authority and created opportunities to connect people, mobilize labor, and develop infrastructure. In this sense, ceremonies like this not only displayed the cacique's power but also established criteria to define who was a good, generous, respectable leader. The exchange of textiles was at the heart of the political culture enacted during communal ceremonies. It was vital for the cacique's reputation.

The categorization and classification of mantas was central to this economy's functioning. Plain, painted, and colored mantas were the most common types and were treated as separate, strictly differentiated categories linked to social class: commoners and captains wove plain mantas, while the cacique distributed the more prestigious decorated mantas. The flow of mantas also followed clear patterns: simple mantas flowed up toward the cacique, and painted and colored mantas moved down toward lower strata. If commoners and captains gave the cacique between one and twenty plain mantas, the cacique would give in return only one or two painted or colored mantas to high-ranking officials. Painting and coloring the mantas, a process monopolized by the cacique, made them valuable enough that the cacique could receive many plain mantas in exchange for a single decorated. In other words, the categorization of mantas created a regime of value that allowed for the "asymmetric reciprocity" upon which the cacicazgo's economy rested.[29]

In this sense, mantas were not a standardized commodity in Indigenous communities, but rather highly individualized items that reflected the prestige of the wearer. Their value varied enormously according to its characteristics: if it was woven in cotton or in wool (a material that became increasingly accessible after the arrival of the Spanish and was employed to produce cheap mantas), if it was thick or thin, if it was black, white, striped, or had elaborate designs. Thinner mantas were more highly valued, as were those that were painted and dyed. In contrast, cheaper mantas were thick, coarse, and color-less. Different sources show that there was a profusion of categories and names to classify mantas. For instance, a list that recorded the mantas given by the encomendero of Oicatá to the Indigenous people of his encomienda distin-guished between ten different types of mantas and detailed their diversity of colors and styles. The list identified black, red, white, striped, and painted mantas, among other types. Especially interesting was the category "mantas de vestir" (mantas to be worn), suggesting that some mantas were not to be worn, which coincides with sources that describe Indigenous houses and palisades as covered with textiles.[30] The quality of the textiles people wore or kept at their homes rendered visible their social standing.

Who could wear or own a painted manta were political questions as much as economic ones, and the circulation of painted and colored mantas was highly regulated by Native authorities. Tomás López, for instance, noted in 1558 that "the caciques of this region had their indios in such a state of subjec-tion that no one could wear a painted manta or eat deer meat" without their consent.[31] Mantas signaled social hierarchy. For a commoner to wear an un-authorized painted manta was to defy the social order. Categories of mantas were thus highly enforced, and the order of mantas essentially reflected the order of society. Value and politics, prestige and hierarchy were different sides of the same coin. As a result, caciques aimed to strictly regulate the produc-tion and circulation of mantas within the cacicazgo, since the circulation of textiles was based on the principles of asymmetric reciprocity that allowed the cacique to accumulate a surplus of textiles. Thus, Indigenous textiles material-ized the cacicazgo's power and economy; they allowed leaders to accumulate wealth while being regarded as generous.

The principles that guided Indigenous manta exchange were reflected in language. The compilers of the most complete Muisca dictionary in 1606 in-cluded entries for "price" (*cuca*, precio de la cosa), "cheap" (*acucaza*, barato), "ex-pensive" (*acuca yn puyca*, cosa cara) and other terms associated with economic calculations. Remuneration was understood as distributing part of the yield, as explained in the definition of *bquysqua*: "paying someone in the same matter in which they worked." It provided the following examples: "*Abago bquysqua*, I give him some maize for the maize he helped me pick. *Aiomgo bquysqua*, I give him some potatoes for those he helped me pick. *Aspquago* is the pay or remuneration for any handwork; *chiego* is the piece of land they give him to plant."[32] Labor and remuneration were part of communal economies and were performed in ceremonies in which food and clothing circulated among kin groups. Perhaps for this reason, there was no word to describe a "poor person," as the dictionary attested ("pobre, no hay vocablo particular").[33] Rather, kin groups gathered together in celebrations to augment the community's base, which was then apportioned and distributed among them.

In essence, cloth circulation established a political economy. All Muisca households wove cloth, and these textiles mediated each household's participation in wider economies, either in larger trade networks or in cacicazgos. In fact, cloth production was possible only because of the existence of larger provisioning networks, and as woven cloths flowed downhill and raw cotton went uphill, textile circulation maintained and reinforced these economic ties. Mantas were neither a currency nor a commodity defined by a nominal exchange value. Rather, mantas circulated in each of these two realms. In the trade realm, the production and circulation of textiles depended on and strengthened an interethnic, decentralized economic space that encompassed both the highlands and the lowlands. In the reciprocal realm of cacicazgos, cloth exchange was tied to community labor distribution, infrastructure building, and systems of authority. It guided both the sense of who was a good, generous leader and the sense of who was a good commoner. Textile circulation in both realms, interregional markets and cacicazgos, entailed different forms of calculation and two logics of exchange: in markets they participated in straightforward trade to provision households, while in the cacicazgo textile flows were presented as an exchange of gifts in search of reputation and distinction in their communities.

From Boi to Mantas

Between the 1530s and 1560s, as Spanish conquistadors took control of the Andean highlands, distributed Native communities in encomiendas, and established a royal tribunal for the administration of the kingdom, the cloth economy became embedded in the emerging institutions of the Spanish empire. This was a gradual process that came along with the empire's own process of self-definition. In other words, it took place as the empire also defined its own institutional systems of labor and surplus extraction and how it would tax Indigenous communities in its global domains, under the encomienda system.

The Spanish empire in its own way distinguished between two economic realms that were similar in concept to the two realms of Indigenous cloth transactions, though they differed in the way they were executed. One realm was tributary, consisting of taxes to pay allegiance to the king and church; the other took a market form, permitting the exchange of all manner of goods, services, livestock, real estate, and even human captives relying on a base cash unit, the golden peso (peso de oro). These two realms meshed with the Indigenous gift and trade economies in a way that could be described as parasitic or predatory: the goal of the Crown in establishing its own institutions was to drain surplus from Indigenous communities to pass it on to Spanish encomenderos, the royal treasury, and the church, while aiming to maintain the economic dynamics and composition of Indigenous social groups.

The encomienda was key to this institutional setup. It was part of the tributary economy in the sense that the Crown demanded a payment from Indigenous communities, yet yielded it to encomenderos in recognition of their services. By the time the encomienda reached the New Kingdom, in the 1540s, the monarchy's evolving legal statutes defined it as annual tributes Native people paid to encomenderos. Twenty percent of that tribute in turn went to the royal treasury, a tax called the royal fifth (quinto real). In the crown's colonialist rationale, Native people paid this in exchange for evangelization, which it thought a path to salvation. The goal of this form of organization was to preserve local "customs," especially systems of governance and economics, while transforming Indigenous spirituality.[34] In other words, the new tributes aimed to replicate Indigenous economies, while evangelization aimed to reform their beliefs.

To set up a system of this kind, imperial officials expected tribute to be paid in the types of products Native peoples used as offerings to their caciques in precolonial times. Inspectors visited local communities to identify the goods that could be demanded from Indigenous communities and then developed elaborate lists organizing Indigenous people into colonial categories, as I showed in chapter 2. During their inspections, visitadores aimed to identify the key items that would allow them to simplify, standardize, and regulate colonial tribute. They asked local communities "if they knew what indios paid in pagan times to their caciques and lords, and in which ways and what amounts they did so."[35] That way, they could calculate a rate that roughly corresponded to pre-Hispanic levels. The Crown even asked local officials to set tribute rates below those paid to precolonial Indigenous leaders. The tribute rate depended as well on the size of the working-age male population in each encomienda—those whom imperial administrators called "useful indios," as I explain in chapter 2. For this reason, part of the inspectors' task was listing and counting the tributary population. With all this information, visitadores could determine the share of tribute that corresponded to the crown. Magistrate Francisco Briceño and bishop Juan de los Barrios established the first tribute rate in 1555, based on a restricted, scattered visitation carried out by Juan Ruiz de Orejuela. It was

Tomás López Medel who set the first generalized tribute rate, as the kingdom's visitador between 1558 and 1560 (see chapter 2). The visitadores who came after him, like Angulo de Castejón in the 1560s, Juan López de Cepeda in the 1570s, Miguel de Ibarra in the 1590s, and Luis Enríquez in the 1600s, were supposed to adapt the tribute rate set by previous visitadores to current circumstances.[36] Throughout the sixteenth century, these rates consisted of a combination of payments in gold, labor, and, above all, Native textiles.

In the 1560s, the inspectors' field incursions revealed a remarkable diversity in the types of products Indigenous communities paid to their encomenderos. Since Indigenous cacicazgos produced such a variety of goods, tribute was quite heterogeneous and consisted of a wide array of local products depending on what was available to each Indigenous group. In some communities, tribute payments included quantities of corn, potatoes, chickens, eggs, and textiles, as well as the labor of varying numbers of Native men and women who worked in the encomendero's residence and agricultural fields. In other cases, it consisted of honey, beans, ceramics, thread, coca leaves, cotton, salt, containers, and hammocks; often different products were paid at different times of the year. In fact, in 1562 in the Province of Tunja alone, an imperial official recorded forty-one types of goods given as tribute payments. Each good was measured using different standard units: some based on length and volume, others based on weight, others that created equivalence between sacks of produce and the amount of land needed for such yields.[37] In addition to these products, Native communities performed labor in a variety of enterprises, from mining to cattle herding to cheese production, which came to be known as personal services (servicios personales).

These arrangements were outright extraction of community resources, but they were practical for settlers and Native peoples on the ground. A community would give encomenderos a mix of products, as well as the labor of men, women, and youths for the encomenderos' own enterprises. But this was less practical for the Crown, since it became nearly impossible for officials to keep clear records of such a variety of transactions. The diversity and complexity of the system made it extremely difficult to ensure that the Royal Treasury received its fifth. This was especially the case for personal services, which were repeatedly prohibited by imperial mandates.

Thus, visitadores aimed to replace these varied and diverse economic arrangements with a standard transaction that they could monitor more easily: the payment of one or two kinds of goods at most. The legislation specified that the items for tribute should be local—Native communities could not leave their settlements to find these items or to gain access to the raw materials needed for their production—and that the tribute itself needed to be a continuation of pre-Hispanic economies, theoretically lessening the burden on Native communities. But to fulfill both requirements was simply impossible: most precontact Muisca communities of the highlands paid tribute to sihipquas in textiles they wove using cotton, a product of the lowlands that did not grow in the cold Andean highlands. In fact, most Indigenous products of the highlands, like mantas, salt, gold, ceramics, coca, shells, and in some cases even wood and rock, were part of a network of extended transregional commercial networks (see chapter 1). And that continued to be the case throughout the sixteenth century.

The decision to set tribute rates in mantas was consistent with the requirements laid out by imperial officials in the sense that they were a widely available item that encapsulated the economic exchanges of highland cacicazgos. They taxed Native communities not in "local" items—as law dictated—but in items available through their commercial networks. Historian Germán Colmenares argued that the logic of the system was designed to maximize colonial profits: royal officials taxed Native peoples in whatever products they did not have—Popayán in mantas and the New Kingdom in gold—so that encomenderos could take advantage of exchange rates by selling products to Native peoples at higher rates and then receiving those goods in return as tribute.[38] Nevertheless, this is imprecise, since many Indigenous people of Popayán had their own types of mantas and many Indigenous people of the New Kingdom had access to gold in the same types of economic networks in which they gained access to cotton. Furthermore, tribute records suggest that both regions were taxed in a combination of mantas and gold, and at different times both encomenderos and Native communities complained to the audiencia regarding the products paid as tribute. Rather, by selecting mantas and gold as the main items for tribute, imperial officials considered not what each individual village produced but rather the whole system of exchange. This was clear in other non-Muisca regions that were taxed in Muisca mantas, because they got hold of these textiles through trade, like the case of the Teguas in the mid-seventeenth century.[39] In other words, imperial officials did not invent the system themselves; rather, they identified the prominent role of textiles in Indigenous economies and overlaid tribute requirements on existing networks of exchange.

The declarations of the cacique of Pausaga to visitador Miguel de Ibarra in 1594 reveal the complexity of the system. He stated that the community paid tribute to their encomendero in mantas and "some of them weave mantas in this town although they go to get their cotton to Subachoque and other neighboring towns."[40] The cotton was not even grown in Subachoque itself, but rather was traded there from production sites in warmer areas like the Eastern Plains or the Magdalena River valley. This shows that the notion that mantas were a local product was a clear fallacy, but there were no other fairly standard yet wholly local products they could use for tribute, since precolonial societies had been deeply interconnected by trade. Similarly, Native peoples of the cold lands accessed gold—a product of the lowlands—in exchange for salt and mantas. López wrote that by trading these two products, the Muiscas "bring to the kingdom great amounts of gold every year, from which they pay tribute to the encomenderos."[41] Mantas were thus at the core of the Andean tribute system, whether Native peoples paid in mantas or in gold, since the economic value was always traceable back to mantas. In other words, the Crown's search for a "local good" that synthesized the Indigenous economy reflected a misunderstanding of how economic interactions worked in the northern Andes—ignorance of the region's characteristic trade networks.

Mantas came to embody the overlapping of European and Indigenous social systems and economies, and they also revealed the tensions and contradictions between them—especially regarding Indigenous ritual. As noted above, the exchange of mantas within the cacicazgo took place in elaborate ceremonies known as biohote or iebzasqua in which commoners planted and harvested the cacique's fields and built his houses and palisades. In return, the cacique gave them large quantities of maize beer and food. Because of the quantity of fermented beverages commoners drank during these celebrations, Spaniards labeled these events borracheras and condemned them as anti-Christian ceremonies.[42] Visitadores stressed that tribute amounts and the timing of payments should depend on the characteristics of pre-Hispanic economies. At the same time, however, officials stigmatized Indigenous ritual events, which enabled textile exchange. The depredation of Muisca ritual created an ambivalent situation: while in theory colonial administrators sought to preserve Indigenous economies, they also strove to eliminate the political cultures guiding the economy. In this sense, the imperial manta economy created opposing incentives: it encouraged encomenderos to allow caciques to collect tribute through existing systems, a process that in Indigenous economies was tied to ritual and to ceremonies like the biohote and iebzasqua, while expecting friars and officials to persecute Muisca ritual gatherings.

The 1560s and 1570s were the most critical decades for the tensions surrounding Indigenous rituals of manta exchange. Imperial authorities and, in some cases, friars fought fiercely against borracheras, while encomenderos overlooked them, or in some remarkable cases even defended the right of

Indigenous peoples to host them—like Juan de Céspedes in Ubaque, who questioned the royal tribunal's investigation, saying that "just like the Spaniards had their sacred holidays, the indios had their own."[43] Despite official persecution, the ceremonies remained widespread. In 1563, for example, the encomendero Gonzalo García Zorro declared that it was widely known, "público y notorio," that Native peoples hosted these ceremonies, and Francisco de Santiago noted that he "has seen many Indigenous borracheras."[44] In 1569, an Indigenous witness in a legal proceeding against the borracheras testified that he knew about these ceremonies because "as a boy he was stolen and taken to Choachí . . . where he saw borracheras with his own eyes and listened to them with his own ears. After he fled Choachí, he continued to hear and know about borracheras everywhere he passed by."[45] Wherever he went, he saw or heard about these ceremonies. When colonial officials asked him why had he not denounced them to the royal authorities when he knew the great damage that borracheras caused to the "evangelic law," he said that "he thought that everyone knew about these ceremonies just like he knew about them, because it is not possible that the mestizos and interpreters that spend time among the indios do not know about them."[46]

However, the use of mantas for tribute provided officials, encomenderos, caciques, and commoners with a standard to calculate and debate a new type of economic relationship—a form of tribute that broke the norms of the Indigenous gift economy. Colonial officials envisioned a parasitic system perpetuating an Indigenous economy and profiting from it. In the new setup, Indigenous households remained in control of production but had to surrender textiles to encomenderos receiving nothing in return. They continued to access cotton through their own extended trade networks, weave mantas in their households, and deliver them to their caciques. But now the encomenderos expected caciques to hand the mantas over to them, while friars and officials attacked the Indigenous rituals of manta exchange.

This was a big leap from precolonial times, when manta gifts established a political bond between sihipquas and commoners. People paid their respects personally, in the name of their kin units. Commoners expected food and beverages, kin leaders anticipated painted textiles, and the cacique amassed many plain textiles. People acted upon this framework to aim to improve their social positioning and material wealth. In the colonial tribute system, textile exchange lost its tangible reciprocal character, as the encomendero's contribution consisted of providing evangelization—and Indigenous peoples paid tithes to friars in kind, too—in exchange for a fixed rate of cloth. In this sense, textiles became a measure of extraction. The Crown hoped to keep Indigenous economies unchanged, and encomenderos' role in the textile economy built on the caciques' power, but their participation also changed this economy.

Weaving an Economic Space

The overlap between the Indigenous gift and trade economies with the Spanish tribute and market economies meant that encomenderos started accumulating large amounts of goods that were not designed for their consumption; this volume posed specific challenges. In contrast to colonial products such as pearls, emeralds, gold, silver, sugar, dyes, or even furs and brazilwood, there was no demand for mantas in European or Asian markets.[47] Nor did encomenderos wear mantas—in fact, in the only cases I have found of Europeans described as wearing mantas, they were trying to disguise their identity by passing as "indios."[48] Mantas remained markers of Indigeneity, and visitadores in their inspections routinely inquired if there were any mestizos or non-Indigenous persons living among Indigenous communities, dressed in mantas. In other words, imperial officials expected mantas to render visible individuals' legal identity as "indios."[49]

Since the manta was not an item for their consumption, for encomenderos and officials to find ways of making mantas profitable to them they needed to engage with Native markets. In so doing, they involved themselves in Indigenous economic systems by using them as a way of attracting Indigenous people to their estates or mines and paying for their labor. In 1568, Melchor Pérez de Arteaga described the economy of the Province of Santa Fe by saying that the Indigenous inhabitants produced cotton mantas and the Spaniards lived from selling those mantas and Indigenous produce in the mines, and from trading in cattle and derived products at seaports.[50] Three years later, in 1571, Fray Gaspar de Puerto Alegre described Spaniards' economic activities, saying that "the occupations and enterprises of Spaniards" were based upon the economy "of the indios, dealing and contracting with mantas in Popayán and other places." According to Puerto Alegre, encomenderos had become manta merchants. They also produced "flours, cheeses, biscuit [vizcocho], hams, and Spanish products."[51] Others described the colonial economy in similar terms: settler wealth relied both on Spanish goods and on the circulation of mantas in long-distance trading networks. Settlers sold mantas as clothing for Native people in the mines, in Popayán, and in other regions.[52]

The flows of mantas configured a distinctive regional economic space in the northern Andes. Historian Carlos Sempat Assadourian coined the term "colonial economic space" to argue that specialized regional economies and the flow of goods in internal markets wove together larger territories in Latin America.

For him, most of South America—from Ecuador to Chile and Argentina—was threaded together in an "Andean economic space" that revolved around the Potosí silver mines, largely reproducing the boundaries of the Inca empire. Potosí silver and the centralized authority of the Viceroyalty of Peru were powerful magnets moving large contingents of labor to the mines, and which assembled together specialized regional economies like Argentina's mule herding and Quito's textile workshops.[53]

The New Kingdom of Granada was not part of this Andean economic space; it had its own economic sphere, spun in a regional circuit that connected the highlands and the lowlands through the flow of Indigenous textiles. Manta circulation in larger Indigenous trade networks marked the limits of the New Kingdom's economic space, as the mining zones of Antioquia, Pamplona, and Mariquita turned into lively centers of textile exchange in the sixteenth century. The new economy was an extension of the Indigenous gift and trade economies, simultaneously adjusting and transforming them. Some of these markets boomed with the advent of colonialism, as Indigenous people concentrated in the gold mines of Antioquia and Popayán and the silver mines of Santa Agueda and, later in the sixteenth century, Mariquita. The result was a coherent economic system that stemmed from a pre-Hispanic economic network, with its own supply chains and internal markets, but which now had mining as one of its central axes.

This economic space was shaped by the New Kingdom's topography. The gold deposits were associated with the geologic formation of the three distinct ranges of the northern Andes, and in particular with the distribution of igneous and metamorphic rocks among them. These rocks flowed down mountain streams and were especially abundant in the central and western ranges. For this reason, the mining centers were in the lower sections of the central and western mountain ranges—in the hot lands—where Indigenous peoples did not live in large concentrations.[54] In the early sixteenth century, most Indigenous people working the mines came from encomiendas in the surrounding areas and from those in the cold lands. By 1565, the Indigenous population working the mines had reached around eight thousand people.[55] The activity was so intense that by the 1580s, many placer deposits had been depleted in the zones of Anserma, Zaragoza, Cáceres, and Cartago. These new population hubs required maize, salt, pork, beef, and mantas to feed and clothe Indigenous and African miners. The agglomeration of Indigenous people made the mines ideal places to trade in mantas.[56] In 1579, a new law required that each worker be given two mantas yearly.[57] The demand for mantas in these new centers certainly presented an opportunity for encomenderos receiving their tribute payments in textiles to turn a decent profit, as well as for Spanish merchants who would carry loads of mantas to the mines and sell them to Spanish miners. The miners would, in turn, use the mantas as payment for Indigenous labor.[58]

Even in the mining centers, encomenderos participated in regional markets and networks of manta circulation that had clearly grown from Indigenous roots. The gold and silver mines were in the hot lands, and since precolonial times Indigenous commercial networks had connected the cold lands and hot lands by exchanging finished textiles and salt for raw cotton, coca leaves, gold, and other goods. The system consisted of carrying mostly finished goods to the lowlands and raw materials to the highlands. The new boom of silver and gold mining promoted by Spaniards built on and expanded these pre-Hispanic circuits. Encomenderos and miners sought to attract labor to the mines by providing mantas as payment to Indigenous laborers who ventured to the lowlands. They aimed to use this culturally significant item, which conveyed honor and prestige, to channel labor to the lowlands and thus convert Indigenous surplus into Spanish forms of wealth.

Encomenderos also dealt with mantas by redistributing them back to Indigenous people—usually those who belonged to their encomiendas—in exchange for labor. They operated within the basic realm of exchange of cacicazgos, in which textiles were deployed as a way of mobilizing labor. This flow of mantas from encomenderos back to Native people appears in colonial documents, usually in the lists of mantas that the encomendero gave to Native people as payment for "personal services." The relationship between the encomendero and Indigenous people in this case seems to be an extension of the relationship between the community, the captains, and the cacique. If the cacique rewarded commoners and captains with food and valuable mantas in exchange for working in their plantations and houses, the encomenderos used the same forms of exchange for labor in their haciendas. The flow of mantas was crucial to channeling Indigenous labor, and the encomienda economy seemed to work broadly under the same principles as that of the cacicazgo. In other words, encomenderos played the role of caciques, receiving textiles and using them as a reward for labor.

Imperial officials, in turn, auctioned mantas off to the highest bidder, transforming them into a unit of currency that could be entered into the royal treasury's books. The auctions, called almonedas, were supposed to be announced by a town crier and took place in the central square in the presence of a magistrate, three officials, and a scribe, who would record the date, buyer's name, numbers of mantas, and price paid. In 1565, the king decreed that this type of sale, which was frequent in medieval Iberia, was the official procedure to turn any tributes paid by Indigenous people in goods into profit.[59] The account books do not include much information about the people who bought mantas in almonedas, but they were usually men with Spanish names, such as Cristóbal Camelo, Jorge del Cardo, Bartolomé Marín, or Bernardino de Buenmayor, probably merchants who dealt in mantas.[60] In the case of Diego de Hernández, he was described explicitly as a "trader of the royal street" (tratante de la calle real). The prices fluctuated but usually were around one peso (un peso de buen oro). If they were sold at that price to Spanish merchants—who did not use mantas but expected to resell them at a profit elsewhere—we can assume that the value of mantas was higher in other locations.[61]

Mantas clearly became a key good and means of exchange, transcending Indigenous networks and markets, in many ways defining European officials' and settlers' economic expectations. Textiles were the thread knitting together the New Kingdom's economic space, which involved the production and circulation of metals. Unlike the Andean economic space, which was powered by Potosí silver, the system in the New Kingdom was anchored on an Indigenous item.

The Rules of the Game

An Indigenous good that marked the personal status of people wearing it, and therefore was singular and individual, became a standardized commodity and a type of currency used to measure units of labor that Indigenous people owed as tribute and configured the New Kingdom's economic space. This placed mantas at the center of imperial accounting and for settlers' economic enterprises. Throughout the sixteenth century, caciques, commoners, settlers, and officials engaged in often heated discussions in court about mantas' worth and their commensurability in gold and Spanish currency—that is, to identify exactly how much mantas were worth and establish their equivalence in metals.

Questions about the value of mantas encapsulated disagreements over how much labor Native people could be expected to pay to their encomenderos and the imperial administration—about the reasonable amount of time people should spend working to satisfy the empire's tax demands—and the amount of revenue they could keep for themselves. These discussions stemmed from the fact that the imperial administration was instrumentalizing as a currency a good with a high use value for Indigenous people. For visitadores, accountants, and other imperial officials, the challenge was to make mantas into a clear standard of value. This entailed determining exactly what could be considered a standard manta for tribute and reaching a consensus on what it was worth, setting an equivalence in golden pesos. Yet mantas were a plural kind of good, with many varieties and customizations that gave them value. Their production cost and their value also shifted according to market fluctuations, given that they depended on interregional cotton trade. This tension between tribute requirements set on the basis of an abstract, standard manta and the plurality of objects that resulted, taking into account fluctuating market prices, artists' skills, and availability of materials, resulted in frequent discrepancies in the cost of tribute, opening opportunities for gain and dispute.

These tensions were grounded in a type of social aesthetics that involved forms of appreciating, reading, and observing textiles. Mantas were produced in different colors, degrees of coarseness, and degrees of quality, and they circulated in very specific social contexts. A manta's quality was judged according to its thickness: the thinner the better. By the 1560s, Indigenous households had incorporated European animals and products like hens, eggs, sheep, and wool into their economies, and they added a new variety of inexpensive mantas to the mix, woven with sheep's wool. Woolen mantas were usually thicker, meaning that cotton remained the standard for quality.[62] Through implicit agreements like this, Indigenous people knew how to value different types of textiles.

To participate in this economy, encomenderos and imperial officials had to learn to evaluate textiles the way Native peoples did: they needed to be able to discern a costly textile from a cheap one and reach agreements about exactly which type of textile Indigenous people could fairly expect to pay. Visitadores, in particular, started to refer to tribute mantas with the expression "of the brand" (de la marca), which usually meant thin, white, and cotton, though on occasion these were made of wool.[63] They sometimes indicated the measurements of these mantas, which were roughly just under two meters square ("dos varas y sesma de ancho y otro tanto de largo").[64] Yet the definition of a manta de la marca was broad enough to leave plenty of room for interpretation; so was its equivalent in pesos. In this sense, mantas set the rules of the game: they opened possibilities for people to calculate their worth, aim to increase their profit, and advance their personal interest. In other words, by assigning value and identifying which mantas were refined and worthy, Indigenous forms of perception laid the groundwork for negotiation and calculation, even for cheating and manipulating the legal system.

Both encomenderos and Native peoples made elaborate calculations to assess the value of mantas. They frequently complained about the type and quantity of mantas they were supposed to pay or receive as tribute. Encomenderos often claimed that the textiles were too coarse and demanded that caciques pay in high-value mantas. Caciques and commoners, on the other hand, usually expressed that the encomenderos underestimated the value of mantas, especially when compared to the exchange rates between gold and mantas in transregional markets.

Many of these disagreements ended up in litigation and recorded in colonial archives. Such was the case of Fusagasugá, a Muisca cacique, who in 1558 asked the audiencia to allow him to pay his cacicazgo's tribute in gold, rather than in mantas, because prices in the market for mantas were so high that the cacique would be losing an important amount of value if he gave the mantas to his encomendero rather than trading them. For example, an Indigenous trader could obtain a large amount of gold in exchange for a thin, delicate, painted manta in a mining area, and use part of that gold to pay his tribute. Since tribute in mantas was given by number rather than value, if he instead delivered the same manta as tribute, he would lose part of the value, because the manta was more valuable than the amount owed in gold. It was much more profitable for him to sell the mantas in exchange for gold and pay the value of tribute in gold to his encomendero, saving the remaining amount for himself and his community. For this reason, the cacique preferred to pay his tribute in gold, a foreign good that could not be extracted from his cacicazgo or indeed the highlands of the Andes. The audiencia's response is even more revealing. Royal authorities did not accept his proposal and instead forced the cacique and the community of Fusagasugá to continue to pay tribute in mantas.[65]

Some caciques sought flexibility, hoping to pay however was easier for them each year. For instance, in 1594 the cacique of Pausaga told the visitador Ibarra that Indigenous people should pay in "both gold and mantas, because some indios get gold more easily and others get mantas."[66] Neither cotton nor gold was a local, completely accessible product in Pausaga, but they could get hold of them rather easily through Native markets.[67] Whether it was more advantageous for Indigenous people to pay tribute in mantas or gold depended on fluctuating "conversion rates" between the two products, as well as the price they could get for each according to the official tribute rates and in transregional markets. Therefore, the flexibility would allow leaders to make the decision best suited for their economic pursuits.

Imperial officials, however, tried to restrain the flexibility of tribute payments. During visitations, they relentlessly inquired about the practice of "commutation," which referred to the substitution of tribute items—for instance, paying an equivalent amount of tribute in gold, labor, or other products instead of mantas. Officials forbade encomenderos from commuting mantas for gold or other products, and were even more emphatic in banning the substitution for labor (personal services), even threatening to strip encomenderos of their encomiendas.[68] Officials' insistence on this was a matter of clarity for royal accounts: as explained above, the ability to calculate the king's royal fifth relied on their ability to reduce payments to a series of standardized amounts. For this reason, only magistrates and visitadores were allowed to establish quantities and values for commutation in cases in which it was indispensable.

Standardizing the economy of such a diverse geographical expanse based on textiles resulted in some puzzling situations. In 1564, for instance, the vecinos of the gold-mining areas of the Province of Quimbaya complained about the tribute rate Tomás López had set. He had established that tribute should be paid in mantas, but Native communities in this region had easy access to gold. The Quimbayas had one of the most developed gold industries of northern South America. Today, a large proportion of the items in the collection of the Gold Museum in Bogotá were produced by these groups.[69] Still, López opted to fix tribute in textiles. Unsurprisingly, the vecinos complained that the Native communities of the area had no cotton to weave mantas, and even if they did, they would not know how to produce them. This was probably an exaggeration, since the Quimbayas had an active textile economy in precolonial times.[70] But witnesses testified that the Native peoples of this area in the mid-1560s did not weave mantas but rather bought them from merchants who came from the Muisca territory—what they called the "New Kingdom of Bogotá"—and that the Native economy of the area revolved around gold. In some cases, it was their encomenderos who bought mantas woven in the cold lands and gave them to Native people.[71] The vecinos complained that the tribute rate was absurd and that the Native communities of this region should pay their tribute in gold or by providing laborers for the gold mines now owned by European settlers.

As encomenderos used the mantas to pay for Indigenous labor, mantas also came to define what Indigenous peoples considered fair or unfair remuneration for their labor. When asked if Indigenous servants had been paid fairly, Indigenous witnesses would often respond that they had seen them and they were well clothed, meaning that they had received nice mantas as payment. On occasion, the encomenderos' engagement with the manta economy might have made prestigious mantas accessible to commoners who performed certain duties that were not as widespread or valuable in precolonial times, like working in mines.[72] This also meant that Indigenous peoples, friars, and others often assessed the degree of exploitation in relation to mantas: whether the encomendero and imperial officials were requesting too much from Indigenous communities. Juan de Avendaño spoke candidly about this in a 1573 letter to the king, explaining that "the tribute in mantas the indios pay, they do with great work ... bringing cotton through trade by land from long distances." He added that "the encomenderos go to their villages to ask for the mantas and pick the thinner ones, and when they are not [thin] they tear them and punish them."[73]

The following year, in 1574, a conflict associated with mantas broke the relationship between the mestizo cacique of Turmequé, Don Diego de la Torre, and his encomendero, who was also his half brother, Pedro Torres. Don Diego reported to the audiencia that while the tribute rates set the value of a manta at five tomines and gave the Indigenous community the capacity to decide whether they would pay in mantas or gold, the encomendero was actually demanding mantas, which he credited against the tribute at a price of five tomines each but which he then sold at double the price. Following this scheme, over the span of twelve years the encomendero had accumulated enormous wealth that should actually belong to the community of Turmequé. Don Diego claimed that the encomendero owed the community of Turmequé eight thousand pesos.[74] As I will show in chapters 5 and 6, this conflict over mantas detonated a massive Indigenous freedom project that took Don Diego to Spain twice, where he personally met King Philip II and advocated for political change in the New Kingdom, deeply impacting the kingdom's governance.

These cases prove that the tribute system's valuation of mantas created room to maneuver and opened space for a whole series of calculations and disputes between encomenderos and Indigenous peoples, giving a material, tangible character to colonial extractive institutions. By setting up a tribute system in mantas, the value of Indigenous textiles came to be associated with the value of labor in a changing economy. It was a mutually transformative process: Indigenous forms of exchange influenced how the tribute system and thus the broader imperial economy developed, but the creation of that imperial economy also opened new avenues to acquire textiles and changed how and what was valued in Indigenous textiles.

An Economy of Mantas, Gold, and Silver

Whenever we think of the economy of the early modern Spanish empire, gold and silver come to mind. These metals were powerful motivators of Spanish imperial expansion. It is difficult to grasp the attraction they held for the first conquistadores. As Inga Clendinnen has written, perhaps the best allusion to it are the words of Hernán Cortés himself when he explained to a cacique in Mesoamerica that Spaniards suffered from a disease of the heart, for which the only cure was gold.[75] Indigenous author Felipe Guamán Poma de Ayala evoked another iconic scene in his twelve-hundred-page letter to King Philip III, in which he included a drawing of the Inca Guayna Capac asking conquistador Pedro de Candía, "Is this the gold you eat?" to which Candía replied, "This gold we eat."[76]

Conquistadors dreamt of entire cities covered in gold. They drained lakes, climbed mountains, and launched conquest campaigns in the name of gold. Entire expeditions were wiped out in dense tropical forests while in search of metals. Similarly, the silver produced in early modern Hispanic America redefined the world economy and consolidated the first global currency: the real de a ocho (Spanish dollar). Distinctive societies emerged in the silver-producing areas of the Andes, such as the cosmopolitan city of Potosí, at 4,000 meters (13,200 feet) above sea level, while the Mexican Bajío was an engine of global capitalism in the sixteenth century.[77]

Spaniards were ravenous for precious metals, and the New Kingdom's settlers were no exception. But mantas were instrumental to amassing metals; they provided access to Indigenous labor. The Spanish had to engage in a transcultural economy in which they aimed to transmute mantas into gold for export and to transmute gold into mantas for internal payments. Encomenderos operated within preexisting social and political groups governed by caciques and depended on caciques to collect their tribute. After draining this surplus, encomenderos acted partly as manta exporters, sending large quantities out to mining areas and other districts, and partly using manta redistribution to compensate laborers in their estates. Many Spanish merchants in practice acted as manta suppliers. Encomenderos, merchants, and miners acted upon Native economic networks and used the redistribution of mantas as a way of contracting labor.

The manta economy was therefore neither an implanted economic system derived exclusively from the empire's needs nor the unaltered persistence of an Indigenous economy. It was, rather, a hybrid economic system that wove Indigenous and Spanish economies together.[78] Manta exchange configured a distinctive colonial space in the Northern Andes: a regional economic system that stemmed from precolonial Indigenous trade networks, that increasingly involved metal extraction as one of its axes, and that was largely independent of other economic systems in Spanish South America. Furthermore, the colonial economy of mantas shows how Indigenous peoples were forced to adapt and accommodate to colonial pressures, coercive labor, and all kinds of burdens, but also how encomenderos had to adjust to local arrangements and blend into Native economies. The economy of mantas suggests that we must complement studies about how Indigenous peoples were forced into colonial markets, into coercive forms of labor and consumption, with others exploring how Spaniards were drawn into the inner workings of Native economies.

Through the manta economy, Indigenous peoples maintained a firm grip on the production of the most important objects that moved the economy. Their notions of value dominated the system. Even if the surplus that remained in Indigenous hands decreased and was siphoned off by Spanish settlers, mantas were the thread weaving kingdom together and facilitating the functioning of its economy, and they remained so during the sixteenth and early seventeenth centuries. However, as we will see in chapters 7 and 8, in the last decades of the sixteenth century Indigenous peoples confronted a new push to disenfranchise them, as audiencia officials passed regulations aimed at dispossessing them of their lands and closely monitoring their economies—seriously attacking the economic autonomy they were able to attain through mantas and other economic activities, like salt production.

By 1560, the kingdom had a specific institutional architecture: an infrastructure of governance dependent on flows of paper between Santa Fe de Bogotá and Madrid and whose economy was largely moved by Indigenous textiles. New challenges emerged in the following decades, however, as Indigenous peoples envisioned opportunities for justice and freedom and acted upon them in ways that challenged, reshaped, and transformed the kingdom. The next part examines these visions of Indigenous freedom.

PART II   INDIGENOUS FREEDOM

It was almost dawn, possibly in 1580, when twenty-three Spanish soldiers gathered their arms to depart from the city of Cartago into the mythical mountains of the "indios Pijaos." This large and mountainous territory lay to the southwest of the Audiencia of Santa Fe in the central range of the northern Andes, which the Spanish often referred to as "the impenetrable mountain." The territory had been largely ignored by imperial authorities during the first decades after the Spanish invasion in the 1530s, seen as a marginal territory. Yet since the late 1550s it had increasingly attracted the attention of Spanish officials.

The soldiers' departure was not completely voluntary; it was part of an imperial logic that combined fear and destruction. A group of Pijao soldiers had assaulted and nearly burned down the Spanish settlement of Quindío, a small town created in the effort to aid travelers and secure transit along the royal road that connected the Audiencia of Santa Fe to the cities of Popayán, Quito, and Lima. Not only had the attack been lethal, but the Spanish feared that failure to retaliate would only embolden Pijao forces to launch new, deadlier attacks. In this way, the departure of the twenty-three soldiers was part of a complex economy of fear, and they needed to move quickly. The governor of Popayán, Juan Atuesta Salazar, asked Captain Pedro Sánchez del Castillo to put together a group of men to head into the steep mountains in search of the attackers.

Although we lack basic facts about the soldiers' incursion, we do have an undated personal account from a soldier named Juan in a letter he sent to Madrid, most likely written in 1582 or 1583.[1] In a rush, the men gathered the available arms and provisions in Cartago, but felt underequipped and underprepared for an incursion into Native territory. Along with the twenty-three soldiers, an unidentified but crucial group of Native allies left Cartago in search of the Pijao soldiers. They first headed to the highest point of that section of the mountains—to the cold moors (páramos)—and roamed for two long days until they found what they believed to be the Pijaos' main highway. After six more days on that path, they reached a built environment they described as a Pijao settlement. This was an unexpected and unprecedented success. Until then, most military incursions into Pijao territory had been complete failures. The soldiers felt a mix of excitement and angst. They interpreted their success as a sign of divine intervention. They saw their God acting with them at every step. When Captain Sánchez del Castillo noted the presence of a large group of Pijao men hunting nearby, Juan wrote, "our Lord, who never forgets his own, sent a great rain shower with a great storm, and the indios sheltered in their homes." When a Pijao man stumbled on a soldier in the vanguard and nearly revealed the soldiers' presence to the Pijaos, Juan wrote, "our Lord desired that the indio was drunk, so he did not see us."

The soldiers followed the drunken man to his house and waited for everyone to fall asleep. The soldiers agreed to attack the Pijaos that night; they gathered their arms and prepared. Captain Sánchez del Castillo cried, "Santiago y a ellos"—invoking Santiago Matamoros or St. James the Moor-Slayer, the medieval patron saint of soldiers and horsemen who was said to appear on the battlefield to behead Muslims and aid Christians, and whose image and devotion later took on a new life in the New World, sometimes even recast as Santiago Mataindios (James the Indio-Slayer).[2] Responding to their captain's cry, the soldiers surrounded the house quietly and, "with God's help," took six men, four women, and their children captive without firing a single arquebus. They then tortured and intimidated one of the captive men, interrogating him about the locations of nearby Indigenous houses. After initially resisting, he broke under torture and agreed to lead the soldiers to a larger Pijao site.

Led by the captive, the soldiers traveled up and down the mountain until they spotted seven large longhouses—the size of barracks, Juan recalled—at the top of a hill. They surrounded the largest house and opened fire as they closed in on the house. Native men and women fled from within. They were not soldiers and did not turn to defend themselves, but merely sought refuge. The Spanish soldiers fired their arquebuses toward the fleeing people, aiming to kill as many as they could. As people ran, the soldiers entered the largest house, which they had surrounded, and found eighty men. With chilling brevity, Juan wrote: "All were put to the sword." The soldiers took twenty-four women and twelve children to sell as slaves and imprisoned the highest Native authority, whom the soldiers called the "cacique."

The soldiers shared a feeling of success. Not only had they retaliated and inflicted fear in the Pijaos; they also had taken slaves and valuable goods from the Indigenous houses. The Spaniards' descriptions of those goods give a sense of the hybrid material cultures of the Pijao villages. "We found a great source of silver," wrote Juan. "I personally took a sword, a silver vase, and fifty minted golden pesos." Other soldiers took a pair of silk socks, velvet pants and shirts, felt capes, other shirts, shoes, linens, more than a hundred pesos in gold dust, and a golden Indigenous figure worth about two hundred pesos, along with many letters "for Your Majesty and other lords." From these items and documents, the soldiers inferred that the assailants responsible for robbing a Spanish merchant named Sancho García resided in these longhouses. The soldiers burned the houses, ruined the crops and plantations they found, and turned for home with a feeling of glory and success. "We hurried down the mountain very contentedly," confessed Juan in his letter. On their way back to Cartago, they impaled the cacique and left his body as a scar on the landscape, as a sign of power and vengeance. His body became a marker in the cross-cultural economy of fear that characterized interactions between Spaniards and Pijaos.

At night, they found a safe place to camp. Juan was on guard that night when he noticed strange movements. "I felt the coming of the indios," he recalled, and he shouted, "To arms, to arms!" The soldiers reacted immediately, waking in a disciplined and trained military posture, and stood guard all night. At daybreak they advanced, hoping to exit Pijao territory. Signs that the Pijaos had been nearby in the night were everywhere. The soldiers walked with caution and prepared for battle. The air was tense. The captain sent forth a group to scout the terrain, Juan among them. They continued along the path and crossed a small hill, only to be ambushed by more than a hundred Indigenous attackers.

They were trapped. The Pijao soldiers closed a circle they had organized like "two half-moons," killing three men and taking three others captive before the soldiers could react. Juan was struck by two spears, one in his back and another in his thigh. As a last resort, Juan played dead: "Seeing the multitude of indios, I dropped down among the dead."

The soldiers' feeling of success and glory faded and gave way to rage, impotence, and emasculation. The sense of power that had momentarily boosted their confidence gave way to vulnerability. In an appalling action, probably to counter their fragility and to vent their anger, the soldiers slaughtered the Pijao women and children they had taken captive and whom they had planned to sell as slaves. They went back to Cartago, in Juan's words, "very far from content."

This "impenetrable mountain" was the domain of the Pijaos—an Indigenous sovereign world that was growing at the expense of the kingdom. It was a complex Indigenous coalition that has been severely misunderstood, even explicitly distorted. The reasons for this historical erasure are grounded in the archive and in historical methods: the documentary trails included in archives are mostly one-sided narratives, like Juan's story described above, that center the perspective of Spanish invaders, immortalizing their distortions and biases, and leaving simplistic, stereotyped visions of Indigenous peoples. Like his contemporaries, Juan deemed the Pijao peoples untamable ("indios indómitos"), people whose very nature was fierce. In his view, they were incorrigible barbarians. His letter makes no mention and betrays no awareness of Indigenous aspirations, aims, or forms of social and political organization.

Part II confronts these methodological challenges to narrate two ambitious, transformative Indigenous political projects that emerged between 1550 and 1590 and had an enormous impact on the history of the New Kingdom of Granada. Both projects were spearheaded by Indigenous persons—even if one of them is identified as mestizo—who deployed their own strategies and used the means within their reach to fight oppression, in a determined search for justice and freedom. Yet their methods and definitions of justice and freedom were remarkably different. The Pijao coalition is the first of these projects, which I examine in chapter 4. Contradicting a long historical tradition that has presented the Pijaos as pre-Hispanic peoples who were able to temporarily resist Spanish conquest through violence but were eventually defeated, I argue that the Pijaos were a new coalition that emerged in the 1550s in response to the Spanish invasion. They acted on the background of Carib political frameworks, played into Europeans' simplistic ideas and fears of "indios," and mobilized these fears to establish an expansive anticolonial system that dismantled the kingdom's institutions and grew dramatically in the second half of the sixteenth century.

The second project, the subject of chapters 5 and 6, was carried out by a man called Don Diego de la Torre—a mestizo Muisca cacique who traveled twice to Spain in the 1570s and 1580s, met personally with King Philip II, and gave him advice about the good government of the New Kingdom of Granada. During a crisis of governance, in which the audiencia faced serious accusations of corruption and lost extensive territory to the Pijao coalition, this Indigenous intellectual opted to travel to Spain and meet with the king to redress the kingdom's problems. Torre fought at Hispanic courts with paper weapons and deployed legal concepts in a quest for Indigenous freedom and justice. He offered a political utopia for Muisca communities, who projected in him a new form of leadership that relived long-gone Indigenous political categories, as well as Muisca terms used to refer to high-ranking Spanish officials or even the king himself. His vision had a long-lasting yet often unacknowledged impact on the development of the kingdom.

Both projects speak to the meaning of colonialism and anticolonialism in Indigenous political practice: how and why specific groups of Indigenous peoples chose to advocate for specific versions of empire or sought to get rid of the empire altogether. They also speak to the difficulty of retrieving those projects from historical archives. Colonial archives are full of misleading, mythical, and fictional language, as imperial agents tried to make sense of Indigenous politics, which remained beyond their grasp. I argue that both the Pijaos' anticolonialism and Don Diego de la Torre's litigation were radical Indigenous freedom projects that have not been recognized as such, in part due to the violence of colonial archives that reduced them to a basic, mythical language of cannibals and dangerous outsiders. In this sense, this part of the book is a quest to understand how Indigenous peoples with different political traditions envisioned freedom and how they set forth to attain it.[3] In reconstructing them I join a series of authors who have reflected on the silences of the past, experimented with interpretive methods to retrieve unknown histories, and used them to unravel histories of Indigenous power.[4]

4

DEVOURING THE EMPIRE

The introduction to this section of the book described an incursion into the heartland of what Spanish officials called "the Pijao frontier." Both terms, *frontier* and *Pijao*, had a fraught history. While *frontier* identified a border region, a land beyond the reach of the imperial administration, *Pijao* referred to a sovereign group of Indigenous peoples that had taken over the central Andean range and aimed to destroy every trace of Spanish Institutions. The word *Pijao*, with its multiple spellings, captured the intensity of the experience of those twenty-three soldiers.[1] It was a mystical, powerful name that inspired fear and caution. In 1576, the thirty-five-year-old Spanish soldier García Martín Montañez explained that uttering the word *Pijao* "scares the peoples of any nation, Spaniards and all others." Montañez described the Pijaos as "bellicose, butcher-like, evil, perverse, untamed people ... the most cruel, thieving, and treacherous of any province of the Indies."[2] To Montañez, the Pijaos were violent by nature. They were "unashamed" (desvergonzados), by which he meant that they were not intimidated by the Spaniards. They came to Spanish and

Indigenous homes to take captives and blocked the major bridle paths. Those who risked crossing them without great armies were "all murdered and eaten."

In the imperial ethnic lexicon, the Pijaos were classified as "caribes," a category reserved for seditious Indigenous groups that fought against the empire and were purported to eat human flesh—a legal category that made people subject to enslavement.[3] In his letters to the king, Montañez assured that the Pijaos were in fact terrible cannibals. He claimed that they ate Christians, both Indigenous and Europeans, "like the Spaniards have beef." They "have public butcher shops where they slaughter and weigh the meat of Spaniards and [their] indio allies," he informed. After butchering and dining on the bodies, they "spike their heads on sticks, facing towards their places of origin." He claimed they had depopulated entire towns by eating them. The Pijaos, he wrote, no longer fought with darts and clubs, but used iron spears, swords, and other weaponry they had taken from Spaniards, and dressed in the clothing they had stolen from their enemies. This made the Pijaos strong and frightening. Bernardo de Vargas Machuca, the author of one of the most important early modern Spanish treatises on military strategies and the use of arms, considered the Pijaos the third-most-famous Indigenous group of the Indies due to their bellicosity, surpassed only by the Mapuches in Chile and the Chichimecas in Mexico.[4] Rumor had it, Montañez claimed, that the Pijaos had a proverb saying that upon eating their last Indigenous neighbor they would reach the Spanish, devour them, and burn their homes.

Ingestion offered the Spanish a powerful vocabulary to describe the Pijaos' world. According to the Spanish, the Pijaos ate people and consumed cities; they devoured the empire both literally and figuratively, feeding upon Spaniards and their Indigenous allies. It was through these acts of eating that the region formerly known as the Province of Ibagué became Pijao territory. This chapter considers how a group of Native people who the Spanish classified as "caribes" remade the central mountain chain of the northern Andes into a new political formation that fed off and antagonized the empire. It confronts the difficult question of how to understand this Indigenous world, whose peoples owned silk socks, velvet underclothes, and felt capes; who were thought to have large butcher shops where they sold human flesh; and whose name when uttered instilled fear in the people of any nation.

I argue that the Pijaos emerged in the mid-sixteenth century as a political coalition articulated by a forceful and expansive anticolonial agenda, which stretched from a couple of hundred people in a restricted area around the Saldaña River in the 1550s to several thousand people spanning the entire central Andean range and the Magdalena and Cauca river valleys by the end of the century (figure 4.1). Indigenous peoples and Europeans understood this process of expansion through a language of eating: for Europeans, it was cannibal destruction; for the Pijaos, it was consumption through captive-taking. Rather than a stable ethnic group, the Pijaos were a coalition united by a common enemy. They spread a message of radical freedom from the New Kingdom's oppression and waged war against everyone who did not join their cause, destroying Christian symbols and executing a full-fledged attack on the modes of life promoted by the Spanish empire. This Indigenous political project mobilized Spaniards' stereotypes and fears of cannibals against them. What the Spaniards saw as a massive feast of bodies was in fact the incorporation of new peoples and groups into the Pijaos' political framework. In this sense, a mythic language of man-eating came to describe a decades-long process through which the Pijaos established a multiethnic, autonomous territory.

Indigenous political reactions to Spanish colonialism in the sixteenth century came in all forms. In the 1560s, when the Pijao coalition was growing, a neo-Inca state governed in the jungles of the Amazon, in the region of Vilcabamba (the exact place has yet to be located); a popular outburst took over the Andean countryside, a "dancing sickness" known as Taki Onqoy that envisioned a utopia of free communities; the mobile Indigenous peoples of southern Chile who called themselves reche (true men) appropriated the horse, rebelled against the encomienda system, and reclaimed their freedom, beginning a centuries-long process of ethnogenesis in which they would establish an identity as Mapuches; and the diverse, semisedentary peoples of northern Mexico that the Spanish identified as Chichimecas maintained complicated relations with the mines of Zacatecas and Guanajuato and its adjacent populations.[5] These are just some of the Indigenous political reactions that most troubled Spaniards. While sharing features, each of these projects was grounded in a different form of Indigenous organization and political imagination, established a different form of interaction with Europeans, and had its own goals and aims—whether it was the return of the Inca or escaping colonial pressures.[6]

In a world full of stereotypes, the Pijaos' aims and strategies remain silenced behind layers of fabrications and colonial formulas.[7] Europeans left hundreds of documents describing the Pijaos as fierce, apolitical, cannibalistic brutes, pre-Hispanic peoples who were so barbarous that they brought the conquest to a temporary halt but whose submission was inevitable and predictable, destined to ultimately be overcome by European superiority. Colonial descriptions established an enduring interpretation of the Pijaos, which echoes in how they are depicted in historical works and public narratives of the past up to the time of this writing: they are often described as "unconquerable" (inconquistables)

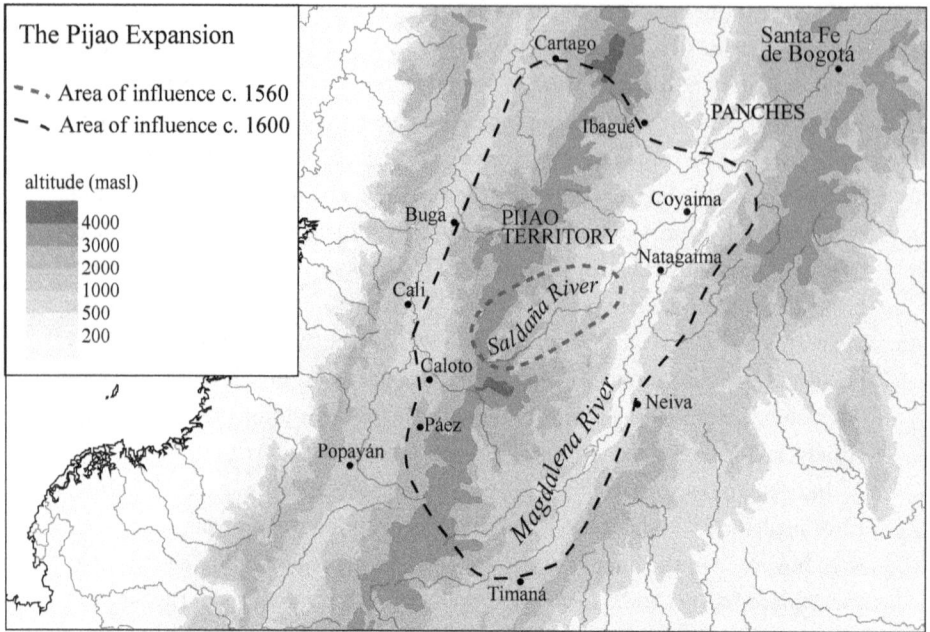

The Pijao Expansion

- - - Area of influence c. 1560
- - - Area of influence c. 1600

altitude (masl)

4000
3000
2000
1000
500
200

Cartago

Santa Fe
de Bogotá

Ibagué

PANCHES

Coyaima

Buga

PIJAO
TERRITORY

Natagaima

Cali

Saldaña River

Caloto

Neiva

Páez

Magdalena River

Popayán

Timaná

FIGURE 4.1. The Pijao expansion c. 1560 to c. 1600. Map by Santiago Muñoz-Arbeláez.

yet ultimately subdued.[8] Historian Juan David Montoya questions this static and linear view of the Pijaos, arguing that colonial narrations and stereotypes created a distorted idea of coherence amid diversity. He suggests instead that the term *Pijaos* was a misnomer, a generic tag Spaniards coined to refer to a variety of Indigenous groups with no common agenda or identity and whose only resemblance was that the Spanish regarded them as enemies.[9]

In contrast, here I argue that the Pijaos established a political coalition operating on a flexible model of politics that prevailed in the lowlands and central Andean range and spread a message of freedom from and war against the New Kingdom. The coalition formed and grew through interethnic pacts and alliances, often resorting to intimidation and violence. The Pijaos were not a pre-Hispanic group or a bunch of disconnected, fragmented peoples. They were not a coherent ethnic group, either, nor did they develop a common ethnic identity. They were a contingent political coalition assembled together under the common banner of vanishing the kingdom from its territories.

In this sense, I contend that the coalition's goal was not only to escape the kingdom and its institutions but also to eliminate them—the very essence of anticolonialism. The attacks themselves were not directed against the Spanish as persons, as attested by some documented cases of Spanish refugees who were welcome in Pijao territory. Instead, the Pijaos opposed Indigenous subordination to Spanish imperial systems, burned Spanish cities and the villages of Indigenous peoples allied with the Spanish, and attacked Christian symbols and priests. These attacks were directed toward Indigenous and European audiences, and they aimed to undermine Spanish legitimacy and systems of rule. At the same time, they established bonds and alliances and incorporated captives into their body politic as kin, building on existing Indigenous political frameworks. They did not follow a single ruler nor have a system of tributaries; they were a conglomerate of groups with different leaders, all of whom were skilled at war and formed a ruling council.

The whole scheme made sense from the point of view of the political traditions of Carib groups, who had a flexible understanding of politics, grouping and regrouping in times of battle while avoiding permanent subjugation to centralized rule.[10] This formed a particular type of configuration. Political rebellions in the old Inca domains were constantly envisioned in Andean political imagination as a return to a political system embodied by the Inca—what historian Alberto Flores Galindo has termed an "Andean utopia."[11] The Pijaos' political imagination was not centered around the figure of a single, millenarian ruler but rather emphasized the dismantling of such type of authority. It was a form of Carib anticolonialism, with a fluid arrangement of groups structured around the destruction of centralized rule. In this way, the Pijao project takes shape as an even more stark and radical opposition to Spanish rule than Vilcabamba or the Mapuches in the sense that they made no pacts or treaties with Spaniards, nor did they establish any communication channels. They aimed for the complete uprooting of the empire's institutions.

While we have no political manifesto to understand the making of the Pijao project, we can trace it through the description of their actions in Spanish reports. In this sense, the Pijaos' political agenda becomes visible through a logic of practice. That is, lacking a formal articulation of their political project, we can reconstruct it by analyzing and actively interpreting fragmentary descriptions of their actions, in the light of histories and ethnographies of Indigenous peoples in the circum-Caribbean and the South American lowlands. Through this method, it is possible to detect the Pijaos' sophisticated reading of the Spanish empire and Christianity, their careful inversion of imperial symbols, and their explicitly anticolonial project that unambiguously aimed to recruit allies and vanish imperial settlements.

An "Impenetrable Mountain"

In the early 1500s, a diversity of ethnic groups lived in the central Andean mountain range and the valleys of the Magdalena and Cauca Rivers, which divided it from the eastern and western ranges. Many of these groups had a strong resemblance to other groups of the circum-Caribbean, especially the Caribs, but with large variations and with presence of Quechua, Chibcha, and other linguistic groups. It is likely that the name Pijao is a colonial label that took on a new life as the new political coalition emerged in the sixteenth century.[12] The coalition's creators were a small band of people who lived near the Saldaña River, a tributary of the Magdalena. They lived on high terraces near rivers and had a deep tradition of ceramics, agriculture, and stonework.[13] It is probable that their language, which came to be known as the Pijao language, was from the Carib linguistic family or closely related to it.[14] The Panches, Pantágoras, Yareguí, and Carares of the lowlands around the Magdalena River were also likely Carib. The Antioquia, Caramanta, and Quimbayas, toward the Cauca River, were probably from the Chocó linguistic family. Other groups, like the Nasa (frequently referred to as Páez in colonial documents) and Misak (referred to as Guambianos) to the south, were from the macro-Chibcha linguistic family. To the south, the Ingas were merchant groups of the Quechua linguistic family; colonial inspectors tended to classify them as Quillacingas, merging them with a separate ethnic group in what today is Nariño.[15] All these linguistic groups left traces in current-day toponymy, revealing the region's heterogeneity.[16] The peoples of the mountain range had rich economies, involving gold mining and ceramics—both products often reached the Panches and Muiscas through interethnic trade networks—intensive production of seed crops, and exploitation of fish stocks.

Like other peoples of the circum-Caribbean, many groups of the central Andean mountain range had a flexible model of politics, in which they did not follow a single leader but rather formed alliances in times of war by establishing kin networks and absorbing captives of war into their own organization. Some leaders derived authority from success in warfare or gained followers by offering utopias, such as preaching the "end of all evil"—a phenomenon known as prophetism, which was quite common among the Tupí-Guaraní—rather than hereditary nobilities. According to some anthropologists, like Pierre Clastres, this political model favored flexible, fragmented societies and avoided the creation of robust state structures. It also made the societies that inhabited the lowland valleys and the hills extremely heterogeneous in their ethnic and linguistic composition.[17]

If its inhabitants were diverse and held flexible ideas of politics, the mountain range itself was both topographically forbidding and geopolitically strategic. It was the central range of the northern Andes and the steepest of the three. Europeans often referred to the region as an "impenetrable mountain": a harsh and coarse land with many dangers. It was "an enormous massif of ancient metamorphic and igneous rock," surrounded by two of the region's largest rivers: the Magdalena River to the east and the Cauca River to the west.[18] Both river valleys descend sharply nearly to sea level, resulting in highly variable landscapes and a climate that changes rapidly between the region's six ice-coated peaks and the sea-level hot lands at its base. There is no way to pass over the mountain range without ascending more than 3,000 meters (9,850 feet). The Quindío road—an Indigenous route the Spanish described as full of dangerous paths and precipices—was the main avenue across the mountain range, and merchants traversed it with dread. Many sections of the road were too dangerous to travel on horseback, and Europeans were forced to walk or ride on the backs of Indigenous porters (cargueros), who remained prominent figures on the Quindío road for centuries.

This peculiar geography proved difficult for the Spanish to classify in their cold/hot dichotomies. The Spanish early modern ethnographic eye projected its notions of civilization onto the Indigenous peoples they encountered in the New World. These notions assumed that societies with centralized forms of authority—those who feared their leaders—were more advanced than others. Those who did not fear their leaders could be classified as behetría: anarchic groups that changed their political leaders when they did not fulfill the group's expectations. For imperial administrators in the New Kingdom, as noted in chapter 1, this division took on a geographic character: the cold plateaus of the Andes came to be seen as centralized, sedentary societies, while the hot lowlands exemplified behetría.

But the steep, broken slopes of the central Andean range were difficult to locate in this rigid scheme. The peoples inhabiting these landscapes could easily move from warm lowland valleys to snowy peaks. Spanish observers claimed that these peoples had no caciques or lords and lived in behetría. In 1560, for instance, the visitador Tomás López Medel described them using many tropes that other Spanish observers used to describe lowland peoples, although they lived high in the mountains. López described the rebels as poorly dressed people living "with no caciques or natural lords." He went on, saying: "They live in thatch huts, distant from one another," although the lands were "more cold than warm" and were connected by "a path that wended through the mountains."[19]

The Spaniards' rigid divisions between cold and hot, cacicazgos and behe-tría, and civilized and unruly peoples were poorly suited to describe the Pijaos and their neighbors—peoples that resembled the other hot-lands groups but moved efficiently and easily between cold and hot lands through the broken Andean landscape. In the early seventeenth century, the president of the au-diencia, Juan de Borja, described it in the following terms: "The said range is the roughest one known in all the Indies, with very high hills and deep brooks, thick woods and many falls and cliffs of great danger, without the mildness of the flatland, with a disposition better suited for wild beasts than for the habi-tation of men."[20] In Borja's pastoralist vocabulary of empire, the broken land-scape made its inhabitants adopt the behaviors of predators rather than flocks.

Control of the impenetrable mountain and its inhabitants eluded the mon-archy. Conquistador Sebastián de Belalcázar and his crew first tried crossing it in the late 1530s, when they departed Quito to explore northward after par-ticipating in the conquest of Peru. Violent confrontations with Native peoples forced them to find an alternative route. In the early 1540s, Hernán Venegas, a conquistador residing in Santa Fe de Bogotá, left to fight the Panches in the Magdalena River valley, founded the city of Tocaima (1544) in Panche terri-tory, and advanced uphill. In 1550, Andres López de Galarza, a magistrate of the Audiencia of Santa Fe, sent a group of soldiers with orders to found a city. They set off inland, confronting Native peoples in a site they called the Val-ley of Spears (Valle de las Lanzas) because their Indigenous adversaries fought with long, pointed rods rather than bows and arrows. The Native fighters were skilled warriors and besieged Galarza and his men, who sent messengers back to Santa Fe de Bogotá for help. Beltrán Anzueta and others came to their res-cue. When reinforcements arrived, the soldiers achieved some military success, took possession of the area in the name of Emperor Charles V, and founded the city of Ibagué, named after one of the Indigenous caciques of the area. Later, Spaniards divided the Native peoples of the region into encomiendas. This was a familiar pattern of Spanish colonialism: a system that distributed Indigenous communities among Spanish settlers, asking them to pay settlers tribute in ex-change for protection under the encomienda system, and aimed to populate the landscape with cities for Spaniards and villages for "indios," where all lived up-holding Catholic values in physical spaces organized around chapels and under the tutelage of a priest. Ibagué was a first step toward this goal, and settlers felt secure and in control. Beltrán Anzueta wrote a few years later: "We pacified the Natives [naturales] and discovered very rich gold mines in that valley."[21]

The city of Ibagué provided a point of entry to the mountains, which the Spanish perceived as their own, even if their presence had been but fleeting.

The settlers felt much more comfortable traveling on the impenetrable mountain in search of riches. In 1552, Domingo Lozano, one of the founders of Ibagué, brought thirty men to explore the area and found the Native inhabitants living peacefully, paying tribute, and providing services to the vecinos. Two years later, Francisco de Trejo, Belalcázar's son-in-law, left the Audiencia of Santa Fe in 1554 with sixty men to visit the city of Ibagué and the neighboring Indigenous territories. He reported that the Native peoples there were at peace and served his party, carried their provisions, and led them to the Province of Coyaima. The Indigenous people of Coyaima received the soldiers peacefully, served them, fed them, and even gave them some gold. In such peaceful times, Trejo sent thirty men to explore an area near the Saldaña River that was ostensibly under the leadership of Francisco de Barrios, the archbishop of Santa Fe's nephew.[22]

While Trejo and the rest of the soldiers waited for them to return, Native soldiers from the Saldaña River attacked the thirty men by surprise. The assault was unpredictable and vigorous. The soldiers fled, leaving their horses, clothing, and provisions behind. Few managed to escape alive. One of them was Juan Ribero, who later told others about Trejo's unfortunate expedition to Saldaña and reported how the men had been destroyed (desbaratados). Despite its brutality, the Spaniards saw the assault as an isolated incident.[23]

Shortly afterward, however, similar events took place in the Province of Buga, on the western face of the mountains. In 1555, Captain Gerardo Gil de Estupiñán had departed Jerez to explore the Saldaña River with thirty soldiers when the Native inhabitants of the area staged a surprise attack, killed many of the party, and stole their provisions and arms. A few days later, a group of Indigenous people took over the city of Jerez, burned it down, and took all the settlers' belongings. In retaliation, Captain Estupiñán sent twenty soldiers in pursuit of the Native attackers. Only two soldiers returned. Pedro de Castro Mora, one of the survivors, expressed a deep sense of betrayal. The Native peoples of Buga, he initially thought, were at peace and serving as guides for the Spaniards in the search for the assailants. They had told the soldiers they saw signs of men ahead, but then the Spaniards found themselves in the middle of an ambush. "Only this witness and another man escaped."[24]

There were two attacks on two sides of the mountains in a short period of time. A new Indigenous movement was starting to take control of the mountain range. Spanish soldiers and settlers found themselves under increasing pressure, but their testimonies revealed Europeans' inability to grasp Indigenous politics. They noticed that the coordinated attacks relied on extended communication networks. The Native peoples of Saldaña, who had killed Francisco de Trejo and his men, and the Native peoples of Buga, who had killed Estupi-ñán and his soldiers, were on opposite sides of the impenetrable mountain, yet Espinosa suspected that "they had news of each other." While Espinosa provided evidence that these suspected interethnic Indigenous information networks motivated different peoples to rebellion, he also dismissively explained their actions as a natural trait of "indios": "the condition of indios of being in the thrall of novelty, and to be cruel when they detect weakness and find themselves within reach of victory." Similarly, Nicolás Martín, a thirty-five-year-old vecino of Cartago, had learned that "the indios are of the sort that, on realizing that they can have a minor victory, they seek to do the greatest ill and call on others to do the same."[25]

Although the soldiers remarked on the connections between the events, their conceptual vocabulary was inadequate to describe this emergent Indigenous world. It was as impenetrable to them as the mountains themselves. Reverting to the familiar language of pastoral colonialism, Europeans attributed Indigenous political action to natural traits. Native peoples, in Europeans' view, were ferocious and untamed; their actions could only be explained as a reaction to a lack of corporal punishment, a lack of domestication. In this way, that the Pijaos had a political strategy did not occur to the Spaniards: their politics remained unthinkable, hidden behind layers of stereotypes and misconceptions.[26]

Despite the limitations of the written record, it is possible to reconstruct the dynamics and chronology of the coalition's expansion from the first attack around 1554 near the Saldaña River against Francisco de Trejo through the 1570s. The first assaults of 1554 probably began with an alliance between the peoples of the Saldaña River and the Coyaimas. At that time, however, the people of Natagaima and Combeima, who occupied territories near the Saldaña, remained in encomiendas and serving encomendero Juan Bretón, though they gave him "nothing besides one load [roza] of corn and some potatoes [turmas]" and no priest had "dared to be among them."[27] Echoes of the assault had reached far in the central Andean range, fueling major opposition to Spanish rule in 1557 in all the central Andean range and spanning both shores of the Magdalena River valley, spreading well beyond the contours of the Saldaña River and involving the Muzos, Panches, Páez, Sutagaos, and Quimbayas.[28]

While in several of these areas the uprising was short-lived, in the heart of the Saldaña River area the early Indigenous assaults led to an expansive agenda in the 1560s and 1570s, when the coalition flourished through the continuous plunder of Spanish cities, including Ibagué, Timaná, and Neiva. They completely burned down Neiva in 1569, taking thousands of Indigenous people captive, according to several accounts. In 1572, they burned down the city of San Vicente de Páez—founded in 1562 by Domingo Lozano to contain the first acts of sedition in the area near Popayán—established a kin alliance with the Páez (Nasa), and began systematic attacks on the mines of Caloto.[29] These were not marginal territories, of little interest for Spaniards. On the contrary, Spaniards had placed high hopes in the mining potential of Neiva and Caloto.[30]

In the takeover of these cities, the Pijaos projected a full inversion of Spanish power. The destruction of San Vicente de Páez illustrates this point. The city was located in the territory of the Nasa people (called Páez by Spanish settlers), who spoke a completely different language and lived far away from Saldaña. The Indigenous advance began by quashing Diego de Santacruz's expeditions, which had tried to "pacify" the Pijaos, as well as the group led by Domingo Lozano, who had been searching for gold mines near Pijao territory with eighteen soldiers when the Pijaos attacked, leaving no one alive. Then they besieged the city of Páez for two months, "fighting the Spaniards, eating their food, and killing and eating their indio allies." According to Andrés Najara, a local encomendero, the Spanish took shelter in one house, which became their stronghold for two months. Najara recalled sheer desperation: men and women fighting day and night with any object they could find, frantically trying to reinforce the building with rocks and dirt, and praying and crying for help. They managed to slip a few letters past the siege via the hands of Indigenous allies, in which they begged for help from nearby cities. A few of the Spanish, including Najara himself, survived until Captain Bartolomé Marin's men arrived to rescue them. Pedro Cleves described the survivors as naked, alienated, and destroyed. Francisco de Belalcázar recalled: "Those who survived told so many sorrows that it was worthy of crying."[31] Najara witnessed the city's destruction: a peaceful settlement populated by Christians and served by obedient Indigenous people became a deserted collection of ruins.

Radical Anticolonialism

The killings of Trejo and Estupiñán and the sacking and burning of the cities of Páez and Neiva were the first expressions of a new Indigenous order that redefined the modes of living and political allegiances of the Native peoples of the rugged central Andean range and its foothills. These isolated acts of violence triggered an avalanche that swept away Spanish institutions and replaced them with Indigenous control. The Indigenous world that resulted from these first assaults progressively expanded to become a radical project of

Indigenous sovereignty that paralleled and inverted the dynamics of Spanish institutions and forms of colonialism, sacking and burning cities, desecrating Catholic symbols, depopulating Spanish villages, and obstructing arteries of commerce—unleashing a disciplined and systematic attack on the kingdom's infrastructure.

What made Indigenous dominance inexplicable to the Spanish was that the Pijaos were a comparatively small group of people. While the Spaniards estimated the Muiscas of the plateaus of the eastern range to be more than thirty thousand people, they believed the Pijaos were less than two hundred people—three hundred at most—who lived in a relatively small area surrounding the Saldaña River.[32] That very basic demographic observation disquieted the Spanish—how was it even possible that such a small group could besiege colonial cities in such a large territory, exposing the vulnerability of the kingdom?

Looking carefully at Spanish reports, it is possible to tease out fragments of the Pijao political agenda—a radical and inclusive opposition to the kingdom, at the same time fierce against the Spanish and its allies and flexible enough to encompass and accommodate those who joined their common goal. By embracing this political program, the Pijaos established a territory that became a viable alternative to the kingdom.

We get a glimpse of this structured, methodical opposition to the kingdom in numerous testimonies about Pijao advances on both sides of the mountains. Their political program basically consisted of three elements: (1) spreading a message of Indigenous freedom to convene Indigenous peoples who had accepted vassalage to the kingdom to join their cause, (2) waging war against Spanish settlements and destroying Christian symbols, and (3) taking captives whom they then incorporated into their coalition. As early as 1558, a variety of witnesses in the city of Ibagué contended that the Native peoples of the Saldaña River convened and induced the Native peoples in Ibagué's surroundings, who were not Pijaos, not to serve the Spaniards but instead to join them in their territory to fight against Spanish rule. Witnesses specified that the core instigators were people of the Saldaña River, located in a strategically central position, who would convoke other peoples like the Coyaima, Doima, Cacataima, Buga, and others near Saldaña, and between the 1560s and 1590s reached the more distant Indigenous peoples of Páez (Nasa), Neiva, Mariquita, Timaná, Cartago, and others, forming an expanding web of alliances.[33]

Witnesses did not describe the specific content of the Pijao message, other than just to say that they "convened" Indigenous people and "induced" them not to serve Spaniards. It is likely that the peoples of Saldaña resorted to a prophetic message that promised to get rid of all evil by waging war against the Spanish—the sort of message that was common in Tupí-Guaraní politics—and invited others to join in ceremonies that included gift exchanges, music, and beverages, as the Muzo did.[34] There is evidence that the 1557 Quimbaya rebellion was motivated by such a message, apparently proclaimed by Panche messengers. According to at least one Indigenous witness, it was said that a gold figure in the shape of a man spoke condemning Spanish violence and called Indigenous peoples to arms, saying "that he was the father of all the indios and all of them were his children and his heart ached from seeing them mistreated by the Christians . . . that all of them might as well die before serving Spaniards."[35]

The Pijao expansion might have been triggered by a similar message of freedom or death. Historical sources make clear that the Pijaos resorted to an elaborate courtship strategy. In Spanish court documents, Indigenous and Spanish witnesses reported that the Pijaos presented gifts to the Native peoples of surrounding areas, inviting them to join the Pijaos' cause, and thus embedded them in reciprocity networks, drawing them into the Pijao coalition.

One of the key milestones of the coalition was the alliance with Páez (Nasa) groups, themselves a diverse people responding to different leaders; they lived to the southwest, closer to the governorship of Popayán.[36] According to several local witnesses, this alliance took place in a ceremonial gathering in the town of Toboyma, which brought together more than two thousand individuals. A long list of Páez and Pijao leaders attended the meeting and decided to join in "confederation." The witnesses declared that the Páez political ties to the Pijaos were established by kin: daughters of Páez leaders were married to the Pijao leaders, who could have many wives. Polygamy was an ancient practice, and so was alliance-making through intermarriage; it was an available vehicle that enabled growth and integration to achieve common goals.[37] The Pijao coalition used these mechanisms to expand their territory and military might through alliances and kinship bonds.[38]

However, if their invitations were rejected, the Pijaos resorted to violence. In 1558, a Native interpreter called Ycaco declared that a group of armed Indigenous people from Coyaima killed a Native man from Doyma and warned his compatriots that his murder was their responsibility because they "served the Christians and did not rebel." Don Diego de Calambás, the Indigenous cacique of Guambía and the closest Indigenous ally to the Spanish in the area, found himself in a similar situation. Andrés Najara recalled being in Guambía when a group of Pijaos, Páez, and Toribio people attacked Calambás. Najara fired his arquebus thinking to intimidate them and halt the assault. To his surprise, the

Pijaos fired an arquebus of their own in response, which frightened Najara and dissuaded him from further engagement. He could only watch as the Pijaos killed Calambás and took his body, which was never found again.[39] These are just two examples of the tactics of intimidation the Pijaos put forth as incentives for others to join them in their opposition to the kingdom, dissuading them from collaborating with Spaniards.

Rumors of such assaults spread quickly through Indigenous networks, magnifying the challenge to Spanish rule. In every Andean marketplace, Indigenous merchants talked about the Pijaos and how they were destroying Hispanic settlements and killing or capturing every Spanish ally or those who served the colonizers.[40] This caused anxiety among Native peoples and settlers alike: encomenderos and soldiers believed their Indigenous subjects and allies expected protection from the Pijao attacks. When Spaniards failed to provide protection, their Indigenous allies might flee and join the rebel forces. In 1577, a Spaniard from Timaná named Bernardino Velásquez articulated how the Pijaos' actions had stoked skepticism of Spanish rule among Native peoples in neighboring cities. In his words: "The indios of peace complain asking 'what are the Spanish good for,' if we let them [the Pijaos] take them and kill them."[41] If the premise of the encomienda system was that Spanish settlers protected the Indigenous peoples of their encomiendas, the Pijaos' actions laid bare the vulnerability of Spanish rule, leaving the Spaniards' Indigenous allies and vassals asking themselves why they served the colonizers if they were not protected in return. The fact that it became a rumor that was replicated, magnified, and distorted was part of the intended effect of the poetics of violence put on display in the assaults: to intimidate Pijao enemies.

This strategy was remarkably successful for the Pijaos. It had the dual effect of garnering support from a broad array of Indigenous peoples while shattering the legitimacy of Spanish rule, even in places not directly in their territory. By the late 1570s, Spanish officials reported that the Native peoples of Ibagué, Cartago, Tocaima, and Mariquita—four imperial cities on the outskirts of the Pijao territories, whose Indigenous inhabitants were not Pijaos—were always on the verge of rebellion because "they are induced, convinced, and gifted by the Natives [naturales] of the Saldaña River and its provinces not to serve their encomenderos but to rebel against them." Twenty-three-year-old Pedro Alvarez reported that every city and town as well as every vecino near the Pijao borderland lived in continuous danger and great fear, thinking that at any point the Native peoples in their service would switch sides and rise with the Pijaos against them.[42]

Incorporating groups of people who joined the coalition, either voluntarily or as captives, was a key part of the process of expansion. The Pijaos' military advances against Spanish cities and Indigenous settlements allied with the Spanish yielded a large number of captives and newcomers who lived among the Pijao. The protocols for this type of incorporation went completely under the radar of Spanish observers, who, as I will describe below, mostly obsessed over the consumption of some captives' bodies—what Europeans termed cannibalism. In other words, most reports of Pijao raids and assaults on Spanish settlements limit themselves to stating that the Pijao either killed or ate thousands of Indigenous and European travelers or residents, reproducing the cannibalism myth. It is much more likely, however, that most of the population was taken captive and absorbed into Pijao settlements, rather than eaten. There is scattered evidence of this. In 1570, Joan Váez, a soldier son of a conquistador who lived among the Pijaos for one year, reported that while the Pijaos numbered no more than two hundred, they had more than two thousand captives and allies living among them, who aided them in war. There were also other reports of Spanish and mestizo women taken captive by the Pijaos. Váez himself said that during this time he met one of the Pijaos' women captives, a Spanish woman from Antequera. "They took her captive in the episode of Trejo in Saldaña and this witness saw her and spoke to her. A Pijao cacique took her as his wife and they had two sons and a daughter." Andrés Najara and Diego de Castro testified that it was publicly known that the Pijaos had two or three Spanish girls living among them as wives of powerful men.[43]

Captive-taking and exchange of people likely played an important role in the Saldaña River region since before the arrival of Spaniards, as it was a common practice among many South American lowland peoples. In such groups women were often incorporated as wives, but male captives, too, married into their new social groups and formed families. In some groups, captivity was connected to ritual anthropophagy: captives and abducted children were conceptualized as pets, adopted by families, and in certain cases sacrificed and eaten.[44] Pijao groups could have had similar dynamics for captives of war and people abducted during attacks on European cities, while they probably incorporated others who voluntarily joined their cause through kinship networks. In both cases, the newcomers were absorbed into Pijao groups and became a key part of social life.

Even some Europeans were welcome in Pijao territory. The very essence of Pijao politics was to convene people to join them in their wars and to stop serving Spaniards. For this reason, their territory became a sort of refuge zone from imperial justice.[45] Joan Váez himself claimed to have fled to the impenetrable mountain to avoid prosecution in the kingdom: "This witness knows all this because he lived one year among the Pijaos fleeing justice. The Pijaos saw him coming out of [the kingdom by] his own will, so they did not bother him and, therefore, he saw all they did, as he has stated."[46] Individuals such as Váez, fleeing from the empire, were apparently welcome in Pijao territory. Instead of an impenetrable mountain, Pijao territory became mountains of hope for those who aimed to escape or oppose the kingdom; there they could become unreachable.

This made the Pijao territory a multiple, hybrid world that convened people from different backgrounds. Indigenous peoples of many ethnic groups lived there, both voluntarily and as captives, as did mestizos and Europeans. The peoples of the Saldaña River had sparked a process of expansion, building on a shared cultural and political background of Carib groups that enabled integration in times of war and promoted fragmentation and decentralization in times of peace.[47] They established alliances with the Coyaimas, Natagaimas, Páez, and many others, creating a heterogeneous coalition of the kind that had existed in many other areas of the circum-Caribbean. For Spaniards, this became an absolute mess. Sometimes Spanish reports include the name Pijao alongside other ethnonyms, such as Páez, Toribios, Putimaes, Coyaimas, Guauros, and Natagaimas. When colonial documents initially referred to the Pijaos as a group of a couple of hundred people, they were alluding to the peoples around the Saldaña River who motivated the rebellion, but the word soon became a vague referent to the different coalitions among these groups, who acted alongside each other but whose allegiances also shifted over time and who even engaged in rivalries with each other. In this sense, for Spaniards the term *Pijao* more often than not came to refer to the larger political network that controlled the mountains, which was not reducible to a single ethnicity. It became a catchall phrase, meaning something like "all the people coalescing against European rule in the central Andean range."

Yet *Pijao* was not a completely artificial term employed by colonial authorities without empirical grounding. On the contrary, it was a coalition, a network built by Indigenous people over time in their effort to combat European colonialism, as exemplified by the way their neighbors and allies defined them.[48] A seventeenth-century dictionary of the Páez (Nasa) language gathered by Spanish priest Castillo y Orozco lists the term *Pijao* both as meaning a "nation of indios" and as a synonym for "foreigner" (extranjero), "fierce" (arisco), and "maroon" (cimarrón). It also includes it as an example of the term *ambi*, which it defines as "anything that's fierce and maroon, those of a diverse nation who are not Christians" (cosa arisca y cimarrona, los de diversa nación que no son cristianos).[49] While these definitions are filtered through the mind of a Spanish priest and his Indigenous collaborators—thus adopting concepts like "nation of indios," which were probably far from the way sixteenth-century Nasa people thought about ethnicity—it does give a sense of the conglomerate nature of the Pijaos. In other words, it shows that the seventeenth-century Páez—their key allies and co-conspirators, who established kin bonds with the Pijaos and for decades fought alongside them—defined the Pijaos as a composite group, a conglomeration of maroons united by their opposition to Christianity.

In this sense, the coalition was a dynamic polity that, while united by a common message against colonialism, grouped peoples of divergent opinions and political visions.[50] Groups could come into or break out of the coalition. Such was the case of the Páez themselves, who joined in alliance in the 1570s, or the Coyaimas and Natagaimas, who dropped out in the early seventeenth century to join forces with the Spaniards against the Pijao coalition. But the general trend throughout the second half of the sixteenth century was growth. By the early decades of the seventeenth century, the Pijaos had grown from two or three hundred men in the mid-sixteenth century to at least six thousand men under arms.

Their territory, covering a large slice of the central Andean range, was divided into about twenty-eight different sections or provinces, each centered near a different river source. Amoyá (initially an ethnonym of a group acting alongside the Pijaos) had become by the early seventeenth century a key political hub and population center; Spaniards commonly referred to it as the "main fortress" and described it as the site with the most difficult access.[51] It was surrounded by many other territories, like Otaima, Mola, Cacataima, Ambeima, Yrico, Natagaima, Anatoima, Maito, and Beuni.[52] Each of these territories had its own organization.

The coalition did not have a centralized political ruler, but rather a series of interconnected leaders, each governing their own province, yet acting in coordination with others. European records describe these leaders as courageous and remarkably skilled at war. They were able to maintain leadership if successful in battle, and could be replaced by other courageous men if they fell or failed to achieve victory.[53] Leaders apparently hosted meetings (juntas) to agree on a course of action. These meetings usually entailed sharing knowledge and visions, in ways that Spaniards often interpreted as black magic and described as led by sorcerers, framing such meetings as the devil's creation.[54] For instance, in his manual about war in the Indies, Bernardo Vargas Machuca described the visions of one sorcerer (mohán), saying he drank jopa, a stimulating substance, which enabled him to foresee an imminent Spanish attack and warn everyone to flee before the assault.[55] Vargas Machuca also noted, however, that they had silent spies spread throughout the mountains, tracking every movement and sharing information among them. Leaders had vast information networks, which they used to anticipate Spanish assaults and to plan their own assaults on Spanish cities.

The mountains themselves were the Pijaos' main weapon. In this they were different from many Indigenous groups of the Americas who reinvented themselves as dominant peoples—like the Mapuches, Comanches, or Sioux—in large part by appropriating new technologies from colonizers, like the horse or the rifle. The Pijaos, too, used firearms, but topography gave them the most advantage. They were masters of the slopes: they used verticality strategically to invert the geographies of the kingdom in their favor. For instance, they would pile large rocks around narrow crossings and dangerous precipices in such a way that when the Spaniards crossed below, the Pijaos could knock the rocks down and tumble their enemies off the cliff. They identified narrow paths and sites with limited visibility to surprise soldiers and merchants in ambushes, or corner them near precipices and then "rush against the Spaniards at diverse points with great fury and clamor."[56] Spanish troops suffered some of their most significant losses in these ambushes.

In their mastery of the mountains, the Pijaos also took advantage of the empire's inefficient bureaucratic divisions and the lack of coordination between administrative entities. The mountains occupied a gray area theoretically dividing the Audiencia of Santa Fe and the Gobernación of Popayán, which was subordinate to the Audiencia of Quito. This meant that military assaults launched from cities like Ibagué and Neiva, in the northeastern section of the mountain range, were coordinated by Santa Fe de Bogotá, but those from cities like Cartago, Buga, and Cali were organized between Popayán and Quito. The lack of synchronicity between these administrative divisions left ample room for the Pijaos to slip between jurisdictions. When Santa Fe attacked, the Pijaos moved closer to Popayán, and when the latter mobilized troops, they escaped toward Santa Fe. Furthermore, they attempted to block every trading party trying to cross Pijao territory or to travel between Santa Fe and Popayán, making communications between Santa Fe and the Viceroyalty of Peru fragile and unreliable.

As time went by, opposition to Spanish colonialism solidified patterns of interaction between peoples, creating enduring social bonds. Some of these practices had ancient roots, while others were forged by the practicalities of living in war against Spanish colonialism—a form of life and landscape-building that could be described as both fugitive and insubordinate.[57] They lived in large homes on the most remote and hidden parts of the mountains: near the tops of hills and sources of rivers, or around cliffs and brooks, which they used as escape routes in the event of an attack.[58] Usually each longhouse stood by itself, though sometimes there could be two or three in close proximity. They built tunnels under their homes to escape surprise assaults. A diverse material culture flourished in Pijao households, combining goods they raided from European traders and neighboring cities with items of Indigenous origin. They owned velvet and silk clothing, metal armor, swords, knives, and arquebuses. Most of these items were strictly forbidden to the commoners living in colonial villages. Access to some of these items, traditionally restricted to Spaniards or to some Indigenous elites, might have attracted commoners and even mestizos of low means to join the Pijaos.

On the mountains, hidden in dense forests, they would clear sections for tillage and grow corn, beans, yucca, and many other tubers and roots; they aimed for these agricultural spaces to be undetectable to Spanish eyes.[59] They also hunted deer, birds, and rodents to complement their diet. They would roast and bake these foods, coat them in corn flour, and carry them into battle in containers made from gourds. Concealed crops and movable food products were well suited for war. The longhouses of some war leaders were surrounded by large statues made out of wood and ceramic, and in some cases—such as the longhouse of Ucoche, a Pijao leader in Coyaima in the 1570s—"many heads of indios and Spaniards" were displayed as trophies in front of the house.[60]

War shaped subjectivities and everyday practice in other ways, too. Even the Pijaos' worst enemies described them as courageous warriors who would only truly respect those who proved brave and strong, rather than accepting hierarchy and authority for its own sake. A gendered notion of bravery was central to the Pijaos' values. Men occupied themselves in war and could have many wives, and boys learned to fight, resist, and hide any weakness from a very early age: "They are very brave and determined in war, they withstand great pain and trouble, and are of notable valor and courage in embracing death and any kind of torment without complaining or showing a sign of sentiment, as if they were completely insensitive."[61] Upon death, they were buried with great solemnity in caves, accompanied by drinks and food. From youth, boys' and girls' bodies were molded differently through cultural practices. In the Saldaña River region, the Pijaos boarded boys' foreheads to achieve a long hollow shape, and broke and stretched their noses to be long and curved.[62] Girls' legs and arms were corded very tightly so that their torsos were wide and their extremities thin. These cultures of the body—marked by enduring pain and praise for strength—built a character difficult to defeat in war. War and fugitivity forged new subjectivities, patterns of interaction, and territory in the contest for sovereignty in the central Andean range.

That these broad patterns existed in Pijao territory does not mean that everyone in their territory shared the same lifestyle or conformed to traditional ideas of community. The territory was diverse, grouping people from many ethnic and cultural backgrounds, and the forms of organization of the Pijao peoples allowed for a general framework of incorporation, rather than imposing a homogeneous culture. This is evident in language. Historian Santiago Paredes has argued that the language of the people of Saldaña, Coyaima, Natagaima, and some other surrounding territories became a lingua franca used by Native peoples of different ethnicities to communicate with each other. Pijao names and concepts invaded other languages and left traces in their lexicons and naming practices—traces that endured throughout the imperial period and are still evident in southwestern Colombia today.[63] In the heterogeneous and irregular landscapes of the central Andean mountain range, the Pijao coalition both built upon and cemented common ideas of politics that were remarkably flexible, allowing for the creation of macropolitical units that could, however, rapidly dissolve to form other arrangements.

Rituals of Consumption

Hemmed in by their rigid dichotomies, the Spanish did not have the conceptual tools to understand or explain the Pijao expansion. The dissonance between an overwhelming, emerging Indigenous power and the Spaniards' incapacity to come to terms with it is at the core of the making of the Pijao project—a territory full of myth and fantasy that was nonetheless built by very real people in an increasingly tense environment. If the Pijaos' politics were unthinkable for Spaniards, their allegedly rapacious appetite for human flesh consumed much of the would-be colonizers' attention—their worst fears seemed to be coming true. As a result, a mythical language of eating and consumption came to symbolize the Pijao expansion.

The Pijao notoriously used violent displays as a means of upending the kingdom—for instance, by exhibiting mutilated bodies around their homes or at key points on the road. They played into Spanish fears and inverted the lifeways and symbols of colonialism to create an autonomous Indigenous territory. For this reason, some of the scenes I will discuss in what follows are quite graphic. I do not aim to disturb the reader, but I believe that we must seriously consider violence as a form of expression and political strategy. After all, both sides made use of it: Spaniards raided Pijao settlements, took everyone they could put their hands on, tortured prestigious leaders and warriors, mutilated the bodies and left them as marks in the landscape, and enslaved the rest of the Pijao men, women, and children, auctioning them off to the mines or cities, even marking the faces of children with symbols of property.[64] Violence was a pervasive language of interaction; it is what shook Spanish settlers and what they recorded in detail. It also had political effects. Examining the Pijao "poetics of violence"—to use Neil Whitehead's term—in this light illustrates the Pijaos' political aims and how they were understood and misunderstood by Europeans; how an image of them eventually got fixed into history.[65]

Consider the display of violence in the 1570 Pijao attack on the town of Guambía. This town was the home of the main allies of the Spanish, the Manba Sabala people of Francisco de Belalcázar's encomienda in a profitable mining area in the jurisdiction of Popayán. After the Pijaos took control of the settlement, "they found Father Duarte Moreno, a clerical priest of that province who was in church saying mass when these indios killed him and killed many other indios amigos inside the church and in its surroundings. After killing him, they quartered him in the church and took the chalice and the paten, they butchered the flesh of the doctrinal father on the paten and drank maize beer in the chalice, raising it in the air like priests do, and mocking them."[66]

Spanish soldiers who arrived later found the settlement in flames and the paten and the church floor stained with blood. They could gather only a few remaining limbs and pieces of the priest's body to give him an appropriate burial.[67] The inversion of symbolic regimes was clear in this ritual mockery of the Catholic mass. The Pijaos mimicked and inverted Christianity's anthropophagy—the consumption of the body and flesh of Jesus Christ through the host. This motif appeared frequently in colonial art after the Council of Trent, which insisted that the body of Christ was truly present in the wafer (known as the doctrine of transubstantiation). Mimicry by the Pijaos of fundamental tenets of Christianity shows that they had basic knowledge of Christianity and acted on it. As many Pijaos were maroons or captives taken from villages living under Spanish rule, they had witnessed basic sacraments such as mass, confession, baptism, marriage, and burials. They also knew that the chapel and the church were the core of Spanish colonialism; the destruction of the village and consumption of the priest targeted the essence of the colonial symbolic order.

As I will explain below, ritual consumption of human bodies was a nuanced, textured Indigenous cultural practice associated with violence, revenge, and incorporation of others into their body politic. By eating the priest in this manner, the Pijaos took possession of the ritualized space of the church and inverted its meaning. They shocked, intimidated, offended; they asserted control; they claimed the space. Their mockery was a ritual of destruction and creation, erasing the landscapes of the kingdom and giving birth to an Indigenous territory where Spaniards were unwelcome outsiders. It was a ritual of anticolonialism, one that upended Spanish colonial symbols of power to make visible Indigenous power.

Spaniards described these events by resorting to a rhetoric of cannibalism. They spoke of the Pijaos using a vocabulary of ferocity and ingestion, characterizing them as predators who ate the Christian flock. Some scholars have discarded Pijao anthropophagy as a Spanish invention.[68] After all, European images and descriptions of cannibalism were so gross and simplistic that no one could truly be believed to engage in such dehumanizing acts. For centuries, Europeans had resorted to stories of man-eaters to project their own fantasies of virtuosity vis-à-vis a bestial, subhuman, immoral other, creating epic narratives about European heroes against non-European villains.[69] But it was in the sixteenth-century Caribbean that the term *cannibal* appeared and its associated imaginary took shape, combining medieval notions of cynocephali (men with dog snouts) and of the "indio" in the context of Atlantic debates about Indigenous people's humanity.[70] During the early days of print, lively woodcuts and engravings depicting this trope saturated European book markets, showing "indios" enjoying a roasted human calf while engaging in conversation. The resulting image was a crude archetype, an imaginary ontologically similar to ideas about "witches" or "sorcerers," which motivated fear and hatred and resulted in persecution of and discrimination against targeted populations.[71]

Descriptions of Pijao anthropophagy included all the tropes and stereotypes applied to cannibals. Take, for instance, the description of Pijao cannibalism in 1608 by Juan de Borja, one of the most acute observers of the Pijao:

> The most bizarre and despicable vice known among them is the fiery inclination to eat human flesh, which they highly value and prefer its taste to all other things raised for man's maintenance. Even though it is their ancient custom, they are now so crammed and grim with Christian flesh that most of their unrests and wars are impelled by the taste and delight of this cruel vice, slaughtering and cutting into pieces the people they take and enacting in their bodies infamous cruelties, slicing them into small lumps and eating them bit by bit in their presence, and roasting the tender creatures as a whole in a barbecue, as a kind of grill, and take

them in a bag to eat them on the road or hanging them with a cord by the neck. And to add to the dreadful inhumanity of these barbarians, it has been seen in this war that they have disinterred and eaten the fallen and buried soldiers even ten days after being interred, ignoring the stink and corruption of the rotten cadavers.[72]

Borja believed it was the taste of human flesh that moved them and explained their wars and opposition to the kingdom. In his limited understanding, he believed it was an inherent trait of their existence: the source of both nutrition and delight.

However, that the European notion of cannibalism was so crude does not mean that some groups did not ingest the bodies of their enemies.[73] We should start by differentiating anthropophagy, the practice of consuming body parts, from cannibalism, the European imaginary of man-eaters. In a way, anthropophagy is a problem of classification: what constitutes anthropophagy depends on where one draws the limits of humanity, on how one defines who is a human and who is not. Many Indigenous groups used definitions of humanity that excluded neighboring groups and Europeans.[74] Among many Indigenous groups, anthropophagy was an act of war perpetrated against those who may not have been seen as human, in the context of violent confrontations. Even Borja's horrific descriptions resemble documented practices of anthropophagy among Carib groups in Guayana, like the feared Kanaima, a secret, violent ritual in which people disinterred dead bodies and consumed bodily fluids.[75] Borja also stated that the Pijaos' appetite for human flesh had increased after the Europeans' arrival and that they were especially fond of Christian bodies. While he recognized that anthropophagy was an "ancient custom," he saw it not as a timeless trait of pre-Hispanic peoples but rather as a language of violence stoked by the kingdom's expansion and invoked amid violent colonial encounters.[76]

There are numerous examples of these encounters that show how the Pijaos themselves deployed anthropophagy as an intimidation strategy. Take, for instance, the report on the incursion by Captain Asencio de Salinas and his soldiers into the Province of Ibagué in 1556, in which they sought to punish the Native people who had killed Francisco de Trejo. As soon as they saw the soldiers, the Indigenous people formed large groups and shouted to the European soldiers defiantly that they were knaves, that they should visit the Pijao territory in the Saldaña River region and the Province of Mayma, where the Pijaos would kill them and eat them, as they had done with Trejo's and Estupiñán's soldiers.

Similarly, Antonio de Mesa, the alcalde of San Sebastián de la Plata, recounted that when the Pijaos entered the city of Timaná in 1575, "they killed

Spaniards removing their hearts, beheading them, and dismembering them to eat them."[77] They often found mutilated bodies missing eyes, heads, hearts, stomachs, intestines. Domingo de Herrera said he once found two burned huts with the bodies of at least forty children between eight months and three years of age, which the Pijaos had left to be found. Herrera and a group of soldiers trailed after the Pijao warriors and reached a point where they were able to see them on top of a cliff but could not climb there, nor could their arquebus fire reach them. "Standing there, at those heights, we saw them kill many creatures they had taken. They cut them into chunks and showed them to this witness and his companions and, right in front of them, ate the raw flesh."[78]

A conversation between the Pijao leader Yanbaro and settler Domingo de Herrera in the early 1570s is illustrative of the performativity of anthropophagy. Herrera had taken Yanbaro—a man reputed for his courage—and his soldiers captive. Herrera was tying Yanbaro down when Yanbaro dared Herrera and his Indigenous allies to eat him: "He said they should eat him, because he and his companions had eaten the fathers, mothers, and sisters of all the indios that used to live in that province, and that he and his companions had depopulated and eaten all the indios of the valley of Neiva."[79] Yanbaro's daring, threatening invitation to eat him reinforces that anthropophagy was a language of violence projected and directed toward an enemy, conceptualized as a form of revenge, an unending cycle of violence. Yet it also highlights that Yanbaro was not afraid of being eaten, perhaps revealing of a widespread attitude toward the afterlife that might have a resemblance to the Tupí preference to be eaten by enemies rather than buried.[80] Anthropophagy was not necessarily a matter of fear but an act of war and revenge that could be expected after being captured by an enemy, especially in the internecine conditions of violence unleashed by the expansion of Spanish colonialism.

The visuality of these acts of violence indicated that anthropophagy was part of the Pijao poetics of violence. It was a performance directed to an audience, composed of both the Spanish and their Indigenous allies, whom it was meant to shock and intimidate. Violence was inseparable from witnessing, imagining, and anticipating. The oral images of cannibalism dispersed through large geographic expanses, resulting in a widespread rumor and reputation about Pijao might and ruthlessness. In other words, the Pijaos played cannibals, turning the Spaniards' fantasies and fears against them.

By displaying this form of violence, the Pijaos offered the basic elements for the mythic language Europeans used to explain why their world was being destroyed and to stigmatize the Pijaos as "fiery, undomesticated savages." Eduardo Viveiros de Castro argues that Amazonian peoples' anthropophagy was a form of incorporation of others: simultaneously a form of adopting the point of view of enemies and making the enemies their own. For Neil White-head, the "transculturation of enemies" was a central part of the logic of Tupían warfare and the meaning of revenge: the Tupí aimed to transform captives into Tupí, at the same time as the Tupí, through the intimacy of eating, became the other, adopting their point of view. Some European individuals came to be remarkably immersed in Tupían culture in this way—like Hans Staden, a German man who fell captive to the Tupí and was incorporated into a ritual process of anthropophagy before returning to Europe and writing an evoca-tive narrative about his experience.[81] That transculturation might have been the purpose of ritual anthropophagy among the Pijaos as well. Anthropoph-agy simultaneously served as a way to assimilate others into their society—captives and newcomers ceased to exist as a differentiated identity, as others, thus becoming Pijaos—and established a common language of violence with Europeans. The fact that their enemies, like Bernardo de Vargas Machuca in the war manual cited above, described Indigenous peoples at war against the Spanish almost as supernatural creatures, as "nocturnal birds" who "walk on air" and need no food or sleep, might just be a testament to that.[82] Whether they wanted or not, Europeans became participants in a culture of anthro-pophagy: cannibalism and anthropophagy became the dominant concepts that both Europeans and Indigenous peoples adopted to express a very real, very concrete situation—the advancement of a self-governing Indigenous co-alition that completely uprooted the kingdom.

The theatrical, scandalous imagery of anthropophagy got the Pijaos the attention they sought: it rapidly transformed into a mythical language that abandoned any concrete evidence and ceased to describe concrete situations, instead serving as a vague, abstract referent to offer a moral explanation of the inversion of colonial power. I have found more than one hundred denun-ciations of Pijao anthropophagy in archives in Spain and Colombia, many of them simple letters to the king that barely reveal any exposure to or knowledge of the Pijaos and just mention that they were these terrible cannibals destroy-ing the kingdom.[83] Settlers and officials offered outrageous, clearly inflated numbers of people eaten by the Pijaos. In 1558, Joan Vaez Crespo estimated that the Pijao peoples had consumed more than forty thousand Indigenous vassals of the kingdom in the city of Neiva alone.[84] Juan de Borja stated in 1610 that the Pijaos had destroyed fourteen Spanish settlements and devoured over one hundred thousand individuals, and that they craved human flesh as the most exquisite of meals.[85]

This hyperbolic rhetoric describing tens of thousands of bodies consumed by the Pijaos was the Spaniards' way of coming to terms with the actual growth of Pijao power as an alternative political framework that was sidelining the kingdom; it gave them a vocabulary to grapple with the fact that they were being defeated by a people they deemed inferior. In this way, the act of eating human bodies offered a powerful metaphor for Pijao expansion: it was both a social practice amplified in response to colonial violence and a story that Indigenous peoples and Europeans told about themselves and others. The Pijaos did not literally eat entire villages, but the rhetoric of cannibalism allowed both the Pijaos and European settlers to talk about the Pijaos' expansion, the colonial cities and villages they destroyed, the captives they took, and their creation of a multiethnic configuration uniting thousands of people and ruling a territory spanning hundreds of square miles.

Contested Sovereignties

In the second half of the sixteenth century the Pijao coalition emerged as an overt attack on the material and institutional aspects of Spanish infrastructures of governance carried out by a mishmash of ethnic groups under a structured organization. They grew exponentially by spreading a message of freedom, convening and courting Indigenous peoples to join them, and waging war and incorporating captives. A complex mixture of people found in the impenetrable mountain an alternative to the extenuating, demeaning life of the kingdom. The Pijaos achieved this through a spectacle of violence that mobilized Europeans' deepest fears. Their coalition was associated with a language of predators, rather than obedient herds. They devoured the kingdom, leaving cities in ruins and heads on sticks, and transforming colonial provinces into Indigenous territories. There was nothing natural or inherent about the violence of the Pijaos—it was not an inherent characteristic of static Indigenous groups, as the Spaniards described. Instead, it was a result of brutal interactions with imperial violence.

Archival descriptions of the Pijaos and their landscape are cast in language that blurred fiction and reality. Europeans told the most dreadful and abhorrent stories about the Pijao territory, but that territory was also where those stories just might prove true. The land had its own mystique, as impenetrable as the Pijaos were unthinkable. The Spanish used an emotionally charged language to speak of the symbolic inversion of the landscape. They were outraged, shocked, and scared by Pijao built environments, cultures of the body, gender roles, and material cultures. They saw themselves as the targets of an extreme, unprovoked violence waged against them by infidels. They claimed that the Pijaos went against the very laws of nature. The Spanish, however, had physically and symbolically attacked Indigenous ritual worlds of spirituality and politics whenever they had the chance—just like the Spanish described the Pijaos' actions against them. The Spanish profaned and destroyed Indigenous sacred spaces and burned their spiritual figures. The Pijaos inverted this economy of destruction; they turned the kingdom upside down and devoured it to remake it into a frightening space where the scales of power no longer favored Europeans.

Europeans' rigid views of politics and ethnicity made them unable to grasp the complexity of the Indigenous world they faced, and so they reproduced a mythic language of cannibalism. And we still lack the conceptual vocabulary to accurately represent the Pijaos' political choices, ambitions, and actions. Some of the terms used by borderlands historiography to describe Indigenous politics and maroon societies are too abstract, not applicable, or utterly unhelpful. The Pijao territory was, of course, an "Indigenous ground," but that does not really describe their agenda, instead merely giving an idea of the power balance in relation to Europeans.[86] The Pijaos did not form an "empire" with tributary networks or a centralized administration.[87] The Pijao organization was something new, in the sense that it emerged as a territory and a political framework in the sixteenth century. However, the concept of ethnogenesis emphasizes the emergence of an ethnic identity, which does not describe a political coalition like the Pijaos.[88] Nor did they have a "parasitic" economy, such as those that scholars have associated with some maroon societies: they stole from Europeans, but they did not so much feed off the colonial economy parasitically as they sought to sabotage or destroy it, in a pattern more closely resembling predation.

Instead, the Pijaos were a political coalition aiming to disassemble Spanish rule. It was a web of alliances based on a Carib political framework: proclaiming a clear political message that allowed them to channel the efforts of multiple ethnic groups into a common cause and incorporate newcomers and captives into their social systems, while also avoiding centralization. It is striking that, in the context of a plummeting Indigenous population, the result of epidemics, violence, and strenuous labor conditions, the Pijaos managed to expand their territory and enlist a population of several thousand. The significance of this demographic expansion cannot be overstated. On the one hand, it opens the possibility that the Pijao project is tied to the history of flight from the New Kingdom, as its expansion might have even included some of those who were marked absent or missing in colonial censuses as far away as the Muisca territory.

On the other hand, it forces us to come to terms with the stark success of their anticolonial project in the sixteenth century. It proves that the history of the Pijaos is not that of a marginal, pre-Hispanic group but one of consolidation of a deliberate political project. The Pijaos did not tolerate Hispanic settlements, nor did they establish alliances, diplomatic channels, or exchange networks with Europeans; rather, they consumed colonial landscapes and people, making them Pijaos. They aimed to entirely uproot the Europeans and their allies from their mountains by targeting the two basic tenets of Spanish colonialism: the Spanish capacity to protect Indigenous vassals—the premise of the encomienda—and Catholic symbols. Destruction was a political act, and so was consumption. Both implied knowledge of Christian rituals and imperial institutions—a theory of empire they rendered visible through their attacks.

I believe Pijao anticolonialism has deep methodological implications for the study of Indigenous politics. It means reclaiming Indigenous political ideology: how Indigenous sovereignty projects operated on the basis of specific Indigenous political cultures and practices, used available political instruments and diplomatic vehicles, and developed different aims and ambitions. It means discerning between different kinds of Indigenous projects and examining how these projects were grounded in ideas about politics and views of empire. In this way, the Pijao project was an especially radical version of anticolonialism.

Pijao dominance was uncontested until the first two decades of the seventeenth century, when important members of the coalition separated from it—like the Coyaimas and Natagaimas—and when Juan de Borja assumed the presidency of the Audiencia of Santa Fe and redesigned a military strategy to match the fighting power of the Pijaos. That final phase of war, marked by the separation of the Coyaimas and Natagaimas and Borja's genocidal enterprise, will be explored in chapter 8. While Borja's incursion ended the Pijao coalition I examine in this book, it was not the end of the Pijaos—who resurged as a group in the twentieth century—nor the end of the processes of making and unmaking macropolitical unities that forged special alliances between groups in the central Andean range. In the centuries to follow, new political and ethnic groups and territories would emerge by establishing bonds through different means—in some cases warfare, in others even deploying the empire's own legal system.[89]

A drastically different Indigenous freedom project emerged in parallel to the Pijaos, in the 1570s and 1580s, in the Muisca highlands of the eastern range. This project was led by Don Diego de la Torre—a man who studied the empire's legislation and governance procedures and used them to promote a new vision of the kingdom. The next chapters will turn to his story.

A MESTIZO CACIQUE

In the 1570s, when the Pijao coalition was actively devouring the New King-dom's governance infrastructures, Don Diego de la Torre—the ruler of the Muisca cacicazgo of Turmequé, in the cold highlands of the eastern Andean range—developed a different kind of Indigenous freedom project: one that put its bets on the empire's legal frameworks and, in particular, in the transforma-tive power of the king. The king, indeed, was the epicenter of Spanish political culture, the ultimate judge. The empire's administrative organs were designed as extensions of his body, as audiencias and oidores served as his ears and paper flows enabled communication with the king. In cases in which these instru-ments were thought to be compromised or corrupt, individuals all over the empire envisioned the possibility of talking directly to the king and ask him to provide justice in their provinces.[1]

This was exactly Torre's situation: after engaging in conflicts with the audi-encia magistrates and being stripped of his cacicazgo, Don Diego fled to King Philip II's court to present his situation and advise him on the good govern-ment of the New Kingdom of Granada. Torre belonged to a privileged group of Indigenous nobility who presented themselves as loyal vassals and framed their presence in the king's court as intended to help the monarch understand what was happening in their localities. This vibrant community of Indigenous transatlantic travelers moved ably within the empire's legal systems and deployed the empire's juridical categories to claim justice and seek royal support.[2] In the case of Don Diego, his presence at court unleashed a full transformation of the audiencia. We now turn to the role Torre played in the kingdom's transformation in the 1570s and 1580s, in a context of deep turmoil over the meaning and mechanics of Indigenous authority, evangelization, and the place of mestizos in the empire.

Don Diego de la Torre was a puzzling figure whose life story is worthy of a novel. He was a bicultural character in a world that had few words to describe him. He was born in 1549, about two decades after the Spanish invasion, to Catalina, the eldest sister of the cacique of Turmequé, and Juan de Torres, a prestigious conquistador and encomendero. According to Muisca inheritance patterns, Torre was heir to his uncle's cacicazgo. He was brought up in between worlds: he learned Spanish and Muisca, as well as how to read and write, and received training in both Spanish law and the cultural role a cacique must perform. Torre had a close familiarity with both his father's and his mother's worlds, in a time when the empire was still defining its ideas about "mestizos"—a nascent label used to refer to individuals resulting from Indigenous-European unions. As Frank Salomon and Stuart Schwartz put it, "People of mixed birth formed not so much a new category as a challenge to categorization itself."[3] The label was drawn from a vocabulary used to describe crossbreeding in animals and was framed in a genealogical system that conceived of religion as embedded in people's bodies and bodily fluids: in blood, milk, and semen. In such a system, to carry the blood of non-Christians was to bear a stain. It cast an aura of doubt and suspicion that rendered individuals dangerous to society at large.[4]

In part for these reasons, Torre became a highly public and controversial figure. In 1574, three years after he was appointed cacique, he engaged in a series of legal disputes with his half brother, Pedro de Torres, the encomendero of Turmequé, over the size of tribute payments required of the Native people of the encomienda. From Don Diego's perspective, Pedro expected a larger quantity of textiles than was fair. These legal clashes escalated to involve elites and imperial officials of the city of Tunja and the Audiencia of Santa Fe. The audiencia magistrates ultimately removed Torre from the cacicazgo. In response, he traveled all the way to the king's court in Madrid between 1574 and 1579—even surviving a storm that sank his ship—and met personally with

Philip II. His return to South America only increased the anxieties of the royal tribunal's magistrates: Torre retained the support of Indigenous communities, and the magistrates worried that he might cause unrest upon his return. After his arrival, audiencia authorities accused Torre of organizing a rebellion and arrested him twice. He escaped from jail, hid on the moors for a while, and then traveled back to Spain in 1584, this time as a prisoner accused of treason. In Madrid he met Alonso de Atahualpa (the grandson of the last Inca), married a Spanish woman called Juana de Oropesa, had children, and died. He was a cacique, a transatlantic traveler, and a mestizo heavily involved in the New Kingdom's political networks.[5]

Don Diego de la Torre's multifaceted character has inspired multiple interpretations. In the 1960s, Colombian historian Ulises Rojas wrote a five-hundred-page biography of Torre depicting him as a refined Spanish gentleman who took pity on Native peoples and defended them much as Antonio de Montesinos or Bartolomé de las Casas had defended the Native peoples of La Española or Chiapas. To Rojas, everything about Torre was Spanish. His attire, his ideas about nobility, and his most innate values looked to Spain. Rojas, who rigorously read and transcribed the files about Torre kept in Seville, dismissed all evidence that he participated in Native rituals as false accusations intended to discredit and dishonor him. Torre's true character was, to Rojas, that of a Spanish gentleman.[6]

More recently and from an ethnographic perspective, Joanne Rappaport has examined how Torre conceived of and acted upon his complex social classification as a mestizo. Rappaport argues that "mestizo" was not a stable category, nor were mestizos a socially or racially defined group in the New Kingdom during the early modern period. Mestizos, rather, tended to stop identifying as such during their lives, blending instead into other social categories. Torre and Don Alonso de Silva, his ally and the mestizo cacique of Tibasosa, exemplified this unstable quality of the "mestizo" label in a very particular way. They were "insiders-outside" who defended their good Christian blood while at the same time fighting for their right to lead Indigenous communities.[7] Historian Max Deardorff adds to this, arguing that Don Diego was part of a wave of mestizo activism of the 1570s and 1580s in the New Kingdom and Peru that confronted legal discrimination toward the descendants of "indios" and instead sought full enfranchisement by appealing to the Spanish monarchy's more inclusive notions of "Christian citizenship."[8]

Here I focus on Torre's political project, which was intimately connected to his identity, his understanding of Hispanic law, and the place of Indigenous peoples in the Spanish empire. My contention is that Torre advanced a bold and innovative political project aimed at transforming the governance of the New Kingdom of Granada. This project was based on his interpretation of the Spanish empire's legal principles, particularly of the New Laws, and on his particular position within the empire as a bicultural cacique. This broad argument unfolds in this chapter and the next. This chapter, centered on Torre's life until his travel to Spain, situates his early struggles for his cacicazgo through his interactions with the Indigenous people of Turmequé, Spanish encomenderos, and the Audiencia of Santa Fe, and within an imperial context that was increasingly adverse for people labeled as mestizos. I challenge Ulises Rojas's depiction of the community of Turmequé as naïve by instead showing the community's deep engagement with Spanish governance in the preceding decades, and thus highlighting changes to the meaning of Indigenous authority in the face of evangelization and Spanish institutions. I argue that, in the eyes of the community of Turmequé, Torre emerged as a successful contender for the cacicazgo precisely because of his bicultural skills. He was not a champion of ignorant and defenseless "indios," as Rojas depicted him, but part of community politics, and he acted against a background of frameworks for political action among the Muisca in the 1570s and 1580s, when Indigenous politics had been deeply changed. Those same traits, however, vilified him in the eyes of Spaniards, who depicted him as a dangerous mestizo. For the Spanish, the fact that Don Diego combined legal knowledge and writing and used them to promote a specific vision of Spanish institutions made him unfit to lead an Indigenous community. The next chapter examines Torre's travels to the king's court and how he shaped his rhetoric to capture the monarch's attention.

Turmequé

Turmequé was a major Muisca cacicazgo located in a vast Andean valley in the Province of Tunja, on the border between the domains of Tunja and Bogotá. The people of Turmequé inhabited a diverse landscape crisscrossed by three rivers and adjacent to a high-altitude moorland (páramo) called Guaneche, where the Bogotá River is born. Most of its landscapes were cold and fertile agrarian lands in rugged hills at an altitude of around 2,400 meters above sea level (about 7,875 feet). The seventeenth-century chronicler Lucas Fernández de Piedrahita—one of the few chroniclers to show interest in pre-Hispanic history—noted that Turmequé had great military power and played a strategic role in the wars between the rulers of Tunja and Bogotá before the Spanish conquest. He estimated that Turmequé had about three thousand inhabitants at the time of the conquest; however, this turned out to be a gross underestimation. During his visit in 1560, Tomás López recorded a population of 1,457 Indigenous men who fit the category of "useful indios," or those of appropriate age and physical condition to pay tribute. This suggests that the total population of Turmequé would have been between 5,800 and 7,300 at that time, even after the marked demographic collapse that followed the European invasion, making Turmequé one of the New Kingdom's largest and wealthiest encomiendas in the second half of the sixteenth century.[9]

During his inspection, López inquired about the relationships between Indigenous communities and encomenderos. The instructions for visitas required inspectors to personally visit the localities, but due to his tight schedule and many responsibilities, López did not actually reach Turmequé (see chapter 2). He instead requested that the cacique and other Native authorities travel to meet him in the city of Tunja, about forty-five kilometers away (roughly twenty-eight miles), and asked them questions about the population, economy, and overall situation of the cacicazgo. The records of these interviews offer an overview of the environment Don Diego de la Torre grew up in. López learned from the cacique and a series of witnesses that four encomenderos had held Turmequé transitorily before Juan de Torres—a testimony to the encomienda transfers that were common in the early decades after the conquest. Three of them—Gómez del Corral, Gaspar Rodríguez, and Diego García Pacheco—held it only briefly and witnesses said little about them. By contrast, the cacique and other Native authorities accused Guillermo de Aguayo y Villaviciosa and Juan de Torres of misdeeds of varying seriousness. The strongest accusations were made against Villaviciosa, the first encomendero of Turmequé in the 1540s, who had killed four Native people by throwing them to the dogs—a practice common enough to have its own verb in the colonial lexicon, *aperrear*—in an obsessive quest for more tribute.[10]

The caciques and commoners also reported that Juan de Torres had requested that commoners carry loads of wheat, corn, and textiles to the hot lands, especially to the ports in Vélez or to the silver mines in Mariquita. Although he did not force commoners to do this, he did offer incentives, giving each of them a manta and relieving them of their annual tribute if they made the journey. However, several commoners died during the long and difficult journey between the cold and hot lands, either at treacherous river crossings or due to the drastic changes in altitude and weather. López also found that while the Native people of Moyachoque, a subunit of Turmequé, were supposed to pay Torres 560 mantas annually, they instead worked in his textile workshop (telar) as payment. This practice of trading tribute for work or other kinds of payment was illegal at the time.[11]

López firmly believed that imperial officials should demand retribution to achieve justice—a phenomenon known as the doctrine of restoration. Thus he imposed a penalty on Juan de Torres, and sought to address the hardships Torres imposed on the Native commoners of his encomienda by giving them spiritual guidance and compelling the encomendero to abide by the New Laws and the policies that isolated Native peoples from Spaniards. López required Torres to provide the commoners with instruction in Catholicism, to construct a permanent church building—with a bell, ornaments, and paintings approved by the bishop—and to maintain a priest who would live in Turmequé year-round. From then on, Torres should observe the laws regarding the treatment of Native people, especially keeping them out of the mines, avoiding making them work outside their villages, and avoiding making them do tasks that involved carrying products away from their lands. Torres had three days to leave Turmequé and take his family and workers with him. From then on, the Native people of Torres's encomienda would only be required to pay tribute to him according to the official rates and in the official products (mantas and gold). He was not allowed to ask for any other kind of payment or work. Furthermore, López sentenced Torres to pay fifteen golden pesos to the Crown to cover the costs of the trial, and to pay three hundred cotton mantas to the Native people of Turmequé as restitution for the harm he had caused.[12]

By the time Don Diego de la Torre became cacique, the people of Turmequé had more than twenty years of experience dealing with Spanish institutions, settlers, and the legal system. Five different encomenderos and at least two inspectors had come through its valleys. The caciques and commoners had witnessed the harm caused both by strict inspectors like López—who wanted to establish villages and reform Indigenous routines to align their lives with the precepts of Christianity—and by encomenderos who sought new economic ventures. They had reacted against unwanted policies and practices both within and outside the confines of the law. For instance, after López first sought to resettle the Native people of Turmequé in towns, the Indigenous captain Guatavica fled with his subjects to the moorlands to avoid life in gridded villages.[13] The Native people of Turmequé had also used the legal system to address mistreatment, and witnessed the positive rulings and limited penalties imposed. As early as 1560, during an inquiry responding to accusations of mistreatment of Turmequé commoners by Andrés Riquel, a Native man named Pedro stated that if Riquel had acted wrongfully, "he and others would have gone to the city of Tunja or to the *cipaes* of Santa Fe to take legal action against him."[14] Here again, Pedro invoked the Muisca concept of "cipa" to refer to the magistrates of the Audiencia of Santa Fe, in a widely used tradition in the sixteenth-century New Kingdom of Granada, and showed that he was well aware of his right to use the legal system to challenge the wrongful actions of outsiders.

In his biography of Torre, Ulises Rojas depicted Native peoples as defenseless victims who needed protection and painted Torre as their champion. Rojas went so far as to reproduce the language that Torre had employed to describe Native peoples. In his letters, Torre frequently referred to them as "ovejas mudas" (mute sheep) or "míseros indios" (wretched indios) and framed them as victims. As we will see in chapter 6, however, Torre did not use such terms to describe specific traits he attributed to the Muiscas. Rather, he deployed such words as part of an argumentative strategy that invoked medieval and early modern Hispanic legal concepts to tailor his message to his audience: the king and his advisers. At the same time, the people of Turmequé—who had a history of ample engagement with imperial institutions—understood not only the value of Torre's strategy but also that the qualifications for the position of cacique had shifted. They knew the options available to them and made strategic choices as they faced increasing pressure from colonial institutions. In this sense, Don Diego de la Torre became a viable contender for the post of cacique in the eyes of the Native people of Turmequé not because they were defenseless, but rather because they were politically savvy enough to understand the necessity of leveraging Spanish legal concepts against the empire.

Becoming Cacique

The Muiscas, like many other Indigenous groups of the Americas, were not naïve victims of the empire. They were historical agents who studied, analyzed, and engaged the empire and its institutions. The Turmequé commoners supported Don Diego de la Torre in the midst of ongoing, profound changes in the Muisca cacicazgos' concepts of power and authority, as well as in Native authorities' role in the cacicazgos. Around the same time, other caciques of neighboring communities, who saw themselves as Catholic subjects, were losing the support of Muisca groups for failing to fulfill the role expected of them by their communities. Those expectations included the complex use of ritual, symbolic, political, and economic languages that shaped interactions between Muisca communities and their authorities. These interactions—established through rich symbolic languages and ritual practice—created a set of ideas regarding how leaders should be chosen and how they should exert their authority, as well as which demands were just or unacceptable.

The ceremonies they called iebzasqua or biohote in the Muisca language, in which community members gathered to dance, eat, and work, were crucial in the cultural politics of these Indigenous groups. Colonial authorities called these gatherings borracheras and associated them with the cult of the devil, as discussed in chapter 3. Most of these practices directly contradicted the teachings of friars as well as the audiencia's policies, which constantly sought to enforce what they called a "life in good order" (vida en policía). Caciques, acting simultaneously as leaders of Native communities and agents of the empire, had to absorb many of the contradictions that resulted from Native communities' incorporation into the empire. Some caciques who reinvented themselves as Christian subjects and condemned Native ceremonies as idolatry, like Don Francisco of Ubaque, could not get their communities to follow them. Meanwhile, other caciques who followed Native customs too closely found themselves in trouble with colonial authorities and friars.[15] It was a difficult time to be an Indigenous cacique.

During the allocation of encomiendas, imperial officials unified many levels of Indigenous political authority under the simplified category of "cacique"—a term they had borrowed from the Arawak and used to categorize all Indigenous authorities in the empire.[16] The fact that Indigenous hierarchies were dismantled and that Native leaders suddenly occupied a single political stratum created new tensions and opportunities. Among the cacique's new roles was active participation in the legal system. During these decades the audiencia witnessed a boom in Native legal activity related to how Native communities had been divided and given to encomenderos. The caciques used the Hispanic legal system in a series of legal battles to expand their cacicazgos—primarily by adding new subjects. They not only complained in court but also used the monarchical legal apparatus and appropriated its language and procedures to respond to the new situations created by the conquest. Not least, they often did so with their encomenderos' support. By the 1570s, the cacicazgos' cultural politics had radically changed. Since caciques played a dual role as Native authorities and imperial agents, their communities expected them to be skilled in Indigenous political practices and ritual languages as well as in the empire's legal structures.[17]

In that sense, rather than assuming that Native commoners blindly followed Torre, we must explain historically how Torre, as a lettered cacique, managed to retain the support of his community. Joanne Rappaport has shown that the inheritance of the cacicazgo by Torre and Don Alonso de Silva—his contemporary and the bicultural cacique of Tibasosa—was contested rather than natural. In Tibasosa, three pretenders to the cacicazgo claimed authority through different forms of kinship, each claiming he was the true heir. Rappaport argues that the dispute over the cacicazgo was "a struggle over which model of chiefly authority would prevail."[18] A look at Torre's trajectory might give us a better sense of how he envisioned his role as a cacique.

We know little about Torre's early years. In 1557, when he was eight years old, his father registered him at a school for mestizos in Diego del Aguila's house in Tunja, an institution that resulted from the gendered and sexualized violence of colonialism. The school had been established one year earlier by the king's decree, probably in response to letters and petitions by settlers. The king indicated concern for the large number of mixed-race children abandoned or left unattended by their Black and Indigenous parents, who were busy in the service of Spaniards. Many of these children were orphans who roamed freely in the city of Tunja. Torre would later write to the king that the cause for this neglect was that Indigenous women were separated from their infants in order to breastfeed Spanish newborns and to provide domestic service to Spaniards in the disruptive, gendered dynamics of colonialism. By establishing a school, the king and the audiencia hoped to educate these children in the Catholic faith and what they saw as "good" customs.[19] Indeed, Torre noted that in school he learned to love God and the king through strict discipline and whippings—illustrating the methods teachers used to inculcate the empire's morals and ethics.

In Diego del Aguila's school for mestizos, Torre met some of the men he would be in contact with throughout his life. Among them was Don Alonso de Silva, the mestizo cacique of Tibasosa, who would later join Torre in his legal disputes to keep his cacicazgo. He also met Sebastián Ropero, Miguel de Partearroyo, Antón de Rojas, Diego de Carvajal, Cristóbal de Sanabria, Andrés Camacho, and Martín de Requejada, all of whom communicated with him through oral or written means in the ensuing years and were called to testify when Torre was prosecuted by the Audiencia of Santa Fe in the 1580s. Although, as Joanne Rappaport has shown, the category of "mestizo" did not create a fixed social or racial identity, institutions such as the school for mestizos run in Diego de Aguila's house did create enduring social bonds among individuals who did not fit the empire's rigid legal and social categories.[20] Their shared experience gave rise to a tight network of lettered mestizos who would remain in touch, maintain epistolary contact, and coordinate actions.

Torre continued to study subjects such as grammar, morals, religion, reading, arithmetic, and music at the Dominican convent in Tunja. He was probably trained through the intellectual conversation about the morality of empire that Dominican friars like Antonio de Montesinos and Bartolomé de las Casas had initiated and which spread throughout the Hispanic Atlantic. These friars sustained a profound philosophical discussion about whether the Spanish empire had the right to wage war and establish institutions such as the enco-mienda in the New World.[21] It is quite possible that Torre had access to the writings and teachings of Las Casas and the School of Salamanca at the Dominican convent. He probably also learned about the unorthodox methods of Juan del Valle, the Dominican bishop of Popayán who excommunicated enco-menderos who mistreated Indigenous peoples, and about Fray Francisco de Carvajal and the many other Dominican friars who denounced the excessive violence against and destruction of Indigenous communities during the sixteenth century, as explored in chapter 2.

Furthermore, during his early years in Tunja, Torre must have met or seen Tomás López Medel, or at the very least heard about his inspections of Turmequé. It is difficult to assess the kind of contact that Torre, as the eight-year-old son of the encomendero and heir to the cacicazgo, might have had with the visitador general of the kingdom. Native authorities met with López in Tunja, but it is unclear if Torre joined them. Whether or not they met personally, it is most likely that Torre learned about López's operations in Turmequé. Not only was López's visit the most important event at the time, but López also prosecuted Torre's father, Juan de Torres. Since López's work consisted of reversing a series of regulations that the encomenderos were not abiding by, it is easy to see how López—as the eyes of the monarch, the ultimate judge of the empire—may have influenced Torre's understanding of imperial adminis-tration. López's visit probably reinforced the idea of a distant monarch who had the right intentions but who was ill advised and misguided by a corrupt administration. This background explains why, years later, Torre sought help from Philip II when he was at odds with the local administration of the audi-encia. As we will see in the next chapter, his Dominican education would help him craft a narrative for the court.

When Torre's uncle Don Pablo—the former cacique of Turmequé—died, Torre was too young to take over the cacicazgo. Don Pablo had instructed the community to regard Torre as heir to the cacicazgo and asked them to obey Torre after his death. In the meantime, until Torre reached the necessary age to become cacique, a regent (called Don Diego as well) assumed his duties. However, the commoners of Turmequé continued cultivating Torre's fields and providing resources for him to acquire tunics, capes, and other kinds of European clothing—indicating that they saw him as the heir to the cacicazgo. In August 1571, when Torre was twenty-two years old, a group of twelve Native authorities who called themselves the caciques and captains of Turmequé— the regent included—appeared before the Audiencia of Santa Fe to request that Don Diego de la Torre assume his post as cacique.

Torre brought witnesses to the audiencia to support his appointment. The testimonies of these witnesses give a sense of the many overlapping cultural influences and forms of identity that shaped Torre's early years. Don Diego the regent said that he had only been appointed to serve as cacique temporarily, until Torre was old enough to rule. Six more Native men from Turmequé also testified. All of them were described as chontales (meaning they did not speak Spanish); most of them served as authorities; some were Catholics and some had not been baptized. They all said that Don Diego de la Torre was the heir, that he was the son of Don Pablo's eldest sister, Catalina, and that they obeyed and respected him as cacique. Torre presented some Spaniards as witnesses: people who had talked to Don Pablo or Catalina in Juan de Torres's house. Antonio Cubidez and Teresa de Sanabria said they had met Catalina de Moyachoque, that she was a Catholic and a ladina (an Indigenous woman who spoke Spanish), and that it was well known in the kingdom that she had married Juan de Torres, that they lived as husband and wife, and that Don Diego de la Torre was their son.[22] Juan de Penagos had served as judge for a long time and had been to Turmequé to rule in judicial matters. He had talked to Don Pablo and knew that the other pretender to the cacicazgo, Perincho—Don Pablo's brother—had died. After collecting this information, the audiencia produced the necessary documents for Don Diego de la Torre to be appointed cacique of Turmequé in September 1571.

By the time Torre became cacique, his father, Juan de Torres, had died and his half brother Pedro de Torres had inherited the encomienda. Pedro had been born in 1534, just before his father sailed for the Indies. In 1557, Pedro arrived in the New Kingdom of Granada to be trained in the administration of the encomienda.[23] He became the encomendero of Turmequé a decade later, in 1567. Torre's appointment as cacique, therefore, resulted in a very unusual situation in which the encomendero and the cacique were half brothers. But rather than establishing bonds between them, the new position revealed their conflicting understandings of the encomienda as an institution and of the value of mantas Indigenous peoples owed to their encomenderos.

In May 1573, only a couple of years after Torre began his tenure as cacique, his half brother Pedro denounced him to the Audiencia of Santa Fe for unsettling the Native people of the encomienda—in what he described as "appeals and rampage" (llamamientos y alborotos)—and requested Torre's dismissal from the cacicazgo. The initial disagreement between the half brothers was over the value of Indigenous textiles: while the established rate for tribute indicated that each manta was worth five tomines, Pedro de Torres sold them for ten. Torre claimed that the Native people of Turmequé should be allowed to pay their tribute in gold and that the encomendero owed them about eight thousand pesos in good gold. In essence, Torre aimed to alter how tributes were being paid in the encomienda. Pedro de Torres was incensed and denounced him at the audiencia.[24]

Pedro de Torres's appearance at the audiencia set off a series of legal battles that revolved primarily around the nature of mestizaje and the place of mestizos in the empire. Historian Max Deardorff has shown that during the 1560s a new model of citizenship formed in the Spanish empire characterized by a racialized, post-Tridentine ideal of a "good Christian," which rendered people of mixed origin like Don Diego suspicious.[25] Building on this logic, Pedro de Torres and his allies argued that Native cacicazgos should be led by Native people, and that Don Diego de la Torre should not be cacique because he was a mestizo. Even worse, they claimed he was an illegitimate mestizo born from adultery, which made him unpredictable and untrustworthy. Pedro de Torres claimed that Don Diego was playing the legal system—an accusation that Pedro de Torres asserted laid bare Don Diego's dangerous character. According to Pedro de Torres, Don Diego had organized two hundred Native commoners to give false testimony against Pedro de Torres in the audiencia. Furthermore, he argued that Torre was promising freedom to the Native people of the encomienda, telling them that they were not Pedro de Torres's subjects and were not obliged to work for him.[26]

In sum, Pedro constructed Don Diego as a racialized being within the specific frameworks that marked difference in the Spanish empire, and argued that these qualities made him suspicious. Pedro argued that the fact that Torre was a mestizo predisposed him to politically subversive ideas and actions. By contrast, Don Diego de la Torre argued that his condition as a mixed-blood cacique was actually an asset, a quality that made him even more suitable for the position. In his deposition to the audiencia, Don Diego framed his arguments within a Christian moral framework: he would make a better cacique due to his paternal lineage. His "good" Spanish and Christian blood and the fact that he descended from a conquistador made him even more suited to the task and placed him above any Indigenous pretender.[27] Don Diego then arrived at the audiencia the following day accompanied by the Native authorities of Turmequé to lodge a claim against his half brother.[28]

The audiencia magistrates sided with the encomendero and wrote to King Philip II in April 1575 asking him to ban mestizos from serving as caciques. While waiting for a response, they ruled that Don Diego de la Torre would no longer serve as cacique of Turmequé and replaced him with a man called Don Pedro. Torre was barred from setting foot on the lands of Turmequé under threat of permanent expatriation from the Indies. Finally, they sent Juan Solano de la Cueba, the bailiff (alguacil) of Tunja, to burn Torre's houses, palisades, and fields. The magistrates aimed to erase every symbol of Torre's cacicazgo from the landscape. On January 18, 1576, Philip II confirmed the ruling of the Audiencia of Santa Fe by decree and forever prohibited mestizos from holding appointments as caciques and authorities of Native communities.[29] The decentered processes of lawmaking in the Spanish monarchy were again exposed. A local struggle over Indigenous textiles in Turmequé and Tibasosa had produced a rippling process of political contention—a debate about race and politics—that resulted in an empire-wide policy defining the place of mestizos in the empire.[30]

Mestizo: The Perils of a Label

Don Diego's struggle for the cacicazgo unfolded as animosity toward mestizos increased and conflicting ideas about their place in the kingdom surfaced in religious spheres. The kingdom's archbishop at the time, Fray Luis Zapata de Cárdenas, fought to regain control of the evangelization project, which until then had been weak, indeed nearly absent, characterized by the scant presence of both secular clergy and religious orders like the Franciscans and Dominicans.[31] Zapata arrived in the New Kingdom from Peru intent on implementing the Tridentine reforms and the "cédula magna del Patronato" of 1574, which stipulated that Indigenous languages be used for evangelization.

This implied an ambitious program that included appointing a chair (cátedra) who could teach Indigenous languages to the friars, produce standardized materials—like dictionaries and catechisms in Indigenous languages—to enable the friars to preach relatively homogeneous messages to Indigenous peoples, and visit local parishes to oversee their discipline and working methods. As part of the process, the archbishop compiled a set of instructions, norms, sermons, and a catechism that the friars could use on the ground. Zapata's instructions were extremely detailed: they covered everything from how a friar should gesture to the cross to the expiration date of the communion wafers. They included sample sermons and guides for confession, as well as instructions on practical matters like how to perform an Indigenous wedding, what degrees of kin were eligible to marry, and how to handle monogamous Indigenous couples who wanted to legalize their non-Catholic unions.

Zapata's instructions had a clear structure: like López, he prioritized matters of civil training over spiritual instruction. He instructed the friars to disallow Native people from living outside the villages, to make sure they kept clean houses and slept in European-style beds, to punish nudity, and to enforce a specific dress code and hairstyle. He expected friars to keep a book with the names of Indigenous parishioners and to work with local justices (alcaldes) to maintain a jail, where they would confine those who defied these rules. He also expected them to punish any Indigenous people who engaged in Indigenous ceremonies, such as "borracheras." Zapata placed a special emphasis on their sacred objects. He ordered the friars to surreptitiously learn where Indigenous people under their purview kept their sacred objects and notify their superiors, so that a secular official could destroy them and punish those who kept Native beliefs alive. He instructed the friars to place crucifixes, statues of the Virgin, and other Catholic symbols in the exact same places where Native people practiced their religion, since he expected that they would return to the shrines. Zapata hoped that replacing Indigenous sacred objects with Catholic regalia would draw people to Catholicism.[32]

To begin such an ambitious program, Zapata had to solve a key problem: the lack of priests in Indigenous parishes, which led to insufficient instruction of Native peoples and which, as he frequently attested, resulted in the continuity of what he described as the "bad customs" and "cult of the devil" among Indigenous peoples. Imperial evangelization policy required bishops to ordain only friars who could prove they spoke Native languages.[33] Zapata sought to circumvent this issue through an unprecedented approach: he opted to name many mestizos and creoles—the latter descendants of Spaniards born in the New World—as friars. Of the 124 clerics he ordained, 39 were creoles, 22 were mestizos, and the remaining 63 were Iberians. In 1582, the audiencia appointed Gonzalo Bermúdez to a new chair in Muisca language, which they aimed to make into a "general language" of the "indios"—a kind of lingua franca that could be used to communicate with all Indigenous peoples. Bermúdez's responsibilities included giving two daily lectures on the Muisca language, testing the clergy's proficiency, and giving mass every Sunday. It also entailed composing "the most general possible vocabulary of the general language of the indios"; this task would have to wait until the early decades of the seventeenth century.[34] Zapata expected this new workforce to reinforce the evangelization process.

Both the decision to appoint mestizos and to evangelize in Muisca were controversial. Many people openly questioned whether the Muisca language had the nuances and subtleties needed to convey Catholic teachings and whether mestizos could master the word of God. Detractors claimed that the Muisca language lacked basic terminology—even the concept of "God." They posited that it would be simply impossible to speak about the immaculate conception in Muisca without using obscene language and evoking impure thoughts. They also suggested that, since priests were the interpreters of God on earth, they should be exemplary individuals. And mestizos, along with illegitimate children, people with deformities, and those who had suffered any kind of mutilation, were untrustworthy. These controversies unfolded amid global discussions over ordaining non-European people as clerics in places like New Spain, Peru, Africa, Goa, Brazil, and Japan. In these scenarios, the question under scrutiny was ultimately who could become an agent of the empire—a question connected to ideas about the nature of non-European peoples. These discussions infantilized Indigenous people and were often accompanied by allusions to their low spiritual nature, their stupidity, and even their darker skin. In two very similar decrees of 1576 and 1578, Philip II forbade the audiencia and the bishop from naming mestizos as either caciques or clerics, but Zapata completely ignored the king's prohibition and reproofs and continued to ordain mestizos as priests.[35]

In an environment that was increasingly hostile toward mestizos, Zapata justified this move by arguing that they would be able to preach more effectively due to their mastery of Indigenous languages. Just as in the case of Don Diego de la Torre, the debate focused on the role mestizos should play in the mediation of the empire. In Torre's case, audiencia officials saw his command of the empire's legal system as a threat and banned him from serving as cacique—a decision that was later backed by the king. To Zapata, those same traits made mestizos ideal clerics: their mastery of Native languages would allow them to preach more effectively to Native peoples. Furthermore, drawing mestizos into clerical roles was the only feasible way to strengthen the secular clergy and redirect the evangelization project.

Presumptions about the people classified as mestizos made their place in the empire a matter of significant controversy. During Don Diego de la Torre's life, "mestizo" emerged as a social category that provoked anxieties and mixed reactions. Due to the bicultural background of most individuals classified as mestizos, they could work effectively as mediators and bring the empire's institutions to Native communities. As cultural brokers, they became central mediating figures. Alonso de Silva, for instance, faced no resistance to serving as a scribe for the audiencia. Other mestizos found occupations in the borderlands, fighting the Pijaos or Carares, or as part of the incursions to the eastern plains. Their skills were highly valued in such occupations, but the audiencia found them much more dangerous in positions that involved leading or preaching to Native communities. They acquired leverage and power and, for that reason, became a potential threat. Other individuals—such as ladinos and lenguas (interpreters)—caused the same kind of reaction among imperial officials and settlers. Thus, imperial administrators saw the political activity of mediators between Indigenous communities and imperial institutions as a site of concern, where potential disruptions and fractures to Spanish rule could emerge.

In Search of Justice

Prohibited from returning to Turmequé and with his houses and palisades burned to the ground, Don Diego de la Torre felt the weight of being labeled a dangerous mestizo by audiencia magistrates, and decided to make a bid for the monarch's attention. He sought his community's support to embark on a journey to Philip II's court in Madrid. According to Ulises Rojas, the Native people of Turmequé built a new palisade for him in Chiramita (today Chiratá), where he gathered the community to communicate his travel plans and his intention to reclaim his right to the cacicazgo and fight for their rights. Torre held his baton (macana) firmly in his hands and stuck it forcefully in the middle of the field.[36] It was an act of authority, a material sign that would stand as a reminder of his presence while he was away. The community gave him the support he needed and provided the resources necessary to finance his trip, mainly in emeralds and gold, which he would use to pay for passage on transatlantic ships, food, and accommodation while away. This support again revealed that the people of Turmequé saw litigation in Spanish courts as an effective political mechanism and thought it worthwhile to pursue Torre's representation in the empire's highest justice court: the king's court.

By seeking royal favor against local authorities, Torre's actions again resonate with the parallel struggles of mestizo clerics. In particular, Torre's story resembles the case of Gonzalo García Zorro, a legitimate son of a conquistador and an Indigenous woman from Tunja who occupied a prominent role among the kingdom's elites. In 1578, García Zorro successfully pleaded for a position in the cathedral chapter (cabildo) of Santa Fe and became not only the first mestizo canon of the kingdom but also one of the first in the empire.[37] The Council of the Indies named García Zorro to this position, yet the local ecclesiastic administration refused to recognize him as canon because he was mestizo. At this time of creation of and debate about new models of subjecthood, the actions of people like Diego de la Torre or Gonzalo García Zorro could destabilize colonial stereotypes but could not eliminate them completely. While Zapata had no problem advocating for mestizo clerics, he did not expect them to ascend the Church hierarchy or gain influence. Therefore, Zapata opposed García's appointment as canon. Like Don Diego, García was jailed—though in an ecclesiastic jail, from which he fled and attempted to travel to Madrid to seek the king's support. However, the aligned forces of the audiencia magistrates and archbishop caught García on the way and he never reached the court.[38]

For Don Diego de la Torre to stand before the king, he would have to avoid the audiencia's roadblocks. It would be a long trip, full of mishaps. He left with two Native guides from Tibasosa. Juan Navarro, a mestizo from Tunja who had already been to Spain, came along as well. In August 1575, Torre set out on his way through the Carare region. When he was in Tamalameque, an Indigenous messenger sent by Alonso de Silva alerted him that the audiencia had ordered the authorities to jail him. They had no intention of allowing him to reach the king's court. Torre changed his route to avoid capture, taking a lesser-known path through Valle de Upar to Rio de la Hacha. Reaching Cartagena, he hid there for two weeks while Navarro found passage for both of them on a ship that did not belong to the authorities. Torre and Navarro finally boarded a ship to Havana, but as they passed through the Caribbean a storm nearly destroyed the ship. Torre ended up in Haiti and then traveled to Hispaniola, where he spent eight months. In Santo Domingo he met Gregorio González de Cuenca—the president of the Audiencia of Santo Domingo—and gained his trust. There he was able to study the books of royal decrees for the New Kingdom of Granada, Peru, and Mexico. González de la Cuenca sent Don Diego to Spain entrusted with private correspondence for the Council of the Indies. He arrived in Seville, where he stayed only a few days before continuing his journey to Madrid. After two long years of navigating the Atlantic, Don Diego finally arrived at his destination in 1577.[39]

Torre later wrote that his voyage to Spain and especially his two-year stay in the Antilles were crucial in convincing him of the need to plead for the well-being of the kingdom's Native peoples.[40] Torre had come a long way since he was first appointed cacique. His legal battles with his half-brother and the Audiencia of Santa Fe had taken him on an Atlantic journey that positioned him to voice his concerns in a new venue—the monarchical court of the largest empire of the day. A new phase of struggle began, one centered on a larger and deeper legal agenda pertaining to the essence of the kingdom: the interactions between Native peoples and Europeans. The next chapter examines how Torre developed a voice, a language, and a perspective from which to address the king—and how this rhetorical strategy reshaped the kingdom's politics.

6

AN INDIGENOUS INTELLECTUAL IN KING PHILIP'S COURT

When the audiencia magistrates heard that Don Diego de la Torre was on his way to Madrid, they scrambled to recall the legal documents relating to his removal as cacique, which were already on their way to the king's court. This was a savvy legal tactic aimed at disarming Torre and disrupting his strategy at the king's court: after all, if Torre did not have the case files when he arrived in Madrid, he would not be able to ask the Council of the Indies to review them. Torre first learned about this move in a letter from his friend Don Alonso de Silva, the mestizo cacique of Tibasosa, and he immediately informed the officials in Madrid, probably hoping to pursue his lawsuit at the king's court in spite of this setback.[1]

However, the files never arrived. This practical problem forced a change in Torre's agenda. Without the files, he could not present to the king the issue that affected him directly—his removal from the cacicazgo—so he opted instead to inform the monarch about irregularities in the kingdom's administration more generally. Since no one at court doubted his legitimacy as cacique, Torre ignored the audiencia's ruling as well as the royal decree deposing him, as if they had never happened. At court, he called himself "cacique of the peoples of Turmequé" and informed the king and the council of the many injustices of local governance. Like other Indigenous transatlantic travelers, journeying to the royal court gave Don Diego the opportunity to reinvent himself: to break away from the "dangerous mestizo" stereotype and present himself as Indigenous nobility.[2]

Torre had fled the kingdom for Madrid hoping to be reinstated as cacique of Turmequé, but during his travels and while at court his aims and strategy shifted. He developed an ambitious narrative that aimed to transform power relations in the kingdom, especially among commoners, Indigenous nobility, imperial officials, and European settlers, and which delineated a new political project for the kingdom. This chapter explores Torre's political vision and practice by closely following the records he left in archives on both sides of the Atlantic. Through a careful juxtaposition of Hispanic law and political theory, Torre conveyed a message of renovation: Indigenous peoples were free vassals of the king, protected by law, who lived faithfully as Christian subjects; however, settlers and imperial officials were harming them. To him, Indigenous nobles were the only officials loyal to the king. I argue that between the lines of Torre's writings lay a new blueprint for the kingdom, one that gave Indigenous authorities control over local affairs and upheld the free status of Indigenous vassals. Torre communicated this project to the king and the Muisca peoples in their own media and communication frameworks, initiating a snowballing political phenomenon that quickly rolled out of his control and took on a life of its own. The king initiated legal procedures to inspect the audiencia, ultimately demoting all the magistrates and setting off a wave of reform. In contrast, the Muisca interpreted Torre's return from Spain by reinvigorating Muisca political categories that had not been used for Indigenous leaders since the conquest, such as "cipa" and "hoa." In this sense, Torre's project shaped a particular kind of Andean utopia, oscillating between Spanish bureaucratic procedure and Muisca political frameworks: a return of the cipa in a time when Muisca political thought was enmeshed with Spanish politics.[3]

During his time at court, Don Diego wrote many letters to the king and the Council of the Indies. He addressed representatives of the Crown in both text and images in which he deployed a wide array of genres, and he left behind the largest archival record of any Indigenous person of the northern Andes.[4] Simultaneously, however, Torre's contemporaries framed him as a seditious mestizo. In the years between his first meeting with the king around 1578 and his death in 1589, Torre was accused of leading a rebel army of mestizos against the kingdom, inviting Indigenous peoples to disobey their encomenderos and audiencia officials, and asking them to call him "child of the sun" (hijo del sol) and pay him tribute. For this reason, Torre's political project is muddled by diverging accounts. While his opponents claimed that he was plotting a rebellion to overthrow the Spanish monarchy, Torre argued that he was a loyal Spanish vassal. Here I have tried to avoid taking his word for granted, assuming that his testimonies were a clear reflection of his beliefs or his identity, or assuming that his opponents' words were merely false accusations intended to harm him. Such a position would do a disservice to the savviness of Torre's legal tactics. It would assume that he articulated his intentions without guile, that he was transparent in his claims, and that all testimonies against him were mere inventions. Instead, I propose that Don Diego moved proficiently in a world of linguistic and cultural difference, and that he was skilled and strategic in his communications.

As a bicultural intellectual, Don Diego de la Torre addressed imperial authorities and Native peoples in their own registers. He carefully crafted his legal claims with a deep awareness of transatlantic discussions about justice and the legitimacy of the Spanish empire in the New World. When he addressed Native peoples, he did so through Indigenous media and Native networks. Like Felipe Guamán Poma de Ayala, the renowned Peruvian author of *Nueva crónica y buen gobierno*, Torre wrote to the king with concerns about problems unleashed by the Spanish empire in his local area. Unlike Poma, he did not mix an Andean perspective into his writing. In this sense, he was a different kind of Indigenous intellectual: he separated registers of cultural communication.[5]

Unfortunately, we have only a record of Torre's communications with imperial authorities and lack direct evidence of how he interacted with Native peoples. But careful analysis of the archival traces of his interactions with Indigenous groups reveal that his message was remarkably coherent. Through a close look at the testimonies of Native people, mestizos, and Spaniards included in his legal files in Bogotá and Seville, analysis of their descriptions of Torre and his interactions with Native peoples, and careful examination of his own texts, Torre's political project begins to take shape. Torre tried to transform the social and political structure of the New Kingdom of Granada, but he strove to do so using the Spanish empire's legal pathways. He offered a radical reading of the New Laws in which Native peoples would be treated as free vassals of the Crown and the Native nobility would be given preeminence. He did not plan a rebellion against the king, but his vision and ideas about how the kingdom should work were revolutionary in the context of the sixteenth-century New Kingdom—perhaps even more so because they were rooted in his reading of the empire's own political principles.

Torre's political program rocked the kingdom. The decades between 1570 and 1590 were a political mess. In addition to the Pijaos' expanding coalition, administrative chaos overtook the Audiencia of Santa Fe. Charges of corruption and conflict among imperial officials became routine. In the span of a decade, the king appointed two high chancellors as visitadores to try to figure out what was happening, and the audiencia jailed one of them. The audiencia, the entity that the king established to serve as his ears and his image, had gone awry. In this context of crisis, an Indigenous cacique traveled to Spain to address the king, armed with pen and paper and quoting the New Laws and other royal ordinances according to his readings of the theory and practice of empire. His visit unleashed a substantial reform of the kingdom's institutions. In response to his requests, the king replaced all of the audiencia magistrates, thus setting the stage for a new phase in the kingdom's history.

This sequence of events is so complicated that it is worth outlining from the outset. Don Diego arrived at the king's court for the first time in 1577 and eventually met with the monarch, though the precise date of this meeting is unknown. In 1579, Don Diego traveled back to the New Kingdom of Granada with visitador Juan Bautista Monzón, the most senior magistrate of the Audiencia of Lima, who was commissioned to inspect the audiencia. As Torre traveled, the rumor of his return caused turmoil; the audiencia magistrates imprisoned him in April 1580, just after his arrival. A few weeks later, however, his half brother, Pedro de Torres, asked the audiencia to temporarily release Don Diego to appease the community of Turmequé, who had fled to the páramos (moors). By this point, Don Diego and Pedro had reconciled. Don Diego soothed his community and, convinced that Monzón would bring change, returned to prison after ten days. Pedro was jailed soon after as well. Feeling pressure from Monzón, who was already charging magistrates with crimes, audiencia officials and encomenderos began plotting against him and defying his orders—a bold move that put the audiencia in clear violation of imperial hierarchies of power. Facing such opposition, in October 1580, Monzón decided to send Don Diego to the king's court to personally report the situation to Philip II and deliver secret information. But an even more emboldened audiencia tracked down Don Diego as he traveled down the Magdalena River and once again imprisoned him, in November 1580. In February 1581, after an arduous imprisonment, in which the prison burned down, nearly killing him, Don Diego fled to the páramos, from where he corresponded in code with fellow mestizos, asking them to prepare to fight in case Monzón called them to arms.

Now in outright sedition, the audiencia imprisoned Monzón in September 1581, and retained secret correspondence sent to him by the king, while the archbishop excommunicated Monzón. In January 1582, Philip II responded by removing the audiencia magistrates and naming Juan Prieto de Orellana as visitador. As such, he would be responsible for finishing Monzón's inspection. Prieto de Orellana took care to study both the charges against the magistrates and those against Monzón and Don Diego. For this reason, he dispatched Don Diego's case to Spain, and off Don Diego went once again to the king's court, this time to be tried for sedition. During this second stretch at court, Don Diego prepared some of his most moving writings and images, some of which he presented in person to the king. This moment marked the peak of his intellectual production. Meanwhile, Prieto de Orellana produced thousands of pages of research about the complicated events of the kingdom, which included the voices of many witnesses.

This chapter offers an intimate analysis of Don Diego's intellectual and political projects and the turmoil they caused, revealing how his political project transcended his own expectations and he came to be seen by many Indigenous peoples as a new cipa, restituting a precolonial political category to envision a new kind of authority, and by others as a threat to the stability of the kingdom. For this reason, in the sections that follow I piece together documents from different time frames, especially those produced during Prieto de Orellana's visit to the kingdom and during Don Diego's second visit to Madrid, to clarify his rhetorical strategy and the impact he made on Indigenous commoners and authorities, European settlers, and the king.

Addressing the King

Since first arriving at the king's court in 1577, Don Diego had prepared a series of petitions and letters that aimed to attract the attention of Philip II and his staff. He did so after a revealing journey through the Caribbean and in a context in which he could access important volumes in the royal library, like the books of royal ordinances sent by the king and the Council of the Indies to the audiencias. In this context, his writing was injected with emotion and aimed to call attention to the contrast between imperial legislation and the situation of the New Kingdom's Indigenous peoples.

These elements of Torre's narrative are most visible in the documents he prepared for the king and the Council of the Indies during his second trip to Spain in 1584, which built upon the documents he wrote during his first visit to the court and should therefore be considered a continuation of, rather than a break with, his early writing. His most important and renowned writing is the *Relation about the Grievances Done to the Natives* [Naturales] *of the New Kingdom of Granada* (hereafter *Relation*), commonly referred to as the *Memorial de agravios*.[6] The account is organized into bullet points enumerating twenty-two ills that affected the good government of the kingdom, and it includes two maps. The *Relation* is the most complete surviving account of Don Diego de la Torre's vision of the kingdom and how he thought its governance should be transformed.

The *Relation* criticizes two pillars of the kingdom: the tribute system and the evangelization project. Adhering to blood purity discourses, Torre denounced many encomenderos as being not of noble origin but rather people of "low blood," which made them unworthy of encomiendas. He claimed that the encomenderos treated Indigenous people like slaves. Some encomiendas, called royal encomiendas, were titled to the King himself and were administered by the staff of the audiencia. Torre argued that the conditions under the royal encomiendas were even harsher than those under the conquistadors' descendants, due to the corruption of imperial officials. He also described how Indigenous women were forced to abandon their own children to breastfeed Spanish children, how imperial bureaucracies placed untenable labor demands on Indigenous people, and how corrupt local governors avoided prosecuting crimes committed against Indigenous subjects.[7] These were just some of the most common recurring themes of the twenty-two points included in his account.

Four elements structure Torre's rhetoric: an emphasis on the gap between law and practice, a consistent depiction of Indigenous peoples, the use of a highly emotional vocabulary, and a critical perspective on most of the kingdom's imperial agents. In each bullet point, Torre followed a similar pattern of expression. He evoked the New Laws and imperial theories of good government, and then contrasted them with the kingdom's harsh realities. These points are lengthy and, therefore, difficult to quote in their entirety. In one of them, he argued that despite the king's ruling lowering tribute rates below pre-conquest levels—the broad aim being that Indigenous peoples receive the Catholic faith with "love"—Indigenous peoples were paying tributes in excess. Consider an extract:

> His Majesty has ordered and commanded that the Natives [naturales] must pay tributes to their encomenderos in ways in which they receive no harm, so that they understand that after they came under your royal embrace and government they are better treated than they were in the times of their cacique lords, so they more lovingly receive the aspects of our sacred Catholic faith, yet this has not been performed according to your royal intention in the visitations and rates done to date to determine what they need to give and tribute, instead the wretched indios

have been greatly harmed and deceived . . . since the poor Natives [na-turales] do not know how to express the harm and deceit done to them, they lack remedy, and if an unfortunate leader [principal] of theirs has moved to claim redress, they [the encomenderos] have destroyed and devastated him, for which reason they suffer like wretched people and mute sheep.[8]

Torre went on to argue that although the laws stated that tribute should be paid in goods that Indigenous people could produce on their own lands, the two products paid in the highlands—mantas and gold—came from the lowlands.[9]

In a harsher tone, he stressed that despite the New Laws' proclamation that Indigenous peoples should be "treated as free people, as they are," they were treated as commodities in practice.[10] After contrasting the ideal image of the kingdom as laid out in the king's laws with on-the-ground realities, Torre issued a call to action. Following a common Christian line of reasoning, he reminded the king that his royal conscience was "burdened" by the mistreatment of his Indigenous vassals, and that addressing these issues would help unburden it. In this way, Torre repeated a Christian rhetorical expression employed by many others beseeching the monarch to take steps to remedy situations they deemed problematic.

Torre's call to action was tied to the rhetorical construction of the "indio." Torre alluded to Native peoples by employing the "wretched indios" formula, describing them as well-meaning but vulnerable vassals who needed the king's protection, as blind and mute sheep waiting for a good shepherd. He often grouped himself under that label—"we the wretched" (nos los miserables). Imperial tropes are so dominant in Torre's narrative that they often give the sense that he was writing not about the Muiscas, Guanes, Uwas, or other ethnic groups of the kingdom but about a generic type of "indio." He includes no ethnographic detail and says nothing about their history, customs, kin structure, or ways of life. Furthermore, there was no place in Torre's narrative for the powerful and sovereign Pijaos, the Carares, or any other group that questioned the king's rule or persecuted Christian subjects. The people of Torre's own cacicazgo had reacted in myriad ways to Iberian rule: fighting, fleeing to the moors, and using Hispanic courts for their own ends, as we saw in chapter 5. Yet in the *Relation*, "indio" was a passive category of good and loyal vassals, "as loyal as any native from Castile." In the text, descriptions of Indigenous peoples coincide with the images and expectations articulated by the New Laws and Spanish theories of empire—and, since he was making a legal argument, his descriptions were apt for his goals.

The concepts of "freedom" and "wretchedness" were key to Torre's rhetoric. Don Diego used them to make his central argument: that Native peoples, who were free vassals of the king, were being exploited and the monarch had the moral obligation to act. He included an emotional language, using words like *love, freedom, suffering, corruption, diabolical cruelty, justice,* and *enslavement.* These concepts helped him emphasize the monarch's responsibility to protect the "indios" as a special category of vassals. Indigenous peoples were endangered victims who would soon perish because of the many harms Europeans caused them. Torre emphasized that they would be annihilated, with terrible consequences for His Majesty's patrimony. Not only would his conscience be burdened, but such an outcome would be detrimental to the king's material wealth.

The last pillar of Torre's argument identified the flaws of imperial institutions and bureaucrats. He argued repeatedly that the local administration was corrupt, that its agents took valuables from Native peoples without reporting them to the king and, thus, without paying the royal fifth, and that it acted with extreme cruelty toward Native peoples. There were multitudes of useless and dispensable local officials (gobernador, contador, tesorero, corregidor, etc.), who all took hefty salaries from the wealth generated by Indigenous communities. In Don Diego's descriptions, the audiencia's magistrates were corrupt and thrived from violence against the Indigenous people. In their short time spent visiting encomiendas, visitadores were unable to grasp the complexity of local relations. The conditions Indigenous vassals experienced at the encomenderos' hands were bad, but they were even worse in royal encomiendas, due to the inefficient and corrupt staff administering them. Torre only favored one post: the *protector de naturales,* or protector of the Natives.

In the hostile administrative context Torre described, only one class of vassal was unfailingly loyal and reliable: caciques and other Native authorities. He argued that these local Indigenous nobles should play a more central role in imperial administration. They were the only ones who could communicate effectively with Native peoples and took an interest in their well-being. Don Diego claimed that the king should honor them as local nobility (nobles de la tierra).[11] But instead they were humiliated by corrupt audiencia magistrates.

Reading between the lines, the matter boiled down to which officials should mediate between the empire and Indigenous communities. As he argued vigorously against visitadores, encomenderos, magistrates, and corregidores—and instead highlighted Native nobles—Torre described a kingdom in which Native nobles protected Indigenous vassals. He envisioned a kingdom that would prioritize Native peoples' welfare, one in which they would be treated as free people without the burden of coercive labor. Since Don Diego believed that the visitadores, corregidores, and audiencia magistrates were unable to create and maintain such a state of affairs, it was the local nobility's duty to report any wrongdoing to the king.

Don Diego attached two maps to his *Relation*, which followed the same narrative thread but in a visual format (figures 6.1 and 6.2). One map depicted the Province of Santa Fe, the other the Province of Tunja. At the center of each one stood the provincial capital, Santa Fe and Tunja respectively, surrounded by Indigenous villages represented by icons of chapels, which indicated that Indigenous peoples were true Christians. On the Magdalena River, Torre drew canoes paddling upriver from Cartagena to Vélez—the nearest port to the city of Santa Fe at the time—by Native peoples; this boga system, with its devastatingly harsh tasks, had long been controversial. As a side note, Don Diego wrote: "In this river there was an infinity of indios, all of which have been consumed in the cruel *boga* in such a way that from fifty-thousand indios there are none left."

Torre's maps adapted the geographies of the kingdom to the empire's visual regimes. In this sense, the lines, icons, and texts composed a reading of landscapes and peoples that predicted how the king would read the territory. There was no place on the map for the Carares or Pijaos, who were devouring the kingdom along the Magdalena River and in the mountains toward Peru. Nor was there a place for the people who had fled to the páramo or set fire to the church after the first efforts to settle Indigenous communities into Christian villages. Instead, Torre depicted the kingdom appropriating the symbols of the reducciones, the Indigenous villages where "indios" lived as true Christians. He also included distances, roads, rivers, toponyms, water supplies, and other elements that the king's cosmographer asked about in the questionnaires it circulated to local officials globally about geography, as part of a far-reaching knowledge collection enterprise known as Geographic Relations of the Indies between 1569 and 1577.[12] In essence, the maps revealed how Torre tailored the territory to the eye of the recipient, the king.

Torre's discourse was rooted in Iberian theological and juridical discussions, but it differed strongly from the ideas promoted by others, such as Tomás López (chapter 2). While López was disheartened by the violence of the kingdom's institutions, he believed that it was all for the good of Native peoples, who would eventually be brought to the Catholic faith and taught to live in a godly manner. To him, restoration meant correcting the wrongs of the encomenderos and settlers by directing all energy toward evangelization, but he did not advocate for structural change. By contrast, Juan del Valle and

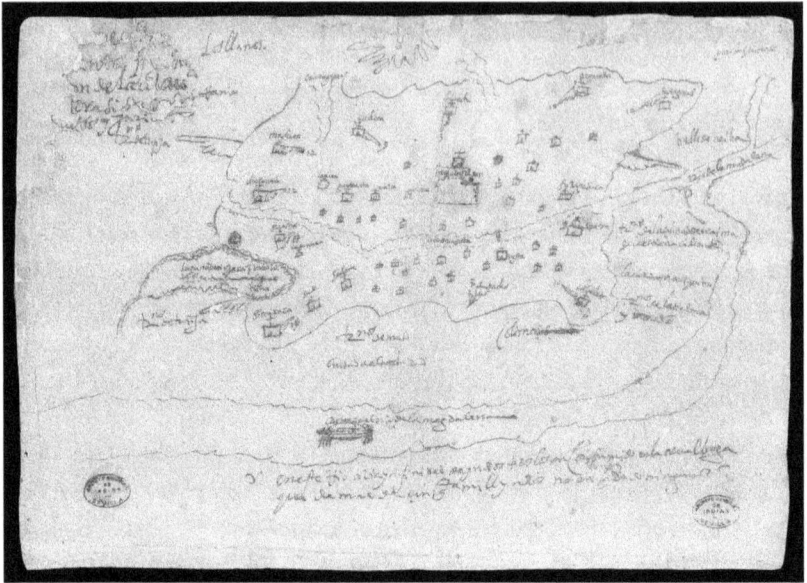

FIGURE 6.1. Province of Santa Fe, in the New Kingdom of Granada, by Don Diego de la Torre, 1584. AGI, Mapas y planos Panamá, Santa Fe y Quito, 8.

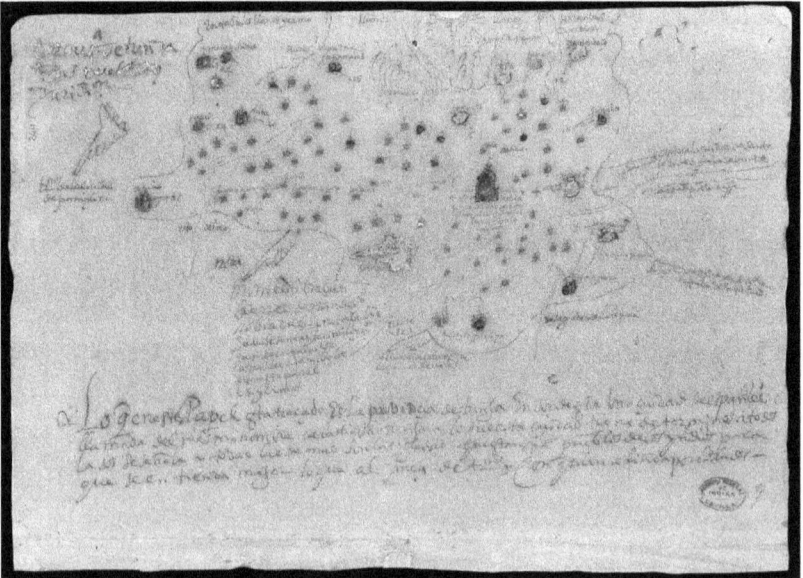

FIGURE 6.2. Province of Tunja, in the New Kingdom of Granada, by Don Diego de la Torre, 1584. AGI, Mapas y planos Panamá, Santa Fe y Quito, 7.

Bartolomé de las Casas had abandoned the idea of a right of conquest altogether, believing that there was no way to rectify the devastation that Spain had wrought in the New World.[13]

In contrast to these Spanish writers, Don Diego neither challenged the empire's right to rule nor placed strong emphasis on evangelization. He took a pragmatic approach by reinforcing the notion that Native peoples were free vassals of the Crown and that they were near extinction. To Torre, the monarch's conscience was burdened, and to relieve this burden the monarch had to ensure that the legislation protecting Native peoples was enforced, so that they would be treated as free people. By using imperial legislation to make this case, Torre simultaneously sought to change the power dynamics at the level of the audiencia, to challenge the power of the encomenderos, and to reenvision the colonial tribute economy. It was an ambitious goal that placed a great deal of emphasis on the transformative power of the king himself. Arguing in favor of imperial laws was a radical idea in a place like the New Kingdom. For that reason, Don Diego focused more on correctly applying legal formulas than on presenting evidence of what was happening on the ground. Torre's position on evangelization offers an example of this.

Faking Idols

Torre's reaction to evangelization was directed against the aggressive program advanced by archbishop Fray Luis Zapata de Cárdenas since 1574. As examined in the previous chapter, Zapata outlined a minute set of evangelization instructions with the intent of radically altering Indigenous lifestyles. To do so, he built up a large workforce of mestizo, creole, and Spanish clerics that depended directly on the secular Church. A couple of years after his arrival, Zapata remained frustrated by the lack of results. In a letter to the king, he expressed his concern for the "spiritual health of my sheep, the indios." He went on: "After visiting and gathering information about the natural indios of this kingdom, I have found that the biggest impediment for the conversion of the unfaithful is that, once the indios are made Christian, they return to their infidelities." He insisted that this was because they did not believe in a single God who was responsible for the creation of all things. Instead, they thought that the things of the world were created by their false gods, whom they also held responsible for their health and sickness.[14]

In Zapata's view, Indigenous peoples were violating the natural law in their rites and ceremonies by honoring human figures and idols made of wood and cotton, adorned with gold and emeralds and perfumed with incense (moque), while church buildings lacked ornaments and were falling down. He argued that punishment and surveillance were required to make Native peoples understand that once they received baptism and converted to Christianity, they must cease activities offensive to God, and that he, "as the person in charge of knowing and punishing all the heresies and idolatries against the Church," would do whatever was necessary to ensure this outcome.

Zapata expressed a feeling common among Catholic officials engaged in evangelization, who were stunned, were frustrated, and felt deceived when they learned that Native peoples often continued their ritual practices even after receiving some Catholic education.[15] After consulting with "people of science and conscience," as well as the president and magistrates of the audiencia, the archbishop opted for a more aggressive approach to shock Native peoples into rethinking their beliefs. He determined that the best way to spread God's message was to destroy all Native sacred objects, to confiscate gold and emeralds from Indigenous peoples, and to use these resources instead to build and decorate churches once the king's royal fifth had been paid.

The events that followed Zapata's proposal looked more like pillage than like a theologically centered anti-idolatry campaign, such as those that took place in seventeenth-century Peru.[16] The Audiencia of Santa Fe appointed two magistrates to lead this campaign and notified the archbishop to appoint a Church representative. Ostensibly worried that deceitful and corrupt audiencia magistrates would hide the real earnings of the campaign from him, Zapata chose an accountant, Domingues de Espejo, to fill the position. In May 1577, the two magistrates, an audiencia accountant, and the Church accountant left for the Indigenous villages of Bogotá and Fontibón to launch the campaign. The four officials produced documents that illuminate the nature of their activities. In both villages, a procession of Native authorities met the officials and forfeited jewelry, human-shaped figures, and many other valuable items. In entry after entry, the officials described the items and assigned their value in pesos and tomines. Their report followed the format of tribute accounts meant to calculate revenue, rather than adhering to the format of a theological investigation. The report reveals financial motivation, rather than an inquisitive or rigorous inspection of Native religious practices. It was plunder, not a deep investigation of Native thought.[17]

Juan Prieto de Orellana's 1583 visita provides a vivid picture of these inspections. Indigenous vassals testified to the violence of the campaign. Witnesses from all over the Province of Tunja stated that they had been brutally tortured. They said the commissioners had beaten many caciques, including those of Busbanza and Cormechoque, and had then tied a rope around their testicles and pulled. In some cases, the commissioners hung the rope from the ceiling and threatened to hang their victims by their testicles, or tied the same rope to a horse before setting it loose. These tactics were intended to frighten the caciques who had not produced any "idols" into accepting the charges and delivering any golden items to the joint commission of the archbishop and the audiencia. Even the campaign's interpreter, the ladino Luisillo, demanded that the caciques give him painted mantas, threatening to tell officials that they were hiding treasures if they refused. News of these punishments spread swiftly across the cold lands, terrifying Indigenous authorities.[18] The caciques later testified that in order to avoid the officials' rage, they had found as much gold as they could, melted it into saint-like figures (santillos), and then surrendered the figures to the commission. They purposely produced the "idols" the campaign expected to find in order to surrender them to the commission. However, this tactic of producing fakes in order to avoid torture was not always successful, as officials requested even more figures.

The news of these violent inspections must have reached Don Diego de la Torre through letters from his allies in the kingdom. What we know for certain is that they became a critical part of his discourse at court. Yet Torre denounced the inspections from a particular angle, which once again demonstrates how he structured his narrative strategically to make his case before the king. Instead of triggering a theological debate about whether Zapata's violent approach to evangelization was appropriate, he opted for a practical lens that was more likely to earn the monarch's support: Torre argued that imperial officials were hiding their true earnings from the king and thus withholding his portion. In choosing this optic, he presented the campaigns not only as an aggression against Native peoples but also as an offense to the Crown. From surviving documents, it is not completely clear whether Torre's claim was factually accurate. What we do know is that the commission's reports were simply itemized descriptions of confiscated goods, since Zapata had strategically chosen an accountant to represent the Church on the commission. His utmost concern was that Crown officials did not defraud the Church of its earnings. Accurate or not, Torre chose the angle he thought would more effectively catch the monarch's attention.

A Triumphant Return

The fact that Torre stylized his letters to fit within broader imperial genres made them extremely effective. After Torre presented his narrative to the king and the councilors, Philip II sent him back to the New Kingdom with an inspector who would assess the situation: visitador Juan Bautista Monzón, a magistrate in Lima. Unlike many visitadores, Monzón's main task was to inquire about the Audiencia of Santa Fe, rather than to count the Native population and establish rates of tribute. The king instructed Monzón to find out how the president, magistrates, prosecutor, and other officials performed in their posts; if they abided by the laws and applied the ordinances of the king and his ancestors, especially in matters of conversion and the good treatment of Native peoples; if they had dealt correctly with judicial cases; and if they kept strict records for the treasury and had always taken care to separate out the king's portion. The king commanded the president, magistrates, prosecutor, and other officials of the audiencia to respond promptly to the visitador's calls, answer his questions, and submit to the penalties he imposed. After his inquiries, the visitador was to send the documents back to the Council of the Indies so its members could redirect policy accordingly.[19]

Monzón's visita offers striking evidence that Torre's narrative influenced Philip II's thinking and led him to take action—a chain of events that is exceptional in the history of the Spanish empire. In a study of a hundred or so Indigenous people who traveled from the viceroyalty of Peru to the Royal Court in Madrid during the sixteenth and seventeenth centuries, historian José Carlos de la Puente found that in only a few exceptional cases did the council commission local judges and inspectors to inquire and send reports directly to Spain for resolution.[20] Such cases were generally neglected and brought little actual change. Torre's case was different. The king personally commented on the documents that Torre gave him. Most importantly, Philip II sent him back to the New World with a visitador whose authority surpassed that of every level of government in the New Kingdom. This was a remarkable, unprecedented accomplishment.

In addition, it is possible that Torre's writing and performance at court influenced the monarch's ideas about mestizos in general. As shown in the previous chapter, the ordination of mestizos as clerics had been controversial in the kingdom. On this issue, Philip II had sided with the Audiencia of Santa Fe from the start. Whenever he received a letter informing him of new mestizos ordained as friars, the king wrote to the archbishop reprimanding him and saying he should not ordain mestizos as clerics under any circumstances.[21] But for some reason, while Torre was in Madrid, Philip II changed his mind. When he received complaints from audiencia magistrates about the new appointments of mestizo clerics in 1579, the king remained silent. It seems possible that Torre's talent with the written word, his mastery of imperial rhetoric, and his prudence and rectitude had complicated the king's ideas about mestizos. And perhaps Torre's complaints against the audiencia led the king to distrust the information he received from the magistrates and the archbishop.

In April 1579, Torre traveled back to the kingdom, feeling both successful and cautious. He knew that, even with a visitador at his side, the powerful local governing networks of Santa Fe would resist change. But penetrating the audiencia's power struggles would be more difficult than Torre could foresee, the events to come more frustrating than he anticipated. While Torre was in Madrid, the audiencia wrote to the king asking that Torre be held there and prevented from returning to the kingdom. They wrote on February 16, 1577:

> There is at the court a mestizo from this kingdom called Don Diego de Torres from Turmequé, one of the mestizos that His Majesty ordered to pull from his post as cacique. In other letters we have informed His Majesty of his life and customs, and it is convenient that under no circumstance he be authorized to come back to these parts. We have opted to write again, since we have now heard that he has written letters to the Indigenous caciques, especially to the cacique of Bogotá, the head of all the indios, naming himself the "lord of the deep lands of Turmequé" and promising them freedom and other vanities. With the trust they have in him, if he were to return to these lands he could hide deep in the plains, where he could get together with the indios and mestizos of the kingdom in a way that it would be difficult to remedy, due to the size of the land.[22]

It was clear that the magistrates saw Torre as a threat to their power and preferred that he stay in Iberia. "In no way should he be allowed to pass to these parts," they reiterated, "since he is very able with weapons and horses, and as he has bad habits and is an accomplice of the indios knowing their language and being of their nation."[23] If Torre and his bicultural skills had been sufficiently threatening to justify removing him from the cacicazgo, he posed an even greater threat after visiting Madrid and meeting with the king. The magistrates foresaw that his return would inspire various reactions among Native peoples and would most certainly challenge their authority by aligning the interests of the king with those of the kingdom's Indigenous population.

A Child of the Sun

The indios of this kingdom are unruly, they do not want to pay their tributes, to recognize the authority of their encomenderos, or to follow Your Majesty's commands. Some have published that Don Diego, the mestizo, is their king and some others that he is the son of the sun, and that they will only obey him.

—MIGUEL DE OROZCO, 1580

Upon his return to South America in 1579, Torre prepared for a new challenge: to bring the news of his meeting with the king to the kingdom and especially to

Indigenous communities without alarming the Audiencia of Santa Fe and the encomenderos. Torre's messages had already intimidated the audiencia magistrates, who accused him of sending letters to Native caciques from Madrid. In Cartagena, Torre and Monzón took separate roads to circumvent opposition from imperial officials and to avoid suspicion that they acted together. Torre stopped in Tolú, Ocaña, Pamplona, Soatá, Sogamoso, and Duitama, where he stayed with local caciques and spoke with them. Rumors of Torre's return to South America spread almost immediately—the news reached the Andes before he did. By the time he got to the highlands, many caciques were aware of his arrival and sent messengers asking him to visit their communities on his way back to Turmequé. They all wanted to hear about Torre's visit to Castile and his interview with the monarch.

Torre's return provoked great suspicion among imperial officials, as witnesses later testified to visitador Juan Prieto de Orellana in his 1583 investigation. Prosecutor Miguel de Orozco accused Torre of agitating the Indigenous vassals during his journey by telling them about his meeting with the king. In a strange fabrication, Orozco claimed that Torre had bragged about his relationship with Philip II, telling the commoners that when he had knelt to kiss the king's hands, Philip II told him to stand up, indicating that the king wanted him to "rise with the kingdom."[24] Orozco also claimed that Torre told the Indigenous vassals that he had come to free them, that they should stop paying tribute, and to ignore any demands that did not come directly from him. Not only had Native peoples stopped paying tribute, Orozco stated, but they also stopped obeying the encomenderos and royal officials. He went on to say that although the audiencia had removed Torre from his cacicazgo and banned him from entering Turmequé, he was living in his old cacicazgo and had persuaded the commoners to recognize him as their cacique, to give him mantas, and to plant his fields—in other words, to treat him like a cacique.

Orozco furthermore accused Torre of underhanded political maneuvering and of convincing the Native peoples beyond Turmequé that he was their lord (señor absoluto) and that they owed their loyalty and obedience to him alone. Orozco claimed that Torre had restored the long-extinct Muisca political concept of "hoa"—the term *hoa* meant "son of the sun" and "king, lord, and cacique of all the land"—since many commoners and even caciques had started using *hoa* to refer to Don Diego. According to Orozco, Torre had assumed the authority to name and remove caciques as he pleased and had instituted a new tribute system through which he received goods from many Native communities. Caciques and commoners were excited and confused (alterados), Orozco claimed, and they spoke publicly of Torre as their king, the son of the sun, and the only master they obeyed.

It would be naïve to take the word of Orozco and the rest of Torre's adversaries at face value. Historians have commonly discarded these claims as utterly untrue, deliberate fabrications by imperial officials, and have dismissed all references to Torre's participation in Native rituals as fictitious. After all, his own writings suggest that Torre was more comfortable in Spanish environments than in Indigenous contexts. It is true that the authorities of the audiencia had an extraordinary capacity to produce legal fictions, and thus even the testimonies of commoners and mestizos recorded by imperial officials in cases connected to Torre must be read with caution. It is also true that prosecuting Torre was in the audiencia's interest, as he challenged the magistrates' authority, denounced them at the king's court, and jeopardized their position. Because of this, they aimed to contain his influence, whether removing him from his cacicazgo or jailing him, and they spared no effort in pursuit of this goal. But to dismiss all accusations as inventions is as problematic as reading the audiencia's paper trail as unmediated truth. It is highly unlikely that the audiencia forced every witness to testify against Torre. Moreover, many of the testimonies were recorded after 1582, during Juan Prieto de Orellana's visit, when most of the audiencia magistrates' power had faded.

The testimonies included in the audiencia's paperwork show that Torre's figure became fertile ground for different readings and interpretations; he was construed in different ways. The news that a Muisca cacique had met with the king stirred up latent social struggles and unleashed new forms of political imagination. The swirling discussions about Torre's return became sites of utopias and dystopias. Indigenous leaders and commoners projected new possibilities onto Torre's arrival; they saw it as an opportunity to rethink or even break free from some of the quotidian routines of colonialism. Imperial officials, on the other hand, saw him as a threat to the established order—even more so for having returned from Madrid. For this reason, it is difficult to access Torre's words and actions behind layers of rumor and expectation. Instead of finding Torre, we find many readings of him by others.

The testimonies do show, however, how Indigenous leaders and commoners made sense of Torre's return to the kingdom and how it afforded them an opportunity to reimagine their role in the empire. The witnesses included Muisca commoners and nobility, mulatos, ladinos, mestizos, friars, encomenderos, and other settlers. Each of them had a different degree of exposure to Torre's ideas and had learned about his return and its significance in different ways. For instance,

Rodrigo, the son of the cacique of Tibaná, was on his father's lands when he first heard the commoners talking about Torre's return from Spain. He set out for Turmequé, where he saw Torre among a massive gathering of Native vassals. Although he had not spoken with Torre, he did hear other commoners saying that Don Diego told them the king was outraged at the archbishop and the audiencia magistrates for taking their shrines as part of Zapata's evangelization program.

The audiencia pressed Rodrigo to tell them more about the gathering: had he seen Don Diego drinking chicha (maize beer) or participating in their festivities? Rodrigo responded that he had been present only briefly and did not know exactly what they had done, but he had heard someone saying that the caciques, captains, and commoners wore their feather costumes, played instruments, sang, and drank all night to celebrate Don Diego's return. He said he did not know if Torre participated in these activities, but he had heard from a commoner from Turmequé that Don Diego was constantly going in and out of his palisade during the ceremony and sat in a tall chair covered in painted mantas.[25]

A Spanish-speaking Indigenous person (indio ladino) from Icabuco testified that he was in the central plaza of Tunja when he first heard about Torre's return. There he ran into another ladino from Turmequé named Toray, who told him that Native peoples would no longer be required to pay as much gold and mantas to their encomenderos as before, nor would they be obliged to work in the encomendero's residence. Instead, everyone was going to live on their own land and work there. Toray explained that this change was due to Torre's return from the king's court: the king had sent Torre back to the kingdom to eliminate illegal labor demands (servicios personales) and to reduce tribute rates. Toray also mentioned that a great number of Indigenous commoners had gathered together to celebrate Torre's return and had given him great quantities of gold and mantas.[26] In response to the prosecutor's insistence, Toray denied hearing rumors about Torre telling the Native commoners that the king was angry and that they would not live in colonial gridded villages anymore.

Diego de Paredes stated that the Native peoples of the whole Province of Tunja were unsettled and that they claimed they were as free as Spaniards.[27] Miguel Diez, a sixty-year-old resident of Tunja, was in Gámeza to collect tribute for the encomendero Gonzalo Suárez when the cacique told him that the commoners of Icabuco and Turmequé did not pay tribute and neither would Gámeza. Diez then left for Icabuco, where he spoke with Franciscan friar Juan Gutiérrez. Gutiérrez told him that the Native vassals did not want to hear mass anymore and that he heard them saying they would not pay any tribute until Torre returned from Santa Fe.²⁸ Mestizo Juan Ropero was in Monga collecting tribute when the cacique told him about a great cipa (un cipa grande) called Don Diego de la Torre, who had come from Castile after meeting the king—again recalling the Muisca political concept of "cipa," used to refer to the highest level of authority. In Indigenous networks, word was that Torre had visited Duitama and Sogamoso personally to tell the commoners they would pay less tribute, that they would no longer be required to do any other work or service for their encomenderos, and that they would be able to keep their sanctuaries and dances. Ropero corrected the cacique, saying that Torre was no cipa and that he would get in trouble for this kind of remark.²⁹

This is a brief sample of the wealth and diversity of testimonies gathered during Torre's prosecution. If the records had all been crafted by the prosecution, one would expect them to be fairly homogeneous, repeating the exact same statements, as one often finds in Spanish colonial paperwork. Yet in this case, each witness reveals different degrees of exposure to Torre's ideas. They often refute the prosecution's information or deny knowing what the prosecution is asking.

At the same time, some testimonies make outrageous claims and appear to be fabricated to indict Torre. Such is the case of Friar Alonso Osorio's testimony, in which he claimed to have seen Torre transcribing a book about Lope de Aguirre's infamous rebellion. By then, Aguirre was a renowned figure in the Spanish Atlantic. In 1560, he had sailed through the Amazon as part of Pedro de Ursúa's expedition in search of El Dorado, but he ended up murdering Ursúa, separating from the king, and reversing the expedition's aims to take over Peru and place it under a new sovereign—Fernando de Guzmán, a young nobleman to whom the soldiers pledged loyalty and whom they declared as their prince after Ursúa's murder. Before he was killed in Barquisimeto in 1561 by his own men, Aguirre wrote an emotional, exhilarating letter to Philip II, reprimanding the king for being cruel and ungrateful, depicting monarchs and politicians as bloodsucking men unworthy of salvation, and declaring himself to be in permanent rebellion ("y yo rebelde hasta la muerte por tu ingratitud, Lope de Aguirre, el peregrino").³⁰ Friar Osorio claimed Torre was copying Aguirre's book so as to follow exactly the same route with thirty armed mestizos and take over the kingdom.³¹ By associating Torre with the empire's most notorious villain, Osorio described him as a threat to the king's sovereignty: a tyrannous rebel who wanted freedom from the empire. Not only is this interpretation completely unsubstantiated, but it is also at odds with the other testimonies and with Don Diego's advocacy at the king's court.

Other testimonies seem exaggerated or misinformed, probably due to the nature of orality and the alterations that occurred as messages were transmitted by word of mouth. Miguel Diez, for instance, reported hearing that the king had sent Torre to fight against the Turks because he was so brave. While undoubtedly false, it was a rumor that people of the time would have believed—after all, mestizos like Inca Garcilaso de la Vega fought in the Guerra de las Alpujarras, and many corregidores as well as low- to midlevel imperial officials had fought in battles in the Mediterranean and the Low Countries—a testament to the astounding mobility of officials in the Spanish empire.[32]

That rumors about Don Diego gained so much traction, however, implies that Torre had become a mythical figure: commoners, caciques, encomenderos, friars, and officials projected many different meanings and ideas onto his gestures, actions, and words. To be sure, the many meanings projected onto the figure of Don Diego de la Torre were at least partially rooted in his engagement with written and oral communication through a plurality of media. During the years after his return, Torre strengthened his epistolary networks, writing to caciques, the visitador, and other mestizos, often in a coded language. He also spoke in Spanish and Muisca in highly ritualized contexts and transmitted his messages through a network of town criers (pregoneros). In this way, Torre embraced the challenge of communication in this complex setting, and his words and actions sparked a proliferation of utopias and dystopias—highly imaginative scenes in which people envisioned Torre as eliminating tribute, fighting the Turks, or planning a full-fledged rebellion following in Lope de Aguirre's footsteps.

But common threads of argument emerged from the plurality of voices. Almost all witnesses stressed that Native communities recognized Torre as an authority above the regular caciques, whom the witnesses referred to as either hoa or cipa. The redeployment of this precolonial category is especially significant. As examined in chapter 1, during the distribution of encomiendas Muisca authorities had been flattened into the categories of "caciques," "captains," and "principals." Since then, the category of "cipa" had been reserved for the audiencia magistrates, who came to fulfill the functions of the highest level of Indigenous political authority. That Indigenous peoples were retrieving this prestigious term to identify Torre suggests that they viewed him as a potentially unifying agent, as a powerful new figure who could advocate for a common Indigenous agenda, even following colonial protocol. The blending of Muisca and Spanish political thought was such that calling Torre hoa or cipa could be misinterpreted, both by the audiencia and by Indigenous people, as it could be used to refer to either an intermediary in the Spanish bureaucracy (as the magistrates) or the return of a pre-Columbian authority. Unlike Andean utopias further south in the old domains of the Tawantinsuyu (the Inca empire) that envisioned the "return of the Inca" as an alternative to Spanish colonialism, the return of the cipa or hoa in the figure of Don Diego de la Torre was not incongruent with the Hispanic monarchy; rather, he was a leader who could act in coordination with the king. It was its own type of Andean utopia that projected the ideals of freedom and self-governance, but under the framework of Spanish politics.[33]

Almost all witnesses commented on the fact that caciques and commoners did not want to pay their tribute to their encomenderos after Torre's return. Indigenous vassals received Torre in great ceremonies, offering gold and mantas, and he, in turn, spoke to them in their own language. In these gatherings they said that he spoke of freedom, tributes, and the responsibilities of Native peoples as vassals of the king. He also spoke about his trip to Madrid and about Monzón's visita. Witnesses insisted that Torre had installed a system of messengers to communicate with caciques and gather information about Indigenous communities. Juan Coro, a yanacona (Indigenous migrant) from Peru, said that while he was staying in the town of Chinguina, one of Torre's ladino messengers arrived to count how many commoners resided in that village. These messengers were not Torre's invention. They were often referred to using the Indigenous category "guaysiga," had extensive genealogical knowledge and prestige, and could serve as regents or represent sihipquas. Some Native witnesses affirmed that Torre had punished those who did not comply with his requirements.

What is truly remarkable is that most of these messages are strikingly similar to what Torre wrote in his letters to the king: namely, the need to abolish personal services, reduce tribute rates, and recognize Native peoples as free vassals of the Crown. It is unsurprising that Don Diego told the Native commoners that he had met with Philip II, that the king knew how they were treated, and that he would solve these problems. Although the audiencia's prosecutor tried to present Torre's message of freedom as seditious—arguing that he intended to agitate Indigenous peoples and provoke them into rebellion against the Crown—in truth it was quite the opposite. Torre's concept of Indigenous freedom—a broad notion defined as the absence of servitude and slavery, not the dismantling of the empire—was grounded in Spanish law and imperial theory, and he discussed in these terms with the king himself.[34] Nor should it come as a surprise that Torre told caciques and commoners that their economic obligations to their encomenderos were about to change, or that they should ignore any special instructions from their encomenderos unless

Torre approved them. Torre knew that encomenderos and local officials opposed Monzón's reforms, and it is logical that he would have wanted to be informed about any encomenderos giving special instructions regarding different kinds of labor or additional tribute.

The growing power of Don Diego's figure also lent itself to scams and opportunities for profit. Apparently, a few impostors who claimed to be Torre's messengers had visited caciques demanding tribute, though audiencia authorities claimed they were Torre's real representatives. The fact that these impostors were able to fool Indigenous communities into giving them tribute for Torre reveals the many interpretations of Torre's arrival that circulated at the time and the uncertainty they caused. The idea of an Indigenous leader with close ties to both Indigenous communities and the king created an intriguing intellectual environment that could yield unexpected outcomes like the establishment of a new system of tributes.

What is clear is that political rumor about Torre rocked the kingdom after his return. That a visitador was working in tandem with someone like Torre, who had such a strong influence on the Indigenous population, posed a threat to the audiencia magistrates, and they decided they could wait no longer to limit Torre's power. In March 1580, colonial officials imprisoned Torre and set a curfew to restrain political organizing among Indigenous commoners and caciques in response. After his arrest, the people of Turmequé decided to abandon their villages.[35] Don Diego's half brother, the encomendero Pedro de Torres, requested Don Diego's temporary release so he could speak to the commoners of the encomienda and calm them down. The audiencia granted the request, and Torre visited Turmequé for ten days and then went back to jail.[36] But matters escalated quickly after that. Monzón removed two magistrates from office and placed them under arrest, including the audiencia president, Lope de Armendáriz, who refused to step down and actively disavowed the visitador's commands. In this context, Monzón asked Don Diego to travel to Spain and deliver secret messages to the king. Evidently, he was the only person in the kingdom Monzón deemed trustworthy enough for such an important endeavor. However, the audiencia intercepted Torre on his way to Madrid, arrested him, confiscated the letters he carried for the king, and exhibited him in the central plaza as a trophy.

Suffice it to say, the audiencia had gone rogue, disavowing the authority of a visitador named by the king, whose authority exceeded the audiencia's, and confiscating secret correspondence to the king. Those were seditious moves, defying the king's authority and systems of governance. As a testament to the audiencia's corruption, a magistrate named Cortés de Mesa murdered a witness who was in prison and then was condemned to death himself. It was the second time a magistrate of the Audiencia of Santa Fe was sentenced to death, less than two decades after Montaño's sentence had been carried out, as we saw in chapter 2. These are the only two cases of audiencia magistrates being condemned to death in the history of the Spanish empire, a fact that reveals just how outrageous and unprecedented the actions of these magistrates were. The state of chaos and confusion had erupted into a situation in which the entity of government that ostensibly represented the king and his advisors had turned extraordinarily seditious and its representatives of justice were being executed.

Matters had gotten so out of hand that Pedro de Torres, Don Diego's half brother, switched sides, denounced the magistrates, and shifted his support to Monzón and Don Diego. It was rumored throughout the kingdom that Diego de Ospina, a wealthy encomendero from the lowlands, had gathered a troop of armed men and was prepared to seize control of the kingdom if the confrontation with Monzón worsened. Torre fled prison in February 1581 and hid in the moors near Turmequé. From there he wrote coded letters to the visitador, saying that he was gathering forces through his mestizo network to counter Ospina's troops in case of a confrontation. These letters later served as evidence against him: the audiencia magistrates used them to claim that he was organizing a mestizo rebellion.

While historians have dismissed the claim as utter lies by the audiencia, Torre himself acknowledged looking for armed men to support the visitador.[37] The evidence gathered in the trial included Torre's letters, which corroborated his claim about organizing men—many of them mestizos—to fight in support of the visitador and the Crown in case of an insurrection by Ospina and the corrupt audiencia magistrates. But the magistrates continued to take the lead. They jailed Monzón after the archbishop excommunicated him. Monzón wrote that no other court in the Indies had committed as many and as serious felonies as had the Audiencia of Santa Fe. He urged the king to punish the magistrates, pointing out that if he did not, it would be impossible to control any other tribunal in the empire, since they would interpret inaction as permission.

In response, the king named a new visitador, Juan Prieto de Orellana, who ultimately dismissed all of the audiencia magistrates. Things settled down at the audiencia following Prieto's arrival; for Don Diego, however, the results were sour, as Prieto sent him once again to Madrid to face charges of sedition. Amid the chaos and unrest of the kingdom during the 1570s and 1580s, it was incontrovertible that Torre's presence ignited strong reactions among

Indigenous peoples. He was not a rebel, as the prosecutor claimed, but his reading of imperial law was critical, even revolutionary, in the context of the sixteenth-century New Kingdom. Whether or not Torre demanded that Native commoners call him hoa is less revealing of his influence than is the fact that caciques and commoners resurrected a political category that had been out of use for more than forty years, since precolonial times, to name him. In order to understand the events that shook the administration of the kingdom, we must look beyond Torre's identity and past the constrained debate concerning what he said, felt, and meant. His words and actions were the initial sparks, but as they were disseminated through different means of communication, they took on new dimensions and meanings. Nicolás Gutiérrez, one of the first Spaniards to learn the Muisca language, who had an intimate knowledge of Muisca customs and frequently testified about them in Hispanic tribunals, commented on Torre's influence among Native peoples: "The indios expect that a man of their own nation will free them from His Majesty's dominion, as well as the rule of the Spaniards, and that this man ought to be Don Diego de Torre."[38] Indigenous peoples placed high hopes on Don Diego's capacity to transform the kingdom. Yet the events that transpired after Prieto de Orellana's arrival augmented Don Diego's frustration and feelings that he had been deceived, as he headed back to Spain under suspicion of rebellion.

A Death Scene: Exile at the Court

Torre's attitude toward his tormented return to Spain is vividly depicted in one of his least known yet most evocative pieces. It is a hand-drawn, sepia-toned broadsheet that Torre composed for Philip II during his second visit to the court in 1584, the same year he wrote his *Relation* (figure 6.3).[39] The document plays with and iterates between genres: it is at once a drawing and a letter directed to Philip II. The scene depicts Don Diego's half brother, Pedro de Torres, on his deathbed. By this time, Pedro and Don Diego had made their peace and been imprisoned and released on different occasions by the audiencia magistrates. Don Diego described Pedro as an outstanding vassal: the son of a man who had shed blood in the conquest of the New Kingdom of Granada, who held one of the richest estates in the region and spent its profits in the service of the king. However, in an effort to hide their crimes, the magistrates had arrested Monzón and all those who had helped him, including Pedro and Don Diego. Pedro died in prison and, to make matters worse, the audiencia magistrates refused to grant his family permission to give him a true Catholic funeral.

In this sense, the drawing renders visible a scene that never occurred. It is the image of a loyal vassal denied justice and eternal peace. The image depicts

FIGURE 6.3. Drawing of Pedro de Torres on his deathbed, 1584. Archivo General de Simancas, *Guerra y marina*, legajos, 0071, 140. 44 × 58 cm.

two spaces simultaneously. The lower half shows the deceased holding a crucifix, a candle on each side of his prone form. His family and friends gather around him positioned hierarchically: the men to the left, the women to the right, and two rows of children in the middle. The right side represents the Christian family: the mother, sister, niece, aunt, and children pray for him. The left side represents the political sphere. At the center of the drawing a hand points the viewer's attention to an inset image depicting a prison cell where Don Diego himself is held hostage (figure 6.4). Don Diego, who was both family and a political ally of Pedro de Torres, occupies the very center of the image, well dressed but in chains and under the surveillance of a second figure. Indeed, this mortuary of his brother is also his self-portrait.

By placing himself at the center, Don Diego conveys the suffering and sadness caused by the injustice and tyranny of audiencia rule, which appropriately reflected his emotions during his final years in Madrid. He left for Madrid in April 1583 in the company of Alonso de Torre Blanca, a mestizo from Tunja. They arrived in Seville in August and spent some time there before leaving for Madrid. In October 1584, Torre received a new appointment to meet Philip II. This was when he prepared some of his most interesting

FIGURE 6.4. Detail: Don Diego's self-portrait, 1584. Archivo General de Simancas, *Guerra y marina*.

materials, consisting of a wide variety of letters, memoriales, and other written work, as well as maps and drawings. Knowing Philip II's interest in geography, he prepared the two maps of the New Kingdom analyzed previously. He also wrote his *Relation*, which Philip II read in the company of the Council of the Indies and, in January 1586, sent to the Audiencia of Santa Fe, asking that they inquire into and reply to each of its twenty-two claims.

It was a time of deep personal change for Torre. Soon after arriving in Spain he wed a Spanish woman called Juana de Oropesa, and by 1586 they had children. Yet, rather than success or contentment, Torre's writings conveyed suffering and hardship. Like most Indigenous visitors to the Hapsburg court in Madrid, he spent his final years facing poverty and pleading for royal favor. Although the king gave him at least twelve sizeable royal grants to cover his expenses at the court during both of his trips, Torre wrote letter after letter to the king stressing his precarious financial situation.[40] The language employed in his evocative letters emphasized that he, as a noble vassal distant from his motherland, was tormented by poverty. Being away from Turmequé meant that he did not have access to tributes or any of his regular sources of income, which had made him a wealthy man in the New Kingdom.

Torre had this in common with other transatlantic Indigenous travelers. Such was the case of Don Alonso de Atahualpa, the grandson of the last emperor of the Incas, who traveled to Philip II's court to contest the dispossession of some of his land by the Audiencia of Quito. Although Atahualpa had a valuable estate and fortune in South America, he had no access to these resources in Madrid and soon became deeply indebted. In an act characteristic of the kind of solidarities wrought by distance within the community of Indigenous transatlantic travelers, Torre agreed to serve as Atahualpa's guarantor and traveled to Seville—where Atahualpa had been imprisoned for his debts—to bail him out of jail. In 1589, when Don Alonso de Atahualpa died in Madrid, Torre took care of the legalities so that Atahualpa's natural daughter could inherit his fortune in Peru and Quito.[41]

In Torre's case, however, not only economic adversity afflicted him. Due to the many reactions unleashed by his return to the kingdom, the prosecutor accused him of rebellion (motín y levantamiento) and ordered his incarceration. The audiencia's newly appointed president and magistrates refused to allow him to return to South America until he was cleared of the charges. The king's court was to serve as his prison. In response, he explained his actions as a defense of the New Laws and the king's will. He argued that he had done everything in his power to stop the Spaniards' terrible cruelties against the "wretched indios," actions that went against His Majesty's will and laws.[42] Although absolved of the charges of rebellion on July 20, 1587, Torre never returned to his native Turmequé, and never again set foot on the fractured terrain of the New Kingdom of Granada. He would not walk the páramos (moors), sleep in his cercado (palisade), or speak to his subjects again. He died in Madrid in 1590 at forty years of age from unknown causes.[43]

An Indigenous Intellectual

The political culture of the kingdom and the principles and values sustained in its laws opened up a wide range of opportunities for Indigenous peoples to make claims to justice. Don Diego de la Torre was especially well positioned to use the ideal of a kingdom of free Indigenous vassals to imagine new futures. The son of a prestigious Native woman and a Spanish conquistador, Torre envisioned a kingdom that applied imperial laws and ordinances strictly; one governed by Indigenous nobility where Indigenous peoples were treated as free vassals of the Crown. His political project ultimately transcended his own expectations, becoming the utopia of a new cipa who worked in tandem with the king to guarantee Indigenous people the freedom so frequently enunciated in the empire's laws and statuses. Due to the nature of colonial communication and legal records, his project was illegible to many of his contemporaries and has remained illegible ever since.

In a crisis of governance in which the audiencia gained a reputation as the most corrupt entity in the Indies, and in which the Pijaos and Carares had established autonomous Indigenous sovereignties that isolated the kingdom from Peru and the Iberian Peninsula, a cacique sought to bring reform to the kingdom by requesting the king's support. Torre's case illustrates the contested nature of politics in the early modern Spanish empire. Empire-making was not only the king's project, nor was it exclusively defined by Spaniards. Torre meticulously crafted his oral, written, and visual expression in order to speak to the king and to the Muiscas in their own languages and visual traditions. His reports to the king and the Council of the Indies framed the New Kingdom within transatlantic debates about good government and theories of empire. In these texts, Native persons were one kind of vassal. They were miserables: helpless people in need of the monarch's protection. They were Catholic vassals who suffered under tyrannical and unlawful local power. Torre's depiction of Native peoples was built on medieval and early modern Hispanic law. Meanwhile, he communicated with caciques and commoners in ways that resonated with their particular experience of colonialism. He spoke to the king and to Native peoples in different registers, but his overarching message was remarkably coherent.

Torre was a unique Indigenous intellectual who left by far the most extensive written and visual record of any Native person from the northern Andes during the early modern period. He wrote and traveled in the 1570s and 1580s, during a time of intense activity among Indigenous intellectuals in the Spanish empire. During this time, Captain Garcilaso de la Vega, known as "El Inca," inscribed the Incas' history in a biblical time frame; a team of Nahua painters (tlacuilos) from central Mexico wrote a bilingual Nahuatl-Spanish history of New Spain in text and images in collaboration with Fray Bernardino de Sahagún; and Cristóbal Choquecasa left a testament in Quechua about Andean thought and his own encounter with Christianity. It was a time of creative Indigenous political thought, as Indigenous leaders were actively engaging in debates about good government and identifying possible futures in the empire, sometimes arriving at very concrete proposals, such as the initiative of a group of caciques from central Peru who offered payment to Philip II so he would not make the encomiendas perpetual.[44]

These thinkers' frame of reference was not local. Rather, they were members of the Spanish global empire and moved with ease within that scale of thought. Their thinking oscillated fluidly between the Scriptures, Aristotle, Renaissance humanism, and Indigenous cosmologies. Indigenous intellectuals' writing and visual creations during this period were deeply influenced by global interactions and usually combined elements from different cultures, in a style that scholars characterize as "hybrid," "syncretic," or "mestizo."[45] Torre's writing style, however, strongly contrasts with works by other Indigenous intellectuals and does not fit within the traditional frames used to understand Native and mestizo literacies in the Iberian Atlantic. When placed in that context, Torre's writings appear deceptively simple: mere echoes of Hispanic traditions of thought, stripped of any trace of their Indigenous roots. This, I claim, is a result of Torre's approach to communication in a colonial context. Rather than combining elements from different visual and philosophic traditions, he separated registers. He expressed himself like an accomplished political strategist who accommodated his message to his audience, making his claims to the Crown in the languages and logics of Spanish law while also readily communicating in Indigenous contexts. Unfortunately, due to the nature of colonial archives we have records only of his interactions with the imperial administration.

Torre's narrative choices were very effective. The king and the Council of the Indies responded promptly to his most important requests. Philip II personally requested detailed information about every point that Don Diego mentioned in his *Relation* and sent him back with the visitador Monzón to redress the audiencia's wrongdoing. Subsequent events—the arrival of Juan Prieto de Orellana as the new visitador, the dismissal of the audiencia president and magistrates—were effects of a process Torre had unleashed. That the Council of the Indies cleansed the audiencia as a result of the visitas triggered by Torre's claims is evidence of his unprecedented achievements. I know of no other case in the history of the Spanish empire—or any European empire, for that matter—in which the writings and petitions of an Indigenous person prompted the removal of all the members of the highest court of governance in their kingdom or viceroyalty. Torre was a radical political strategist who transformed the kingdom by using the empire's self-image against the highest administrative organ of the kingdom, thus dismantling the audiencia.

Torre's vision of the kingdom was never realized, but his elaboration of it had a lasting effect on the New Kingdom of Granada. The replacement of the audiencia magistrates, in particular, laid the groundwork for drastic reform and a new approach to governance more closely aligned with the Crown's agenda. In 1587, while Torre was in Madrid, Antonio González assumed the audiencia presidency and prepared a dramatically transformative agenda. From then on, settlers would forfeit control over Indigenous labor. As the encomienda lost ground to the corregimiento, managing Indigenous workers would become the province of Crown officials. The mita—an institution borrowed from the Incas by the Spanish administration to great success in Peruvian mining ventures—was imported to the kingdom in an effort to boost silver mining. Since Zapata's approach to conversion had become an evident failure in Torre's time, a new, Jesuit-led model of evangelization took shape in the early seventeenth century. Paradoxically, Torre's radical political project resulted in the strengthening of extractive imperial institutions, the decline of ethnic autonomy, and waning power of Indigenous nobility. Those transitions are the subject of the next part of this book.

PART III   NEW IMPERIAL DESIGNS

On September 22, 1572, King Philip II personally dictated and signed a decree allowing a wealthy settler named Antonio de Sepúlveda to drain Lake Guatavita.[1] The king did not often find himself thinking or writing about the bodies of water of the New Kingdom of Granada. However, Guatavita was not just any lake. A circular volcanic crater filled with water, Guatavita was the subject of many legends. Stories circulated of how in pre-Hispanic times new Muisca sihipquas were appointed there through a ceremony. Naked and covered in gold dust, the heir to the Muisca sihipqua would board a colorful raft full of gold pieces, emeralds, and feathered items, accompanied by other Indigenous authorities who were also naked and bore offerings. Large crowds gathered on the shores, playing music, singing, dancing, and burning incense. When the raft reached the middle of the lake, the heir raised a flag to command silence and then tossed his offerings into the lake, as did his companions. Then the music and festivities resumed, the raft returned to the shore, and the heir would be accepted as cacique. Such stories inspired the imagination of many Spaniards, who described this ritual in their writings, awed by the immense wealth that must lie at the bottom of the lake. Many envisioned the ceremony as the origin of the legend of El Dorado.

By the mid-sixteenth century, Philip II considered the Indigenous sacred objects presumed to be at the bottom of the lake to be untapped wealth that could improve the empire's finances. "They say," he wrote, that Guatavita "is a guaca (shrine) or sanctuary," and he asked Sepúlveda to extract "all the gold and silver, pearls, precious stones, and any other things you find . . . draining the lake or extracting it by any other ingenuity." By describing Guatavita using the term *guaca*, the king used the Hispanicized form of a rich, complex Quechua term the peoples of the southern Andes used to refer to objects that connected their sacred ancestors to the landscape and that could have many layers of meaning and many uses. By contrast, the Spanish used *guaca* to describe what they viewed as idolatrous religious practices. By adopting that term for Guatavita, the king deployed a colonial lexicon that had been used for decades to justify the pillage of Indigenous sacred objects throughout the Andes.

Philip II granted Sepúlveda permission to relocate enslaved Africans and to purchase tools like hammers, hoes, and machetes, asked him to pay all costs, and ordered him to record all his earnings in the books of the audiencia. Sepúlveda would keep half of the earnings and the rest would go to the Crown. Philip II envisioned an enterprise that would forcibly displace people and move tools across the Atlantic to extract sacred Indigenous objects from the bottom of the lake and employ them to the economic benefit of the empire. While this imperial utopia would be fruitless—the depths of the volcanic lake appeared to be endless—the attempt to drain it left a deep gouge in one of its edges, as well as modest earnings for the royal treasury. The gouge itself is a reminder of the competing ideas of the landscape, of wealth, and of the sacred upon which colonialism was built.

Philip II's desire for the great wealth that lay at the bottom of Guatavita laid bare the lengths to which the monarch and his officials would go to increase his revenue: he would drain lakes, seize Indigenous wealth, deplete Indigenous landscapes, and reshuffle people across continents. This hubris also illustrates the central place of mining and the allure of metals in imperial imagination, which took precedence over almost any other consideration and set the bar for the kingdom's success. Part III, the book's last, examines the king's officials' efforts to increase the revenue extracted from the kingdom between the 1590s and the 1620s, which inaugurated an aggressive form of economic governance that marked a final stage in the formation of the kingdom.

Historians have long debated the appropriate categorizations for the early modern Spanish empire's economic systems. Constrained by a conceptual vocabulary that marked a distinction between feudalism (a precapitalist form of domination based on serfs who labored on lords' lands in exchange for protection) and capitalism (with many definitions, which may emphasize wage labor, capital accumulation, and profit-seeking behavior, or else world-system analysis), scholars in the 1970s and 1980s debated whether Europe or Asia commanded the world system economy during that early modern period and how to accommodate colonial Latin American economies in this scheme.[2] More recently, John Tutino has shown that the region of the Bajío in New Spain—a thriving commercial society based on a silver-mining economy with a peculiar system of labor based on noncorporate wage workers and a keen profit-oriented mentality—established its own form of silver capitalism, thus becoming an engine of the world economy tying China and Europe.[3] While this analysis tells of the Bajío's extremely dynamic capitalist society and resonates in other places, like the thriving city of Potosí in the Bolivian highlands, the question persists of how to categorize regions that were less obviously capitalistic, such as the New Kingdom of Granada.[4]

While the New Kingdom does not fall squarely into contemporary models of racial capitalism, neither was it a feudal system resembling medieval Europe. The following chapters argue that, beginning in the 1590s, the kingdom's administration passed a series of political reforms that introduced a new form of economic governance based on the expropriation and commodification of Indigenous landscapes and the alienation of Indigenous and African labor. These policies and procedures reconfigured the institutions that governed Indigenous lives, distributed their labor, and disposed of their territories; they forged new ways of being "indios." They also aimed to populate mines with enslaved peoples from the African continent. The new scenario, in which racialized populations were impoverished and transformed into wage laborers or slaves to provide commodities for global commodity chains, is not unlike other versions of capitalism.[5] The new form of economic governance remade the kingdom by transforming the peoples of the cold lands into mobile laborers, importing enslaved peoples from Africa, and re-creating contested lowland landscapes as gold and silver mines.

The case of Micaela Sánchez illustrates the types of transitions that occurred at the turn of the seventeenth century. Sánchez was an Indigenous woman from Ubaque, an area in the cold lands, who appeared at the Audiencia of Santa Fe in 1668 to bail her son, Tomás de Cerquera, out of the tribunal's prison. He had been arrested for "avoiding his obligation . . . to work the mines of Mariquita," in the hot lands. Sánchez implored the tribunal to free him. She promised that her son would reside under her surveillance in the gridded village and, when it was time for the next labor drafts, she would make sure he left for the lowland mines "without any excuse," as required by the Spanish administration. If Cerquera faltered, Sánchez promised, she would pay the tribunal's fine herself.[6]

Mining itself was not new. The empire had been extracting silver from the Santa Agueda and Victoria deposits of Mariquita since the 1550s, and they had been extracting gold from Antioquia since the 1540s. But up to that point, Crown policy had strictly prohibited encomenderos from forcing the Native peoples of their highland encomiendas to work in hot-land mines, as part of the Crown's broader effort to restrict encomienda activities under the New Laws of 1542.[7] The law required the visitadores who traveled the kingdom to ensure that Native peoples were paying tribute to the encomenderos according to rates established by the Crown and in products they could easily access near their areas of residence. Whenever they found Native peoples working in mines or performing other tasks not approved by the royal tribunal, the visitadores prosecuted the encomendero. The Crown's penalties for such infractions ranged from small fines to stripping the encomendero of his encomienda. Prosecution of such behavior was crucial to fulfilling the empire's stated aim of protecting Native peoples. By the time of Cerquera's arrest and Sánchez's intervention, however, the forced displacement of Indigenous men from the highlands to work in lowland mines—which the empire's intellectuals and bureaucrats had attacked both rhetorically and legally—was organized, supervised, and regulated by imperial officials.

By the 1590s, silver production in Santa Agueda had declined, but new, very promising deposits had been found near Mariquita in the sites known as Las Lajas and Santa Ana.[8] In the early years of the seventeenth century, Juan de Borja, president of the audiencia, visited Las Lajas and voiced his high expectations of the mines' potential. In a letter from November 1605, he informed the king that "one hundred indios and fifty blacks would extract more metal from these mines than five hundred indios would in Potosí."[9] He believed that even a small input of laborers would immediately ramp up production, yielding more per capita profits than Potosí. One year later, Borja wrote to the king to argue that the silver mines of Mariquita were "the only remedy of this kingdom"—in the face of economic impoverishment and the success of the Pijao coalition in contesting the New Kingdom's sovereignty, the mines offered an untapped source of wealth that could stabilize the kingdom's rule.[10] His optimistic projections, however, assumed an adequate supply of labor. The problem of acquiring such labor was emblematic of imperial officials' frustrations with the kingdom's geography: the densely settled, mostly agrarian cold lands lacked mineral deposits, while the hot lands were rich in mineral deposits but lacked human laborers. His diagnosis led to an evident solution, in his colonial mindset: move Indigenous people from the highlands to the lowlands to satisfy the empire's hunger for metals.

To this end, Borja created a new institution charged with forcing Indigenous men from the highlands to work in the lowland mines. The people of the kingdom used the terms *conducción* and *mita* to describe these labor drafts. *Conducción* literally meant "conducting" or "driving," and *mita* was borrowed from Quechua and inspired by the Inca labor drafts. In the 1570s, viceroy Francisco de Toledo had made the mita the basis of colonial labor in Peru by requiring Indigenous communities to pay a tax to the empire in manpower.[11] Borja's mita required every community of the cold lands to send 2 percent of its male population every year to the silver mines of Mariquita in the Magdalena River Valley.[12] To meet this obligation, Indigenous men had to abandon their communities and set off on long and arduous journeys.

The activities of the encomenderos that clerics and officials had so insistently attacked were now an institutionalized practice of the empire, under the administration of an imperial official. That the labor drafts had become mandatory and regulated by imperial authorities made the mita no less terrifying and deadly. Settlers realized that Indigenous lives were ravaged in the mines. In 1644, for example, the encomenderos of Mariquita complained that only 398 Indigenous people remained in the province, out of an original population of 12,000—so many had been compelled to go to the mines and then were consumed by them.[13] From all points of view, the mita was a catastrophic, devastating institution. We can see the imprint of the labor draft system in the archival paper trail, which shifts from lawsuits by visitadores against encomenderos to lists of men forced to abandon their communities for long periods, requests by communities hoping to free themselves from the mita, and complaints about the toll it took on Indigenous lives and communities. The neutrality of the term *conducciones* and the stark simplicity of the lists of men forced to labor in the mines contrast sharply with the voices and testimonies of the communities that sought to free themselves from the empire's demands.

In sum, this new form of economic governance introduced a system that extracted people from the cold lands and metals from the hot lands to increase the empire's revenue. The chapters of this part examine the enclosure of the

Indigenous economies of the cold lands, projects to eliminate the threats of Indigenous sovereign polities like the Pijaos from the hot lands, efforts to establish new mines in Mariquita, and the emergence of a diverse society around Mariquita's silver mines. Chapter 7 uses a legal landscape painting from 1614 to explore the dispossession of Indigenous lands and policing of Indigenous bodies in the cold lands. It addresses a series of measures that included provisions to limit and enclose Indigenous lands to only what was strictly necessary for their survival so that Crown officials could sell the remaining lands to Spanish settlers, as well as the creation of a new bureaucratic post that governed Indigenous peoples' daily lives and sold their labor to Spanish settlers. These measures, I argue, further undermined the Andean Indigenous communities' independence and ethnic autonomy, which they had been struggling to maintain in the face of decades of colonial pressures.

Chapter 8 surveys the administrative provisions that transformed the Pijao territories and Magdalena River valley into silver mines during the first decades of the seventeenth century. It concentrates on audiencia president Juan de Borja's genocidal project, in which he gathered armies to exterminate the Pijaos and all other Indigenous groups of the hot lands who did not comply with the kingdom's demands. In addition, Borja followed imperial guidelines to create a new post—the accountant of the audiencia—who became a protagonist in the administration of the kingdom. Among other things, the accountant advocated for the introduction of thousands of enslaved Africans to the mines. The influx of African and Indigenous peoples to Mariquita's mines gave rise to a diverse society composed of dislocated individuals who had had their ties with their communities of origin severed and remained in the mines either under coercion or attracted by the possibility of making profit from the silver economy. In essence, Borja's presidency laid bare the kingdom's cold and calculating administrative rationale and its insatiable hunger for precious minerals—acquired at the expense of Indigenous and African communities.

LANDSCAPES OF PROPERTY

The landscapes of the Bogotá savannah on the Andean plateau come to life in Juan Aguilar's 1614 painting, as bulls and cows graze on lands rich with pastures and water, scattered rural villages, and roads (figure 7.1). This colorful image of the savannah is one of a kind: it is the only sixteenth-century painting of the northern Andes that captures the landscape in detail. It presents an idyllic rural image that strongly resembles contemporary scenes of the Andean plateau. For this reason, the painting seems to depict an almost timeless countryside, where few things change over time. But rather than an unchanging agrarian landscape, the painting reveals intense struggles between colliding social and political ecologies, and between societies with different ways of inhabiting the earth and shaping their environments.

In fact, this painting illustrates the dispossession of the lands called Muyquyta—which housed the headquarters of the cipa (the highest level of Muisca authority) and the homes and farmlands of the Muisca community of Bogotá—and their transfer to the personal property of Francisco Maldonado de Mendoza, the encomendero of the Indigenous community of Bogotá and

FIGURE 7.1. Painting of the swamps and floodlands of Bogotá, Juan Aguilar, 1614.
AGI, Mapas y planos Panamá, Santa Fe y Quito, 336.

one of the wealthiest men in the kingdom. This process of enclosure started in 1540, when the town council of Santa Fe started assigning lands to settlers, and was boosted by a series of political reforms in the 1590s that established new mechanisms to regulate access to land and labor; by 1614, when the painting was made, it had brought important changes to the landscapes of the savannah. The painting, titled "Painting of the Swamps and Flood-Lands of Bogotá" (Pintura de los pantanos y anegadizos de Bogotá), was presented as evidence in a trial that reinforced Maldonado's ownership of the territory.

As settlers like Maldonado gained title to former Indigenous lands, they aimed to replace the landscape's carefully designed architecture of water—which fed its agriculture and fisheries—with pastures devoted to intensive cattle ranching. In this sense, the painting is a map of colonization and dispossession. This chapter examines the deep transformations of Indigenous landscapes and labor as imperial officials pushed a specific version of the enclosure of the commons that sought to remake Indigenous peoples after the image of poor agrarian laborers in Castile, deploying textual technologies like maps and minted coins to dispossess Indigenous people of their lands and to quantify and dispose of their labor.

The presence of cows, bulls, and horses in the painting offers the first evidence of the changes that European occupation provoked in Indigenous landscapes. These animals arrived on the Andean plateau in the late 1530s, along with the Spanish conquistadors, and dispersed throughout Muisca agricultural landscapes in the following decades. The arrival of cattle formed part of a broader global flow of microbes, flora, and fauna that boarded European vessels for transoceanic travel and completely reshaped environments, demography, and food systems globally.[1] While the Muiscas invested communal labor to create raised agricultural beds by carving out water canals, which in turn provided abundant fish, the Spanish model of pastoralism left cattle to roam mostly unattended, with often disastrous results for Indigenous crops. Bulls, cows, sheep, and pigs multiplied in landscapes that already had been profoundly transformed by Indigenous occupancy and where they had few predators, often creating devastating environmental damage.[2]

The presence of Indigenous settlements hints at these colliding ecologies. In the upper-middle section of the painting, the artist locates the "old palisade of the cacique," the headquarters of the cipa—formerly one of the most majestic Muisca sites—accompanied now by a small Spanish-style construction in a settler-owned estate. The Indigenous community of Bogotá now resided in the place referenced on the map as the "pueblo de Bogotá," located at center-right: a gridded village structured around a chapel, created through the forced resettlement projects initially carried out by Tomás López Medel in the late 1550s. Thus, the painting reveals how power was reshaped, as the Indigenous community of Bogotá was forced to abandon their built environments and adjust to life in new settlements under Christian symbols.

But perhaps the most poignant evidence of these colliding ecologies is in the allocation of property—the question of who had the authority to claim landscapes and ecosystems as their own. In the painting, most lands are referenced as Spanish estates, while only a few are marked as belonging to the Indigenous community of Bogotá, just a small parcel in the center-right section of the painting. The painting itself, as a work of art done to provide evidence in court, was an instrument in the process of dispossession. While the encroachment of Indigenous lands started in the 1540s, it was the reform of the 1590s that made landed property the main system for organizing human relations in the countryside.

Through a series of reforms initiated during this decade, the Audiencia of Santa Fe changed the system that allocated Indigenous labor, which had until then been ruled mostly by the encomienda system. These reforms included revising and validating land titles (composiciones de tierras), installing a new governor of Indigenous life charged with administering labor (corregidor de naturales), abolishing any type of custom arrangements between encomenderos and Indigenous communities (servicios personales) and instead channeling Indigenous workers as paid daily laborers (jornaleros), and merging Indigenous villages whose populations had declined (agregaciones). In sum, the reforms paved the way for Spanish settlers to accumulate lands into private estates, increasingly transform them into pastureland to raise pigs, sheep, and cows, and create mechanisms for forcibly assigning Indigenous workers to them. While the encomienda remained alive in the New Kingdom until the eighteenth century, these reforms made landed property the main basis of wealth and power.[3]

In the previous chapters we saw how Don Diego de la Torre's travels to the king's court resulted in the dismissal of the royal tribunal's entire cabinet, giving the new administration the political power to carry out a deep transformation. This chapter argues that, rather than resolving the issues Torre had raised, the resulting reforms instead targeted Indigenous autonomy. They aimed to encroach on Indigenous economies, which despite demographic decline and coercive labor under the encomienda system had remained in control of some of the kingdom's most vital enterprises, like salt and manta production, and food provisioning.

Indigenous peoples had engaged in long-distance, interethnic economic networks since pre-Hispanic times and continued to do so throughout the sixteenth century. In these trade networks they sold and purchased textiles, ceramics, utensils, and food.[4] Some of these products were crafted, and some took advantage of Andean ecological tiers to commercialize different crop varieties. But they all depended on a network of specialized economies built on deep traditions of material culture and the transmission of knowledge across geographic space. While the king and the Council of the Indies conceived of wealth in terms of minerals such as gold and silver, encomenderos and settlers had learned that engaging in these economies usually meant dealing in Native textiles and, not least, competing economically with Native peoples.

The political reforms of the turn of the seventeenth century introduced a new property regime that gave different categories of people different kinds of legal access to land. They limited Indigenous lands to the minimum—barely enough for survival—and created a mechanism to forcibly deploy Indigenous wage labor on Spanish estates and in cities. New governance procedures that leaned heavily on textual technologies such as censuses, letters, instructions, titles, and money accompanied the reform. Native people and settlers would come to depend on the pieces of paper known as titles in order to call a place home, build a house, plant gardens, or raise crops and domestic animals.

The reforms were an early iteration of the enclosure of the commons, whose best-known example is eighteenth-century England.[5] But while in England the reforms created a dispossessed proletarian class that used wages to pay for sustenance, the New Kingdom's Indigenous communities were left with just enough land for subsistence and coerced into work not because of their own economic need but by pressure from imperial officials. The wages they earned were used not for provisioning, since that was covered by subsistence farming on their communal lands (resguardos), but instead to pay taxes and tithes. Coin weighed and marked with the King's seal in royal mint houses was less a means of exchange in popular economic circuits than a textual technology the kingdom used to monitor the economy and calculate taxes. Through these measures, imperial officials installed a form of economic governance directed at dispossessing Indigenous peoples of their lands and economic enterprises, transforming people into wage laborers, and increasing the empire's tax revenues, thus raising funds to pay for transatlantic wars. In this sense, I see this schema as a peculiar model of racialized early capitalism in which people, by virtue of being categorized as "indios," were spatially insulated, disconnected from the profits of their own economic enterprises, and pushed into wage labor at the whim of imperial officials. This chapter draws on environmental history and political ecology to expose the rationale of this form of economic governance, revealing the reforms' effect on Indigenous ecosystems as well as Indigenous communities' calls against environmental violence.

Waterscapes to Pastures

The abundance of water was foundational to the Indigenous ecologies of many areas of the Andean plateau, like the Bogotá savannah. In this region, poor drainage and dense acidic soils that are slow to absorb excess water created conditions in which rivers overflowed easily during the rainy seasons. In response to these conditions, the Muiscas dug deep ditches to form elevated agricultural terraces in a manner similar to the techniques seen in other parts of the Americas.[6] They developed regular and irregular ditches that varied greatly in size, each addressing a specific challenge: regular ditches were built to contain water, while irregular ditches drained it. Through these strategies, the Muiscas made this area of overwhelming supply of water into rich "yards and planted fields"—Muyquyta, as they called it.[7]

The seasonal overflow of water had profoundly informed Indigenous rural engineering for centuries, and created distinctive ecologies with many types of flora and fauna.[8] Ditches not only helped drain water away from the plantations but also served as artificial fish ponds. There is some evidence of this in language. The Muisca term for the species of fish now called capitán (*Eremophilus mutisii*), *chichinegua*, is a composite of the words for "ditch" (*chichine*) and "fish" (*gua*), meaning "the fish in the ditch."[9] The ditch bottoms became repositories of high-nutrient soil, which the Muiscas then used as fertilizer. Muisca cultivators most likely practiced polyculture farming, planting corn, potatoes, and herbs alongside one another.[10] A rich variety of birds, amphibians, and rodents came together around Indigenous crops and fisheries.[11] Furthermore, since water maintains its temperature longer than air, the canals would have shielded the crops from the savannah's frigid temperatures before dawn. Thus, by creating terraced fields, the Muiscas of the savannah could control flooding, store water during dry seasons, protect crops from frost, maintain a repository of high-nutrient soil to use as fertilizer, and sustain fisheries on their plantations.

These hydraulic systems relied on care by the community. Much of the work was done by hand, possibly in festive gatherings.[12] In floodable areas, every arable piece of land was a feat of individual and collective labor as well as engineering. It is likely that this work entailed forms of property that have gone unacknowledged: Muisca leaders likely had well-monitored systems for assigning arable lands. Ditches may have separated plots assigned for individual or communal purposes, with some restricted to elites and others for commoners. In fact, Spaniards noted that commoners' cultivated fields were directly in front of their residences and that they demarcated their landscapes with fences formed by gardens and lines of trees (cercas de árboles).[13]

Muyquyta was a combination of bodies of water (interspersed with agricultural terraces), Muisca households, and the majestic palisades and symbols of power of the cipa (chapter 1). However, as Spaniards took over Indigenous homelands, Muisca ecologies and landscapes of power faced fierce competition from expanding pastoralism. In the Bogotá savannah, for instance, city council (cabildo) officials signed over the lands belonging to Indigenous communities to at least fourteen Spaniards between 1543 and 1586.[14] While actual Spanish occupation of the lands probably did not occur until the 1560s, after the reducciones and after a bridge was built over the Bogotá River, these lands were traded among Spaniards.

One individual, in particular, benefited from this process. In 1586, the recently arrived, Spanish-born Francisco Maldonado de Mendoza married Jerónima de Orrego, the daughter of the prominent conquistador and encomendero of Bogotá, Alonso de Olalla, and began buying titles to lands on the Bogotá savannah with the goal of establishing an estate of his own.[15] In 1592, Jerónima de Orrego renounced her encomienda in Bogotá and Maldonado formally petitioned president Antonio González to assign it to him. In 1593, Maldonado officially took possession as the encomendero of Bogotá. In 1594, the Indigenous community of Bogotá was formally confined to a limited expanse of land (a resguardo, as we will see in the next section). By the end of the sixteenth century, Maldonado held more than 65,000 hectares (about 160,200 acres) of land—fully a third of the Bogotá savannah.

Maldonado became the owner of the largest and most profitable piece of land in the cold lands, and, as the encomendero, he also had access to Indigenous labor. His estate came to be known as the "Meadow of Bogotá" (Dehesa de Bogotá, or El Novillero), which generated huge profits through cattle-raising and as a transit point for cattle from the lowlands—from Ibagué, Tocaima, and Timaná—on their journey to the city of Santa Fe, where they were butchered and sold. The Meadow was by far his largest hacienda. It had pasture capacity for around twenty thousand head of cattle and produced three hundred tons of wheat, maize, and barley.[16] Maldonado's 1610 will made all of his properties an inalienable entailed estate (mayorazgo), meaning they could never be divided among his descendants but would pass intact to his firstborn, Antonio Maldonado de Mendoza, and be inherited in this manner for generations. Maldonado's heirs then received titles of nobility, establishing the house of the marquis of San Jorge, among whose descendants were bishops, viceroys, and the first president of Colombia, Jorge Tadeo Lozano.

Maldonado's estate was based on a perception of the landscape different from that of the Muisca. Where the latter had built a rich and diverse terraced ecosystem, Maldonado condemned the savannah's hydraulic cycles, calling the elaborate constructions of terraced fields and watercourses infertile swamps.[17] He envisioned instead a landscape of pastures where cattle could graze, with contained repositories of water, and some monocrop plantations, especially of wheat and barley. He insisted that to make his lands profitable he had to drain them, which he first attempted by introducing pigs and letting them go feral—a low-budget strategy that in its aims was not unlike the Spanish empire's battles against Indigenous waterscapes throughout the Americas, which often had disastrous environmental consequences.[18]

Through a series of strategic moves over a twenty-year period, the Spaniard Francisco Maldonado de Mendoza managed to seize a large section of the cipa's landscapes of power and the Bogotá community's homelands. Bogotá, with its rich canals and terraces, had once sustained the authority of the cipa. Now, as it became pastureland for cattle grazing, it also transformed into the foundation of another system of power: a European noble house that reshaped the land and fostered other kinds of ecological arrangements. Rather than a crafted waterscape maintained by community care, it supplied grass for animals imported by humans who constantly battled water.

The painting of the Bogotá swamps introduced earlier is perhaps the best evidence of these changes. It was produced in 1614 in the context of a legal suit against Maldonado. A decade earlier, in 1603, the attorney general of the audiencia, Aller de Villagómez, had initiated a lawsuit against Maldonado arguing that, during the composiciones, Maldonado had tricked the audiencia into legalizing a huge slice of the plains as his property without paying the appropriate fees. Villagómez expected the legal procedure to punish Maldonado and reclaim the land for the audiencia, which would then sell it to other settlers for more money. In fact, the lawsuit was inspired by the bid of one settler, Hernando Caicedo, who offered to pay a hefty sum for a small swath of Maldonado's terrain known as "Say's Corner" (rincón del Say), which was occupied by what Caicedo called "maroon indios" (indios cimarrones)—a group of Indigenous people under the leadership of a captain who had abandoned their cacicazgo and had a special arrangement with Maldonado.[19]

Every graphic element on the map depicted a feature of the landscape that was under contention in the lawsuit. While from Maldonado's perspective the abundance of water evidenced the land's swampiness, infertility, and uselessness, for Villagómez it proved exactly the opposite: "What they call swamp is actually the best land and that which is worth the most." Maldonado contended that cattle could roam freely because he had introduced pigs to drain the swamps and make the lands more productive. Villagómez, however, saw the abundance of cattle as evidence that the swamps were highly profitable. The proximity of the villages of Bogotá and Serrezuela (today Funza and Madrid) revealed that the territory lay within easy reach of Indigenous laborers who could work the land. The paths and bridges demonstrated that these lands were ideally situated to provision the city of Santa Fe. The opposing parties highlighted these elements when crafting their arguments. Even the processes of land measurement and the map itself were contested during the trial. The attorney general repeatedly complained about the initial land measurement using adjectives like engaño, "deceit," and corrupción, "corruption," arguing that the composición of the terrain had been carried out by a "vagrant man and soldier who made a living and was entertained by gambling, and knew nothing about lands and their worth."[20] Maldonado also questioned the map's validity, arguing that the inspectors' journey had taken place during a dry period and claiming that, given the fluctuating water levels in the area, they had not been able to fully achieve the "desired effect," which was to illustrate the excess of water.[21]

But what was perhaps the most salient change in the landscape went unmentioned in the suit and is nearly imperceptible in the map itself. Both parties tacitly agreed that these rich, fertile, and well-situated lands should be the property of Spanish settlers and that Indigenous peoples should be forced to provide labor to generate profit for the owners. Maldonado's crime, as framed by the audiencia's prosecutor, was against the king's assets, not against the Muisca community of Bogotá. Submerged in the beautiful rural scene of the painting, we can see the violence of imperial notions of justice and its encroachment into Indigenous lands.

The painting was both an artistic production and a legal document meant to be used as evidence in court. It is signed by Juan de Aguilar Rendón, its painter (signing artwork was uncommon in the early modern period, perhaps a signal that its creator was proud of this piece for its aesthetic qualities), and by a "receptor," who granted validity for its use in court. In this sense, with its vivid green and blue tones, this fabulous mix of cartography and landscape painting indicates a moment when paper became a central tool for claiming territory: when scribes were trained to measure, depict, and describe the landscape, when painters demonstrated their skill by creating hybrid genres representing and embellishing the landscape while crafting documents that supported their patron's legal claims.[22] The painting was not only the work of an artist's imagination or an example of a cartographer's expertise but also part of a legal strategy for accumulation of the old lands of the cipa and the community of Bogotá by a European man. In this sense, the map did not just depict a world but constructed it. It was an instrument of enclosure.

Governing Land and Labor

The dispossession of Indigenous landscapes was part of a comprehensive and systematic enclosure, a system to govern land and labor, that the audiencia made into a systematic political program beginning in the 1590s. It covered everything from land tenure to spiritual guidance, and it brought new administrators to the New Kingdom's countryside. The basis for the enclosure was established by political innovations of the 1590s and 1600s implemented by audiencia presidents, following the general guidelines of the Council of the Indies. Antonio González, the president appointed to lead the audiencia after the dismissal of the magistrates, started the wave of reforms. After his appointment in 1587, he passed several measures, including revising and validating land and encomienda titles for a fee (composiciones), auctioning off bureaucratic posts (such as those of regidor, alferez, alguacil mayor, and even protectores de indios), creating new taxes (alcabalas), expelling foreigners from the kingdom unless they paid a special tax, offering mestizos and illegitimate children the opportunity to purchase legitimacy from the Crown, and selling social status certificates.

The revision of land titles, or composiciones de tierras, resulted from an empire-wide policy: three royal decrees sent by Philip II in 1591 to the heads of every major viceroyalty, audiencia, or independent governorship, instructing governors to revise all landholdings in their jurisdictions to see that settlers had valid titles and that they made the land productive (uso útil).[23] The king required officials to return to the Crown lands that lacked proper titles or had remained unproductive, and to confirm the validity of the remaining titles. Those whose titles were eligible to be validated would pay the king for the confirmation procedure. Unproductive and untitled lands would then be placed under the king's control so that he could dispose of them as he saw fit.[24]

In addition to individual estates (haciendas) and royal grounds (realengos), a third category of property was at play in the composiciones: communal grounds. Communal lands were anchored in Iberian legal traditions, which differentiated between property and possession (the tenancy or the holding of a thing).[25] This category was applied to shared lands in cities (ejidos) and to Indigenous lands—called resguardos in the New Kingdom. Resguardos were a new legal concept through which the king granted Native peoples the right to occupy their own lands collectively, although they remained the property of the monarch. It was a type of communal land designed to produce basic foodstuffs to meet survival needs. These were lands that, at least in theory, Indigenous communities had traditionally occupied. To keep their plots, they had to prove they had held them since "time immemorial"; however, they could not sell or trade them. Thus, while Spanish estates were treated as commodities, Indigenous resguardos were created as a means of survival.[26] The flawed premise of these diverging landholding categories was that "indios" were oriented toward subsistence and that they were not inclined to participate in markets. While the policy was based on mistaken assumptions about the economic activities of Native peoples, it impacted how these groups built their social and natural environments.

The audiencia presidents entrusted the implementation of the new land and labor system to a series of visitadores. As explored in chapter 2, visitadores were highly regarded inspectors who journeyed across large territories to make sure imperial guidelines were being followed. It took three different magistrates to carry out this set of inspections: Miguel de Ibarra visited the Province of Santa Fe between 1591 and 1595; Egas de Guzmán set off for the Province of Tunja and the lowlands in 1595, and his work was completed by Luis Enríquez in 1599 and 1600.[27] Before leaving the audiencia, Ibarra asked the town crier, Gaspar de Valencia, to shout from a corner of the royal street in the plaza of Santa Fe that the vecinos had twenty days to bring a copy of their land titles to the audiencia. Past that deadline, titles that had not been presented at the royal tribunal would be annulled and the lands would be declared property of the king (realengos).[28]

After collecting the titles, Ibarra and his crew left for the inspections. As was the goal of all visitas, Ibarra aimed to render local societies visible to the imperial administration: to know exactly how many people lived in each village, how they were organized, what products they grew, and whether they lived as good Christian subjects and married into Catholic families following Catholic kin patterns, and to record this information in books. The crew inspected the church, made an inventory of its ornaments, and interviewed the cacique, some Indigenous authorities, and the priest. They then turned their attention to the environment. President González had instructed Ibarra to personally walk and measure Indigenous lands and to make the communities build clear and visible boundaries. Ibarra noted that he specifically considered Muisca waterscapes when assigning the resguardos: "The indios of this district have some crops on river plains, riverbanks, brooks, and ravines, which they keep for maintenance during unfruitful years, for which reason the adjudication of resguardos to indios includes these fields."[29] In flatlands, resguardos often had a perfectly rectangular shape. After delineating resguardos, officials could "dispose of the other, vacant lands as Your Majesty instructs."[30]

The task of the inspectors was, to put it simply, to transform the landscape into property by putting it on paper. People with different kinds of knowledge and expertise participated in transcultural field trips and excursions into rural landscapes, usually working alongside Indigenous guides, to produce land titles. They were overseen by the most senior audiencia magistrate while a scribe (escribano) registered the visitador's on-the-ground observations on paper. Other functionaries were often hired to measure territory. After the visita was concluded, the owner kept a copy of the document, which served as a title. The caciques would keep the resguardo's title, and a copy of it was archived in the audiencia.[31]

The composiciones played out differently across the empire, with great regional variation. In areas of Peru, the measure was applied promptly and resulted in the dispossession of Indigenous peoples from their land; in others, its application was slower and communities managed to keep their land or even amass larger swaths. In New Spain, the implementation of the composiciones was delayed and only enforced later in the seventeenth century. In areas like the Huasteca, the composiciones did not necessarily strip Indigenous peoples of their lands but rather forced them to pay for their titles. In different contexts, land titles and maps became key instruments for community appeals and claims-making.[32]

In the eastern Andean plateau, and especially in the Bogotá savannah, the composiciones were applied promptly and served as an effective means of dispossession, as they allowed the Crown's officials to shrink Indigenous landholdings to the bare minimum. In typical colonial fashion, the composiciones introduced a logic in which imperial officials debated and decided exactly how much land was necessary for an Indigenous person to survive, as historian Jorge Orlando Melo has phrased it.[33] The inspector in charge of assigning the first resguardos, Miguel de Ibarra, considered that 1.5 hectares (3.7 acres) was more than enough for an Indigenous family, and proposed that land should be distributed to Indigenous communities according to the number of tribute-payers (a male eighteen to fifty-five years of age).[34] A Spanish settler could receive more than a hundred times that amount of land.

This perverse rationale had acute consequences at this time because the Indigenous population had declined critically—in many places by over 50 percent. While it is difficult to assert exactly how much land Indigenous people lost through the composiciones, some historians calculate that by the turn of the seventeenth century, Indigenous communities in the Province of Bogotá lost access to 95 percent of the lands that had been available to them before the conquest.[35] These calculations vary across time and space, and the displacement and dispossession of Indigenous lands had begun in the 1540s and intensified in the 1580s. However, the political reforms of the 1590s accelerated this process by legitimizing dispossession as the new mode of organizing the countryside.

These measures stripped Indigenous peoples of their lands, but they were still forced to provide labor for settlers' estates. In 1593, González created a new administrative post for this task: the corregidor de naturales, an administrator of Native affairs.[36] The new position was intended to restrict the encomenderos' power by eliminating direct contact between them and the Native peoples of their encomiendas. Instead, the corregidor would deal directly with caciques and answer to the audiencia. Corregidores were micromanagers of "indios": they had to correct bad customs, punish people for holding Indigenous ceremonies, punish thievery and incestuous behaviors, care for the church ornaments, bring European-style beds into Indigenous homes, make sure the houses were clean and well lit, and verify that no mestizo, mulato, or Black people lived among them. González even asked the corregidores to ensure that Native peoples drank clean water and to prevent them from tying textiles around children's heads, so as to protect the next generation from their parents' cultural practices. González expected the corregidor to inspire fear and respect. He illustrated this point by posing a theoretical scenario: when a priest complained about a cacique or commoner, the corregidor should punish the troublemaker without revealing that the priest had informed on them, for, as González stated, "what we desire is that they [the indios] love the priests and fear the corregidor."[37]

The instructions were especially precise with regard to Indigenous economies. Since the first decades after the conquest, the Crown had prohibited Native people from engaging in any commercial activity, arguing that it was for their own good and to protect their integrity.[38] The instructions to the corregidor were consistent with this premise. The corregidor would collect tribute and prevent the encomenderos from setting foot on their encomiendas or coming into direct contact with Native peoples. The corregidor should have close knowledge of Indigenous lands and crops. He was responsible for setting prices for Native produce and selling it. He would place the earnings from such sales in a coffer with three keys (arca de tres llaves). The corregidor, priest, and cacique would each have a key, to ensure that the caciques paid the tributes, taxes, and tithes. In this new arrangement, Native peoples would no longer be able to make transactions without the priest or the corregidor's approval.

Finally, since he deemed it "impossible for the Spanish republic to survive without the service and aid of the indios," González instructed the corregidor to set up a system renting out Native people's labor through what they called a general lease (alquiler general). This meant that the corregidor, at his discretion, could send Indigenous men to provide labor wherever it was needed at a wage that he set. While property law deemed Native people to be minors who needed protection, the instructions for corregidores treated them instead as a mobile workforce.

The corregidor became a key player in the economic organization of the countryside. For Indigenous peoples, he was the new face of the empire. He deployed his intimate knowledge of Native societies for the empire's purposes: distributing Indigenous labor to cities and estates and collecting tribute. It is no wonder that it became a coveted position, attracting settlers who had served the empire around the globe, arrived in the New Kingdom, and sought imperial posts.[39] The corregidor was such an important position that González excluded it from the list of administrative positions that could be auctioned;

the audiencia president appointed corregidores for four-year terms instead. Corregidores administered Indigenous economies beginning in the 1590s and throughout the rest of the colonial period.[40]

Miguel de Ibarra also established guidelines for workdays and wages for Indigenous labor. In 1598, he determined that in addition to the tribute Indigenous peoples paid to their encomendero, part of which went to the king's fifth (quinto real),

> it is convenient to establish that they appear for the labor and benefit of the fields and the breeding of cattle and the trade and commerce of the land, so commerce is not lost and there is an abundance of products and so that the indios are paid for their work and they know that they are obliged to turn up to work instead of roaming idle, playing and wandering, of which many vices and harms come as a result.[41]

Ibarra dictated that settlers should inform the corregidores of their labor requirements, and the corregidores would then lease out the "indios" according to proximity. He also set the pay rates for different types of labor according to task: preparing the soil for cultivation; planting maize, wheat, or barley; caring for cattle herds; building houses; carrying wood; preparing foods (like cheese); or other tasks. Wages were usually set at daily rates in pesos, the Spanish standard of value, though sometimes they included rations of corn and other foodstuffs, as well as mantas, hats, shoes, and other pieces of clothing. Work and wages were gendered: while men were tasked with agrarian and pastoral work and paid in cash, women were usually assigned to cook and more frequently paid in mantas.

Ibarra insisted this system was inspired by that of Castilian peons, the lowest stratum of agrarian workers, who had similarly been "reduced" to villages and subjected to standardization of wages and working hours.[42] In the Indies, however, people were subjected to these requirements because they had been labeled "indios"—an identifier that limited how much land they could expect to have and limited their engagement in some economic activities, like salt production.

During his inspection, Ibarra also took action to remove salt production from Indigenous hands. By 1595, he informed the king that he had effectively "taken possession" (tomado posesión) of the salt mines in Tausa, Zipaquirá, and Nemocón.[43] As I have shown, colonial administrators like Ibarra and González saw minute, precise instructions governing every detail of the production process as forms of restricting Indigenous people's room for profit and instead transferring it to the royal treasury. In 1599, Ibarra's successor, Luis

Enríquez, delineated two different districts (partidos) for salt production in the Province of Santa Fe and specified seventeen instructions for the production of ceramic vessels for salt-making, the provision of wood for the fires to evaporate the water, road maintenance, and even the sale price of salt (two tomines per arroba). In the process, Ibarra and Enríquez dispossessed the Muisca communities of this ancient industry, which had structured the interactions between cold lands and hot lands for centuries. As with the Spanish haciendas, Native people would still provide the labor for each of these tasks through the general lease, as commanded by corregidores and under the surveillance of two imperial officials, but the profits would go to the Crown. Native peoples were forbidden from selling salt to anyone; it was now the Crown's business.[44]

In the early years of the seventeenth century, visitador Luis Enríquez added measures to merge small Indigenous villages, a process they termed aggregations (agregaciones), in response to the decline in the Indigenous population, which was driven by high mortality rates resulting from disease and overwork. The impetus was both religious and economic: Indigenous villages had to provide the resources for a priest to evangelize them year-round. This proved a heavy burden for small Indigenous villages, especially combined with the general lease, the tribute paid to encomenderos and the king, and the requinto for the king. The aggregations reduced the number of Indigenous villages in Santa Fe from 83 to 23 and in Tunja from 125 to 40.[45] It was a massive project that also coincided neatly with the goals of the composiciones by freeing up lands that could then be distributed to Spaniards as estates.

Imperial officials discussed at length which evangelization models should be applied in the newly aggregated villages, a problem that in their minds was not dissociated from labor. Historian Juan Cobo shows that it was precisely the audiencia, under the presidencies of González, Sande, and Borja, that spearheaded a sweeping reform that increasingly relied on the Jesuits.[46] Ever since Archbishop Zapata de Cárdenas ordained more than a hundred friars, some of them mestizos, and ransacked Indigenous communities in search of idols in the 1570s, the evangelization project had focused on persecuting Indigenous rituals, as examined in chapters 5 and 6. Friars had remained scarce, rotating between different villages every two or three months and mostly focusing on sacraments like baptisms, marriages, and burials.[47] In contrast, the new program of evangelization implemented at the turn of the century sought to open spaces for Indigenous leaders to articulate their authority and build links to their communities through the symbolic languages of Catholicism. In other words, they aimed to offer venues for the re-creation of Indigenous cultural practices, not just their destruction. To do so, they sought to make the language of Catholicism available to Muisca leaders by studying the Muisca language carefully, translating the gospel, and creating catechetical material in Muisca—which they hoped would become a kind of lingua franca (lengua general) for evangelization. They also promoted the creation of confraternities (cofradías), through which caciques hosted large meals and banquets to celebrate Catholic festivities, took to the streets to dance in costumes, or drank chicha before starring in bullfighting contests with capes and swords.[48]

If the secret dialogue between friars and corregidores worked as González had envisioned years prior—in which priests secretly informed corregidores of what the "indios" confessed privately—the spiritual reform completed the new system of economic governance, making it an efficient surveillance mechanism in which Christian spirituality was at the service of the empire's material needs. The reform aimed to produce devout Catholic workers, living in Catholic families and sharing common values of Christianity, just like the peoples of Castile. And the priest's surveillance of Indigenous thought and social life—along with the books of records that included information about birth, household conformation, and customs—extended the enclosure to the realm of spiritual life.

In this sense, the composiciones and the birth of the resguardos formed part of a larger remaking of economic governance: a process of enclosure in which most of the adult male population was drafted from Indigenous communities to work long shifts on lands and in enterprises that were not their own. They did so in exchange for a payment that the corregidor stored in a box, from which he paid tribute, taxes, and tithes, as well as the other obligations the empire put on Native peoples. In this new state of affairs, the corregidor disposed of Indigenous labor. In coordination with friars, the corregidores also maintained an intimate knowledge of Indigenous communities, keeping records of their names, ages, skills, and capabilities, and used that information to dictate where they must contribute their labor. It was an age of hubris in which administrators felt entitled to merge and reshuffle populations at will and take over Indigenous enterprises if they stood to benefit. These labor demands and payments added up: Indigenous peoples had to provide tribute in mantas for the encomendero, cacique, and king, plus the king's requinto in cash, along with the tithes and salaries of the corregidores and priest in cash and products like eggs, chicken, and hay—all while producing food for subsistence in their resguardos.

To be sure, these policies did not consolidate a single and coherent model of empire agreed upon and abided by all. There were divergences, factions, frictions, and conflict. The ideal of the kingdom still left space to discuss even the most basic tenets of the empire: if the encomienda should persist, how and who should evangelize, what types of Indigenous labor demands were morally justifiable, and how people's lives should be administered and sur-veilled. But the reforms definitively transformed the kingdom's infrastructure. They prompted the decline of the encomienda as the institutional framework organizing Indigenous labor.[49] Although encomiendas did not disappear in the New Kingdom—they in fact survived until 1810—the legal mechanisms that determined who could benefit from Indigenous labor changed.[50] After the composiciones, documents that proved land ownership, like titles and maps, increasingly became enmeshed in disputes about the rightful organization of the landscape.

Paper Battles

Dispossession happened on paper and was contested on paper. In the case of the old lands of Muyquyta, Maldonado's defense produced the land titles cor-responding to the sections of the estate received from previous owners and land grants, all ratified during the composiciones under González. The visita-dor Ibarra had established the resguardo in 1592, and González had approved the composición in 1597. That year Maldonado made a new petition to displace the Bogotá community to new lands in the warmer region of Tena, aiming to grab their remaining resguardos and add them to his estate. He claimed that the cold weather was affecting their health and that by relocating to Tena they would be cured. The Bogotá cacique, Don Diego, was able to stop these at-tempts at dispossession through a formal complaint.[51] But this did not halt the progressive dispossession of Indigenous lands, as Maldonado used legal means to claim ownership. The 1614 lawsuit eventually favored Maldonado, protect-ing his land rights. In the following decades, Maldonado's descendants would intermarry with some of the kingdom's most powerful families—like the Ospi-nas, Venegas, Berrío, Caicedo, and Dávila families—thus consolidating a lin-eage that remained powerful for centuries.

The use of litigation to enforce land ownership and mediate relations with the Indigenous community of Bogotá continued in the Maldonado family's ad-ministration of the estate, as tensions between Spanish pastoralism and Muisca agrarian waterscapes remained alive. In 1628, Antonio Maldonado de Mendoza, the son and inheritor of Francisco de Maldonado's entailed state, requested the Crown's support to force the Indigenous commoners of Bogotá to fence their village. He praised the corregidor's insistence on keeping the village en-closed, aiming to deter Indigenous people from dispersing. Yet he claimed that many Indigenous vassals of his encomienda had spread out along the savannah to protect their fields from cattle belonging to neighboring estates and residents, as the poor state of the fences in certain sections had left their crops unprotected. The encomendero envisioned an easy solution: that the whole village of Bogotá, including women, the elderly, and children, devote one day per month to rebuilding the fallen portions of the fences and to cleaning and deepening a ditch next to the fence. This simple procedure, if applied rigorously, would keep cattle outside the fence and Native people inside it, restoring order.[52]

Building fences to enclose land, assign it to someone, and declare an owner is an expression of sovereignty, since property is a social arrangement that determines who has access to what, who deserves what. Fences have a deep colonial history. They enabled dispossession by restraining the movement of bodies, both human and nonhuman.[53] That Indigenous commoners were forced to provide the labor to build the fences required to prevent livestock from damaging their fields, while also growing their own subsistence crops and providing labor to adjacent cattle ranches, agrarian estates, and even cities, illustrates the stark inequities and profound exploitation of the new agrarian regime.

Legal languages introduced modes of arguing and rules for presenting evidence that strongly influenced how Native peoples thought of themselves and claimed their right to access their resguardos as Indigenous persons. Joanne Rappaport has argued that this language of jurisprudence and the forms of communal organization that first the Spanish empire and later the Republic of Colombia championed—such as the resguardo and the cabildo—became central to how people defined and claimed indigeneity.[54] Land titles were perhaps the most important genre of paper document to guide Indigenous engagements with literacy, shaping everything from their reading practices to their attempts at forgery, but also molding ethnic identities and how Native peoples imagined themselves in relation to the past. Thus, paper forms and the broader legal frameworks they represented strongly influenced how Indigenous peoples defined their identities.

Indigenous leaders and commoners voiced their concerns about the many problems of the new system of economic governance in ways that would be recorded on paper, written either by themselves or by scribes or lawyers. At first they saw the corregidor as a useless figure—"they do nothing," declared the cacique of Ubatoque—who nevertheless became a costly new actor in the chain of command.[55] The cacique of Pausaga said that before there were corregidores, the communities simply paid tribute to the encomendero, implying that there was no need for an additional bureaucrat in this context.[56] In 1595, a group of encomenderos including Juan de Guzmán, Diego de Maldonado, and Bartolomé de Mazmela echoed the caciques' arguments and petitioned to halt the appointment of corregidores, saying that they were completely useless and burdened Native peoples, who paid the corregidor's salary in addition to their other obligations.[57] But what caciques initially saw as an unnecessary step in an existing process became a thorn in their side when the corregidores started using their connections and networks of cronies to distribute Native labor or overlook violence against laborers.[58]

All levels of Indigenous authority approached Hispanic officials orally and in writing to seek justice, articulating their dissatisfaction, documenting the many forms of violence they experienced, and requesting change—often in evocative terms. One of the most expressive complaints I have found came from the Indigenous leaders of Turmequé in 1672. It elegantly interweaves a critique of environmental violence with the acts of measuring and the politics of evidence in colonial courts:

> We come before you to state the troubles and destructions we have suffered in our town in the form of damage to our crops. There is a neighbor named Agustín Vela with over two hundred mules and horses, bovine livestock, and donkeys in our *resguardo*. Before we can harvest our pittance, which is wheat, maize, barley, and truffles, he brings in his tame and wild mules and destroys [our crops, he] has many lands starting on the Boyacá Bridge, where he has many grazing lands and can keep to his estate without maliciously fattening his mules with our grain by letting them into our crops every year with contempt for the poor because he is so rich and powerful, and ruining and diminishing us. And after we harvest and pile up our crops, he destroys them with his mules and livestock, and because we are poor and do not speak [Spanish], he is oppressing us. When we go to tell him, he says: "Who weighed the damages, who saw them?" and then he releases his dogs on us.[59]

Turmequé's Indigenous leaders' claims for justice juxtaposed the ecological tension between the pastoralist economy of a settler, Agustín Vela, and the agrarian economy of the people of the resguardo, along with a critique of monarchical systems of knowledge production and evidence collection. Vela intimidated the people of the resguardo of Turmequé, saying that because they were poor, they were not fluent in Spanish, and there was no surveyor or painter documenting the assaults on their crops, justice was unavailable to them. Overcoming these challenges, the leaders of Turmequé proved Vela wrong and appeared in court to communicate their outrage and sense of violation. In this way, they revealed what they saw as just and unjust with respect to access to land and the uses of the environment.[60]

The juxtaposition of claims for justice and critiques of imperial knowledge production processes appeared in many Indigenous testimonies. The caciques of Soracá, too, expressed that they faced many hardships but that all colonial inspectors "passed like the wind" (todos los visitadores pasan como el viento), meaning that they rushed to move on to the next village and were not able to really perceive, let alone solve, the causes of Soracá's hardships. They then outlined twenty-seven forms of aggression they experienced from settlers and officials, including gendered and physical violence and excessive work. They requested a "secret investigation" because when they had tried to alert the corregidor of these problems he called them "dogs" and dismissed them. They explained that those who harmed them were allied with the corregidor because they had "bought off the justice system" (compran la justicia).[61] Indigenous peoples voiced their outrage toward the forms of colonial enclosure that took over their lands to transform them into cattle pastures, destroying their crops and selling their labor. But despite the violence of the new system of property and labor, Indigenous economies remained central to the kingdom.

Indigenous Economies

The audiencia presidents' all-encompassing enclosure program did not translate smoothly into practice. The vision of subservient Indigenous villages with subsistence-oriented resguardos, populated exclusively by "indios" and closely administered by corregidores, priests, and caciques who siphoned labor off to settler-owned enterprises, deeply impacted the development of the countryside, but it failed to relegate Indigenous villages to a secondary role. In other words, Indigenous villages and resguardos were never the isolated, subsistence-driven islands that the reform dictated. They remained vibrant epicenters of economic activity for centuries; their population greatly surpassed that of cities, and they attracted a diverse population of people whom officials did not necessarily identify as "indios."[62]

The reach and vitality of Indigenous networks of exchange—extending from the highlands to the lowlands and involving gold, mantas, salt, agricultural products (like coca and cotton), meat, feathers, wood, stone, and crafts—was evident from the information collected in Ibarra's and Enríquez's visits. Indigenous markets continued to offer access to all these products, which were still traded for mantas and salt, relying on the same types of pacts and bonds that had enabled the flow of products in pre-Hispanic times. Indigenous produce was still the main source of food as well. The continuity of these markets is so astounding that ethnohistorian Carl Langebaek has used these late sixteenth-century reports to shed light on the scale and dynamics of pre-Hispanic Muisca trade.[63]

Yet not all was continuous: Indigenous economies had innovated and changed dramatically and creatively. Indigenous peoples had added chickens, pigs, cattle, sheep, and mules to their economies. The adoption of Old World animals allowed them to rely less on deer and guinea pig meat, adding chicken, pork, and occasionally beef, along with eggs and dairy products, to their diets. All these products eventually reshaped local cuisine. Indigenous artisans also began making cheaper mantas using wool (see chapter 3). Indigenous agroecologies began to change as well, combining terraced agricultural landscapes with pastoralism.[64] There is evidence of this in the Maldonado painting, which includes a nonterraced section of the resguardo for the cacique's pigsty and another section with the cacique's residence accompanied by a drawing of a bull (center-right). The cacique was not the only one to keep Old World animals. One of the Indigenous captains, Say, who had an agreement with Maldonado to occupy a section of the hacienda instead of residing in the resguardo, had at least eighty sheep. Juan Platanero, probably a wealthy commoner who lived in the same area, had around 240 sheep and seven or eight pigs. Others in the same area had between ten and fifteen pigs, while some had no Old World animals. In addition, they all had lands that were tilled or terraced.[65] In other words, Indigenous communities found ways to combine their agrarian ecologies with imported cattle ranching, developing a hybrid economy.

Over time, the general lease and daily wages brought income to Indigenous villages in gold dust and gold in bars and bits, and possibly in minted cash—a new form of currency that previously had not been widely available. The move toward a recognizable cash economy took shape in steps, more slowly than in other places, such as the viceroyalties of Mexico or Peru. The Bogotá mint (casa de la moneda) was established in 1620, and seven years later it was consistently producing officially sanctioned silver, gold, and copper coins. Yet even then, the circulation of minted cash remained limited. While gold coins were destined for larger transactions, probably at the hands of wealthy merchants, copper coins were more suited for daily transactions ("para la contratación y comercio por menor de dicho Reino").[66] When minted cash was available in Indigenous villages, it likely was used for specific types of transactions, rather than day-to-day expenditures. Trying to identify the types of transactions that Indigenous people made using minted copper coin is a venture of hypotheticals, since ledgers and accounting books are misleading: while transactions were done with some type of cash money or through the exchange of products, records and ledgers used a money of account that transmuted those several currencies into one standard of value, the golden peso (peso de oro). As with other paper technologies, account books and ledgers abstracted, distorted, and simplified local realities to make them legible, digestible, and computable for decision-making. Perhaps for this reason, I have found no evidence that minted cash overwhelmingly permeated Indigenous markets, trade, or economic interactions in general. In González's instructions, it was the corregidor's job to set wages, assign labor, collect earnings, and deposit them in the coffer with three keys. Tribute was still paid to the encomenderos and the king in mantas, and likely most trade in foodstuffs and Indigenous products continued to be carried out primarily in the varied, dispersed types of economic engagements that characterized Muisca trade, without a specialized merchant class or the use of coin.[67]

From these traces, I would posit that cash was used for the cacicazgo's economic duties to the imperial administration and to purchase European goods. The types of obligations paid in minted cash were the requinto for the king, the tithe, and the salaries of the corregidor and the priest, though those also included other types of products, like eggs, chicken, and herbs. Some cash expenditures went to the church, often sponsored by caciques, who donated cash and paid to be featured in murals and paintings as patrons, or to fund the activities of confraternities, through which caciques increasingly convened community gatherings. Caciques and other wealthy Indigenous persons might also use cash to purchase the types of European items that granted them distinction, such as clothes, horses, furniture, jewelry, candles, and even swords and daggers.[68] These items were often purchased directly from merchants in Santa Fe.

The balance between community lands and income destined for the caciques' personal wealth and that meant for commoners and communal purposes varied across time and space. In some cases, caciques amassed large swaths of land for personal profit; in others, commoners retained access to the majority of resguardo lands. In all cases, the resguardos had complex systems of land attribution, which attracted not only the people of the cacicazgo but also multiethnic populations that leased or occupied lands through a variety of arrangements.[69]

In this sense, Indigenous villages defied the empire's spatial organization that aimed to marginalize and isolate "indios." While officials insisted only "indios" could live in villages—and visitadores aimed to expel any persons who did not fall squarely into this category, such as those with European or African ancestry— the towns attracted a diverse population. Such was the case of Lorenzo Requero, born in the city of Santa Fe to an Indigenous woman of Ubatoque whom he described as related to the caciques. Even though he was from Santa Fe and legally classified as a mestizo, Requero returned to his mother's community in Ubatoque and married a local Muisca woman named Catalina Çimca; they had four children and lived on the newly created resguardo, where they raised cattle and grew fruit trees. While evading the legal label of "indio" proved useful in some respects for Requero—doing so exempted him from tribute and forced labor under the general lease—he worried that his condition as a mestizo would leave him landless. For this reason, Requero asked the visitador Ibarra to assure him that he would be permitted to remain on his lands. His entire life journey made sense from the point of view of Muisca kinship patterns, in which mother and children traveled to the father's residence during his lifetime but never lost their political connections to their mother's kin line and were always conceived of as part of the uncle's household. Once the father died, the children returned to their uncle's community and reclaimed their place.[70] The lands Requero occupied, he argued, were his uncle's and wife's lands.

The empire's racialized vocabulary was poorly suited to designate and accommodate the experience of someone like Lorenzo Requero. The fact that authorities tagged him as "mestizo" made him no less Muisca. Many more individuals like him occupied important roles in the social life of resguardos and Indigenous villages. The caciques rented lands to them and used those resources to pay tribute.[71] In 1668, audiencia president Don Diego de Villalba y Toledo complained that resguardos and Indigenous villages were behaving like Spanish villages and cities, where people of any background rented land and became vecinos even though the law dictated otherwise.[72] Imperial officials made every effort to outlaw this behavior, threatening to jail intruders and confiscating their goods. But further inquiry reveals a different reality. These men and women were not intruders. If the authorities labeled someone as a mestizo, it identified him as an intruder and an outsider—apparently they thought the "foreign" mixture severed every tie the person had with the community. But, as visita records suggest, to Indigenous peoples it was the kin ties and connections that mattered, not the fact of a non-Indigenous parent. In other words, that mestizos were born to Indigenous women made them part of the community.[73] Besides working their uncles' lands, these individuals had various occupations, from shoemakers to carpenters to muleteers. They were involved in transportation and candlemaking, bread baking, and the production of other items that were necessary for commerce or consumption in the town. Officials' binary language, however, left no room for such shades of gray.

In the long run, Indigenous villages and resguardos remained sites where interactions among peoples eclipsed the empire's constraining ethnic labels. Their vibrant agrarian and pastoral economies made them magnetic poles that attracted people who did not fit the ethnic categories the empire sought to enforce. Over time, the imperial administration had no choice but to recognize the role of Indigenous villages in consolidating the rural economy and the broader rural population. Historian Marta Herrera Angel argues that an important step in this process took place in 1622 when Archbishop Hernando Arias de Ugarte, during a pastoral visit, saw the many poor Spaniards, as well as mestizo, mulato, and Black people, who resided near Indigenous villages but far from Spanish cities. Since it was impractical for them to travel to Hispanic settlements to attend mass or confess, Ugarte commanded the village priests to oversee their spiritual education. The measure applied only to poor settlers who could not afford a residence in Spanish settlements.

Herrera Angel posits that Ugarte introduced a seed of change that ultimately subverted the principles of spatial organization in the highlands. It unleashed a demographic transformation that undermined ethnic segregation as the organizing principle of society.[74] Indigenous lands and villages would be increasingly occupied by people who conceived of themselves not as "indios" but rather as vecinos. While in theory the terms *vecino* and *indio* were not opposites, in using them individuals made different appeals and points of emphasis. In this case, *vecino* displaced the ethnic premise of imperial spatial segregation and emphasized instead a person's belonging to and citizenship in the empire.[75] In fact, in 1594, Lorenzo Requero was already using the term *vecino* to evade the empire's constraining labels. By identifying himself as a *vecino*—a category that implied he lived a "vida en policía"—Requero reappropriated a legal label of empire to subvert its vocabulary of differentiation.[76]

By the eighteenth century, the number of vecinos living in or near Indigenous towns had grown enough to be described as a demographic explosion.[77] The richest residents came to be known as orejones, "big eared"; the term was also used in Peru to refer to the young nobility and probably stemmed from Spanish impressions of Inca noblemen's ear enlargement and jewelry.[78] The mixed, heterogeneous, and blurry category of "vecino" had become the dominant demographic force. This group evaded the legal category of "indio": their lands were not the protected reserves called resguardos, their labor was not to be sold coercively, they were not subject to tribute, and the corregidor did not place their earnings in a coffer with three keys. Their legal condition came to be embraced under the phrase "free people of all colors" (libres de todos los colores). An ethnographic study of their kin patterns and how they interacted among themselves and with Indigenous communities has yet to be performed; however, preliminary evidence indicates that many of their cultural practices, economic activities, and customs built upon those of Indigenous societies. As Joanne Rappaport puts it, many vecinos "were immersed in a web of largely indigenous relationships, despite their classification as people of mixed parentage."[79]

Early Modern Enclosures

Between the 1590s and the 1610s, kingdom officials consolidated an early modern Catholic version of the enclosure of the commons that dispossessed Indigenous peoples of the eastern Andean plateau, aiming to remake them after the poorest strata of rural laborers in Castile—so that they had just enough time to work and to pray, as Mercedes López put it.[80] This form of economic governance also transformed Indigenous ecologies by reallocating lands to boost productivity, but in so doing it also undermined highland Indigenous peoples' economic autonomy.

In Muisca aquaculture, notions of community and justice were tied to building a landscape and, in the Bogotá savannah, to the management of water. Since the Spanish invasion, Indigenous communities had struggled to remain key economic players. The production and sale of the two iconic highland products that defined highland peoples' connection to the lowlands—textiles and salt—had remained primarily in Indigenous hands. This gave them subtle leverage in their negotiation with encomenderos and Crown officials. The new property regime laid responsibility for organizing Indigenous labor at the feet of imperial officials, who in turn told Native peoples how they should live their lives, build their houses, raise their children, spend their money, and plant their crops. The reforms brought transformation, and Indigenous peoples made their objections known in tribunals and courts. Ironically, the legal status of the resguardos asked "indios" to prove that the lands they claimed were those they had occupied from "time immemorial," while the measures simultaneously dispossessed, displaced, and reshuffled them.

The idea that an official could lease an entire population was morally troubling even for visitador Miguel de Ibarra, who after seeing things on the ground implored that at least pregnant women and the elderly be exempted.[81] Historians sometimes refer to maroon economies as parasitic, located at the margins of colonial centers and often draining colonial profits through raiding. Colonial economy was parasitic in its own way, designed to systematically deplete Indigenous economies. As Ibarra put it: "Those who govern shall not be satisfied with the fact that indios eat and fill themselves up, if their industries . . . do not provide sustenance for Spaniards."[82]

When designing some of his reforms, audiencia president Antonio González explicitly referenced the aim of financing interimperial war by impinging on Indigenous lands and economic enterprises. The taxes that came out of the composiciones did not produce a major source of income by themselves, but the new structure of imperial governance changed the rules of the game by enabling legal mechanisms to dispossess Indigenous peoples of their lands and to dispose of their labor. Audiencia presidents and corregidores would soon be joined by accountants, as we will see in the next chapter, who aimed to augment revenues. These officials were the new imperial planners, who dreamed of the institutional landscapes they could build to maximize the empire's profit at the difficult economic juncture that existed at the turn of the century. These imperial dreams, as we will see, increasingly brought them downhill—down from the cold lands to the hot lands—as they envisioned highland peoples as mobile laborers who could not only work on nearby haciendas but also move down to the mines in the hot lands. Imperial officials designed new mechanisms to pull Indigenous labor downhill, as they advanced a drastic, genocidal campaign to eradicate the Pijaos from the Andes and the Magdalena River valley. Their ultimate goal was to transform the troubled borderlands into productive mines. This imperial alchemy is the subject of the next chapter.

IMPERIAL ALCHEMY

In 1601, the president of the Audiencia of Santa Fe, Francisco de Sande, appointed magistrate Luis Enríquez to "pacify"—a euphemism for destroy and subjugate—the Carares, a Carib group in the eastern piedmont of the Magdalena River who constantly attacked and robbed the vessels that carried merchandise and passengers along the river between Cartagena and Santa Fe de Bogotá.[1] Following Sande's instruction, Enríquez led a military force of over two hundred Spanish men funded by the cities of Tunja, Santa Fe, Vélez, and Honda, all of which had been affected by Carare raids.[2] After performing a preliminary exploration of the river, Enríquez and his men settled in a site they called Barrancas Bermejas (meaning "red ravine"), where they built a fort protected by a tall palisade. The fort became the soldiers' center of operations for the next three months, where they kept provisions and from where they paddled and poled the rivers and walked into dense tropical forests in search of the assailants, who moved silently and discreetly, leaving almost no trace of their passage.

Enríquez wrote a report describing the military incursion and attached a map depicting the contentious geographies he had traversed (figure 8.1). The artist's brush revealed the tensions between the kingdom and fugitive Indigenous groups: cities represented the Spaniards' domains, while jungles and forests signaled the landscapes dominated by Indigenous peoples. The fort's size was exaggerated on the map, as were the sites at greater risk of Indigenous attack. The presence of the Carares and Yareguíes was overwhelming, though it is not immediately evident in the painting. They loomed out of the forests to haunt Spanish settlements, yet were nowhere to be found. In his report, Enríquez confessed that without their Indigenous allies, like the Simitís, the Spaniards never would have found any of the Carare assailants. Even with the Simitís' help, after a few military encounters the Carares vanished into the forests along the river. Enríquez concluded that the soldiers had only mildly "punished" the rebels, and that the Crown would need to launch new attacks to dismantle the feared assailants of the Magdalena River.[3]

The map captured the uneven geographies of rule and dissidence that had formed over the previous decades: the audiencia perched high in the mountains and connected to Iberia by the Magdalena River, a connection made precarious by sovereign Indigenous groups that confronted the kingdom in the hot lands and the central Andean range. This chapter explores kingdom officials' responses to their precarious control of the hot lands during the first decades of the seventeenth century: they sought to eliminate threats to the kingdom's sovereignty and transform the hot lands into producers of precious metals for the empire. To do so, officials took a structured, rationalized approach to violence, labor, and finance. Thus began the final stage in the consolidation of the kingdom.

That Enríquez and his men likened the Carares to jungles and forests did not mean the Carares were ahistorical remnants of a pre-Columbian past. Rather, the Carares likely formed and grew in size and power during the sixteenth century, probably absorbing refugees and taking captives from other groups, who joined them in their targeted attacks on merchant convoys along the river.[4] At the same time, the Pijao anticolonial project had grown into a powerful interethnic coalition with thousands of people spread over the central Andean range into the Magdalena and Cauca river valleys (chapter 4). Indigenous projects like those of the Pijaos and Carares both contained the kingdom and offered opportunities to people who wanted to escape its institutions. By the end of the sixteenth century, they revealed the kingdom's tenuous claims to sovereignty in the hot lands. The Pijao expansion, in particular, posed such a critical challenge to the kingdom that they were one of the

FIGURE 8.1. Map of the Magdalena River, 1601. AGI, SF, r. 4, n. 29, 30r.

main subjects discussed in officials' and settlers' personal correspondence to the king, in which they urged him to prioritize putting down the "indio bandits" (indios salteadores) so that they could develop the mining potential of the lowlands.

The dreams and expectations for the kingdom relied on exterminating the Pijao coalition, the Carares, and other Indigenous sovereignties who threatened imperial rule and jeopardized commerce and metal production. In this sense, campaigns like Enríquez's against the Carares were coupled with dreams of the kingdom's success. The presidents, lower officials, and settlers often iterated these dreams through a language of mining. They trusted that once the hot lands and transportation arteries were secured, developing the silver mines would enrich them and contribute to resolving the monarchy's financial problems—if they could find adequate supplies of labor. To this end, imperial officials pushed coerced laborers to the hot lands by importing enslaved Africans or Indigenous workers from the cold lands. The mita, which violated the kingdom's legal values, and the massive importation of enslaved Africans— through which human beings became property—came to be seen as the only remedies for the kingdom's financial problems.

The chimeric quest to redeem the kingdom by transforming the hot lands into rich mines of gold and silver is what I call an "imperial alchemy." This chapter examines how a shift in the empire's techniques of governance made the genocide of the Pijao peoples and the development of silver mines in the hot lands—especially in Mariquita—two priorities of government during the early decades of the seventeenth century. Between 1600 and 1630, officials relied on new methods and instruments of governance: new ways to wage war, seeking total annihilation through militias directed by the audiencia president instead of wealthy settlers; increased efforts to draw conscripted Indigenous and enslaved African labor to the mines; and new administrative instruments and routines to measure and evaluate the kingdom's economy and calculate profit.

These methods of governance were the culmination of decades of colonial violence and labor administration, and emerged from the interaction between empire-wide policies and local processes. Yet they brought about a new phase in the history of the kingdom. I argue that the official investment in genocide and forms of coerced labor reshaped the hot lands, opening a new geographic horizon to the kingdom in what had been the territory of the Pijaos or in their area of influence while establishing a dynamic, motley world in the Mariquita hot lands. This expansion toward the hot lands marked the culmination of a century-long process of making the kingdom and colonizing downhill. It completed the enclosure of Indigenous economies and landscapes in the cold lands (examined in chapter 7), but now in order to extract able-bodied men from their communities to ship them off to the hot lands as mobile laborers. In this sense, the mita closed the circle of enclosure, dispossession, and commodification of labor.

In officials' eyes, transforming the hot lands into a rich source of precious minerals would epitomize the kingdom's success, but mining was both a utopia and a dystopia. Such a transformation proved an ever-elusive dream, especially given the challenges of securing labor. The officials' dream of introducing large contingents of enslaved people from Africa and pulling from the New Kingdom's hot lands quantities of silver that rivaled Potosí's output never quite reached the dimensions they expected, but the radicalization of war against the Pijaos and the turn toward the Mariquita silver mines did give the kingdom a new horizon and structure, marking a new inflection in the history of the kingdom.

Genocide as Imperial Policy

In 1595, the former corregidor of the mining town of Almaguer described the Pijao peoples as the greatest obstacles to the kingdom's prosperity. He described the paths that connected the kingdom to Peru, saying, "The Pijaos are the lords of these lands, with their gold and silver mines and many riches."[5] The city of Ibagué had few Native inhabitants, the official reported, because "the Pijaos, their neighbors, eat them." In chapter 4, I argued that from the mid-1550s to the 1600s, the Pijaos formed a sprawling anticolonial coalition that grew rapidly from a few hundred men living around the Saldaña River to a force of several thousand people spread across the central Andean range into the Magdalena and Cauca river valleys. Both Spaniards and Pijaos explained this expansion through a language of eating: they used cannibalism as a metaphor to describe how large contingents of Indigenous vassals of the king were incorporated into the Pijao coalition, as either allies or captives. By the end of the sixteenth century, imperial officials consistently identified the Pijaos as the most urgent threat to the kingdom's claim to sovereignty.

In 1593, audiencia president Antonio González tried to tackle this problem using the available institutional mechanisms of conquest: by signing a private contract, known as a capitulación, with one of the wealthiest settlers of the kingdom, Bernardino de Mujica Guevara. The capitulaciones were one of the main institutions used to subdue Native peoples throughout the sixteenth century. Capitulaciones were contracts between imperial authorities and wealthy individuals that made those individuals responsible for waging war against rebellious groups at their own expense, in exchange for privileges and benefits over the peoples and lands they subdued. In this case, the contract granted Mujica the title "Governor and Pacifier of the Pijao Provinces," and he, in turn, pledged to use his wealth to eliminate the threat the Pijaos posed to the kingdom's security. Under his capitulación, Mujica created a new city, San Miguel de Pedraza, where he stationed 110 armed men under the command of Field Captain Pedro de Jove. Mujica himself commanded operations from Ibagué, where he also had a group of soldiers.

Bernardo de Vargas Machuca led a company to Timaná in 1593. He was a "luckless conquistador" who participated in a series of Indigenous wars after the more renowned conquests of the New World—when revenues were minimal compared to the times of Cortés, Pizarro, or Jiménez de Quesada—and authored the first known manual of counterinsurgency warfare.[6] His involvement in the offensive is indicative of how cumulative knowledge had shaped the Spanish style of war in the Indies, and on the Pijao mountains in particular: they used a type of irregular counterinsurgency that adopted Indigenous tactics. Vargas Machuca's war manual revealed how Indigenous strategy, medicinal knowledge, and even martial culture had reshaped European war. It suggested that soldiers travel "fast and light," wear cotton clothing rather than Spanish armor, remain aware of their surroundings, and use dogs for ambushes or night attacks, and it suggested ways to effectively interact with Indigenous allies. While filled with references to Rome and Greece, the most practical advice was taken from Indigenous cultures and at points even appears to credit Indigenous "sorcery"—an example of what anthropologist Neil Whitehead deemed the efficacy of Indigenous aggression tactics to transculturate their enemies.[7] Vargas Machuca's main point, though, was "that the new defenders of the Indies, unlike the old freelance conquistadors, be recognized as a professional, soldierly class"—a need that was abundantly clear in the efforts to contain the Pijao expansion.[8]

Despite Mujica's enormous expenditure in service of conquering the Pijaos, and notwithstanding Machuca's experience, this method of conquest—which had structured the Spanish conquests of the New World more generally—failed soundly. The Pijaos had mastered the art of the silent attack over half a decade. They ambushed, raided, and confronted their enemies when the Spaniards were most vulnerable. However, when Spanish forces managed to regroup and gather their weapons and prepared to counterattack, the Pijaos disappeared into the mountains, not to be found. This made them unbeatable in a traditional confrontation or through the institutional mechanisms for conquest available in the Spanish empire, like the capitulaciones, that placed war in individuals' hands. The Pijao coalition was simply too strong and experienced for even the wealthiest Spanish settlers to subdue. Vargas Machuca's plea for a professional militia was apt.

By the early 1600s it was clear that the capitulaciones would not work against the Pijaos, and Philip III took a new approach, appointing Juan de Borja to lead the audiencia in 1604 and making war a priority of the government. Borja's appointment was strategic within the logics of seventeenth-century Spanish forms of governance. The Iberian tradition distinguished between two types of officials. The togados were lettered magistrates who wore gowns, had studied at least ten years in one of the four most prestigious law schools in Spain, and could advise the court on legal practice. Meanwhile, the officials de capa y espada wore cloaks and swords and could not vote in judicial matters but could advise the court in every other aspect of governance, including war. Borja belonged to the latter category, even though he had studied arts and law at Alcalá and Salamanca and came from a noble lineage.[9] He was a cousin of the king's most trusted advisor, Don Francisco de Sandoval y Rojas de Borja, duke of Lerma; of the president of the Council of the Indies, Pedro Fernández de Castro y Andrade, count of Lemos and marquis of Esquilache; and of Francisco de Borja y Aragón, who would become viceroy of Peru in 1615. Someone with his relations and education would generally be a togado; his designation as presidente de capa y espada made clear that the king expected him to take a militaristic approach to enforcing the kingdom's sovereignty.

Borja's connections to powerful men gave him strong political leverage as he confronted the two issues most affecting Hispanic rule: Pijao sovereignty and antagonism, on the one hand, and the rise of contraband trade, on the other. In Borja's opinion, the contract with Mujica to dissolve the Pijao coalition had resulted only in a "loss of people, reputation, and treasury."[10] During the seventy years that the Pijaos had ruled the central Andean chain, Borja claimed, they had destroyed fourteen Spanish cities and towns and twenty Indigenous villages, and had killed and consumed a hundred thousand Native allies. Although Borja undoubtedly padded these numbers in his effort to justify military reform, they do reveal the general sense of chaos, devastation, and intimidation the Pijao coalition provoked among settlers and officials. Their ability to move across the empire's jurisdictions made it nearly impossible for a settler belonging to a single administrative division to attack effectively: as noted in chapter 4, if a settler from the Audiencia of Santa Fe organized an attack, the Pijaos would retreat to Popayán, and if the Audiencia of Quito launched one, they would hide near Santa Fe. It was just impossible for a settler to gather the resources and political leverage needed to command a multisite attack, as the capitulaciones system dictated.

In 1605, Borja spearheaded a new modality of war, moving away from settler-led incursions to militias directed by the audiencia president: a confrontation financed by the kingdom's treasury or by neighboring cities and under the supervision of the kingdom's highest political figure. His approach had the dual impact of uniting the municipal councils, settlers, and even governorships against the Pijaos while strengthening the central authority of the Audiencia in Santa Fe. He was appointed audiencia president on August 11, 1604, arrived in Cartagena on July 20, 1605, and left for the mines of Mariquita before even setting foot in Santa Fe. His journey to Mariquita foretold the habits of rule he would adopt in the first part of his twenty-two-year presidency—the longest in three centuries of Spanish rule in the New Kingdom. During these years, Borja was seldom in the kingdom's capital, and instead could be found in forts and fields throughout its territories.

Four months before naming Borja president of the audiencia, the Crown appointed Domingo de Eraso as governor of Muzo and Colima—a hot-land area well known for its emerald production.[11] Eraso had extensive war experience, having participated in many of the wars Spain had waged throughout the Atlantic in the name of Catholicism in the late sixteenth and early seventeenth centuries. He first traveled from Spain to Chile in 1584 and fought in the wars against the Mapuches—the sovereign Indigenous peoples of the southern tip of the Andes whom Bernardo de Vargas Machuca described as the continent's most powerful Indigenous warriors. Eraso had also participated in skirmishes with renowned pirates, including possibly Francis Drake, as he defended the cities of the Caribbean and Pacific against their incursions, and had spent more than a year as the prisoner of French corsairs.[12] Eraso's practical experience in the Mapuche wars made him Borja's most important military leader. Like Borja, when Eraso arrived in Santa Fe in 1606, he immediately left for the Pijao territories.[13]

Borja and Eraso redefined the kingdom's institutions and infrastructures of war by drawing on strategies and institutions from all over the empire. They recognized that it would be senseless to expect their troops to find the Pijaos and subdue them in direct confrontation, given their use of furtiveness as a combat strategy. Instead, Borja and Eraso concentrated on the landscape, trying to eliminate the Pijaos by disrupting their lived environments and impeding their survival strategies. Their style of war turned the environment into a weapon: they first surveyed and mapped the territory, then established forts in strategic sites, periodically marching through the territory wrecking buildings, ruining crops, and destroying any possible food source. In this sense, their war made space and geography the focus of aggressions.

As part of this process, Borja and his men put their effort down on paper, sketching a large, simple map of the Pijao borderlands (figure 8.2).[14] This map was different from the painting of the lands of Bogotá (chapter 7) or the map of the Magdalena River (discussed above). Instead of a colorful depiction of fauna and vegetation, it indicated toponyms and suppressed all natural features except altitude and rivers. It was the visual aid Borja and his crew needed to move through the borderlands. Plain and practical, the map stripped the landscape of superfluous features, resulting in a simple yet informative sketch Borja and his war captains and soldiers could pore over as they discussed tactics or figured out where their Native adversaries were hidden. The fact that the paper of the map is torn along its folds demonstrates that this object was heavily used; it was not a work of art, but rather a tool of war.

The map captures the essence of the contested landscapes of the Pijao borderlands. The artist employed different drawing techniques to depict the rugged terrain, using thin, parallel strokes stemming from wavy lines to describe mountain cusps, as well as tree-like formations to represent bodies of water. The combination of these two techniques gives a sense of depth to the flat surface, rendering topography visible. Rivers, mountain ridges, and Indigenous place names were the main orientation criteria. Some toponyms inscribe on the mountains the contested, mythic geographies of the area Borja and Eraso called an "impenetrable mountain." The map includes, for example, the place

FIGURE 8.2. Extract from a map of Pijao Territory, 1607. AGI, Mapas y planos Panama, Santa Fe y Quito 26.

called Hill of Butchers (Loma de las Carnicerías), where Borja and Eraso believed the Pijaos butchered and sold human bodies.

Yet in its simplicity the map renders visible the five military principles that animated the president-led militias. First, the militias aimed for synchronicity by coordinating attacks from both sides of the mountains—from the administrative centers of Popayán in the southwest and Santa Fe in the northeast— to circumvent the Pijaos' furtive movements between jurisdictions. Second, they used a typology of settlements known as presidios y fuertes, especially designed for the borderlands, which had worked well to control territories in most parts of the Indies where war had become routine. Presidios y fuertes were small wooden forts placed in crucial locations in Pijao territory where soldiers remained all year round. In the map's center-left section, there is a depiction of the San Juan Fort, perhaps the most relevant of these settlements. Third, they carried out what the Spaniards referred to as "las talas" (cutting down) or "correr la tierra" (to run the earth): soldiers routinely surveyed the territory, located the Pijaos' subsistence crops, and then burned or cut them down. When they found Indigenous homes or buildings, they would tear them down and burn them. They would leave some structures undamaged but left smallpox-infected mantas and other contaminated materials in them, attempting to set off epidemics among the Pijaos—as they put it, "sowing smallpox" (dejándoles las viruelas).[15] Fourth, they garnered the support of indios amigos: Indigenous enemies of the Pijao peoples who would support the Spanish. And fifth, when any Pijao children, women, or men were caught, they would be branded and sold individually into slavery in distant locations, usually in the mines of Mariquita, but as far away as Quito.[16] This modality of nonconfrontational war was the most atrocious kind: it turned Indigenous homelands into a weapon against their ways of life.

Many of these conflict strategies had been outlined before the arrival of Borja and Eraso. In fact, in 1601, Don Vasco de Mendoza y Silva, then governor of Popayán, wrote to the king documenting his strategy against the Pijaos and enumerating its every feature: from the need for the New Kingdom and Popayán to coordinate attacks to smallpox-infected materials, indios amigos, and enslavement.[17] However, even if Mendoza had identified the type of actions required to contain the Pijao expansion, and possibly even defeat them, he lacked the political leverage to carry them out. Maintaining troops year-round in the forts required investment from bordering cities, and efforts to dispatch soldiers from Popayán and Santa Fe simultaneously were usually thwarted by petty jurisdictional conflicts. In fact, in the same letter in which Don Vasco de Mendoza y Silva expounded on his strategy, he denounced the lack of support and even outright sabotage by the audiencia magistrates in Quito, who interrupted his military efforts by forcing him to travel to Quito to respond to petty political queries. Only Borja's personal ties to many imperial administrators could produce the political determination to wage this war in spite of local disagreements. In 1605, just four years after Mendoza's correspondence with the king, Borja was beginning to launch the incursion.

The new military strategy changed the landscape dramatically. In 1605 and 1606, Borja and Eraso mapped the territory and established forts, and by 1607 the war had reached its bloodiest point. The new forts and outposts moved people from all walks of life to the impenetrable mountain. Many of them were people who did not have a stable position in the empire's institutional formation. Records describe them as "mestizo," "mulato," "indio," "moreno," or simply "soldado." From the campaign's economic records, we know that most soldiers wore mantas and cotton vests (which were better suited for war in the mountains); ate ham, cheese, and bread; and had few horses, some firearms and swords, and many machetes.[18] These marginalized individuals moved to the front and ran down the mountains to burn Indigenous settlements, destroy their crops, and erase every sign of human presence. Waging war offered a path to glory and distinction in a world that positioned these people as less valuable, as undesirable. Their actions exposed some of the kingdom's harshest dimensions: people who were denigrated as inferior because of their family genealogies or ethnicity joined a war of extermination against other stigmatized people to seek distinction in the kingdom.

The support of Indigenous allies like the Coyaimas and Natagaimas was the most important element of the Spanish strategy in the Pijao borderlands. By the seventeenth century, the Spanish had classified the Pijaos into two groups: those of the hills (de las sierras) and those of the plains of the Magdalena River (de los llanos).[19] The Coyaimas and Natagaimas, who lived in the lowlands closer to Ibagué and Mariquita, belonged to the second group, but despite their cultural resemblance, the Coyaimas and Natagaimas had distanced themselves politically from the Pijaos. It is uncertain exactly when this fracture in Pijao politics took place, since the distinction between the Pijaos of the hills and those of the river plains is not mentioned in earlier reports from the sixteenth century, and because there is evidence from 1600 suggesting that the Coyaimas and Natagaimas initially joined forces with the Pijaos of the hills against all Spanish allies. A Spanish military incursion initially targeted against the Coyaimas and Natagaimas might have forced them to look for new allies in Europeans and part ways with the coalition.[20] Be that as it may, by 1605 the Coyaimas and Natagaimas appear as independent political actors moving alongside Spaniards to dismantle the Pijao coalition.

The new type of war was, by design, a form of genocide: Borja and Eraso aimed to wipe an entire people from the face of the earth by attacking their capacity to feed themselves. In 1607, after a year of continuous warfare on the mountains, Borja wrote that his forces had killed the majority of the Pijaos through hunger and disease and that the ones who remained were living hidden in caves and along the edges of brooks. He predicted that the end of the war was near and that soon a wave of settlers would arrive on the impenetrable mountain to establish cities and extract minerals for the Crown. Borja and his men were resolved to not abandon the war zone until they had killed the last Pijao man and enslaved the last Pijao woman or child.

That imperial officials opted for this brutal war just reveals the scale of the challenge the Pijao project posed to the kingdom's sovereignty and economic ambitions. A few years prior, in the late 1590s, officials in Chile had taken a drastically different approach toward the araucanos—the Indigenous people who would eventually develop an identity as Mapuches—creating parliaments, giving gifts, negotiating, and even creating the post of "captain of friends" (capitán de amigos), whose task was to befriend Indigenous rebels, with the aim of reducing plunder and conflict.[21] In contrast, Borja chose genocide. Pijao anticolonialism had frustrated the kingdom's ambitions for lowland mines and for trade and communications with Popayán and Peru, and the Pijaos had shown no leniency nor any interest in negotiation. As Borja saw it, their project could not coexist with the kingdom.

But complete extermination was not quite so easily accomplished, and the end of the war was not as near as Borja believed. The last stages of the war, from 1609 on, were a protracted incursion against an invisible enemy. Borja's troops remained in the forts surveying the territory and destroying anything they could find. In 1611, the war accountant Andres Pérez Pisa calculated that around 250 Pijao warriors still hid in the mountains, and that they had adapted their lifestyle to the conditions of Borja and Eraso's environmental war.[22] In 1613, Borja withdrew the last troops from the mountains even though some Pijaos remained; in 1616, Pedro Lasso de la Guerra asked that Popayán renew the war effort against the remaining Pijao groups.[23]

Still, genocidal policy forever changed the face of the mountains. It was no longer governed by a coalition of Indigenous groups who aimed to eliminate the kingdom; it had become a territory full of riches waiting to be extracted for Atlantic markets. Imperial officials relegated the Spaniards' Indigenous allies, the Coyaimas and Natagaimas, to royal encomiendas, made their lands into resguardos, and granted the lands surrounding the resguardos in composiciones.[24] The Hispanic monarchy's institutional forms accommodated to the shapes of the mountains and made their way into the everyday lives of Indigenous peoples: the mountains' slopes became landscapes of property, and imperial officials felt closer than ever to the illusory mineral wealth they imagined extracting there. The ultimate imperial alchemy would be to remake the territories in which Indigenous peoples had been masters and hunters—where Europeans and their allies were prey—into silver-producing sites for the empire. After the war, the newly tamed hot lands only needed an influx of laborers to develop this new industry.

Labor

Human labor was essential to making the hot lands into thriving mines. Officials normally expected to draw labor from newly subdued populations, since military defeat implied bringing Indigenous communities to live in villages and the supervision of priests—and living according to Catholic practices meant submitting to the labor demands of the empire. Yet imperial authorities were wary of creating an intensive and coercive labor regime in the hot lands, even after the military defeat of the Pijaos.

In the former Pijao territory and area of influence, fear of revolt inhibited imperial authorities from installing demanding compulsory systems. Borja himself wrote to the king in 1609 and 1614 requesting he "relieve the indios from the villages of the hot lands in this kingdom of the payment of the royal fifth, since they are so poor and miserable." While the Native peoples of the cold lands were "ladinos and have their own economic enterprises [granjerías]" and could pay the tax, those in the hot lands never accepted it.[25] Tribute collectors repeatedly annotated the accounting records stating that they could not gather tribute in the hot lands and that there were no tribute rates for those areas.[26] As late as 1649, collectors stated that "in this corregimiento the indios do not pay royal fifth, being natural from and settled in the hot lands," and in 1657 they noted that "it has been ordered that tribute collection in the hot lands is done gently" and "softly, and mildly."[27] Setting up a coercive labor regime in former Pijao territory seemed like a risky move. Colonial officials feared that intensive labor demands would once again push the Native peoples of the hot lands to rebel.

Social engineering was at the root of the administrators' problem: how to create a productive society of miners who lived under Catholic values and produced revenue for the empire. Crown officials tried many different strategies to overcome the labor shortage. A first experiment aimed to impose the ethnic practices of highland communities on the hot lands: they tried to make the Native peoples into manta weavers (chapter 3), create cacicazgos, and standardize a lingua franca.[28] In essence, they tried to remake lowland peoples by applying some Andean ethnic forms.

Back in 1594, audiencia president Antonio González attempted to solve this problem by populating the hot lands with people from the cold lands. He established a town near the silver deposits of Mariquita with a group of people he described as "vicious indios, thieves, and vagrants of the cold lands." They were mainly Indigenous men and women who had fled their cacicazgos to avoid living in colonial-style villages, paying tribute, and assuming the other imperial burdens of corporate life, and who roamed freely through the cities and towns of the cold lands. The group also included mestizos, mulatos, and other individuals who did not have a clear social position in the empire. Many of them worked as traders or artisans and sold their goods in Indigenous markets or royal avenues. González was obsessed with finding fixed occupations for them and regulating their behavior. In an effort to make the hot lands more productive, the audiencia president relocated the unwanted, masterless peoples who roamed the cold lands to a permanent settlement in the hot lands, expecting they would sell their labor in the mines. In these new sites, he thought, they would have no option other than to become jornaleros (day laborers) and work for pay.[29]

In the early seventeenth century, the audiencia also resorted to the mita to fill the lowland mines with highland workers. González first installed the mita as a labor institution in the New Kingdom in the 1590s to supply nearby cities with labor, albeit forced. But it was Borja, through the new mining legislation of 1612, who used the mita to bring laborers from the cold lands to work as miners in the hot lands. This was a drastic change in imperial policy. Since 1575, the audiencia had restricted how far highland Native peoples could be sent to work, ruling that they could travel only as far as the cities of Santa Fe, Tunja, and Vélez.[30] Borja's new mining instructions, however, forced them to travel all the way to Mariquita, the silver mines on the banks of the Magdalena River. He required at least seven hundred Muisca people, about 2 percent of the population of the highlands, to travel to Mariquita every year. From then on, officials took no issue with legally coercing Native peoples to set off on long journeys or move to different climates, resulting in the separation of families and communities. This scheme provided labor to the mines, but it also took a toll on Indigenous communities. At certain points in the seventeenth century, the death rate for migratory Indigenous laborers was as high as 10 percent. The rate of escapees was 10 percent as well.[31] While the mita impacted negatively on Indigenous communities, it did not make the mines as productive as officials hoped. The push toward the Mariquita mines and the problems of labor occurred in a context in which finances and economic planning became increasingly important for governance in the Spanish empire.

Accounting

During Borja's tenure as audiencia president, an empire-wide innovation of governance made its way to the New Kingdom: a structured approach to numbers and finances. Philip II—the head of the largest empire in the world—filed for bankruptcy five times between 1557 and 1596. The empire's insolvency prompted a keen theoretical engagement with its political economy: a chronically bankrupt monarch seemed to prove that political power was not synonymous with economic prosperity. Most servants of the empire realized that if the empire wanted to shift its trajectory, it would need to rethink its economic policy—to a point that it became common practice for vassals and officials to write arbitrios, short treatises to the king offering advice on political economy. Finances occupied an increasingly central place in how officials thought about their role in the empire.

In this context, Philip III introduced a reform reorganizing the empire's finances. In 1602, he merged the Consejo de Hacienda and the Contaduría Mayor into a single entity and named it the Consejo y Contaduría Mayor de Hacienda.[32] In 1605, he restructured the administration of finances in the Indies, creating new entities called the Accounting Tribunals (Tribunals de Contadores). Each tribunal had five members, kept the kingdom's accounts, and worked separately from the audiencias. The king established three tribunals, one each in the cities of Mexico, Lima, and Santa Fe.[33] He opted to create competing jurisdictions that did not exactly map onto the existing viceroyalties, audiencias, or archbishoprics, in order to avoid concentrating authority in a single entity. The result of this empire-wide administrative restructuring was the emergence of the accountant as a crucial voice in matters of governance.

In accordance with this imperial policy, one of Borja's first moves as president of the audiencia was to create the post of "Accountant-Organizer of the Tribunal of Finances of the Kingdom" in 1605. The new officials were financial administrators responsible for making sure the kingdom's finances were clear and that the Crown received its share of the profits. The accountant quickly became a key figure: he advised the president and corresponded frequently with the king and the Council of the Indies. Andrés Pérez de Pisa started his term as accountant in 1606, and Borja immediately appointed him to the war against the Pijao coalition. Soon afterward, Pérez de Pisa took over the administration of labor in Mariquita, keeping tabs on the Indigenous laborers, salaries, taxes, and loans taken by miners from the treasure, and their repayment.[34] Among other innovations, he established that Indigenous peoples displaced from the cold lands to work in the silver mines had to keep planted fields to provide for their own food, ensuring that their wages were directed toward paying their taxes. He employed instruments of commercial arithmetic and bookkeeping that were widespread in the Iberian Atlantic to devise effective systems of extraction.[35]

The accountants' reports left no stone unturned. For instance, in a 1618 letter from the accountant Juan de Sologuren to the king, Sologuren touched on topics ranging from pirate raids in Cartagena and the English Crown's geopolitical strategy in Virginia and Bermuda to the wars in Lombardy.[36] Accountants did not envision their role in the empire as being restricted to bookkeeping, but rather intervened in questions of politics and proposed new mechanisms and devices to increase the empire's revenues.

In 1622, in one such letter to the king, Sologuren emphatically expressed his frustration: while the New Kingdom had the most natural wealth in the Indies and sufficient mines to become the largest mining center in the New World, eventually surpassing even Potosí, there was no one to work in the mines. Employing the emotional language that characterized correspondence between the monarch and his vassals and administrators, Sologuren said he was "hurt to see that this kingdom that promises by its nature the largest and most secure richness of the Indies, due to the many minerals it has in gold, silver, emeralds and other precious stones, its benign weather, and abundance of fruits and cattle, it is the poorest of the Indies." To him, the only way "to enrich the settlers, His Majesty's treasury, and all the monarchy's kingdoms, would be to introduce four thousand slaves, or two thousand at the least, in the mines of Mariquita." Slaves, he specified, should come not from a single nation but rather from "all nations," to prevent rebellion. He asked that two-thirds be men and one-third women, and that there be five hundred "de los ríos" (from the rivers) and fifteen hundred Congos, Angolas, Haroras, and Hardas. "From the rivers" probably alluded to the region near Cape Verde and present-day Dakar, Senegal, which Iberians called "of the rivers of Guinea" in the sixteenth century and which accounted for a large proportion of the early slave trade. Iberians called the enslaved people from this area "top-quality blacks" (*negros de ley*) and gave them a higher status than those from other Sub-Saharan regions.[37] Sologuren used geographic precedence and linguistic diversity for strategic planning and as a way of preventing coordinated political action.

The incoming peoples from Africa were treated as ciphers who mattered only in relation to their impact on the treasury. Sologuren and his contemporaries called enslaved African and Indigenous peoples "pieces" (piezas)—an objectifying language that stripped them of their humanity and made it easier to look at them as merchandise and assess their worth.[38] Sologuren padded his calculations, estimating that six hundred enslaved people might perish on the passage between Africa and Mariquita. The human cost of the Atlantic crossing went unmentioned: it was just a number to be calculated. At the level of financing, Sologuren proposed that the king pay for the enslaved Africans and then loan them to miners at a rate of 250 ducados (ducats) per year per person for five years. He asked the king to send merchandise worth 103,000 ducados to be traded for 2,600 Africans. In all, he estimated the Crown would see an income of 350 ducados from the lease of enslaved laborers alone.[39] In essence, Sologuren proposed a feasible system that would allow the empire to populate the Mariquita silver mines with enslaved people in order to enrich European settlers and produce a steady income for the Crown. Behind this language of finances and institutional figures lay the fates of thousands of people, to be reduced to letters and numbers in a book of accounts.

Almost every letter written to the king and the Council of the Indies on the subject of the mines echoed Sologuren's thoughts. Accountants imagined that African slavery was the only way to create a wealthy kingdom. The introduction of enslaved people from Africa was not a complete novelty. The port city of Cartagena was the main slave port of Hispanic America during the union of the Spanish and Portuguese Crowns between 1580 and 1640. Between 135,000 and 170,000 enslaved Africans were traded in Cartagena during this time. A number of them traveled upriver on the Magdalena and reached the mines of Mariquita, although it is impossible to know exactly how many came to the region because the transactions were apparently arranged directly between miners and traders who left no detailed records. In 1638, there were around five hundred enslaved Africans in Mariquita. Silver production increased steadily during the first decades of the seventeenth century, especially between 1619 and 1632. However, Sologuren's dreams of completely replacing Indigenous workers with enslaved Africans never came to fruition, and mining labor remained predominantly Indigenous. In fact, cold-land Native peoples who were forced to work the silver mines through the mita supplied about 60 percent of the required labor, while enslaved Africans supplied 40 percent.[40] It was less expensive to pay Indigenous laborers the daily wage (jornal) established by imperial officials than it was to purchase enslaved people. This meant that Indigenous labor continued to be undervalued and used for the roughest tasks, while enslaved Africans provided skilled labor and oversaw Indigenous workers.[41]

As Indigenous peoples and enslaved people from Africa settled around Mariquita, a new kind of society emerged in the surroundings of the mines. During the seventeenth century, Mariquita became a land of "freedmen" (libres) and "foreigners" (forasteros): people of Indigenous, African, or mixed heritage who detached themselves from the responsibilities of corporate structures and ventured to make their own way. Coercive imperial institutions like the mita and slavery disrupted forms of community life, as had the excessive burden placed on Native peoples and Africans to maintain the empire. Indigenous peoples were brought down from the highlands, and many opted to remain in Mariquita and not to return to the cold lands. Many renounced the label "indio" as well. Free people of color were subjected to the expensive tax of the requinto, creating few economic incentives for freedom.[42] Despite this, many enslaved African and Indigenous people fled bondage to live near the mines, sell their labor, and carry on living. This gave rise to a motley world in Mariquita, an assortment of people that transcended ethnic labels.

A 1627 visita by Lesmes de Espinosa Saravia reveals this miscellaneous society. In contrast to the visitas of the cold lands, which were usually organized around Indigenous social units like cacicazgos, in Mariquita the visita was structured around European households, and the visitador recorded the information of all people serving them, either in their households or other economic enterprises. Espinosa found mostly people from the highlands, from places like Zipaquirá, Tunja, Paipa, and Ubaque. But there were also Indigenous people from Antioquia, Pamplona, La Palma, Tocaima, and other lowland communities. In addition, he found people of Pijao descent and free Blacks—mulatos, morenos, and pardos.[43] The experiences and expectations of these people reveal the violent disruptions colonialism had wrought on Indigenous and African communities and how the life at the mines had become their new reality. Blas Moreno was a free Black person who worked as a shoemaker, and Luis, an Indigenous man from Ubaté, worked with him to learn this craft—they called Luis the "indio apprentice" (indio aprendiz). Twenty-six-year-old Antonia, an Indigenous woman from the Magdalena River region, had come to Mariquita as a newlywed, but soon after her husband abandoned her to go serve as a poler (boga) on the Magdalena River, and she decided to stay in Mariquita. Fifty-five-year-old Pablo, a Native man from Tunja, had been kidnapped by Spanish soldiers (lo hurtaron los soldados) when he was young and taken to Popayán before he made his way to Mariquita. "María india Pijao" said she had been under the command of Gaspar Ponce de León since she was four years old and she wanted to keep serving him because "she never met other father or other mother"—she was probably enslaved during Borja's genocidal campaigns.[44] Visitador Espinosa and his crew limited themselves to writing brief snippets about their journeys, clarifying how much these workers should expect as salary in cash, mantas, and other goods and making sure they were paying all their dues—the requinto if they were free or their tributes and taxes if they had encomenderos in their lands of origin.

Tax lists of the 1640s and 1650s also included a considerable population of "fugitive indios, free blacks and mulatos." In some cases, tribute collectors recorded people's places of origin. In other cases, their names are the only traces that remain of the worlds they inhabited. Records list names like Lázaro Tunja, Pedro Popaian, Juan Uvate, or Sebastian Quimbaio, suggesting people who came from the Indigenous communities of Tunja, Popayán, Ubaté, or Quimbayas.[45] In Mariquita, a multilingual and culturally diverse world thrived—the kind that characterized the mines and cities of the Spanish empire in the Indies.[46] From these sources it is hard to say if people found ways of reproducing their forms of communal life in Mariquita. However, the administration deployed a series of strategies to classify and control these populations, including an effort to "reduce" the population to gridded villages led by magistrate Lesmes de Espinoza in 1627. But by the eighteenth century, Mariquita had become a world of forasteros—people who had abandoned community life altogether—a hub of ethnic diversity, and a land of those who the administration vaguely referred to as "free people of color."[47]

Mariquita never became a slave society on the scale of many islands of the Caribbean. Nor did the mines of Mariquita ever produce more silver than Potosí, as Juan de Borja had hoped. In fact, the production of silver in Mariquita—or at least the revenues the Crown extracted from it—steadily declined in the second half of the seventeenth century. In a rather indirect way, Borja's policies eventually strengthened the kingdom's mining economy through enslaved labor, but not exactly in Mariquita and long after he had hoped his efforts would bear fruit. Borja's emphasis on war and defeating the Pijaos secured the kingdom's access to Quito and Peru, and it made communications with Popayán safer. Without the formidable barrier that the Pijaos had erected in the central Andean range, the gold mines of the Pacific coast were within reach. In the late seventeenth century, the Spanish administration made more concerted efforts to control the Pacific region, one of the most humid tropical forests on earth, finding that it was suitable for alluvial gold mining. Mining was developed by the labor of large contingents of enslaved people and governed from the colonial city of Popayán. The kingdom's economy would eventually be fed by the labor of enslaved Africans who worked in extremely precarious conditions in the humid tropical forests of the Pacific coast.[48]

A Kingdom Anew

In 1633, accountant Juan de Sologuren wrote a new letter to the king offering his advice for the government of the Indies, this time referring specifically to the selection of accountants. Following its common practice of selling governing offices to generate income, the monarchy had recently sold the posts of accountant and treasurer of Lima for 120 ducados and 80 ducados, respectively; the post of accountant of the New Kingdom for 40 ducados; and that of Cartagena for 80. To Sologuren, the visionary figure of the accountant, whose role was to advise the king in the empire's financial matters, should not be treated as a commodity to be purchased and sold. He acknowledged that it was done because of the monarchy's lack of liquidity and large debt burden. As the king of Spain, Italy, Germany, and the Indies, Philip IV was engaged in wars all over the world, defending Catholicism against pagans and heretics such as Turks, Tatars, and Protestants of northern Europe, but also moriscos and other separatist movements in Portugal and Italy. The royal treasury was the only thing holding the empire and its Catholic quest together. Still, Sologuren advised the king that the income from selling these posts was barely perceptible and ultimately weakened His Majesty's finances: "Seeing that they can get these jobs for money, they will aim to get that money back, harming the finances they administer rather than working with aptitude and integrity."[49]

Sologuren and his colleagues at the Tribunal of Accounts faced the challenge of making the empire lucrative. Their task was to perfect the kingdom's revenue-producing system. Sologuren repeatedly recommended that, rather than selling bureaucratic posts, the king invest in labor in the mines. Borja's 1606–15 genocidal war against the Pijao coalition cleared for imperial occupation an area that officials had until then seen as a land of promise, rich in metals but where people were unruly, even dominating, and where Europeans had to defend themselves against a powerful Indigenous expansion. In this way, genocide brought utopia, as officials envisioned remaking Indigenous territory into profitable mines for the benefit of the monarchy and European settlers. They imagined Mariquita as the new Potosí, an engine of wealth with potential global impact. For this alchemy to come to fruition, they had to bring workers to the lowlands to extract precious minerals. In the early decades of the seventeenth century, officials made strenuous efforts to displace Indigenous men from the highlands as well as bring enslaved Africans to the hot lands, especially around Mariquita. Schemes to purchase contingents of enslaved people, draft men from Indigenous communities, and settle towns of outcasts transformed Mariquita into an assortment of people detached from their communities who remade their lives around the silver mines.

The administration's goal was to increase revenue, and it initially succeeded in doing so. During the 1590s, the Spanish empire received the largest amount of gold and silver it ever had gotten from the New World.[50] In the New Kingdom of Granada, shipments of gold and silver sent from 1590 to 1610 nearly doubled the amounts sent during the preceding decades.[51] However, since many aspects of the reforms restricted Indigenous economies and many of the measures impacted fiscal collection rather than economic growth, the amounts of silver and gold decreased in the 1610s.[52]

The destruction of the Pijao coalition and expansion toward Mariquita and the "district of the hot lands" (partido de tierra caliente) marked a new phase in a century-long process of consolidating the kingdom. This expansion broadened the kingdom's geographic horizon in its quest to colonize downhill and offered more reliable communication with Popayán, paving the way for the eventual expansion toward the Pacific coast—whose gold-mining economy, powered by enslaved people from Africa, would become the northern Andes' economic engine after 1680.[53] In this way, the years between 1600 and 1630 were pivotal—a key inflection point in the making of the kingdom.

The rationale that inspired this alchemic dream exposed the dramatic tensions beneath the surface of the kingdom. Administrators' efforts to address the labor shortage exposed and reified an existing tension between the theoretical ideal of a kingdom that existed to benefit the king's Indigenous vassals, on the one hand, and the material institutions that subjugated and commodified them, on the other. While in theory the heavenly ideal of the kingdom justified its existence through the notion of salvation (i.e., bringing Native peoples into God's flock) and initially officials had aimed to prosecute settlers who displaced Indigenous peoples from the highlands to work in lowland mines, by the early seventeenth century this displacement was directly managed by imperial officials. The tension between economic gain and justice that had troubled visitador Tomás López in the 1560s, prompting him to reprimand the king for his greed and to remind him that evangelization was the true motive for imperial expansion, had given way to economic thinking. The Tribunal of Accounting offered new strategies for understanding the kingdom's progress by considering one variable: money, an abstract form of assigning and measuring the value of human labor and interactions. Rather than existing for their benefit, the kingdom was built at Indigenous peoples' expense. They provided the labor, sweat, and suffering. The ostensible aim of "protecting the indios," based on the medieval principle of "caring for the wretched," paradoxically paved the way for a system of coercive labor that transformed Indigenous peoples into workers who had no choice but to sell their labor in the mines.

In this new stage, the kingdom was assessed and administered according to the revenue it could produce for a bankrupt empire, an empire that was fighting in all its corners to sustain the ephemeral dream of consolidating a universal Christian monarchy. With this aim, the kingdom's administration developed new instruments, institutions, and practices to measure the economy, commodify labor, and charge taxes. People became ciphers, described through an objectifying vocabulary as "piezas" whose worth was measured in numbers. This is a less-explored facet of early monarchical politics, usually buried under a distinction between the baroque empire of "justice" of the sixteenth and seventeenth centuries and a more modern administrative empire beginning with the Bourbon reforms of the eighteenth century.[54] According to this distinction, it was only at the latter stage that Iberian empires underwent a structural reform to maximize the profit they received from their Atlantic empires—a transformation that meant rethinking the overseas kingdoms as colonies. However, from 1590 to 1630, imperial officials dispossessed Indigenous peoples of their lands and forced them into conscripted labor, centering economic governance as the kingdom's hopes for the future, its alchemic utopia.

EPILOGUE

A new entity, a Christian kingdom of the Spanish monarchy, emerged in the frictions between Indigenous and European peoples in the northern Andes in the sixteenth and seventeenth centuries. In the early 1500s, this region was a site of political decentralization, where myriad Indigenous groups with different notions of politics simultaneously coexisted and confronted each other, while maintaining extended interethnic networks of exchange. After the Spanish invasion, officials made sense of these peoples and territories through a language of heat, separating the cold agrarian landscapes of the Andes from the hot lands, a realm of rich mines but unruly people. Officials aimed to tame (reducir) every aspect of Indigenous lives: their lived environments, languages, spirituality, sexuality, and kinship systems. For this purpose, they installed a royal tribunal (audiencia) high in the mountains and charged it with providing justice. The tribunal officials then crafted a series of textual technologies, mostly involving paper, to inspect, quantify, record, standardize, and surveil Indigenous lives and landscapes.

This gave the New Kingdom of Granada a particular topography: its administrative centers were trapped in the heights of the Andes, from where officials drafted plans to reach deep into the hot lowlands to develop a mining economy powered by coerced Indigenous and African laborers. Officials envisioned an alchemical utopia that drew on genocide, coercive labor institutions, and accounting instruments to transform Indigenous homelands into gold and silver mines to fund a transatlantic war. While the mining economy never quite fulfilled this vision and the kingdom's reach was restricted, it did lead to the development of a form of economic governance that encroached on Indigenous economies, drained their labor, and enslaved African and Indigenous peoples.

The making of the kingdom—its structure, composition, and pliability—was much like the weaving of a fabric: the concatenation and layering of a series of threads made out of human interaction. In this book I have aimed to provide a granular look at its historical production: its principles, technologies, routines of rule, geographies of governance and dissidence, systems for governing labor and seeking profit, and the many people who engaged it. I have argued that the kingdom was an image of politics—an aesthetic ideal that people could put into writing, draw, or map; one full of emotion that could disappoint, enrage, or frustrate; and something about which people could disagree. But it was also an intricate assembly of institutions, techniques, and writing practices carried out by people from diverse backgrounds.

This history contributes to discussions about early modern Spanish imperial politics, economics, and science, as well as Indigenous political participation. It does so by challenging the ideas that this empire was mostly concerned with providing justice and enacting rituals; that its officials only began considering economic governance in the eighteenth century; that it designed pioneering scientific enterprises of massive scale, like the Relaciones Geográficas, that paradoxically were ineffective governance tools; and that Indigenous peoples played only a marginal role in politics.[1] Instead, I have shown that textual technologies allowed imperial officials to conceptualize, standardize, and systematize Indigenous peoples, thus producing a working knowledge of the kingdom's peoples and landscapes, which they then used to shape both justice and the economy. But these technologies also provided a means for subjects to voice their concerns and seek change, and they could become platforms for rebellion.

The kingdom meant different things to different people. Visitador Tomás López in the 1550s was stubbornly committed to installing imperial institutions for the sake of evangelization, which for him took precedence over economic gain—to the point that he reprimanded the king for the burden mining put on Indigenous peoples. Meanwhile, Juan de Borja, a member of European nobility who assumed the presidency of the kingdom in the 1600s, made genocide the pillar of his political program and redesigned labor institutions to force Indigenous and African people to work in the mines to satisfy the empire's explicit quest for economic gain. Despite their differences, men like López and Borja considered what it meant for "indios" to be a part of the global Spanish empire and gave careful thought to the meaning of justice, forms of economic governance, and the strategic use of violence to consolidate the kingdom. In this sense, while rooted in an early modern European lexicon of rule that envisioned politics as a problem of justice and aimed to establish a personal relationship between Indigenous vassals and the Spanish king, the kingdom was a colonial entity that stigmatized "indios" as an inferior class of people, encroached on their lands and economies, and extracted their labor for the benefit of the empire.

The new system was not a total break with the past: it formed from precolonial patterns of human interaction while also reshaping them. Significantly, Indigenous textiles remained a key instrument of exchange, even for Spanish miners and merchants. The same cotton cloths that connected the highlands and the lowlands in precolonial times continued to bind together the mining system, held up the kingdom's tributary economy, and became the center of discussions and negotiations over how much labor Indigenous people owed to the empire and to settlers. The kingdom's officials repeatedly referred to its economy as derived from the Indigenous economy. They theorized it as a parasitic economy—even if they did not use that term—in which Spaniards' capacity to thrive depended on the Indigenous workforce. The result was a constant effort to siphon off Indigenous profits, first by extracting mantas, then by enclosing lands, setting wages in minted coin, distributing labor, and taking over Indigenous industries like salt production. By the early seventeenth century, the kingdom had experimented with forms of dispossession and enclosure common to other forms of capitalism.

Indigenous people engaged actively in the making and unmaking of the kingdom. Many learned to use its paper instruments and navigate its institutions; others developed large-scale anticolonial projects. The case of the Muisca leader who crossed the Atlantic in search of good government, Don Diego de la Torre, illustrates the former. Chosen as a leader by his community, Torre developed a bold political project based on his readings of imperial law that shook the kingdom. Some Indigenous people described him as the new cipa or hoa, adapting pre-Hispanic political concepts to a new context in which caciques dealt with a parade of imperial inspectors, magistrates, scribes, interpreters, and encomenderos, and frequently engaged the Hispanic courts. Torre succeeded in removing from power the factions that had governed the audiencia until then, though his vision was ultimately undermined by a new imperial program that tightened control over Indigenous economies.

On the other side of the spectrum was the radical, anticolonial Pijao coalition. The Pijaos openly defied the kingdom's hierarchies, inverted Spanish symbols of power, deployed and dramatized the elements Spaniards feared most, like cannibalism, and offered an alternative for Indigenous people and others aiming to free themselves from the kingdom. The coalition increased in number and power throughout the sixteenth century using a double-pronged strategy that enabled them to draw new peoples to their cause and wage war against those who did not join them, uniting Native peoples under a forceful banner of destroying the kingdom and affirming Indigenous sovereignty. The Pijao project eventually fell to Juan de Borja's genocidal mission in the first decades of the seventeenth century, although the Pijao people survived and the name resurged as an ethnic identity in the following centuries.

The cases of Don Diego de la Torre and the Pijaos exemplify the dynamism of Indigenous politics: how they defined justice, envisioned freedom, and identified violence or litigation as a means to an end. Both cases challenge us to think about Indigenous political projects in this region on their own terms, while in dialogue with historiographies of Indigenous politics and sovereignty elsewhere. This area had no preexisting lingua franca (like Quechua and Na-huatl in the Inca and Mexica empires, respectively), centralized governance, or a tax system, but it was characterized by extended interethnic Indigenous networks of exchange. Thus, it does not fit squarely into the conceptual models designed for places like Peru and Mexico, where imperial governance re-lied heavily on preexisting Indigenous empires' infrastructures and practices of rule, nor those devised for fringe areas like Rio de la Plata, Chile, or the Mexican north, where dominant Indigenous groups held the Spanish to a marginal, sub-ordinate role. For instance, the conquest of the New Kingdom of Granada did not produce massive archives in Indigenous languages; a privileged class of "in-dios conquistadores" or nobilities like the Incas, who enjoyed specific honors associated with their position; nor wholesale Indigenous empires like the Co-manche in the North American interior or the Mapuches in Chile. While the New Kingdom did not conform to any of these models, the sustained political engagement of Indigenous peoples shaped it, yielding a social system that dealt in Indigenous textiles and in large part reproduced precolonial divisions between the Muisca highlands and the lowlands.

The kingdom was a convoluted entity that emerged from these multiple, col-liding projects, establishing basic tenets for the practice of politics that stood for centuries. Cross-cultural interaction crystallized in a mixture of European and Indigenous institutions, ultimately making the kingdom a transcultural entity formed out of counterpoints and oscillations, as well as exchanges in Indigenous and European terms and goods. Thus transculturation was perceptible not only at the level of language but also in the basic dynamics of human interaction and in the New Kingdom's spatial system, economic formation, and political insti-tutions—a less explored facet for transculturation studies, which tend to con-centrate in other cultural manifestations like literature, music, or foodways.[2]

The kingdom that emerged from these contingent, everyday encounters between Indigenous peoples and Europeans consolidated features of politics in northern South America that endured through the nineteenth and twentieth centuries and, in many ways, still shape politics today. Yet the transcultural nature of this polity has been obscured by a form of understanding geography, politics, and history that has its roots in the kingdom itself. The four key elements of this book—the topography of rule, the vitality of Indigenous politics, the role of textual technologies, and the connections between the politics of justice and economic governance—established a political and geographical imaginary strongly divided between a political administration centered in the cold highlands, which saw itself as a lettered, civilized elite, and the extensive hot lowlands, which they deemed inferior, populated by sluggish, racialized beings. In this view, politics became a factor of topography, as colonial and republican states centered in the highlands aimed to extend their own notions of civilization to the lowlands, stripping Indigenous peoples of historical agency and obscuring the transcultural nature of the kingdom.

This form of political imagination was present in colonial and republican projects that evidently prioritized centralization, like the Viceroyalty of New Granada (established 1717, reestablished 1739), the Republic of Colombia (established 1819), and the Regeneration (1886), and also in federalist, liberal projections of the nation-state, such as the Chorographic Commission (Comisión Corográfica, 1850–62) and the Liberal Republic (1930–46). Each of these projects responded to different ambitions: Philip V initially created the viceroyalty to gather the audiencias of Santa Fe, Quito, and Panamá, along with the governorship of Venezuela, under a viceroy who "represents my royal person,"[3] while Simón Bolívar reunited New Granada, Quito, and Venezuela to form the new Republic of Colombia, which he hoped would be the "largest nation in the world."[4] Agustín Codazzi's Chorographic Commission envisioned a country of regions within a federalist agenda. Meanwhile, Rafael Núñez promoted a new constitution for the Republic of Colombia based on centralized government and Catholicism as forms of national unity—a period commonly known as the Regeneration because of its revival of Hispanism and, in particular, its conservative political orientation. Despite their disagreements over the meaning of politics, these projects were all anchored in a deep political history: a form of geographical imagination that went back to the sixteenth century, at least, and which envisioned the hot lowlands as distinct from and subservient to the cold highlands of the Andes.

Intellectuals and politicians like Francisco José de Caldas (1768-1816), Agustín Codazzi (1793-1859), José María Samper (1828-1888), Rafael Reyes (1849-1921), and Luis López de Mesa (1884-1967) put pen to paper to describe what they considered to be the geographic and racial situation of the republic, using climatic language and suggesting warm weather as a degenerative agent. The mountains were, for these men, both a barrier to and a synonym for civilization.[5] Caldas phrased it candidly: for him, the republic was "enclosed by the famous mountains of the Andes," and in order for it to thrive, administrators would need to "surmount the obstacle of that formidable mountain range, that dreadful wall that until today has kept us apart from all the maritime and merchant peoples." Caldas argued that the climate of the mountains created different types of nature and different kinds of human beings: the cold lands of the Andes were capable of raising "organized societies," while the hot lands were hostile to them.[6] Similarly, Rafael Reyes contrasted the enlightened, lettered city of Santa Fe de Bogotá, high in the cold lands—"the South American Athens," home to bureaucrats obsessed with grammar and the correct use of Spanish—and the hot lands, which in the Bogotá elites' imagination were still ruled by peoples they defined as barbaric and cannibalistic. Reyes envisioned roads and infrastructure as the only way to defeat natural barriers and bring civilization to the lowlands; improved communication would be complemented by coercive labor regimes, the privatization of collective lands, and the promotion of white and mestizo migration.[7] His state-making utopia of infrastructure as a means to "civilize"—a catchall term that encompassed standardizing behavior, dispossession, and enclosure—was shockingly similar to sixteenth-century political programs.

Of course, this was not the only way of thinking about altitude and civilization. In fact, at the end of the eighteenth century, scholars in Lima developed exactly the opposite view of the Andes. To them, the coastal lowlands represented civilization, while the mountains were sites of barbarity, populated by Indigenous peoples they disparagingly called "serranos."[8] In other words, the northern Andean political imagination was not natural. Yet peoples from many backgrounds and political positions systematically adopted it to convey their ideas about the society they participated in. For centuries, elites and intellectuals have deployed this form of geographic and political imagination to articulate ideas about race, history, and the nation's backwardness, to describe a divided society in a fragmented territory, and to establish enduring forms of exclusion.[9]

Historians have noted the significance of the Andean mountain ranges in nineteenth- and twentieth-century Colombian political thought, as well as the forms of exclusion that thinkers of this era associated with the climatic regions created by altitude.[10] What has gone unnoticed is that this form of geographical imagination stemmed from a centuries-old division between cold lands and hot lands anchored in the early history of the New Kingdom of Granada. Lettered republicans reproduced a discourse long used by imperial officials. They rendered natural a perception of the landscape that had been developed over centuries. By tracing this form of geographical and political imagination back to the sixteenth and seventeenth centuries, I have argued that it was a product of a history that predated the republicans: it emerged from contingent interactions between Indigenous peoples and the Spanish empire as a result of empire-making impulses directed from the cold lands to the hot lands, and through the political thought and practice of lowland groups like the Carares and Pijaos and their reactions to highland centralizing projects.

Unsurprisingly, this form of political imagination is anchored in a flawed, racialized vision of history that neglects long traditions of Indigenous political participation. As lettered republicans made an effort to distance themselves from Spanish colonialism, they confined Indigenous peoples to the past, as pre-Hispanic civilizations brutalized by the Spanish conquest, and described themselves as the heirs of that imagined Indigenous past.[11] Stereotyped figures of Native peoples appeared on coins, in paintings, and in constitutions as icons of the new imagined community. Republican elites like Joaquín Acosta renamed the Muiscas the "Chibcha civilization" and called it the third great civilization of the Americas.[12] At the same time, creoles sought to banish any trace of Hispanism from their landscapes. They erased Spanish toponyms: Santa Fe de Bogotá became Bogotá, the Province of Santa Fe became Cundinamarca, and the New Kingdom of Granada became Colombia. In 1813, Bogotá's national printing house published its first edition of Bartolomé de las Casas's *Brief Account of the Destruction of the Indies* to further disseminate the narrative describing the brutality of the Spanish conquest.[13] The new nation-state imagined and projected an idealized version of Indigenous peoples who existed outside of history and whose civilizations were diametrically opposed to the "Spanish" and thus must be studied as a remote, untouched past. As we have seen throughout this book, this was a profound distortion of the colonial past, resulting in an enduring erasure of the kingdom's history that persists even today, as politicians and government officials often continue to imagine Indigenous peoples as living out of history.

If the new nation identified itself symbolically with what its framers saw as long-extinct Indigenous civilizations, in practice it eliminated Indigenous peoples' legal existence and sought to assimilate them into the impersonal category of "citizens," stripping them of the special legal status they had held as vassals of the Crown.[14] Religious conversion and civilizing ideals still characterized policies toward Indigenous peoples, but they were now framed in the language of the nation-state. Paradoxically, in the centuries that followed, people who identified as Indigenous fought to retain the rights granted to them by old imperial institutions, such as the right to the resguardos that had become essential to how they defined their indigeneity. In the late nineteenth and early twentieth centuries, the Nasa leader Manuel Quintín Lame even created an Indigenous Council of the Indies (Consejo Indio de las Indias) to unite Indigenous peoples of the central range of the Andes (Huila, Tolima, and Cauca) and demand unified political representation vis-à-vis the Republic. Lame was instrumental in reviving "Pijao" as an ethnic label, and thus introduced a new way of devouring the empire: appropriating Hispanic institutions of governance (Council of the Indies) to articulate the needs and claims of all Native peoples.[15]

These constraining republican narratives of the Spanish empire erased the ways in which Indigenous peoples had participated in the imperial past, rendering invisible how Indigenous peoples had co-produced the Spanish empire for centuries. In their attempts to de-Hispanize the landscape, the new nations were not erasing a Spanish past but obscuring a mutually constructed order. As I have shown in this book, the creation and administration of the New Kingdom of Granada had not banished Indigenous peoples to a distant past. They participated in the production of imperial institutions and co-defined the kingdom's shapes, forms, and characteristics. In turn, Indigenous peoples' engagement with the empire changed them profoundly. They served as scribes, notaries, interpreters, caciques, and vassals. They wrote to the king, made rights-based claims, and re-created their identities using imperial formulas and by applying Hispanic legal frameworks. They were rebels and instigators who fought against imperial institutions and created radical, anticolonial political coalitions. Indigenous peoples played an integral role in the creation, rejection, and redefinition of the global bureaucratic chains that transformed the mountainous landscapes of northern South America into a "kingdom" of the Spanish empire. The New Kingdom was not the sole creation of Spaniards. Rather, it took the shapes and forms of the mountains and the peoples who inhabited them. The kingdom was coproduced and contingent; it was a tattered fabric used to shroud the rich diversity of ethnic groups that spread over mountains and valleys, thus establishing political geographies that remain alive to this day.

ACKNOWLEDGMENTS

Ideas for this book first appeared when I was a doctoral student at Yale University and have taken shape as I moved on to teaching at Universidad de los Andes, the University of Connecticut, and the University of Texas at Austin. Professors, friends, colleagues, and students at these institutions carried me through the process with support and friendship, as well as warm and challenging feedback. At Yale, I am especially indebted to my stellar mentors Stuart Schwartz and Gil Joseph, and to Marcela Echeverri, James Scott, Francesca Trivellato, Ned Blackhawk, and Johnny Faragher; at Los Andes, to Mauricio Nieto, Marta Herrera, Margarita Garrido, Claudia Leal, Adolfo Polo, Ana Otero, Constanza Castro, Catalina Muñoz, and Camilo Quintero; at UConn, to Mark Healey, Gustavo Nanclares, Sandy Grande, Hana Maruyama, Nancy Shoemaker, Kaveh Yazdani, and Daniel Hershenzon; at UT Austin, to Cristina Soriano, Lina del Castillo, Jorge Cañizares, Joshua Frens-String, Seth Garfield, Matthew Butler, Julie Hardwick, Adam Clulow, Erika Bsumek, Melanie Lamotte, Madeleine MacMahon, and Adela Pineda. Throughout the years, I have benefited enormously from the guidance of Joanne Rappaport, Yanna Yannakakis, Pekka Hämäläinen, Francisco Ortega, and Barbara Mundy and from the friendship of Juan Cobo and Adrián Lerner. I am incredibly fortunate to have such a brilliant, generous, and caring support network. Thank you all for years of friendship and mentoring.

Research and writing were made possible thanks to generous funding from the Wenner-Gren Foundation for Anthropological Research's Book Fieldwork Grant; the MacMillan Center for International and Area Studies, the Beinecke Rare Book and Manuscript Library, the Agrarian Studies Program, the Council on Latin American and Iberian Studies, the Gilder Lehrman Center for the Study of Slavery, and International Security Studies, all at Yale University;

Universidad de los Andes; UConn's History Department; UT Austin's Institute for Historical Studies and Humanities Institute; the Mellon Fellowship in Critical Bibliography at Rare Book School; and the Smith Richardson Foundation.

I am indebted to friends and colleagues who engaged critically with my work. Mark Healey organized a manuscript workshop at UConn, with comments from Pedro Cardim, Jorge Cañizares, Nancy Shoemaker, Adolfo Polo, and Brendan Kane, as well as the participation of supportive colleagues. Among the scholars who discussed ideas contained in this book and offered valuable advice throughout the years, in venues across the globe, are Kris Lane, Joanne Rappaport, Josh Piker, Marcy Norton, Tamar Herzog, Max Deardorff, Yanna Yannakakis, Mónica Díaz, Renzo Honores, Alcira Dueñas, Daniela Bleichmar, Rachel Stein, Jeremy Adelman, Marie Schreier, Dana Leibsohn, Max Deardorff, Kate Godfrey, Sasha Turner, Erin Rowe, Laura Correa, Alida Metcalf, and Jim Sidbury. The Southwest Seminar on Colonial Latin America deserves a special mention, as it has become an esteemed venue for intellectual exchange. Special thanks to Ryan Kashanipour, Alex Hidalgo, Joaquín Rivaya, Dana Velasco, Juliet Wiersema, and Jose Carlos de la Puente. Thanks also to friends and colleagues for their support over the years: Daniela Samur, Corinna Zeltsmann, Bridgette Werner, Gloria Morales, Juan Ignacio Arboleda, Sebastián Díaz, Chloe Ireton, Juan Pablo Ardila, Ana María Silva, Mike Rom, Jonathan Graham, Christine Mathias, Tim Lorek, and Andra Chastain.

Digital and public history projects have taught me much about the nature of collaborative work and the urgency of this kind of work in Latin America. Thanks to my inspiring and creative collaborators: Juan Cobo, Natalie Cobo, Andreína Soto, Pilar Ramírez, Jairo Melo, Adelaida Ávila, Catalina Salguero, Jose Cote, Lisette Arévalo, Antonio Jaramillo, Daniel Ruiz-Serna, Maria Alejandra Orduz, Juan Sebastián Macías, Daniela López, and Erika Mejía.

It has been a pleasure to experience the careful, rigorous editorial process at Duke University Press. Thank you to my editor, Gisela Fosado, for believing in this project and guiding me; to the two insightful, meticulous, and supportive anonymous reviewers; to the careful copyeditor, Sue Warga; and to assistant editor Alejandra Mejía and production editor Michael Trudeau.

My deepest thanks to my family: Juana and Emilio, who give me joy and trouble every day; María Clara and Alberto, this book is for them; Consuelo and Jesús, for their constant support; Daniel, Mariana, Samuel, Pablo, Juana, Coque, and Cami, for laughs and smiles.

NOTES

INTRODUCTION. A KINGDOM IN THE MOUNTAINS

1. Gonzalo Jiménez de Quesada named these lands the New Kingdom of Granada, inspired by the native architecture that evoked the alcázares, or palaces of Islamic rulers in his native Granada. Colonial naming practices followed a common imperial pattern that replicated European place names in the New World to mark possession. By naming this area the New Kingdom of Granada they were labeling it as part of the Iberian monarchy, just like they had done with New Spain and the British would later do with New England. Harley, *New Nature*.

2. On the long process of co-optation that took place in Mexico and Peru during the sixteenth century, see López-Portillo, *Another*; Covey, *Inca*.

3. Guhl, *Colombia*, 45.

4. The Muisca have been commonly called Chibchas, a term that refers to a broader linguistic family that includes many Indigenous peoples between the contemporary territories of Costa Rica and Colombia. Recent studies have demonstrated that the Muisca were in no way a homogeneous cultural group. A basic historiography includes Friede, *Chibchas*; Londoño Laverde, "Cacicazgos"; Londoño, *Muiscas*; Colmenares, *Provincia*; Villamarín, "Encomenderos"; Gamboa, *Cacicazgo*; Muñoz-Arbeláez, *Costumbres*.

5. Whitehead, "Native Peoples"; Clastres, *Society*; Clastres, *Land-without-Evil*.

6. These diverse cultural zones were part of a large territory between the Aztec and Inca empires, which extended roughly from the contemporary territories of Honduras and El Salvador to Colombia and Ecuador, where there were no Indigenous states or empires. While some archeologists have tended to view this region in negative terms—as lacking some essential characteristic for the rise of states—others have suggested that the main trait of the societies that inhabited this region was avoidance of the state, rather than its absence. Willey called the entire zone the Intermediate Area. He shared the assumption of many in his discipline that evidence of state apparatus (large cities, monuments, and wealthy elites) revealed that some societies were more "complex" than others, and argued that the societies of

the Intermediate Area had traits very similar to those in Mesoamerica and the Inca empire, though it remained one step behind them. In contrast, Lange was among those who suggested that the main trait of the societies that inhabited this region was avoidance of the state, rather than its absence. He suggests these political formations privileged diversity over centralization, in which the differences between the wealthy and nonwealthy were less pronounced than in places with centralized Indigenous empires. Finally, other archaeologists have preferred the term *circum-Caribbean*, first coined by Julian Stewart, to highlight the connections between the mainland and the Greater Antilles. While the term *Intermediate Area* places a strong emphasis on the groups related to the Chibcha linguistic family on the mainland, *circum-Caribbean* stresses their connections to Arawak and Carib groups of the Antilles and Venezuela. The difficulty in classifying this region as a "cultural area" is a testament to its complexity and heterogeneity. Lange, *Wealth*; Lange, "Gordon Willey"; Curet, "Interaccionar"; Gassón and Wagner, "Cuestión"; Constenla Umaña, *Lenguas*; Lippi and Gudiño, "Rompiendo"; Hoopes, "Atravesando"; Fonseca, "Concepto."

7. "Epítome," 171.
8. Restrepo, *Nuevo*, 196.
9. AGI, Justicia, 502, n. 3, 8v–9r.
10. Pérez de Arteaga, "Relación."
11. Covarrubias Horozco, *Tesoro*, 1:128–29.
12. AGI, SF, 65, n. 56.
13. Weber, *Bárbaros*.
14. Benton, *Search*, 224–25.
15. Braudel, *Mediterráneo*, 40; Scott, *Art*, x.
16. Murra, *Formaciones*; Mumford, *Vertical*.
17. Cardim et al., *Polycentric*; Ruiz Ibañez, *Indias*.
18. Padrón, *Indies*.
19. Assadourian, *Minería*; Assadourian, *Sistema*.
20. I borrow the expression "aqueous territory" from Bassi, *Aqueous*. On the predominance of people of African descent, see Wheat, *Atlantic*.
21. Lockhart and Schwartz, *Early*; Sellers-García, *Distance*; Erbig, *Caciques*; Roller, *Amazonian*.
22. Colmenares, *Historia*.
23. On emeralds, see Lane, *Colour*.
24. Herzog, *Frontiers*.
25. Herrera Angel, "Transición"; Herrera Angel, *Ordenar*.
26. I borrow the expression "transitional area" from Lockhart and Schwartz, *Early*.
27. Herzog, *Upholding*, 1–11, quote from 9.
28. It was only in the eighteenth century, when administrators started to develop a language of colonies. Elliott, "Europe"; Burkholder, "Spain's America."
29. For Iberian political culture, see Fernández Albaladejo, *Fragmentos*; Cañeque, *King's*; Osorio, *Inventing*; Mazín, *Representaciones*. These scholars reacted against another trend that argued that the Spanish empire was a centralized, rational-

ized model of governance that gave birth to the modern state, like Silverblatt, *Modern Inquisitions*. For a useful review essay, see Cañeque, "Political." Historians of Iberian science reveal the often unacknowledged epistemic and methodological innovations in the production and transmission of knowledge, which anticipated the better-known development of new "scientific" methodologies, usually attributed to English, French, Dutch, and German contexts. These studies reveal that the networks of information and knowledge production were integral to the administrative structure of the empire and were coordinated from entities of governance like the Casa de Contratación and the Consejo de Indias. Barrera-Osorio, *Experiencing*; Brendecke, *Empirical*; Portuondo, "Cosmography." Gómez considers the production of knowledge outside of imperial institutions; Gómez, *Experiential*.

30. Philip Abrams highlighted a tension between a state-system (a cluster of institutions of government) and a state-idea (an illusion that gives coherence to the chaos of political practice); Abrams, "Notes," 81–82. "The state . . . is not an object akin to the human ear. Nor is it even an object akin to human marriage. It is a third-order object, an ideological project. It is first and foremost an exercise in legitimation"; Trouillot, "Anthropology," 128.

31. Cobo Betancourt and Cobo, *Legislación*. On British and Iberian views of colonization as spiritual gardening, see Cañizares-Esguerra, *Puritan*, chap. 5.

32. Covarrubias Horozco, *Tesoro*; Rappaport and Cummins, *Lettered*, 221–27.

33. Latour, *Reassembling*.

34. Blackbourn, *Conquest*.

35. Restall, "New Conquest."

36. White, *Middle*; Hämäläinen, *Comanche*; DuVal, *Native*.

37. Kars, *Blood*; Brown, *Tacky's*; Schwartz, *Slaves*; Reis and Gomes, *Liberdade*; Price, *Maroon Societies*; Tardieu, *Cimarrones*.

38. Valencia Villa, *Alma*; Díaz Díaz, *Esclavitud*; Wheat, *Atlantic*; Brewer-García, *Babel*.

39. On the importance of slavery as a means of governance in Quito, where slaves were also not the main demographic force, see Bryant, *Rivers*.

40. Colmenares, *Popayán*.

41. Stoler, *Archival*; Latour, "Drawing"; Dery, "Papereality"; Rama, *Ciudad*; Burns, *Into the Archive*; Rappaport and Cummins, *Lettered*.

42. In contrast to the Native peoples of Mesoamerica, such as the Nahuas, Mayas, or Mixtecs, who used the Roman alphabet to write their own languages and left extensive archives in Native languages, documents created in the New Kingdom of Granada are mostly in Spanish, with the exception of some dictionaries, grammars, and catechisms created as part of the evangelization project. See, for example, Lockhart, *Nahuas*; Terraciano, *Mixtecs*; Restall, "History." Nor do we have works by Indigenous and mestizo authors describing their visions of the past and colonial society, like those of the Inca Garcilaso de la Vega or Guamán Poma in Peru. Garcilaso de la Vega, *Comentarios*; Poma de Ayala, *Nueva coronica*; Adorno, *Guáman*. For other interesting examples of this written tradition, see Dueñas, *Indians*.

43. Trouillot, *Silencing*; Hartman, "Venus."

44. I build here on a geographical literature on maps, vision, representation, and geographical imagination. See Harley, *New Nature*; Cosgrove and Daniels, *Iconography*; Cosgrove, *Geography*; Cosgrove, *Social Formation*.
45. Hartman, "Venus," 11; Hartman, *Lose*.

PART 1. PRODUCING INDIOS

1. AGI, Justicia, 502, n. 2, r. 1.
2. AGI, Justicia, 502.
3. Gamboa, *Cacicazgo*, 286–313.
4. Avellaneda, *Conquerors*, 120.
5. My use of the concept "scripted conquest" is inspired by Baker and Edelstein's notion of the scripts of revolution. Baker and Edelstein, *Scripting*.
6. AGI, Justicia, 502; Friede, *Chibchas*, 189; Francis, *Invading*.
7. Pagden, *Fall*; Davies, *Renaissance*.
8. Hanke, *Spanish*; Adorno, *Polemics*; Brading, *First*.

CHAPTER 1. LABYRINTHS OF CONQUEST

1. Pérez de Arteaga, "Relación," 131.
2. Francis, *Invading*.
3. Diamond, *Guns*.
4. Todorov, *Conquista*. On the "spiritual conquest," see Ricard, *Spiritual*.
5. Restall, *Seven*. For useful review of works in English, see Restall, "New Conquest."
6. Matthew and Oudijk, *Indian*; Yannakakis, "Allies."
7. Schroeder, *Conquest*.
8. Hämäläinen, *Comanche*.
9. "Epítome," 171.
10. "Epítome," 170.
11. Friede, *Adelantado*, 39.
12. Schwartz, *Implicit*, introduction.
13. "Epítome," 170.
14. Lenik, "Carib."
15. Sauer, *Early*, 109. On the active Indigenous slave trade during the Caribbean phase, see Stone, *Captives*. Specifically on the New Kingdom of Granada: Melo, *Historia*, 90–91.
16. Sauer, *Early*.
17. Díaz Ceballos, *Poder*.
18. The Crown first granted the region between the Magdalena River and Panama to Gonzalo Fernández de Oviedo and then to Pedro de Heredia—since Oviedo did not attend to the grant. Castillo Mathieu, *Descubrimiento*.
19. Throughout the next centuries Native groups like the Malebúes would be able to take advantage of the arbitrariness of that administrative boundary. Herrera Angel, *Ordenar*, chap. 3.
20. Hershenzon, *Captive*.

21. Pérez de Arteaga, "Relación," 126; Herrera Angel, "Desaparición"; Tovar Pinzón, *Estación*.

22. Friede, *Chibchas*, 64.

23. Montenegro, "Conquistadors."

24. Traditional narratives have relegated these large Indigenous contingents to the role of porters or logistical support for Spanish conquistadors. Matallana argues that two hundred Spaniards could not possibly force five thousand Indigenous persons to accompany them, that these Indigenous forces played a key military role, and that they maintained privileged positions after the conquest. Thus, she suggests they should be considered Indigenous conquistadors, a continuum with the Inca northern expansion in precolonial times. Matallana, "Yanaconas."

25. Friede, *Chibchas*, 177–86.

26. The other expeditions were led by Jerónimo Lebrón, Lope Montalvo de Lugo, and Alonso Luis de Lugo. The New Kingdom of Granada received 7.3 percent of total Spanish migrations between 1520 and 1588, but in 1547 the total population of Iberians in the New Kingdom was below eight hundred. Colmenares, *Historia*, 12.

27. Avellaneda, *Conquerors*, 89–90.

28. Juan Esteban Verdero had a devotional book written in Latin, *Horas del Latín*. Diego de Ortega's nephew had several books, among them *Amadís de Gaula* and *Abedecedario de mercancías*, on trade and commerce. Avellaneda, *Conquerors*, 74–75.

29. Avellaneda, *Conquerors*, 75–76.

30. Avellaneda, *Conquerors*, 72. However, Belalcázar could sign his name. Figueroa Cancino, "Primeras," 132n25.

31. Anonymous, "Epítome"; Millán de Benavides, *Epítome*. The *Epítome* is an anonymous text probably composed by Santa Cruz copying verbatim from Jiménez de Quesada's own manuscripts (Figueroa Cancino, "Primeras," 135).

32. Anonymous, "Epítome."

33. Anonymous, "Carta," 98.

34. Ramírez de Jara and Sotomayor, "Subregionalización."

35. AGI, Patronato, 196, r. 15.

36. On lowland South American Indigenous politics, see Clastres, *Society*; Clastres, *Land-without-Evil*; Sztutman, *Profeta*.

37. This was reported by chroniclers, like Pedro Simón and Pedro de Aguado (Lane, *Colour*, 53), but also by testimonies of the Muzo peoples in archival documents (AGI, Patronato, 196, r. 15).

38. Langebaek, *Noticias*, 1.

39. Reichel-Dolmatoff, "Agricultural"; Langebaek, "Caminos"; Langebaek, *Mercados*; Langebaek, *Noticias*. Cardale argues that in Pasto they did have specialized traders, markets, and roads, though she agrees with Langebaek regarding the limited exchange of food. Cardale de Schrimpff, "Caminos."

40. Cardale de Schrimpff, *Salinas*.

41. Langebaek adapts Michael Taussig's ethnographic work to suggest that the peoples of the Andes projected magical powers and primeval fantasies to the peoples of the Lowlands. Langebaek, *Noticias*; Taussig, *Shamanism*.

42. Bray, "Skeuomorphos."
43. Langebaek, *Mercados*, 97–99.
44. Specialists call this type of ceramic Mosquera rojo inciso. Paepe and Cardale de Schrimpff, "Resultados."
45. Langebaek, "Cacicazgos," 33; Langebaek, "Secuencias y procesos." Some archaeologists, however, do see the common iconographic motives as evidence of a common "cultural area": Plazas, *Humano-murciélago*.
46. Kruschek, "Evolution"; Patiño Contreras, "Actividades," 141. The authors are pushing back against Langebaek's contention that the elites controlled the trade as a form of ideological domination.
47. López Medel, "Visita."
48. López Medel, "Visita."
49. For example, AGN, *Encomiendas*, 30, 318r.
50. López Medel, "Visita."
51. Murra, *Formaciones*.
52. Salomon, *Native*; Rostworowski, *Recursos*.
53. The Incas faced other Andean economic systems in places like Quito and Pasto, where they tried to lessen the economic reliance on trade by creating a series of vertical archipelagos to gain products of different niches. It was only in an advanced phase of Inca rule that they were able to gain control over different tiers of the mountain and "close the ecological circuit." Salomon, *Native*; Mayer, *Articulated*.
54. Drennan, "Betwixt." On the extensive trade networks between Panama, Costa Rica, and Nicaragua, see Ibarra, *Intercambio*. On early networks of exchange in Honduras, see Begley, "Intercambio."
55. AGI, Justicia, n. 2, r. 1.
56. This concept of the encomienda had taken shape by the time of the Laws of Burgos of 1513. Lockhart and Schwartz, *Early*, 94. Although the New Laws of 1542 limited the encomienda, colonial authorities had trouble seeing for their implementation in the New Kingdom of Granada.
57. Cañeque, *King's*, 10.
58. Muñoz-Arbeláez, "Contested."
59. Yannakakis, "Costumbre"; Yannakakis, *Time*.
60. Avellaneda, *Conquerors*, 98.
61. After a formal analysis of the central plaza, historian Jaime Salcedo claims that Belalcázar had a strong influence in the foundation of Santa Fe de Bogotá. He argues that Belalcázar adopted a special grid that left its mark on the cities he founded—a kind of rubric that he may have intended to use in legal disputes. Salcedo, *Urbanismo*, 70.
62. Avellaneda, *Conquerors*, 99–100.
63. Friede, *Chibchas*; Mejía Pavony, *Ciudad*.
64. Broadbent, "Site."
65. Gómez Aldana, "Muyscubun." On Muisca naming practices, see Muñoz-Arbeláez, Paredes Cisneros, and Herrera Angel, "Geographies."
66. Combining archaeological and ethnohistorical work, Sylvia Broadbent posited that the current site known as La Ramada was one of those units, which at the

time was known as Catama. Broadbent, "Situación." Other archaeological works support this interpretation, like Bernal Ruiz, "Investigaciones."

67. Friede, *Chibchas.*
68. Salcedo, "Vestigio"; Therrien, "Indígenas."
69. Colmenares, *Historia.* In turn, Salcedo claims the rationale for the location of the cities was to extend over different ecological tiers. Salcedo, "Vestigio," 217.
70. Avellaneda, *Conquerors,* 102–3.
71. Colmenares, *Historia.*
72. Kagan, *Urban;* Díaz Ceballos, *Poder.*
73. Herzog, *Defining.*
74. AGI, SF, 88, n. 25.
75. AGI, SF, 105, n. 27, 566v.
76. Trouillot, *Silencing.*

CHAPTER 2. A KINGDOM OF PAPER

1. López Medel, *Tres.*
2. López Medel, *Tres,* 225.
3. Bataillon, *Erasmo.*
4. On universities and education in early modern Spain, see Kagan, *Students.* On Nebrija, see Hamann, *Translations.*
5. Kagan, *Students.*
6. Clendinnen, *Ambivalent Conquests,* 57–59.
7. Cunill, "Fray."
8. Ares Queija and López Medel, *Tomás,* 129.
9. On the key role of global circulation of officials, see Polo y La Borda, *Global.*
10. The New Laws were copied and printed widely, and circulated throughout the empire. Here I have relied on Antonio Muro Orejón's 1961 edition, which transcribes the manuscript decrees signed in Barcelona on November 20, 1542, and in Valladolid on June 4, 1543, kept at the Archivo General de Indias, as well as the first published version of 1543. AGI, Patronato, 170, r. 47; Muro Orejón, *Leyes.* For a general overview, see Muro Orejón, *Lecciones.*
11. Eugenio Martínez, *Tributo,* 7–22.
12. Friede, *Documentos,* 8:330.
13. Cobo Betancourt, *Coming.*
14. Eugenio Martínez, *Tributo,* 27.
15. Garriga, "Justicia"; Garriga, "Sobre"; Schwartz, *Sovereignty;* Fernández Albaladejo, *Fragmentos;* Herzog, *Upholding;* Phelan, *Kingdom.*
16. Solórzano y Pereira, *Política,* 394.
17. Cañeque, *King's;* Osorio, *Inventing.*
18. Osorio, "Copy."
19. Rama, *Ciudad.*
20. AGI, SF, 98, n. 38.
21. AGI, Justicia, 494, n. 2; AGI, Justicia, 493, n. 1. See also Rappaport and Cummins, *Lettered.*

22. British Library, MS 13993: 1539–85.
23. Gómez, *Sello*.
24. Blair, *Too Much*; Blair and Fitzgerald, "Revolution"; Friedrich, "How to Make"; Castillo, "New Culture."
25. AGI, SF, 80, n. 50, 264v.
26. Herrera Angel, *Poder*.
27. Cobo Betancourt, *Coming*; Cobo Betancourt, *Mestizos*; Masters, *We*; Dueñas, "Indian Colonial Actors."
28. Burns, *Archive*.
29. Rama, *Ciudad*; Rappaport and Cummins, *Lettered*.
30. López Medel, however, built on previous visits from the magistrate Francisco Briceño and the bishop Juan de los Barrios. Cobo Betancourt, *Coming*.
31. Cunill, "Tomás."
32. López Medel, *Visita*, 9.
33. López Medel, *Visita*, 346.
34. *Libro de acuerdos*, 1:241–42.
35. Luis Cortes de Mesa, who was named magistrate in 1575, was the only other magistrate condemned to death in the empire's history. He also served in the Audiencia of Santa Fe in the sixteenth century and was executed there in 1580 during another period of crisis—a testament to the exceptionally unstable conditions of the tribunal.
36. In fact, the monarchy led similar resettlement campaigns in peninsular Spain among Gypsies and other groups who were thought dangerous because they had no fixed domicile or forms of local belonging to the monarchy. Herzog, "Indigenous."
37. It is unclear why imperial officials chose to apply the orthogonal grid to New World cities and villages. While several Iberian cities in the medieval period followed this pattern, it was in the Americas that it thrived, replicating itself consistently throughout the continent. The grid became the main form of urban design in the Indies long before the Ordenanzas de Poblaciones of 1573, the first urban code under Philip II. Scholars debate whether officials were following Roman models (such as Vitruvius), were influenced by Renaissance architectural treatises, or were following the example of Indigenous cities (especially those of the Incas or Mexicas), or if it was just a matter of practicality. Some of these explanations are anachronistic; some are possible. Here I follow Jaime Salcedo, who argues that the grid built on the tradition of the military encampment and the medieval Iberian model of the ideal Christian city. Salcedo, *Urbanismo*.
38. Saito and Rosas Lauro, *Reducciones*.
39. For eighteenth-century Rio de la Plata, see Erbig, *Caciques*.
40. Herrera Angel, "Mensajes."
41. López Medel, *Visita*, 352.
42. AGN, CI, 49, 761r.
43. Herrera Angel, *Ordenar*.
44. Henderson and Ostler, "Muisca"; Correa, *Sol*.

45. "Epítome."
46. Rodríguez Gallo, "Construcción"; Boada, *Patrones*.
47. Mundy, *Death*; Dean, *Culture*.
48. Cobo Betancourt and Cobo, *Legislación*.
49. In the Muisca territory, however, town councils did not take root as a governing device among the Muiscas in the sixteenth and seventeenth centuries. Muisca communities continued to be governed by caciques during this period.
50. Hidalgo, "Echo"; López, *Tiempos*.
51. Mundy, "No Longer."
52. "Epítome."
53. There were other plans to resettle Andeans in Peru in 1556 and 1564, before Toledo. Mumford, *Vertical*, chap. 3.
54. AGN, CI, 49, 768r.
55. Yannakakis, *Time*, chap. 1.
56. Garriga, "Expansión."
57. Lewis Hanke suggests that Philip II invented the questionnaire: "Toward the end of the 16th century, the king sought to organize the avalanche of communications sent to him by ordering that summaries be brought for his deliberation. Philip II asked in 1575 that in correspondence 'the style should be brief, clear, substantive, and decent.' He seems to have invented that plague so typical of the 20th century, the questionnaire, in order to manage the wide variety of questions sent to the Indies in his unceasing demands for information." Quoted in Guevara-Gil and Salomon, "Personal Visit."
58. Rappaport and Cummins, *Lettered*, chap. 6.
59. Friede, *Fuentes*, 199 (doc. 445). This type of tactic was also employed by Dominicans elsewhere. Cunill, "Fray," 232.
60. See his letter to the king from Cali on May 8, 1559. Ares Queija and López Medel, *Tomás*, 349–50.
61. Ares Queija and López Medel, *Tomás*, 347.
62. I borrow the expression "caravans of colonial functionaries" from Guevara-Gil and Salomon, "Personal Visit."
63. Craib, *Cartographic Mexico*.
64. Correa, *Sol*; Correa, "Fundamentos"; Correa, "Análisis formal."
65. Premo, "Meticulous"; Escudero, "New Age."
66. On the social construction of ignorance, see Proctor and Schiebinger, *Agnotology*.
67. Stoler, *Archival*.
68. The visitadores of Muisca communities in the sixteenth and early seventeenth centuries were Diego Angulo de Castejón (1562–67), Juan López de Cepeda (1571–73), Miguel de Ibarra (1593–95), Luis Enríquez (1599–1602), Luis de Valcarcel (1635–37), and Gabriel de Carvajal (1639–40).
69. Ares Queija and López Medel, *Tomás*, 349–53.
70. Ares Queija and López Medel, *Tomás*, 352.
71. On harmful colonialist notions of subaltern humanity, see Hartman, *Scenes*.
72. Mignolo, *Darker*.

1. This kind of dressing also became fashionable in sixteenth-century Lima, where officials came to see the tapado style as an immoral behavior and an offense to God. Guengerich, "Mantos."
2. López Medel, "Epítome," 167.
3. There is evidence of each of these textiles and dressing items in sixteenth- and seventeenth-century documents, though some of them, like topos, could be a colonial innovation following the textile fashions of the southern Andes. *Líquira* is sometimes spelled *líquida* or *liquilla*. Fernández de Piedrahita, *Historia*.
4. Simón, *Primera*, 463.
5. González, *Diccionario*, 278.
6. Boone and Mignolo, *Writing*. On khipus and the ways in which they record information unmediated by language or, as Frank Salomon puts it, as they refer "to cultural 'things' without functioning as a secondary code for speech," see Salomon, "Andean"; Salomon, *Cord*; Urton, *Inka*.
7. López Medel, "Visita de 1560," 74; Weiner, *Inalienable*.
8. "Autos en razón de prohibir," 258.
9. In other cases, Native peoples stole the bodies of their deceased caciques to bury them with their mantas, according to their traditions. Langebaek, "Santuarios." On the clashes between Indigenous and Spanish views of death, see Muñoz-Arbeláez, *Costumbres*.
10. López Medel, "Visita de 1560," 82.
11. Colmenares, "Economía."
12. Torres, "Trade."
13. On mantas in the wider context of Indigenous literacies, see Rappaport and Cummins, *Lettered*.
14. A useful conceptual distinction between "community" and "market" realms is in Gudeman, *Anthropology*.
15. Boada, *Evolution*; Boada, "Producción."
16. Graubart, *Labor*, chap. 1.
17. Boada, "Producción," 294.
18. Reichel-Dolmatoff found that Kogi women were prohibited from weaving in the 1970s. Reichel-Dolmatoff, "Templos," 220.
19. On Indigenous inks: Magaloni Kerpel, *Colors*; Devia and Cardale de Schrimpff, "Estudio."
20. That is the case of Teara, a painter from Bosa who was painting mantas in Fomeque in 1562. AGN, CI, 21, 46v.
21. Vanegas, "Textiles," 48.
22. AGI, Patronato 233, r. 1.
23. González, *Diccionario*, 59r.
24. AGN, VC, 8, 381r.
25. AGN, VC, 8, 375r–v.
26. Murra, *Formaciones*; Salomon, *Native*; Mayer, *Articulated*. For a more general overview of gift giving, see Mauss, *Gift*; Sahlins, *Stone*.

27. Herrera Angel, "Muiscas"; Henderson and Ostler, "Muisca"; Henderson, "Alimentando"; Saignes and Salazar-Soler, *Borrachera*.

28. Londoño Laverde and Casilimas, "Proceso."

29. On regimes of value, see Appadurai, "Introduction." On asymmetric reciprocity, see Mayer, *Articulated*.

30. Londoño Laverde, "Mantas." An alternative explanation could be that the mantas de vestir were more elegant than the others.

31. López Medel, "Visita de 1560," 75.

32. González, *Diccionario*.

33. González, *Diccionario*.

34. On local customs, see Yannakakis, *Time*; Graubart, *Republics*; Herzog, "Immemorial."

35. AGN, VC, 8, 375r–v.

36. Cobo Betancourt, *Coming*; Vanegas, "Fuerza."

37. Eugenio Martínez, *Tributo*. On the history of measurement standards, see Kula, *Measures*.

38. Colmenares, *Historia*.

39. González, "Encomiendas."

40. AGN, VC, 8, 381v.

41. López Medel, "Visita de 1560."

42. Herrera Angel, "Muiscas"; Muñoz-Arbeláez, "Contested."

43. Muñoz-Arbeláez, "Contested."

44. Londoño Laverde and Casilimas, "Proceso," 1407r.

45. "Autos en razón de prohibir," 258.

46. "Autos en razón de prohibir," 251.

47. Warsh, *American*; Lane, *Colour*; Tutino, *Making*; Schwartz, "Indian Labor"; White, *Middle*.

48. Such was the case of Sebastián Saavedra, a "perulero" who had participated in Francisco Hernández de Girón's revolt in Peru, moved to Popayán, and "in disparagement of dressing and being Christian, went to be with the native indios [indios naturales] and took their habit, chewing coca like them and loading himself and painting his body and shaving his beards and doing other things and rites of indios, as native indio [indio natural] in their habit." AGI, Justicia, 1118b, n. 5, r. 2.

49. Rappaport, *Disappearing*; Muñoz-Arbeláez, *Costumbres*.

50. Pérez de Arteaga, "Relación."

51. Puerto Alegre, "Relación."

52. Vanegas, "Textiles," 50–52.

53. On the Andean economic space and internal markets, see Assadourian, *Sistema*; Assadourian et al., *Minería*.

54. West, *Colonial*.

55. AGN, CI, 26, d. 17, 646r.

56. The reference to the mines alludes to the gold mines and the silver mines. In the case of the gold mines, it would correspond to what Colmenares has termed "the

first gold cycle" (1550–1640), the epicenter of which was in Santa Fe de Antioquia, Cartago, and Popayán; exploitation relied on Indigenous labor. The second gold boom (1680–1800) was based on slave labor and its epicenter was in the Pacific lowlands of the New Kingdom of Granada. Colmenares, *Historia*; Colmenares, *Popayán*.

57. West, *Colonial*.
58. AGI, SF, 81, n. 1, 16r, 18r.
59. AGI, Justicia, 640.
60. AGI, Contaduría, 1301 and 1303.
61. On Muisca manta prices in other regions, see also Vanegas, "Textiles," 56.
62. There are some exceptions, like in Iguaque in the 1650s, where local artisans made woolen mantas of great quality ("tienen particular grangeria en hazer mantas de lana que son muy buenas"). González, "Encomiendas."
63. AGI, Contaduría 1321; AGN, VC, 8, 382r.
64. AGI, SF, 101, n. 15, 323r.
65. AGN, CI, 25, 474–92.
66. AGN, VC, 8, 381v.
67. AGN, VC, 8, 381v; 2, 912r.
68. AGI, Justicia, 511, n. 1, 2r; AGI, SF, 90, n. 2, 152r.
69. Reichel-Dolmatoff, *Orfebrería*.
70. Friede, *Quimbayas*.
71. AGI, SF, 81, n. 1, IV, 35r.
72. AGI, SF 81, n. 1, 1r, 16r.
73. AGI, SF 83, n. 14, 338r.
74. AGN, CI, 472r.
75. Clendinnen, *Ambivalent*, 13.
76. Guamán Poma de Ayala, *Primer*, 371.
77. Tutino, *Making*; Lane, *Potosí*.
78. On these hybrid colonial economies in the Andes, see Larson and Harris, *Ethnicity*.

PART II. INDIGENOUS FREEDOM
1. AGI, SF, 87, n. 33, 358r–359v. The folio is undated and only the first two letters of the author's last name are readable ("Juan Sa[. . .]").
2. Myers, Simmons, and Pierce, *Santiago*.
3. I understand freedom here in its roughest form, as defined by Covarrubias in the sixteenth century: "opposing servitude and captivity." Covarrubias Horozco, *Tesoro*, 911.
4. Trouillot, *Silencing*; Hartman, "Venus"; Hämäläinen, *Indigenous*.

CHAPTER 4. DEVOURING THE EMPIRE
A version of this chapter was first published in the *Colonial Latin American Review* 33, no. 2 (2024): 239–65.

1. Among its multiple variants, it was spelled *Pijao*, *Pixao*, *Pexao*, *Vijao*, and *Vejao*.
2. AGI, Patronato, 233, r. 1.
3. Van Deusen, "Indigenous"; Lucena Salmoral, "Leyes," 61.
4. Vargas Machuca, *Milicia*, 140v.
5. Stern, *Peru's*; Covey, *Inca*; Boccara, *Vencedores*; Velasco Murillo, "Borderlands." For a methodological debate around the Taqui Onqoy, see Ramos, "Política"; Mumford, "Taki."
6. Native sovereignty projects took place across the hemisphere and share common elements, such as the strategic use of geography, the embrace of political flexibility in alliance-making, the formation of composite groups through captive-taking and kinship, and the use of violence as a form of interethnic communication. In many cases, these elements led to the creation of new types of social and ethnic groups. Ferguson and Whitehead, *War*; Salomon and Schwartz, "New Peoples"; Bushnell, "Indigenous." Despite these commonalities, war and aggression were also framed with culturally defined conceptions of violence, political ideals and practices, and diplomatic vehicles. Herrera Angel, *Conquistador*. On the return of the Inca, see Flores Galindo, *Buscando*. On other Indigenous projects, see García, *Etnogénesis*; Carvalho, "Formal"; Langfur, *Forbidden*; Weber, *Bárbaros*.
7. Trouillot, *Silencing*.
8. Ortega Ricaurte, *Inconquistables*; Bernal Andrade, *Pijaos*.
9. Montoya Guzmán, "Fabricación."
10. Clastres, *Society*.
11. Flores Galindo, *Buscando*. On the political ideology around the coming of the Inca in the eighteenth century, see Serulnikov, *Subverting*.
12. Montoya Guzmán, "Fabricación."
13. Llanos Chaparro and Gutiérrez Abella, "Bajo."
14. Paredes Cisneros, "Lengua."
15. Ramírez, *Frontera*.
16. Reichel Dolmatoff, "Toponimia."
17. Clastres, *Land-without-Evil*; Clastres, *Society*.
18. West, *Colonial*; Guhl, *Colombia*.
19. López Medel, "Visita de 1560."
20. AGI, Patronato, 196, r. 27.
21. AGI, SF, 80, n. 56.
22. AGI, Patronato, 233, r. 1.
23. AGI, Patronato, 233, r. 1.
24. AGI, Patronato, 233, r. 1.
25. AGI, Patronato 233, r. 1.
26. Trouillot, *Silencing*.
27. López Medel, "Visita a Natagaima."
28. Friede, *Quimbayas*, 78.
29. Montoya Guzmán, "Fabricación."
30. "Carta," 103.

31. AGI, Patronato, 233, r. 1.
32. Encomendero Francisco de Belalcázar posited, "It is publicly known that the Pijaos are not more than two hundred indios." Most witnesses supported this estimation, except Pedro de Cleves, who believed they were around 250. AGI, Patronato, 233, r. 1.
33. AGI, Patronato, 233, r. 1.
34. Clastres, *Land-without-Evil*.
35. Friede, *Quimbayas*, 77–94; Friede, "Aportación," 311.
36. Rappaport, *Politics*; Paredes Cisneros, "Nombres."
37. On polygamy in Indigenous sovereignty projects in North America, see Pearsall, "Having."
38. AGI, Patronato, 233, r. 1.
39. AGI, Patronato, 233, r. 1.
40. AGI, Patronato, 233.
41. AGI, Patronato, 233, r. 1.
42. AGI, Patronato, 233, r. 1.
43. AGI, Patronato, 233, r. 1.
44. Staden, *Hans*, xciii, xcvii; Viveiros de Castro, *Enemy's*; Viveiros de Castro, "Cosmological."
45. On regions of refuge, see Aguirre Beltrán, *Regiones*.
46. AGI, Patronato, 233, r. 1. In 1559, after joining Francisco Hernández Girón's revolt in Peru, Sebastián de Saavedra was accused of taking on Indigenous costume to evade justice and plot rebellion. Saavedra might have been in the Pijao territory, like Vaez. Yet spatial referents in the testimonies are vague and oscillate from northern Quito to the Pijao territory. AGI, Justicia, 1118b, n. 5, r. 2.
47. Rappaport has explored this among the Nasa, and Clastres has studied this form of organization for the South American lowlands more broadly. Rappaport, *Politics*; Clastres, *Society*.
48. In this I differ from Juan David Montoya, who argues that *Pijao* was essentially a colonial misnomer—a catchall term Europeans used to describe multiple individual groups waging war against the Spanish. Montoya Guzmán, "Fabricación."
49. Castillo y Orozco, *Vocabulario*, 15, 27, 38.
50. On these divergent ideas of freedom in a eighteenth-century slave revolt in Guyana, see Kars, *Blood*.
51. Diego Sánchez listed the Amoyá separately from the Pijaos: "Ha estado en la dicha Provincia de Saldaña y río del y en los indios a ellos comarcanos que son los Pijaos, Coyaymas y Amoyá e Cagatayma e otras de aquellas provincias." AGI, Patronato, 233, r. 1. On its centrality in the seventeenth century, see AGN, CI, 48bis, d. 15, 911r. "Amoya donde se considera la principal fortaleza y centro de la guerra por ser la mayor población de indios la que hay en ella." AGI, Patronato, 196, r. 27.
52. Other provinces mentioned in 1606 are Calucaluima, Culuculvima, Paloma, Vlulu, Vulima, Namay, Luluma, Tumbo, Totumo, Quitala, Orli, Maulu, Tunure, Zearco, Natagaima, Atarora, Aparoje, Vmbeche, Valleviciosa, Macuri, Canchuma, Vulira, Bintima, and Totorambo. AGI, Patronato, 196, r. 27.

53. Among the names of leaders I have found in archives are Capera (who apparently had a brother who governed on the opposite side of the Magdalena River), Bonbon, Cuchapan, Ytupeque, Coromuto, Yambara, Chilamba y Coera, Caynma, Cayama, and Botoza.

54. As noted in chapter 3, Spaniards frequently described these gatherings as borracheras (drunken binges), obscuring their ritual and cultural meanings. On this subject for other contexts, see Saignes and Salazar-Soler, *Borrachera*; Herrera Angel, "Muiscas"; Muñoz-Arbeláez, *Costumbres*; Muñoz-Arbeláez, "Contested."

55. Vargas Machuca, *Indian*, 172–73.

56. AGI, Patronato, 196, r. 27. On topography, see also McEnroe, "Sites"; Scott, *Art*.

57. Harney, *Undercommons*.

58. In 1607, the audiencia president Juan de Borja, a man who made the genocide of the Pijao his prime presidential proposal, paradoxically offered a detailed report of Pijao values as part of a genocidal campaign to destroy them. The following paragraphs are based on Borja's rich document describing Pijao peoples and landscapes in the early seventeenth century. AGI, Patronato, 196, r. 27.

59. On "agricultures of escape," see Scott, *Art*, chap. 6.

60. While the display of heads as trophies was grounded in precolonial practices, this practice was vamped up by colonial violence—much like anthropophagy, as we will see in the next section, or like scalping in North America. AGI, Patronato, 233, r. 1.

61. AGI, Patronato, 196, r. 27.

62. Alicia Dussán and Gerardo Reichel Dolmatoff found these corporeal practices were still active in Coyaima in the 1940s. Dussán and Reichel Dolmatoff, "Grupos."

63. Paredes Cisneros, "Lengua."

64. Rappaport, *Disappearing*, 173–76.

65. Whitehead, *Dark*.

66. "This witness knows this because an Indian woman named María of his encomienda was there and those indios kept her captive, so she saw everything, until she fled." AGI, Patronato, 233, r. 1.

67. AGI, Patronato, 233, r. 1.

68. Bolaños, *Barbarie*.

69. Heng, *Empire*.

70. Vignolo, *Cannibali*; Hulme, *Colonial*.

71. Federici, *Caliban*.

72. AGI, Patronato, 196, r. 27.

73. Modern historians and anthropologists have long debated the nature and veracity of these reports. Anthropologist Marvin Harris famously argued that anthropophagy was a nutritional problem explained by a lack of protein and population-control needs. His view of anthropophagy is anchored in "cultural materialism," which he defined as "the simple premise that human social life is a response to the practical problems of earthly existence." Harris, *Cannibals*; Harris, *Cultural*. Others, like William Arens, argued that anthropophagy was a myth, a

story Europeans told about non-European peoples. Arens, *Man-Eating Myth*. Historian Frank Lestrigant, however, took a more nuanced perspective by showing how French views and explanations of cannibalism combined firsthand observation and cultural expectations from the early modern to the modern period. In this sense, anthropophagy was both a practice of some indigenous peoples of South America and a matter of discussion in which Europeans projected, exposed, and debated their ideas of otherness. Lestringant, *Cannibale*.

74. Herrera Angel, *Conquistador*.
75. Whitehead, *Dark*.
76. Pineda, "Malocas"; Ferguson and Whitehead, *War*.
77. AGI, Patronato, 233, r. 1.
78. AGI, Patronato, 233, r. 1.
79. AGI, Patronato, 233, r. 1.
80. "The Tupi would rather be buried in the bellies of their enemies, . . . for they say that it is a wretched thing to die, and lie stinking, and eaten with worms.'" Whitehead, "Native American," 218.
81. Viveiros de Castro, *Enemy's*; Viveiros de Castro, "Cosmological"; Staden, *Hans*.
82. Vargas Machuca, *Indian*, 42–43.
83. These include official reports and personal letters to the king and Council of the Indies available in AGI, Santa Fe and Quito, as well as AGN, Caciques e indios. Municipal minutes (actas capitulares) from nearby cities left notes expressing concerns, for example in the Archivo Histórico de Cali and Archivo Central del Cauca (now called Centro de Investigaciones Históricas José María Arboleda Llorente, in Popayán). The most important published accounts replicating these discourses are Simón, *Primera*; Ordóñez de Ceballos, *Viage*; Vargas Machuca, *Milicia*.
84. AGI, Patronato, 233, r. 1.
85. Borja, "Don Juan," 474.
86. White, *Middle*; DuVal, *Native*.
87. Hämäläinen, *Comanche*.
88. Sidbury and Cañizares-Esguerra, "Mapping."
89. Pineda, "Rescate"; Rappaport, *Politics*; Paredes Cisneros, "Nombres."

CHAPTER 5. A MESTIZO CACIQUE

1. Ruiz Ibañez, *Hispanofilia*.
2. Puente Luna, *Andean*; Pennock, "Aztecs"; Dueñas, *Indians*.
3. Salomon and Schwartz, "New Peoples," 444.
4. Martínez, *Genealogical*; Schwartz, *Blood*.
5. In archival documents the rendering of his name varies considerably, as often happens, since nomenclature at the time was not as rigidly standardized as it is today. Common renderings include Diego de Torre, Diego de la Torre, and Diego de Torres. Here I have opted to use Don Diego de la Torre, the form he used in many documents.

6. Rojas, *Cacique.*

7. Rappaport, *Disappearing.*

8. Deardorff, *Tale.*

9. Fernández de Piedrahita, *Historia.* If we use a ratio of three or four women, children, elderly persons, and men who were unable to work per working-age man, the total population would be between 5,800 and 7,300. Jaramillo Uribe, "Población"; Tovar Pinzón, "Estado."

10. AGN, CI, 18, d. 5, 235v.

11. They called this practice conmutación. AGN, CI, 18, d. 5. See chapter 3.

12. Since Juan de Torres had previously been encomendero in Bosa, where he was found guilty of severe mistreatments, he was also sentenced to exile from this town for two years and to pay thirty mantas to the community of Bosa. The judicial inquiries about this process can be found in AGN, CI, 67, and a transcription of the final sentence is available in Ares Queija and López Medel, *Tomás,* 591–93.

13. AGN, CI, 67, d. 28, 904r.

14. AGN, CI, d. 28, 905r. See chapter 2 on the concept of "cipa."

15. Muñoz-Arbeláez, "Contested."

16. On the creation of a lexicon for the Indies based on terms learned in the Caribbean, see Lockhart and Schwartz, *Early.*

17. Muñoz-Arbeláez, *Costumbres;* Gamboa, *Cacicazgo;* Cobo Betancourt, *Coming.*

18. Rappaport, *Disappearing,* 154.

19. The decree was a response to procurator Pedro de Colmenares, who had informed the council of the many mestizo and Indigenous orphans who remained in the kingdom and were in pressing need of a Catholic education. The school, however, seems to have trained the prominent mestizo sons of conquistadors, rather than orphans. AHRB, Fondo Archivo Histórico de Tunja, vol. 1, legajo 4, 108r; Rojas, *Cacique,* 8.

20. Rappaport, *Disappearing.*

21. Nesvig, "Mendicant."

22. Ulises Rojas introduced Don Diego de la Torre's mother as Catalina de Moyachoque and stated that she had married Juan de Torres. In his will, however, Juan de Torres left no evidence of that marriage. Witness testimonies show that even if they did not wed legally, their relationship was public and they lived as husband and wife. AGN, CI, 61, 422v–423r, 424v–425r.

23. It is uncertain whether Don Diego was ever considered to be an heir of the encomienda.

24. Corredor, "Laberinto."

25. Deardorff, *Tale.*

26. AGN, CI, 61, 428r–v.

27. Rappaport, *Disappearing,* 156.

28. AGN, Encomiendas, 21, 404r; Hoyos García, "Lenguaje."

29. AGN, CI, 37, 499v, and in the *Recopilación.*

30. Deardorff, *Tale;* Cobo Betancourt, *Mestizos.*

31. Cobo Betancourt, *Coming.*

32. Cobo Betancourt and Cobo, *Legislación*.
33. AGI, SF, 234, r. 3, n. 49, IV–5r.
34. AGI, SF, 234, r. 3, n. 49, 5r–6r.
35. Cobo Betancourt, *Mestizos*.
36. Rojas, *Cacique*, 23–24.
37. Rappaport, "¿Quién es mestizo?"
38. Cobo Betancourt, *Mestizos*, chap. 3; Deardorff, *Tale*.
39. A couple of months after his arrival in Madrid, the king approved his request for permission to visit the court in a decree of November 24, 1577. Rojas, *Cacique*, 43.
40. Rojas, *Cacique*, 428.

CHAPTER 6. AN INDIGENOUS INTELLECTUAL IN KING PHILIP'S COURT

1. AGI, SF, 85, n. 48, 689r.
2. On Indigenous transatlantic travelers, see Puente Luna, *Andean*; Pennock, *Savage*; Caballos, *Descubrimiento*.
3. On Andean political utopias as the return of the Inca, see Flores Galindo, *Buscando*.
4. These archives are spread across the AGN (especially in CI, 37, ff. 251–506; CI, 61, ff. 14–600; and Encomiendas 21, ff. 392–594) and AGI (especially in EC, 822A–6C, twelve volumes in total), with an interesting printed copy of charges against Torre and visitador Monzón kept in the New York Public Library (Rare Book Collection, KB+ 159–). There are numerous additional documents in other collections and local archives, such as the Archivo Histórico Regional de Boyacá.
5. On Indigenous intellectuals, see Ramos and Yannakakis, *Indigenous Intellectuals*. On Guamán Poma, see Adorno, *Guáman*.
6. See, for example, his first memorial in Rojas, *Cacique*, 53–60.
7. Rojas, *Cacique*, 417.
8. AGI, Patronato, 196.
9. Rojas, *Cacique*, 419.
10. Rojas, *Cacique*, 422.
11. Rojas, *Cacique*, 434.
12. Cline, "Relaciones," 367. On the maps of the *Relaciones geográficas*, see Mundy, *Mapping*.
13. Adorno, *Polemics*; Friede, *Don Juan*.
14. Muñoz-Arbeláez, *Costumbres*, chap. 3.
15. There are interesting parallels here between Zapata de Cárdenas and Fray Diego de Landa in Yucatán. See Clendinnen, *Ambivalent Conquests*, chap. 6.
16. Cobo Betancourt, *Coming*; Mills, *Idolatry*.
17. AHSB, libro 2, 15r–139v. Thanks to Juan Cobo for providing access to these sources. See also Cortes Alonso, "Visita."
18. Some vivid descriptions are included in AGI, EC, 824B, pieza 6, 1–225.
19. See Monzón's commission in Rojas, *Cacique*, 102–4.
20. Puente Luna, *Andean*.

21. Cobo Betancourt, *Mestizos*, 78–79.
22. AGI, SF, 16, r. 21, n. 76.
23. AGI, SF, 16, r. 21, m. 76.
24. AGI, EC, 826b, 201r–v. 48, 675r.
25. AGI, EC, 826b, 24r–v.
26. AGI, EC, 826b, 21v–22r.
27. AGI, EC, 826b, 36r.
28. AGI, EC, 826b, 24v–25r.
29. AGI, EC, 826b, 34v–35r.
30. Galster, *Aguirre*.
31. Rojas, *Cacique*, 107.
32. Polo y La Borda, *Global*.
33. On the return of the Inca, see Flores Galindo, *Buscando*. The revival of the cipa or hoa is more similar to the appeals to Inca symbols and genealogy within the baroque political culture of seventeenth-century Quito, as Carlos Espinosa has studied. Espinosa, *Inca*.
34. For an early modern Spanish definition of freedom as "opposing servitude and captivity," see Covarrubias Horozco, *Tesoro*, 91r.
35. Rojas, *Cacique*, 286.
36. Rojas, *Cacique*, 137.
37. Rojas, *Cacique*, 169.
38. AGI, EC, 826, 5v.
39. Vargas, *Pincel*, 81–90; for a visual analysis, see Zalamea, "Drawings."
40. On September 7, 1585, the king ordered Antonio de Cartagena to pay Torre 100 ducados (37,500 maravedís). On March 6, 1590, Torre was again granted 100 ducados. Between these dates Torre also received several royal grants to cover his living expenses. Rojas, *Cacique*, 451.
41. Puente Luna, *Andean*.
42. Vargas, *Pincel*, 88.
43. Rojas, *Cacique*, 504.
44. Garcilaso de la Vega, *Comentarios*. On the Florentine Codex: Magaloni Kerpel, *Colors*; Peterson and Terraciano, *Florentine*. On Huarochirí and Cristóbal Choquecasa: Salomon, Urioste, and Avila, *Huarochirí*; Durston, "Notes"; Puente Luna, "Choquecasa." On the proposal of the caciques: Stern, *Peru's*, xxxviii; Lamana, "Agencia." On Indigenous intellectuals in general: Ramos and Yannakakis, *Indigenous Intellectuals*.
45. Gruzinski, *Pensamiento*; Russo, *Untranslatable*. On the problems of "hybridity" as a conceptual framework: Dean and Leibsohn, "Hybridity."

PART III. NEW IMPERIAL DESIGNS
1. AGI, SF, 528, L. 1. Thanks to Juan Cobo for pointing me to this document.
2. Colmenares, *Historia*; Assadourian, *Sistema*; Stern, "Feudalism."
3. Tutino, *Making*.

4. Lane, *Potosi*; Barragán, "Working."
5. See, for instance, Beckert's concept of "war capitalism"; Beckert, *Empire*. Scholars who define capitalism in terms of primitive accumulation and the dynamics of capital would not find resonance to what the kind of economic systems of New Kingdom of Granada. See a comprehensive discussion on the global history of capitalisms and, specifically, on the role of precious metals in the Spanish empire in the great divergence between Europe and Asia in Yazdani and Menon, *Capitalisms*.
6. AGN, CI, 25, 809r.
7. *Recopilación*, Book 6, title 12; Yazdani and Menon, *Capitalisms*.
8. Ruiz Rivera, *Plata*.
9. AGI, SF, 18, r. 6, n. 45.
10. AGI, SF, 18, r. 7, n. 54.
11. On the mita among the Incas and its adoption under the Spanish empire, see Assadourian, "Acerca."
12. Bonilla, *Minas*.
13. Ruiz Rivera, *Plata*.

CHAPTER 7. LANDSCAPES OF PROPERTY

1. Crosby, *Columbian*.
2. Environmental historians have long debated whether it was Old World cattle or Indigenous occupancy that desiccated the landscapes of the Valley of Mexico. Melville, *Plague*; Sluyter, "Colonialism"; Candiani, *Dreaming*; Skopyk, *Colonial*; Conway, *Islands*.
3. Friede, "Encomienda"; Colmenares, *Historia*, chap. 4.
4. Langebaek, *Mercados*.
5. Thompson, *Making*; Thompson, *Customs*; Ash, *Draining*.
6. Indigenous peoples built ditches and terraces in the regions of the San Jorge River in Colombia, Cuenca del Guayas in Ecuador, Guayanas, Llanos del Orinoco, Cuenca del Lago Titicaca, La Sierra del Ecuador, and Valle del Casma, in addition to the better-known chinampas of Central Mexico; Valdez, *Agricultura*. For an early treatment of this subject, see Parsons and Denevan, "Pre-Columbian."
7. Boada, *Patrones*, 100; Rodriguez Gallo, "Água"; Rodríguez Gallo, "Construcción."
8. Lleras and Langebaek suggest that due to the flooding conditions, the Muisca occupied elevated fields at the foot of the mountains, with small labor investments. Bernal, Boada, and Broadbent show the great amount of labor involved in building terraces and hydraulic systems for agricultural fields in the plains. Broadbent, "A Prehistoric"; Broadbent, "Agricultural"; Bernal Ruiz, "Investigaciones"; Rodríguez Gallo, "Permanencias"; Cavelier, "Perspectivas."
9. On the nineteenth-century process of scientific assimilation of this type of fish, see Gutiérrez Ardila, *Peces*, chap. 1.
10. Though Boada points that on occasion corn could be planted on its own. Boada, *Patrones*, 133.

11. Among these animals were frogs (*Hyla palustris*), often featured in Muisca hiero-glyphs; guinea pigs (*Cabia porcellus*), an important protein source for Muiscas; and local birds like the Bogotá rail (*Rallus semiplumbeus*), yellow-hooded black-bird (*Agelaius icterocephalus*), and other migratory birds (*Dendroica fusca, Wilsonia canadensis, Mniotilta varia, Elaenia frantzii, Tyrannus tyrannus, Contopus borealis*, and *Coccyzus americanus*).

12. Boada, *Patrones*, 133.

13. Ospina Rey, "Doctrina," 61. It is time to push back against the common assertion that "indios did not have landed property at the time of the conquest" and that, in consequence, they did not mark boundaries or build fences to separate ter-rains. Gonzalez, *Resguardo*, 45.

14. Historian Germán Colmenares suggests that the encomienda in the New King-dom of Granada might have included exploitation of lands, since once communi-ties were assigned to encomenderos they needed to yield part of their lands for the profit of the encomendero. Colmenares, *Historia*, 199–203.

15. Orrego had been briefly married to Fernando Monzón, the son of Juan Bautista de Monzón, the official appointed to carry out a visita of the audiencia after Don Diego de la Torre's meeting with the king, which had enraged the audiencia mag-istrates at that time (chap. 6).

16. Gutiérrez Ramos, *Mayorazgo*, 43.

17. Some Spanish-Muisca dictionaries translate *pantano* (swamp) as *chucua*, which also means "fisheries"—another indication of the different forms of appreciation of the landscape.

18. Candiani, *Dreaming*.

19. The lengthy lawsuit can be found in AGI, EC, 763.

20. AGI, EC, 763, 32v–33r.

21. AGI, EC, 763, 32v–33r.

22. On colonial legal mapping, see Dueñas, "Virgin"; Muñoz-Arbeláez, "Medir." On colonial Indigenous mapping practices in New Spain, see Hidalgo, *Trail*; Pulido Rull, *Mapping*; Mundy, *Mapping*.

23. In the Hispanic legal tradition, land titles granted an "expectation of dominium" (expectativa de dominio), but it was only the improvement of the land (uso útil) that enforced this right; Gonzalez, "Hacienda." On the complex imperial reason-ing that this motivated, see Herzog, *Frontiers*, 114–33.

24. Solano, *Cedulario*, 273.

25. Owensby, *Empire*, 91. On the "possession" and the categories of landholding in the Spanish Indies, see Bastias Saavedra, "Normativity"; Carrera Quezada, *Sementeras*.

26. Gonzalez, *Resguardo*.

27. Eugenio Martínez, *Tributo*, 168–69.

28. AGI, SF, 92, n. 38, 63–85.

29. AGI, SF, 17, n. 80, 5r.

30. AGI, SF, 92, n. 38, 74r.

31. Gonzalez, *Resguardo*, 43.

32. Glave, "Arbitrio"; Dueñas, "Virgin"; Puente Luna, "Widows"; Carrera Quezada, *Sementeras*; Hidalgo, *Trail*; Carrera Quezada and Pérez Zevallos, *Todos*.

33. Melo, "Tierra."

34. In practice, though, the amounts of land varied according to context. Colmenares, *Historia*.

35. Villamarín, "Encomenderos"; Herrera Angel, *Ordenar*.

36. The Crown had first used this office in Castile and the Iberian Peninsula, and then in places like Perú, New Spain, Naples, and the Philippines, as well as many other parts of the empire, to assert royal authority and limit the local nobility's power. Polo y La Borda, "Orígenes"; Graubart, "Learning," 202. Before 1593, only royal encomiendas—those belonging to the king—were administered by "corregidores de naturales."

37. Gonzalez, "Ordenanzas," 186.

38. Gonzalez, *Resguardo*, 30.

39. AGI, SF, 95, n. 16. See a partial list of the first corregidores in Eugenio Martínez, *Tributo*, 547.

40. In the New Kingdom of Granada, however, there are no known cases of the corregidores engaging in the infamous repartimiento de mercancías—forceful sale of goods to Indigenous communities at prices the corregidores determined—that sparked unrest in the southern Andes. Herrera Angel, "Corregidor."

41. Ibarra, "Ordenanzas," 199.

42. On Castilian reducciones, see Herzog, "Indigenous."

43. AGI, SF, 92, n. 38, 408v; AGI, SF, 17, n. 80, IV.

44. Groot, *Sal*.

45. Colmenares, *Historia*, 221; Quiroga Zuluaga, "Proceso."

46. Cobo Betancourt, *Coming*.

47. Muñoz-Arbeláez, *Costumbres*.

48. In 1603, the Jesuits published in Madrid the first catechism and grammar in the Muisca language. In 1606, a group of officials, clergy, and Muisca experts met and produced the most complete dictionary, catechism, and confession guide in the Muisca language known to date; González, *Diccionario*. Some friars traveled to villages after taking Muisca lessons only to find that their parishioners could not understand a word they said; Cobo Betancourt, "Colonialism."

49. Colmenares, *Historia*, 164; Colmenares, *Provincia*, 28; Villamarín, "Encomenderos," 1:141; Assadourian, "Señores."

50. Friede, "Encomienda."

51. Rodríguez Gallo, "Ley."

52. AGI, SF, 107, n. 14, 927-35.

53. For some scholars of early North America, fences reveal the contrast between the fixed European visions of the landscape and Indigenous peoples' mobile, seasonal land use systems. See Cronon, *Changes*; Taylor, *Divided*; Greer, *Property*. On modern fencing systems built to inflict pain, see Netz, *Barbed*.

54. Rappaport, *Cumbe*.

55. AGN, VC, 2, 911v–912r.
56. AGN, VC, 8, 382r.
57. Eugenio Martínez, *Tributo*, 544-46.
58. AGN, CI, 64, 173v.
59. AGN, RB, 7, d. 10, 672–704.
60. Jacoby, *Crimes*; Thompson, *Customs*; Scott, *Moral*.
61. AGN, RB, 7, 159r–170v.
62. Herrera Angel, *Ordenar*.
63. Langebaek, *Mercados*.
64. Skopyk, *Colonial*.
65. AGI, EC, 763, 167r–171v.
66. Colmenares, *Historia*, 410-13.
67. Langebaek, *Mercados*.
68. These items appear frequently in Indigenous wills; Rodríguez, *Testamentos*. For an in-depth analysis of the Spanish clothing of Don Francisco, the cacique of Ubaque in 1583, see Muñoz-Arbeláez, *Costumbres*.
69. Colmenares, *Historia*. On these complicated processes of "commoning" and "uncommoning" and their continuities and breaks with Inca land tenure systems, see Puente Luna, "Widows."
70. Correa, *Sol*, 200; Villamarín and Villamarín, "Kinship."
71. Gonzalez, *Resguardo*, 32.
72. Gonzalez, *Resguardo*, 51; AGN, VB, 13, 1023r.
73. Gonzalez, *Resguardo*, 52.
74. Herrera Angel, *Ordenar*, chap. 4.
75. In fact, Basilio Vicente de Oviedo complained in the eighteenth century that while mestizos should define themselves as "*vecinos de la ciudad de Tunja, y agregados al pueblo de Tequia, de Chita de Soatá, de Sátiva, etc.*," they identified themselves as "*vecinos tales de dichos pueblos*"; Herrera Angel, *Ordenar*, 191. On vecindad and citizenship in early modern Spain and its Atlantic empire, see Herzog, *Defining*; Herzog, "Naturales"; Deardorff, *Tale*.
76. Requero never claimed the label of mestizo, but only declared that he "feared being troubled by the encomendero, the cacique or the corregidor, saying that I am a mestizo." AGN, VC, 2, d. 5, 977r–v.
77. Herrera Angel, *Ordenar*; Bonnett Vélez, *Tierra*.
78. Herrera Angel, *Poder*; on the the term *orejones* and Inca ear enlargement, Hamilton, *Royal*.
79. Rappaport draws on Bonfil Batalla's concept of "deindianization" to describe the "process through which communities or individuals shed their indigenous identity but continue to maintain indigenous lifeways." Rappaport, *Disappearing*, 216-17.
80. López, *Tiempos*.
81. AGI, SF, 92, n. 38, 409v.
82. AGN, VB, 9,169r.

1. The Carares were probably a subgroup of the Yareguíes. Velásquez and Castillo, *Yareguíes*.
2. AGI, SF, 4, n. 29, 30r; Henríquez, "Relación."
3. Córdoba Ochoa, "Comentario."
4. Vargas Machuca, *Indian*, 262.
5. "Relación," 497. See a letter by Caceres describing his incursion in AGI, SF, 85, n. 16.
6. A copy of Mujica's title and the information the audiencia gathered in 1595 about his strategy are in AGI, SF, 94, n. 5. On the capitulaciones to fight the Pijaos, see Martínez, "Intentos"; Córdoba Ochoa, "Guerra," 330-40. I borrow the expression "luckless conquistador" from Kris Lane's introduction to Vargas Machuca, *Indian*.
7. Staden, *Hans*.
8. AGI, SF, 94, n. 5; Vargas Machuca, *Indian*, xxviii.
9. Lucena Salmoral, *Nuevo*.
10. Borja, "Informe."
11. Lane, *Colour*; Rodríguez Baquero, *Encomienda*.
12. AGI, SF, 100, n. 14, 82v.
13. Erazo recounted and documented his life's achievements in a leatherbound and partly printed probanza de mérito of unusual formality and style; AGI, SF, 99, n. 14. See also Valenzuela, "Biobío."
14. "It is impossible to have a military success without first learning about the enemy's lands." AGI, Patronato, 196, n. 27.
15. "De tres meses que los tuve dentro y de haberles muerto y preso noventa y dos indios y talándoles las comidas y quemado sus casas y dejándoles dentro las viruelas de quien han recibido notable daño"; AGI, Quito, 16, r. II, n. 27. Thanks to Marta Herrera Angel for bringing this document to my attention.
16. Lane, *Quito 1599*.
17. AGI, Quito, 16, r. II, n. 27.
18. AGI, Contaduría, 1306.
19. AGI, SF, 103, n. 27, 316v.
20. AGI, SF, 105, n. 39, 714r.
21. Boccara, *Vencedores*.
22. AGI, SF, 99, n. 39, 538.
23. AGI, Quito, 29, n. 5.
24. AGI, SF, 103, n. 27, 316v; Oliveros, "Coyaimas"; Espinosa, *Civilización*; Clavijo Ocampo, *Formación*.
25. AGI, SF, 765.
26. AGI, SF, 98, n. 34, 340-7.
27. AGI, Contaduría, 1346A.
28. Colmenares, *Popayán*; Rodríguez Baquero, *Encomienda*.
29. AGI, SF, 17, n. 99. See also Muñoz-Arbeláez, "Vagabundos."
30. Francis, "Resguardo," 382.
31. Bonilla, *Minas*, 49.
32. Fernández Albaladejo, *Fragmentos*, 134.

33. *Recopilación*, vol. 8, t. i, l. lx.
34. AGI, SF, 99, n. 39; Arango Puerta, "Informe"; Ruiz Rivera, "Andrés."
35. Vilches, "Business."
36. AGI, SF, 101, n. 49, 859–60.
37. Wheat, *Atlantic*, 22.
38. Gómez, "Pieza."
39. AGI, SF, 103, n. 45, 791r–v.
40. Maya Restrepo, "Demografía."
41. Bonilla, *Minas*.
42. Carlos Valencia argues that in Mariquita, enslaved Africans had few material incentives to seek freedom through manumission or to abandon their condition en masse to become maroons or free people of color, since taxes like the requinto made freedom rather expensive. Valencia Villa, *Alma*.
43. AGN, VT, 3, d. 1.
44. AGN, VT, 3, d. 1, 7v–8r, 4r–v, 14r, 41r.
45. AGI, Contaduría, 1346A.
46. Velasco Murillo, *Urban*.
47. Bonil Gómez, *Gobierno*.
48. West, *Colonial*; Sharp, *Slavery*; Colmenares, *Popayán*; West, *Pacific*; Bryant, *Rivers*; Echeverri, *Indian*.
49. AGI, SF, 110, n. 35. This letter echoes a previous letter (arbitrio) Sologuren wrote to the king in 1590.
50. Solano, "Regimen," 651–52.
51. TePaske and Brown, *New*, 287.
52. Colmenares, *Historia*, 381.
53. Colmenares, *Popayán*; Torres, "Trade."
54. On the tension between an empire of justice and economic governance, see Fernández Albaladejo, *Fragmentos*; Eissa-Barroso, *Spanish*.

EPILOGUE

1. On the distinction between judicial and economic governance, see Fernández Albaladejo, *Fragmentos*; on ritual politics, Cañeque, *King's*; on knowledge production, Brendecke, *Empirical*. See the introduction for reference to key debates on the centrality of Indigenous peoples to imperial politics.
2. On transculturation, see Ortiz, *Contrapunteo*; Arnedo-Gómez, "Fernando."
3. AGI, SF, r. 8, n. 263–74; Eissa-Barroso, *Spanish*.
4. Afanador-Llach, "República."
5. AGI, Cuba, 894, n. 1, 1r–v.
6. Caldas, "Influjo." Scholars debate whether it was Caldas or Alexander von Humboldt who discovered the altitudinal distribution of plants. Regardless, it is clear that they were indeed "discovering" a principle that had shaped the way different Indigenous societies had settled the Andes. This realization was far from new to the peasant and Indigenous societies of the Andes, who over millennia had developed a

rich variety of crops by taking advantage of different levels of altitude. See Humboldt and Bonpland, *Essay*. On the relationship between Caldas and Humboldt, see Nieto Olarte, *Orden*; Cañizares-Esguerra, "Derivative." On Humboldt's view of America, see Pratt, *Imperial*. On the economics of verticality in the central Andes, see Murra, *Formaciones*.

7. Uribe, *Frontier*.
8. Méndez, "Indio." Other intellectuals in New Granada, like Diego Martín Tanco and José Ignacio Pombo, did not believe that climate was necessarily tied to civilization, but they did deem Indigenous and African bodies as the main reasons for the stagnation of the kingdom; Nieto Olarte, *Orden*.
9. Safford and Palacios, *Colombia*.
10. Historian Alfonso Múnera argues that the divisive and exclusive notions of Colombia as an Andean republic, which consistently interpreted the population of the lowlands as backward, sealed the fate of a national project that was unable to cope with the diversity of its territories and peoples. Múnera, *Fracaso*.
11. Schmidt-Nowara, *Conquest*.
12. Langebaek, *Herederos*.
13. Casas, *Brevísima*.
14. Méndez, "Incas."
15. Rappaport, *Cumbe*; Rappaport, *Politics*; Espinosa, *Civilización*, 143–47.

BIBLIOGRAPHY

ARCHIVES AND COLLECTIONS

Archivo General de Indias, Seville (AGI)
    Contaduría
    Cuba
    Escribanía de Cámara (EC)
    Justicia
    Mapas y planos Panamá, Santa Fe y Quito (MP)
    Patronato
    Quito
    Santa Fe (SF)
Archivo General de la Nación, Bogotá (AGN)
    Caciques e Indios (CI)
    Encomiendas
    Resguardos Boyacá (RB)
    Visitas Boyacá (VB)
    Visitas Cundinamarca (VC)
    Visitas Tolima (VT)
Archivo Histórico de Cali
Archivo Historico Regional de Boyacá, Tunja (AHRB)
Archivo Histórico de San Bartolomé, Bogotá (AHSB)
Archivo General de Simancas
British Library, London
British Museum, London
Centro de Investigaciones Históricas Jose María Arboleda Llorente, Popayán
Museo del Oro, Bogotá
Museo de Trajes, Bogotá
New York Public Library

Abrams, Philip. "Notes on the Difficulty of Studying the State (1977)." *Journal of Historical Society* 1, no. 1 (1988): 58–89.

Adorno, Rolena. *Guáman Poma: Writing and Resistance in Colonial Peru*. Austin: University of Texas Press, 1986.

Adorno, Rolena. *The Polemics of Possession in Spanish American Narrative*. New Haven, CT: Yale University Press, 2007.

Afanador-Llach, María José. "Una república colosal: la unión de Colombia, el acceso al Pacífico y la utopía del comercio global, 1819-1830." *Anuario Colombiano de Historia Social y de la Cultura* 45, no. 2 (2018): 35–63.

Aguirre Beltrán, Gonzalo. *Regiones de refugio: el desarrollo de la comunidad y el proceso dominical en mestizo América*. Mexico City: Instituto Indigenista Interamericano, 1967.

Appadurai, Arjun. "Introduction: Commodities and the Politics of Value." In *The Social Life of Things: Commodities in Cultural Perspective*, edited by Arjun Appadurai, 3–63. Cambridge: Cambridge University Press, 1986.

Arango Puerta, Mauricio. "Informe sobre la guerra contra los indios pijaos por el contador y veedor Andrés Pérez de Pisa, 1611." *Boletín Museo del Oro*, no. 57 (2017): 58–85.

Arens, W. *The Man-Eating Myth: Anthropology and Anthropophagy*. New York: Oxford University Press, 1979.

Ares Queija, Berta, and Tomás López Medel. *Tomás López Medel: trayectoria de un clérigo-oidor ante el Nuevo Mundo*. Guadalajara: Institución Provincial de Cultura, 1993.

Arnedo-Gómez, Miguel. "Fernando Ortiz's Transculturation: Applied Anthropology, Acculturation, and Mestizaje." *Journal of Latin American and Caribbean Anthropology* 27, nos. 1–2 (2022): 123–45.

Ash, Eric H. *The Draining of the Fens: Projectors, Popular Politics, and State Building in Early Modern England*. Baltimore: Johns Hopkins University Press, 2017.

Assadourian, Carlos Sempat. "Acerca del cambio en la naturaleza del dominio sobre las indias: la mit'a minera del virrey Toledo, documentos de 1568-1571." *Anuario de Estudios Americanos* 46 (1989): 3–71.

Assadourian, Carlos Sempat. "Los señores étnicos y los corregidores de indios en la conformación del estado colonial." *Anuario de Estudios Americanos* 46 (1987): 325–427.

Assadourian, Carlos Sempat. *El sistema de la economía colonial: mercado interno, regiones y espacio económico*. Lima: Instituto de Estudios Peruanos, 1982.

Assadourian, Carlos Sempat, Heraclio Bonilla, Antonio Mitre, and Tristan Platt. *Minería y espacio económico en los Andes, siglos XVI-XX*. Lima: Instituto de Estudios Peruanos, 1980.

"Autos en razón de prohibir a los caziques de Fontibón, Ubaque y otros no hagan fiestas, borracheras y sacrificios de su gentilidad." In *Relaciones y visitas a los Andes*, edited by Hermes Tovar Pinzón, 3:239–66. Bogotá: Colcultura, Instituto de Cultura Hispánica, 1995.

Avellaneda, José Ignacio. *The Conquerors of the New Kingdom of Granada*. Albuquerque: University of New Mexico Press, 1995.

Baker, Keith Michael, and Dan Edelstein. *Scripting Revolution: A Historical Approach to the Comparative Study of Revolutions*. Stanford, CA: Stanford University Press, 2015.

Barragán, Rossana. "Working Silver for the World: Mining Labor and Popular Economy in Colonial Potosí." *Hispanic American Historical Review* 97, no. 2 (2017): 193–222.

Barrera-Osorio, Antonio. *Experiencing Nature: The Spanish American Empire and the Early Scientific Revolution.* Austin: University of Texas Press, 2006.

Bassi, Ernesto. *An Aqueous Territory: Sailor Geographies and New Granada's Transimperial Greater Caribbean World.* Durham, NC: Duke University Press, 2016.

Bastias Saavedra, Manuel. "The Normativity of Possession: Rethinking Land Relations in Early-Modern Spanish America, ca. 1500–1800." *Colonial Latin American Review* 29, no. 2 (2020): 223–38.

Bataillon, Marcel. *Erasmo y España: estudios sobre la historia espiritual del siglo XVI.* Mexico City: Fondo de Cultura Económica, 1956.

Beckert, Sven. *Empire of Cotton: A Global History.* New York: Alfred A. Knopf, 2014.

Begley, Christopher. "Intercambio interregional, conexiones externas y estrategias de poder en el oriente de Honduras durante los periodos V y VI." *Revista de arqueología del área intermedia* 6 (2004): 109–28.

Benton, Lauren A. *A Search for Sovereignty: Law and Geography in European Empires, 1400–1900.* Cambridge: Cambridge University Press, 2010.

Bernal Andrade, Leovigildo. *Los Pijaos: historia e importancia antropológica.* Bogotá: L. Bernal Andrade, 2008.

Bernal Ruiz, Fernando. "Investigaciones arqueológicas en el antiguo cacicazgo de Bogotá (Funza-Cundinamarca)." *Boletín de arqueología* 5, no. 3 (1992): 31–48.

Blackbourn, David. *The Conquest of Nature: Water, Landscape, and the Making of Modern Germany.* New York: Norton, 2006.

Blair, Ann. *Too Much to Know: Managing Scholarly Information before the Modern Age.* New Haven, CT: Yale University Press, 2010.

Blair, Ann, and Devin Fitzgerald. "A Revolution in Information?" In *The Oxford Handbook of Early Modern European History, 1350–1750,* edited by Hamish Scott, 1:244–65. Oxford: Oxford University Press, 2015.

Boada, Ana María. *The Evolution of Social Hierarchy in a Muisca Chiefdom of the Northern Andes of Colombia.* Pittsburgh: University of Pittsburgh, Department of Anthropology / ICANH, 2007.

Boada, Ana María. *Patrones de asentamiento regional y sistemas de agricultura intensiva en Cota y Suba, Sabana de Bogotá (Colombia).* Bogotá: FIAN, 2006.

Boada, Ana María. "La producción textil de algodón en la política económica de los cacicazgos muiscas de los Andes colombianos." In *Economía, prestigio y poder. Perspectivas desde la arqueología,* edited by Carlos Augusto Sánchez, 272–313. Bogotá: ICANH, 2009.

Boccara, Guillaume. *Los vencedores: historia del pueblo mapuche en la época colonial.* San Pedro de Atacama, Chile: IIAM, 2007.

Bolaños, Alvaro Félix. *Barbarie y canibalismo en la retórica colonial: los indios Pijaos de Fray Pedro Simón.* Bogotá: CEREC, 1994.

Bonil Gómez, Katherine. *Gobierno y calidad en el orden colonial: las categorías del mestizaje en la provincia de Mariquita en la segunda mitad del siglo XVIII.* Bogotá: Ediciones Uniandes, 2011.

Bonilla, Heraclio. *Las minas de Mariquita en el Nuevo Reino de Granada: minería y circulación monetaria en los Andes del siglo XVII*. Madrid: Ediciones Doce Calles, Universidad Nacional de Colombia, Universidad Pablo de Olavide, 2015.

Bonnett Vélez, Diana. *Tierra y comunidad: un problema irresuelto*. Bogotá: ICANH, Ediciones Uniandes, 2002.

Boone, Elizabeth Hill, and Walter Mignolo, eds. *Writing without Words: Alternative Literacies in Mesoamerica and the Andes*. Durham, NC: Duke University Press, 1994.

Borja, Juan. "Don Juan de Borja informa sobre la guerra contra los Indios Pijao [25 de mayo de 1610]." In *Relaciones y visitas a los Andes*, edited by Hermes Tovar Pinzón, 4:473–84. Bogotá: Colcultura, Instituto de Cultura Hispánica, 1995.

Borja, Juan. "Informe sobre la guerra contra los indios Pijao [25 de mayo de 1610]." In *Relaciones y visitas a los Andes*, transcribed and edited by Hermes Tovar Pinzón, 4:471–84. Bogotá: Colcultura, Instituto de Cultura Hispánica, 1995.

Brading, David A. *The First America: The Spanish Monarchy, Creole Patriots, and the Liberal State, 1492–1867*. Cambridge: Cambridge University Press, 1991.

Braudel, Fernand. *El Mediterráneo y el mundo mediterráneo en la época de Felipe II*. 2 vols. Mexico City: Fondo de Cultura Económica, 1949.

Bray, Tamara L. "Skeuomorphos, conchas de cerámica en los Andes septentrionales: ideología, emulación e intercambio a larga distancia." *Revista de arqueología del área intermedia* 3 (2001): 11–24.

Brendecke, Arndt. *The Empirical Empire: Spanish Colonial Rule and the Politics of Knowledge*. Berlin: De Gruyter, 2016.

Brewer-García, Larissa. *Beyond Babel: Translations of Blackness in Colonial Peru and New Granada*. Cambridge: Cambridge University Press, 2020.

Broadbent, Sylvia. "Agricultural Terraces in Chibcha Territory, Colombia." *American Antiquity* 29, no. 4 (1964): 501–4.

Broadbent, Sylvia. "A Prehistoric Field System in Chibcha Territory, Colombia." *Ñawpa Pacha: Journal of the Institute of Andean Studies* 6, no. 1 (1968): 135–47.

Broadbent, Sylvia. "The Site of Chibcha Bogotá." *Ñawpa Pacha: Journal of the Institute of Andean Studies* 4, no. 1 (1966): 1–14.

Broadbent, Sylvia. "La situación del Bogotá Chibcha." *Revista Colombiana de Antropología*, no. 17 (1966): 117–32.

Brown, Vincent. *Tacky's Revolt: The Story of an Atlantic Slave War*. Cambridge, MA: Harvard University Press, 2020.

Bryant, Sherwin K. *Rivers of Gold, Lives of Bondage: Governing through Slavery in Colonial Quito*. Chapel Hill: University of North Carolina Press, 2014.

Burkholder, Mark A. "Spain's America: From Kingdoms to Colonies." *Colonial Latin American Review* 25, no. 2 (2016): 125–53.

Burns, Kathryn. *Into the Archive: Writing and Power in Colonial Peru*. Durham, NC: Duke University Press, 2010.

Bushnell, Amy Turner. "Indigenous America and the Limits of the Atlantic World, 1493–1825." In *Atlantic History*, edited by Jack P. Greene and Philip D. Morgan, 191–221. New York: Oxford University Press, 2008.

Caballos, Esteban Mira. *El descubrimiento de Europa: Indígenas y mestizos en el Viejo Mundo*. Barcelona: Editorial Crítica, 2023.

Caldas, Francisco José de. "Del influjo del clima sobre los seres organizados." In *Obras completas de Francisco José de Caldas*, 79–120. Bogotá: Imprenta Nacional, 1966.

Candiani, Vera. *Dreaming of Dry Land: Environmental Transformation in Colonial Mexico City*. Stanford, CA: Stanford University Press, 2014.

Cañeque, Alejandro. *The King's Living Image: The Culture and Politics of Viceregal Power in Colonial Mexico*. New York: Routledge, 2004.

Cañeque, Alejandro. "The Political and Institutional History of Colonial Spanish America." *History Compass* 11, no. 4 (2013): 280–91.

Cañizares-Esguerra, Jorge. "How Derivative Was Humboldt? Microcosmic Narratives in Early Modern Spanish America and the (Other) Origins of Humboldt's Ecological Sensibilities." In *Nature, Empire, and Nation: Explorations of the History of Science in the Iberian World*, 112–28. Stanford, CA: Stanford University Press, 2006.

Cañizares-Esguerra, Jorge. *Puritan Conquistadors: Iberianizing the Atlantic, 1550–1700*. Stanford, CA: Stanford University Press, 2006.

Cardale de Schrimpff, Marianne. "Caminos al paisaje del pasado. Reflexiones sobre los caminos precolombinos en Colombia." In *Caminos precolombinos. Las vías, los ingenieros y los viajeros*, edited by Leonor Herrera and Marianne Cardale de Schrimpff, 43–85. Bogotá: ICANH, 2000.

Cardale de Schrimpff, Marianne. *Las salinas de Zipaquirá: su explotación indígena*. Bogotá: FIAN; Banco de la República, 1981.

Cardim, Pedro, Tamar Herzog, José Javier Ruiz Ibáñez, and Gaetano Sabatini. *Polycentric Monarchies: How Did Early Modern Spain and Portugal Achieve and Maintain a Global Hegemony?* Eastbourne, UK: Sussex Academic Press, 2012.

Carrera Quezada, Sergio. *Sementeras de papel: la regularización de la propiedad rural en la Huasteca serrana, 1550–1720*. Mexico City: El Colegio de México, 2018.

Carrera Quezada, Sergio, and Juan Manuel Pérez Zevallos. *En todos los rincones imperiales: apropiaciones de tierras baldías y composiciones de propiedades agrarias en América y Filipinas (siglos XVI–XIX)*. Mexico City: El Colegio de México, 2022.

"Carta y relación para su magestad que escriben los oficiales de vuestra magestad de la provincia de Santa Marta." In *Relaciones y visitas a los Andes*, edited by Hermes Tovar Pinzón, 3:93–118. Bogotá: Colcultura, Instituto de Cultura Hispánica, 1995.

Carvalho, Francismar Alex Lopes de. "Formal and Informal Alliances between Iberians and Natives in the Heart of Late Eighteenth-Century South America." *Ethnohistory* 70, no. 1 (2023): 65–93.

Casas, Bartolomé de las. *Brevísima relación de la destrucción de las Indias*. Bogotá: Imprenta del Estado, José María Rios, 1813.

Castillo, Antonio. "The New Culture of Archives in Early Modern Spain." *European History Quarterly* 46, no. 3 (2016): 545–67.

Castillo Mathieu, Nicolás del. *Descubrimiento y Conquista de Colombia*. Bogotá: Banco de la República, 1988.

Castillo y Orozco, Eugenio del. *Vocabulario páez-castellano. Catecismo, nociones gramaticales i dos pláticas. Con adiciones, correcciones i un vocabulario castellano-páez*. Paris: Maisonneuve, 1877.

Cavelier, Inés. "Perspectivas culturales y cambios en el uso del paisaje. Sabana de Bogotá, siglos XVI–XVIII." In *Agricultura ancestral, camellones y albarradas. Contexto social, usos y retos del pasado y del presente*, edited by Francisco Valdez, 127–40. Quito: Ediciones Abya-Yala, 2006.

Clastres, Hélène. *The Land-without-Evil: Tupí-Guaraní Prophetism*. Urbana: University of Illinois Press, 1995.

Clastres, Pierre. *Society Against the State: Essays in Political Anthropology*. New York: Zone, 1987.

Clavijo Ocampo, Hernán. *Formación histórica de las élites locales en el Tolima*. 2 vols. Bogotá: Banco Popular, 1993.

Clendinnen, Inga. *Ambivalent Conquests: Maya and Spaniard in Yucatan, 1517–1570*. New York: Cambridge University Press, 2003.

Cline, Howard. "The Relaciones Geograficas of the Spanish Indies, 1577–1586." *Hispanic American Historical Review* 44, no. 3 (1964): 341–74.

Cobo Betancourt, Juan Fernando. "Colonialism in the Periphery: Spanish Linguistic Policy in New Granada, c. 1574–1625." *Colonial Latin American Review* 23, no. 2 (2014): 118–42.

Cobo Betancourt, Juan Fernando. *The Coming of the Kingdom: The Muisca, Catholic Reform, and Spanish Colonialism in the New Kingdom of Granada*. Cambridge: Cambridge University Press, 2024.

Cobo Betancourt, Juan Fernando. *Mestizos heraldos de Dios: la ordenación de sacerdotes descendientes de españoles e indígenas en el nuevo Reino de Granada y la racialización de la diferencia, 1573–1590*. Bogotá: ICANH, 2012.

Cobo Betancourt, Juan Fernando, and Natalie Cobo. *La legislación de la Arquidiócesis de Santafé en el período colonial*. Bogotá: ICANH, 2018.

Colmenares, Germán. "La economía y la sociedad coloniales: 1550–1800." In *Manual de historia de Colombia: prehistoria, conquista y colonia*, edited by Jaime Jaramillo Uribe, 1:223–300. Bogotá: Instituto Colombiano de Cultura, Procultura, 1984.

Colmenares, Germán. *Historia económica y social de Colombia*, vol. 1, *1537–1719*. Bogotá: Tercer Mundo Editores, Universidad del Valle, Banco de la República, Colciencias, 1997.

Colmenares, Germán. *Historia económica y social de Colombia*, vol. 2, *Popayán, una sociedad esclavista*. Bogotá: Tercer Mundo Editores, Universidad del Valle, Banco de la República, Colciencias, 1997.

Colmenares, Germán. *La provincia de Tunja en el Nuevo Reino de Granada: ensayo de historia social 1539–1800*. Bogotá: Tercer Mundo Editores, Universidad del Valle, Banco de la República, Colciencias, 1997.

Constenla Umaña, Adolfo. *Las lenguas del área intermedia: introducción a su estudio areal*. San José: Universidad de Costa Rica, 1991.

Conway, Richard M. *Islands in the Lake: Environment and Ethnohistory in Xochimilco, New Spain*. Cambridge: Cambridge University Press, 2021.

Córdoba, Luis Miguel. "Comentario al mapa del río Magdalena, del oidor Luis Enríquez. 1601." In *Entre líneas: una historia de Colombia en mapas*, edited by Sebastián Díaz, Lucía Duque, Santiago Muñoz, and Anthony Picón, 97–105. Bogotá: Ediciones Uniandes, Editorial Planeta, 2017.

Córdoba Ochoa, Luis Miguel. "Guerra, imperio y violencia en la Audiencia de Santa Fe, Nuevo Reino de Granada, 1580–1620." Universidad Pablo de Olavide, Sevilla, 2013.

Correa, François. "Análisis formal del vocabulario de parentesco muisca." *Boletín del Museo del Oro* 32–33 (2001): 1992.

Correa, François. "Fundamentos de la organización social muisca." In *Los Chibchas: Adaptación y diversidad en los Andes orientales de Colombia*, edited by José Vicente Rodríguez, 25–48. Bogotá: Universidad Nacional de Colombia, 2001.

Correa, François. *El sol del poder: simbología y política entre los muiscas del norte de los Andes.* Bogotá: Universidad Nacional de Colombia, 2004.

Corredor, María Paula. "Entre el laberinto jurídico de la monarquía hispánica: el caso de un cacique del Nuevo Reino de Granada (1572–1578)." Universidad del Rosario, 2016.

Cortes Alonso, Vicenta. "Visita a los santuarios indígenas de Boyacá en 1577." *Revista Colombiana de Antropología* 9 (1960): 200–273.

Cosgrove, Denis. *Geography and Vision: Seeing, Imagining and Representing the World.* London: Palgrave Macmillan, 2008.

Cosgrove, Denis. *Social Formation and Symbolic Landscape.* Madison: University of Wisconsin Press, 1998.

Cosgrove, Denis E., and Stephen Daniels. *The Iconography of Landscape: Essays on the Symbolic Representation, Design, and Use of Past Environments.* Cambridge: Cambridge University Press, 1988.

Covarrubias Horozco, Sebastián de. *Tesoro de la lengua castellana o española.* 2 vols. Madrid: Por Luis Sanchez, impressor del Rey, 1611.

Covey, R. Alan. *Inca Apocalypse: The Spanish Conquest and the Transformation of the Andean World.* New York: Oxford University Press, 2020.

Craib, Raymond B. *Cartographic Mexico: A History of State Fixations and Fugitive Landscapes.* Durham, NC: Duke University Press, 2004.

Cronon, William. *Changes in the Land: Indians, Colonists, and the Ecology of New England.* New York: Hill and Wang, 2003.

Crosby, Alfred W. *The Columbian Exchange: Biological and Cultural Consequences of 1492.* Westport, CT: Greenwood, 1972.

Cunill, Caroline. "Fray Bartolomé de las Casas y el oficio de defensor de indios en América y en la Corte española." *Nuevo Mundo, Mundos Nuevos,* 2012.

Cunill, Caroline. "Tomás López Medel y sus instrucciones para defensores de Indios: una propuesta innovadora." *Anuario de Estudios Americanos* 68, no. 2 (2011): 539–63.

Curet, L. Antonio. "Interaccionar o no interaccionar: el Área intermedia, el área Circumcaribe y las Antillas mayores." *Revista de arqueología del área intermedia* 6 (2004): 83–108.

Davies, Surekha. *Renaissance Ethnography and the Invention of the Human: New Worlds, Maps, and Monsters.* New York: Cambridge University Press, 2016.

Dean, Carolyn J. *A Culture of Stone: Inka Perspectives on Rock.* Durham, NC: Duke University Press, 2010.

Dean, Carolyn, and Dana Leibsohn. "Hybridity and Its Discontents: Considering Visual Culture in Colonial Spanish America." *Colonial Latin American Review* 12, no. 1 (2003): 5–35.

Deardorff, Max. *A Tale of Two Granadas: Custom, Community, and Citizenship in the Spanish Empire, 1568–1668.* Cambridge: Cambridge University Press, 2023.

Dery, David. "'Papereality' and Learning in Bureaucratic Organizations." *Administration and Society* 29, no. 6 (1998): 677–89.

Devia, Beatriz, and Marianne Cardale de Schrimpff. "Estudio de los textiles pertenecientes a la colección del Museo Arqueológico de Sogamoso." Bogotá: Fundación para la Promoción de la Investigación y la Tecnología, 1997.

Diamond, Jared M. *Guns, Germs, and Steel: The Fates of Human Societies*. New York: Norton, 1999.

Díaz Ceballos, Jorge. *Poder compartido. Repúblicas urbanas, monarquía y conversación en Castilla del Oro, 1508-1573*. Madrid: Marcial Pons, 2020.

Díaz Díaz, Rafael. *Esclavitud, región y ciudad: el sistema esclavista urbano-regional en Santafé de Bogotá, 1700-1750*. Bogotá: Pontificia Universidad Javeriana, 2001.

Drennan, Robert. "Betwixt and between in the Intermediate Area." *Journal of Archaeological Research* 4, no. 2 (1996): 95–132.

Dueñas, Alcira. "Indian Colonial Actors in the Lawmaking of the Spanish Empire in Peru." *Ethnohistory* 65, no. 1 (2018): 51–73.

Dueñas, Alcira. *Indians and Mestizos in the "Lettered City": Reshaping Justice, Social Hierarchy, and Political Culture in Colonial Peru*. Boulder: University Press of Colorado, 2010.

Dueñas, Alcira. "The Virgin and the Land Surveyor: Andean Pueblo Boundary Making in the Highlands of Late Colonial Ecuador." *Colonial Latin American Review* 31, no. 3 (2022): 304–26.

Durston, Alan. "Notes on the Authorship of the Huarochirí Manuscript." *Colonial Latin American Review* 16, no. 2 (2007): 227–41.

Dussán, Alicia, and Gerardo Reichel Dolmatoff. "Grupos sanguíneos entre los indios pijao del Tolima." *Revista del Instituto Etnológico Nacional*, no. 1 (1945): 507–20.

DuVal, Kathleen. *The Native Ground: Indians and Colonists in the Heart of the Continent*. Philadelphia: University of Pennsylvania Press, 2006.

Echeverri, Marcela. *Indian and Slave Royalists in the Age of Revolution: Reform, Revolution, and Royalism in the Northern Andes, 1780-1825*. New York: Cambridge University Press, 2016.

Eissa-Barroso, Francisco A. *The Spanish Monarchy and the Creation of the Viceroyalty of New Granada (1717-1739): The Politics of Early Bourbon Reform in Spain and Spanish America*. Leiden: Brill, 2017.

Elliott, J. H. "A Europe of Composite Monarchies." *Past and Present* 137, no. 1 (1992): 48–71.

"Epítome de la Conquista del Nuevo Reino de Granada." In *No hay caciques ni señores*, edited by Hermes Tovar Pinzón, 163–88. Barcelona: Sendai, 1988.

Erbig, Jeffrey Alan Jr. *Where Caciques and Mapmakers Met: Border Making in Eighteenth-Century South America*. Chapel Hill: University of North Carolina Press, 2020.

Escudero, Alfredo Luis. "The New Age of Andeans: Chronological Age, Indigenous Labor, and the Making of Spanish Colonial Rule." *Hispanic American Historical Review* 103, no. 1 (2023): 1–30.

Espinosa, Carlos. *El Inca barroco: política y estética en la Real Audiencia de Quito, 1630-1680*. Quito: FLACSO, 2015.

Espinosa, Mónica. *La civilización montés. La visión india y el trasegar de Manuel Quintín Lame en Colombia*. Bogotá: Ediciones Uniandes, 2009.

Eugenio Martínez, María Ángeles. *Tributo y trabajo del indio en Nueva Granada (de Jiménez de Quesada a Sande)*. Seville: CSIC, 1977.

Federici, Silvia. *Caliban and the Witch: Women, the Body and Primitive Accumulation*. New York: Autonomedia, 2003.

Ferguson, R. Brian, and Neil L. Whitehead. *War in the Tribal Zone: Expanding States and Indigenous Warfare*. Sante Fe, NM: School of American Research Press, 1992.

Fernández Albaladejo, Pablo. *Fragmentos de monarquía: trabajos de historia política*. Madrid: Alianza Editorial, 1992.

Fernández de Piedrahita, Lucas. *Historia general de las conquistas del Nuevo Reyno de Granada*. Antwerp: Juan Baptista Verdussen, 1688.

Figueroa Cancino, Juan David. "Las primeras relaciones del Nuevo Reino de Granada revisitadas (1539–1550): autores y temas centrales." *Historia y sociedad* 34 (2018): 1–21.

Flores Galindo, Alberto. *Buscando un Inca: identidad y utopía en los Andes*. Lima: Instituto de Apoyo Agrario, 1987.

Fonseca, Oscar. "El concepto de Área de Tradición Chibchoide y su pertinencia para entender Gran Nicoya." *Vínculos* 18 (1994): 209–28.

Francis, Michael. *Invading Colombia: Spanish Accounts of the Gonzalo Jiménez de Quesada Expedition of Conquest*. University Park: Pennsylvania State University Press, 2007.

Francis, Michael. "The Resguardo, the Mita, and the Alquiler General: Indian Migration in the Province of Tunja, 1550–1636." *Colonial Latin American Historical Review* 11, no. 4 (2002): 375–406.

Friede, Juan. *El adelantado, don Gonzalo Jiménez de Quesada*. 2 vols. Bogotá: C. Valencia Editores, 1979.

Friede, Juan. "Aportación documental al estudio de la demografía precolombina: los Quimbayas." *Revista Colombiana de Antropología* 11 (1962): 303–18.

Friede, Juan. *Los Chibchas bajo la dominación española*. Bogotá: La Carreta, 1974.

Friede, Juan. "De la encomienda indiana a la propiedad territorial y su influencia sobre el mestizaje." *Anuario Colombiano de Historia Social y de la Cultura* 4 (1969): 35–61.

Friede, Juan. *Documentos inéditos para la historia de Colombia*. 8 vols. Bogotá: Academia de Historia, 1955.

Friede, Juan. *Don Juan del Valle, primer obispo de Popayán*. Segovia: Instituto Diego de Colmenares, 1952.

Friede, Juan. *Fuentes documentales para la historia del Nuevo Reino de Granada desde la instalación de la Real Audiencia en Santafé*. 8 vols. Bogotá: Banco Popular, 1975.

Friede, Juan. *Los Quimbayas bajo la dominación española*. Bogotá: Carlos Valencia Editores, 1963.

Friedrich, Markus. "How to Make an Archival Inventory in Early Modern Europe: Carrying Documents, Gluing Paper and Transforming Archival Chaos into Well-Ordered Knowledge." *Manuscript Cultures*, no. 10 (2018): 1–19.

Galster, Ingrid. *Aguirre o la posteridad arbitraria: la rebelión del conquistador vasco Lope de Aguirre en historiografía y ficción histórica (1561–1992)*. Bogotá: Editorial Universidad del Rosario, 2011.

Gamboa, Jorge. *El cacicazgo muisca en los años posteriores a la Conquista: del sihipkua al cacique colonial, 1537–1575*. Bogotá: ICANH, 2010.

García, Claudia. *Etnogénesis, hibridación y consolidación de la identidad del pueblo Miskitu.* Madrid: CSIC, 2007.

Garcilaso de la Vega, Inka. *Comentarios reales de los incas.* 2 vols. Mexico City: Fondo de Cultura Económica, 2005.

Garriga, Carlos. "La expansión de la visita castellana a Indias: presupuestos, alcance y significado." In *XI Congreso del Instituto Internacional de Historia del Derecho Indiano*, 3:51–80. Buenos Aires: Instituto de Investigaciones de Historia del Derecho, 1995.

Garriga, Carlos. "Justicia animada: dispositivos de la justicia en la monarquía católica." *Cuadernos de Derecho Judicial* 6 (2006): 59–106.

Garriga, Carlos. "Sobre el gobierno de la justicia en Indias (siglos XVI–XVII)." *Revista de Historia del Derecho* 14 (2006): 67–160.

Gassón, Rafael, and Erka Wagner. "¿Cuestión de límites? El no-lugar de Venezuela en la arqueología del Área Intermedia." *Revista de Arqueología del Área Intermedia* 6 (2004): 167–98.

Glave, Luis Miguel. "El arbitrio de tierras de 1622 y el debate sobre las propiedades y los derechos coloniales de los indios." *Anuario de Estudios Americanos* 71, no. 1 (2014): 79–106.

Gómez, Margarita. *El sello y registro de Indias. Imagen y representación.* Cologne: Böhlau Verlag, 2008.

Gómez, Pablo. *The Experiential Caribbean: Creating Knowledge and Healing in the Early Modern Atlantic.* Chapel Hill: University of North Carolina Press, 2017.

Gómez, Pablo. "Pieza de Indias: Slave Trade and the Quantification of Human Bodies." In *Objects of New World Knowledge: A Cabinet of Curiosities*, edited by Mark Thurner and Juan Pimentel, 47–50. London: University of London Press, 2021.

Gómez Aldana, Diego Fernando. "Muysc cubun." Last updated August 29, 2022. muysca.cubun.org/Categoría:Diccionario.

González, Alvaro. "Encomiendas, encomenderos e indígenas tributarios del Nuevo Reino de Granada en la primera mitad del siglo XVII." *Anuario Colombiano de Historia Social y de la Cultura*, no. 2 (1964).

Gonzalez, Antonio. "Ordenanzas de corregidores de 1593." In *La Provincia de Tunja en el Nuevo Reino de Granada: ensayo de historia social (1539-1800)*, edited by Germán Colmenares, 183–98. Bogotá: Tercer Mundo Editores, Universidad del Valle, Banco de la República, Colciencias, 1997.

Gonzalez, Margarita. "La hacienda colonial y los orígenes de la propiedad territorial en Colombia." In *Ensayos de historia colonial colombiana*, edited by Margarita Gonzalez, 333–66. Bogotá: Punto de Lectura, 2005.

Gonzalez, Margarita. *El resguardo en el Nuevo Reino de Granada.* Bogotá: La Carreta, 1979.

González, María Stella. *Diccionario y gramática Chibcha.* Bogotá: Instituto Caro y Cuervo, 1606.

Graubart, Karen. "Learning from the Qadi: The Jurisdiction of Local Rule in the Early Colonial Andes." *Hispanic American Historical Review* 95, no. 2 (2015): 195–228.

Graubart, Karen. *Republics of Difference: Religious and Racial Self-Governance in the Spanish Atlantic World.* Oxford: Oxford University Press, 2022.

Graubart, Karen. *With Our Labor and Sweat: Indigenous Women and the Formation of Colonial Society in Peru, 1550-1700*. Stanford, CA: Stanford University Press, 2007.

Greer, Allan. *Property and Dispossession: Natives, Empires and Land in Early Modern North America*. Cambridge: Cambridge University Press, 2017.

Groot, Ana María. *Sal y poder en el altiplano de Bogotá, 1537-1640*. Bogotá: Universidad Nacional de Colombia, 2008.

Gruzinski, Serge. *El pensamiento mestizo*. Barcelona: Paidos Iberica Ediciones, 2000.

Guamán Poma de Ayala, Felipe. *El primer nueva corónica y buen gobierno*. 3 vols. Edited by John V. Murra and Rolena Adorno. Translated by Jorge Urioste. Mexico City: Siglo Veintiuno, 1980.

Gudeman, Stephen. *The Anthropology of Economy: Community, Market, and Culture*. Malden, MA: Blackwell, 2001.

Guengerich, Sara Vicuña. "Mantos, Sayas, and Golden Buckles: The Tapado Fashion in Viceregal Peru." *Monographic Review / Revista Monográfica* 25 (2009): 45-70.

Guevara-Gil, Armando, and Frank Salomon. "A 'Personal Visit': Colonial Political Ritual and the Making of Indians in the Andes." *Colonial Latin American Review* 3, nos. 1-2 (1994): 3-26.

Guhl, Ernesto. *Colombia: bosquejo de su geografía tropical*. Bogotá: Ediciones Uniandes; Universidad Nacional de Colombia; Jardín Botánico de Bogotá José Celestino Mutis, 2016.

Gutiérrez Ardila, Daniel. *Peces geológicos: pequeña historia de los bagres andinos*. Bogotá: Taurus, 2023.

Gutiérrez Ramos, Jairo. *El Mayorazgo de Bogotá y el Marquesado de San Jorge. Riqueza, linaje, poder y honor en Santa Fé, 1538-1824*. Bogotá: Instituto Colombiano de Cultura Hispánica, 1998.

Hämäläinen, Pekka. *The Comanche Empire*. New Haven, CT: Yale University Press, 2008.

Hämäläinen, Pekka. *Indigenous Continent: The Epic Contest for North America*. New York: Liveright, 2022.

Hamann, Byron. *The Translations of Nebrija: Language, Culture, and Circulation in the Early Modern World*. Amherst: University of Massachusetts Press, 2015.

Hamilton, Andrew James. *The Royal Inca Tunic: A Biography of an Andean Masterpiece*. Princeton: Princeton University Press, 2024.

Hanke, Lewis. *The Spanish Struggle for Justice in the Conquest of America*. Philadelphia: University of Pennsylvania Press, 1949.

Harley, J. B. *The New Nature of Maps: Essays in the History of Cartography*. Baltimore: Johns Hopkins University Press, 2001.

Harney, Stefano. *The Undercommons: Fugitive Planning and Black Study*. Wivenhoe, NY: Minor Compositions, 2013.

Harris, Marvin. *Cannibals and Kings: The Origins of Cultures*. New York: Vintage, 1978.

Harris, Marvin. *Cultural Materialism: The Struggle for a Science of Culture*. New York: Random House, 1979.

Hartman, Saidiya. *Lose Your Mother: A Journey along the Atlantic Slave Route*. New York: Farrar, Straus and Giroux, 2007.

Hartman, Saidiya. *Scenes of Subjection: Terror, Slavery, and Self-Making in Nineteenth-Century America*. New York: Norton, 2022.

Hartman, Saidiya. "Venus in Two Acts." *Small Axe: A Caribbean Journal of Criticism* 12, no. 2 (2008): 1–14.

Henderson, Hope. "Alimentando la casa, bailando el asentamiento: explorando la construcción del liderazgo político en las sociedades Muisca." In *Los muiscas en los siglos XVI y XVII: miradas desde la arquieología, la antropología y la historia*, edited by Jorge Gamboa, 40–62. Bogotá: Ediciones Uniandes, 2008.

Henderson, Hope, and Nicholas Ostler. "Muisca Settlement Organization and Chiefly Authority at Suta, Valle de Leyva, Colombia: A Critical Appraisal of Native Concepts of House for Studies of Complex Societies." *Journal of Anthropological Archaeology* 24, no. 2 (2005): 148–78.

Heng, Geraldine. *Empire of Magic: Medieval Romance and the Politics of Cultural Fantasy*. New York: Columbia University Press, 2003.

Henríquez, Luis. "Relación de la conquista de los Carares [9 de mayo de 1601]." In *Relaciones y Visitas a los Andes*, edited by Hermes Tovar Pinzón, 3:427–82. Bogotá: Colcultura, Instituto de Cultura Hispánica, 1995.

Herrera Angel, Marta. *El conquistador conquistado. Awás, Cuayquer y Sindaguas en el Pacífico colombiano, siglos XVI–XVIII*. Bogotá: Ediciones Uniandes, 2016.

Herrera Angel, Marta. "El corregidor de naturales y el control económico de las comunidades: cambios y permanencias en la Provincia de Santafé, siglo XVIII." *Anuario Colombiano de Historia Social y de la Cultura*, no. 20 (1992): 7–25.

Herrera Angel, Marta. "Desaparición de poblados caribeños en el siglo XVI." *Revista Colombiana de Antropología* 34 (1998): 124–65.

Herrera Angel, Marta. "Mensajes implícitos: el ordenamiento espacial en los pueblos de indios santafereños, s. XVI." *Geopraxis: Revista de estudiantes de geografía*, no. 2 (2005): 13–21.

Herrera Angel, Marta. "Muiscas y cristianos: del biohote a la misa y el tránsito hacia una sociedad individualista." In *Muiscas: representaciones, cartografías y etnopolíticas de la memoria*, edited by Ana María Gómez Londoño, 152–79. Bogotá: Pontificia Universidad Javeriana, 2005.

Herrera Angel, Marta. *Ordenar para controlar: ordenamiento espacial y control político en las llanuras del Caribe y en los Andes Centrales neogranadinos, siglo XVIII*. Bogotá: ICANH, Academia Colombiana de Historia, 2002.

Herrera Angel, Marta. "El poblamiento en el siglo XVI. Contrastes entre el Caribe y el interior andino." *Boletín Cultural y Bibliográfico* xliv (2009): 69–80.

Herrera Angel, Marta. *Poder local, población y ordenamiento territorial en la Nueva Granada, siglo XVIII*. Santafé de Bogotá: Archivo General de la Nación, 1996.

Herrera Angel, Marta. "Transición entre el ordenamiento territorial prehispánico y el colonial en la Nueva Granada." *Historia Crítica* 36 (2006): 118–52.

Hershenzon, Daniel. *The Captive Sea: Slavery, Communication, and Commerce in Early Modern Spain and the Mediterranean*. Philadelphia: University of Pennsylvania Press, 2018.

Herzog, Tamar. *Defining Nations: Immigrants and Citizens in Early Modern Spain and Spanish America*. New Haven, CT: Yale University Press, 2003.

Herzog, Tamar. *Frontiers of Possession: Spain and Portugal in Europe and the Americas*. Cambridge, MA: Harvard University Press, 2015.

Herzog, Tamar. "Immemorial (and Native) Customs in Early Modernity: Europe and the Americas." *Comparative Legal History* 9, no. 1 (2021): 3–55.

Herzog, Tamar. "Indigenous Reducciones and Spanish Resettlement: Placing Colonial and European History in Dialogue." *Ler História*, no. 72 (2018): 9–30.

Herzog, Tamar. "Naturales y extranjeros: sobre la construcción de categorias en el mundo hispanico." *Cuadernos de Historia Moderna*, no. 10 (2011): 21–32.

Herzog, Tamar. *Upholding Justice: Society, State, and the Penal System in Quito (1650-1750)*. Ann Arbor: University of Michigan Press, 2004.

Hidalgo, Alex. "The Echo of Voices after the Fall of the Aztec Empire." *Hispanic American Historical Review* 103, no. 2 (2023): 217–49.

Hidalgo, Alex. *Trail of Footprints: A History of Indigenous Maps from Viceregal Mexico*. Austin: University of Texas Press, 2019.

Hoopes, John W. "Atravesando fronteras y explorando la iconografía sagrada de los antiguos chibchas en Centroamérica meridional y Colombia septentrional." *Revista de Arqueología del Área Intermedia* 6 (2004): 129–66.

Hoyos García, Juan Felipe. "El lenguaje y la escritura como herramientas coloniales: el caso de Santa Fe y Tunja, durante el siglo XVI." Universidad Nacional de Colombia, 2002.

Hulme, Peter. *Colonial Encounters: Europe and the Native Caribbean*. London: Methuen, 1986.

Humboldt, Alexander von, and Aimé Bonpland. *Essay on the Geography of Plants*. Chicago: University of Chicago Press, 2008.

Ibarra, Eugenia. *Intercambio, política y sociedad en el siglo XVI. Historia indígena de Panamá, Costa Rica y Nicaragua*. San Pedro: CIHAC, Universidad de Costa Rica, 1999.

Ibarra, Miguel de. "Ordenanzas de trabajo agrícola de Miguel de Ibarra, 1598." In *La Provincia de Tunja en el Nuevo Reino de Granada: ensayo de historia social (1539-1800)*, edited by Germán Colmenares, 199–203. Bogotá: Tercer Mundo Editores, Universidad del Valle, Banco de la República, Colciencias, 1997.

Jacoby, Karl. *Crimes against Nature: Squatters, Poachers, Thieves, and the Hidden History of American Conservation*. Berkeley: University of California Press, 2014.

Jaramillo Uribe, Jaime. "La población indígena de Colombia en el momento de la Conquista y sus transformaciones posteriores." In *Ensayos de historia social*, 63–120. Bogotá: CESO, Editorial Uniandes, Banco de la República, ICANH, Colciencias, Alfaomega, 2000.

Kagan, Richard. *Students and Society in Early Modern Spain*. Baltimore: Johns Hopkins University Press, 1974.

Kagan, Richard. *Urban Images of the Hispanic World, 1493-1793*. New Haven, CT: Yale University Press, 2000.

Kars, Marjoleine. *Blood on the River: A Chronicle of Mutiny and Freedom on the Wild Coast*. New York: New Press, 2020.

Kruschek, Michael. "The Evolution of the Bogotá Chiefdom: A Household View." University of Pittsburgh, 2003.

Kula, Witold. *Measures and Men*. Princeton, NJ: Princeton University Press, 1986.

Lamana, Gonzalo. "Agencia indígena, racismo, y libertad. Las juntas de las comunidades del Cuzco durante el debate por la perpetuidad de las encomiendas." *Colonial Latin American Review* 32, no. 4 (2023): 572–95.

Lane, Kris. *The Colour of Paradise: Emeralds in the Age of the Gunpowder Empires.* New Haven, CT: Yale University Press, 2010.

Lane, Kris. *Potosí: The Silver City That Changed the World.* Berkeley: University of California Press, 2021.

Lane, Kris. *Quito 1599: City and Colony in Transition.* Albuquerque: University of New Mexico Press, 2002.

Lange, Frederick. "Gordon Willey y el Área intermedia: conceptos, contribuciones y perspectivas." *Revista de Arqueología del Área Intermedia* 6 (2004): 27–50.

Lange, Frederick. *Wealth and Hierarchy in the Intermediate Area: A Symposium at Dumbarton Oaks.* Washington, DC: Dumbarton Oaks, 1992.

Langebaek, Carl. "Cacicazgos, orfebrería y política prehispánica: una perspectiva desde Colombia." *Revista de Arqueología del Área Intermedia* 2 (2000): 11–46.

Langebaek, Carl. "Los caminos aborígenes. Caminos, mercaderes y cacicazgos: circuitos de comunicación antes de la invasión española en Colombia." In *Caminos Reales de Colombia,* edited by Jorge Orlando Melo, Pilar Moreno de Ángel, and Mariano Useche, 35–46. Bogotá: FEN, 1995.

Langebaek, Carl. *Los herederos del pasado: indígenas y pensamiento en Colombia y Venezuela.* 2 vols. Bogotá: Ediciones Uniandes, 2009.

Langebaek, Carl. *Mercados, poblamiento e integración étnica entre los muiscas, siglo XVI.* Bogotá: Banco de la República, 1987.

Langebaek, Carl. *Noticias de caciques muy mayores: orígen y desarrollo de sociedades complejas en el nororiente de Colombia y norte de Venezuela.* Bogotá: Ediciones Uniandes, 1992.

Langebaek, Carl. "Santuarios indígenas en el repartimiento de Iguaque, Boyacá: un documento de 1595 del Archivo Nacional de Colombia." *Revista de Antropología* 4, no. 2 (1988): 217–50.

Langebaek, Carl. "Secuencias y procesos. Estudio comparativo del desarrollo de jerarquías de asentamiento prehispánicas en el norte de Suramérica." *Revista de Arqueología del Área Intermedia* 6 (2004): 199–248.

Langfur, Hal. *The Forbidden Lands: Colonial Identity, Frontier Violence, and the Persistence of Brazil's Eastern Indians, 1750–1830.* Stanford, CA: Stanford University Press, 2006.

Larson, Brooke, and Olivia Harris. *Ethnicity, Markets, and Migration in the Andes: At the Crossroads of History and Anthropology.* Durham, NC: Duke University Press, 1995.

Latour, Bruno. "Drawing Things Together." In *Representation in Scientific Practice,* edited by Michael Lynch and Steve Woolgar, 19–68. Cambrige, MA: MIT Press, 1990.

Latour, Bruno. *Reassembling the Social: An Introduction to Actor-Network-Theory.* Oxford: Oxford University Press, 2007.

Lenik, Stephan. "Carib as a Colonial Category: Comparing Ethnohistoric and Archaeological Evidence from Dominica, West Indies." *Ethnohistory* 59, no. 1 (2012): 79–107.

Lestringant, Frank. *Le Cannibale: Grandeur et Décadence.* Paris: Perrin, 1994.

Libro de acuerdos públicos y privados de la Real Audiencia de Santafé en el Nuevo Reino de Granada. Santafé de Bogotá: Colón, 1938.

Lippi, Ronald D., and Alejandra M. Gudiño. "Rompiendo los límites en el Área Intermedia: hacia una nueva síntesis macro-Chibcha." *Revista de Arqueología del Área Intermedia* 6 (2004): 13–26.

Llanos Chaparro, Juan Manuel, and Sandra Gutiérrez Abella. "Bajo el sol abrasador de las llanuras de Coyaima: aproximaciones a la historia prehispánica del valle del Magdalena tolimense." *Maguaré*, no. 20 (2006): 177–200.

Lockhart, James. *The Nahuas after the Conquest: A Social and Cultural History of the Indians of Central Mexico, Sixteenth through Eighteenth Centuries.* Stanford, CA: Stanford University Press, 1992.

Lockhart, James, and Stuart B. Schwartz. *Early Latin America: A History of Colonial Spanish America and Brazil.* Cambridge: Cambridge University Press, 1983.

Londoño, Ana María Gómez. *Muiscas: representaciones, cartografías y etnopolíticas de la memoria.* Bogotá: Pontificia Universidad Javeriana, 2005.

Londoño Laverde, Eduardo. "Los cacicazgos muisca a la llegada de los conquistadores españoles. El caso del Zacazgo o 'Reino' de Tunja." Universidad de los Andes, 1983.

Londoño Laverde, Eduardo. "Mantas muiscas: una tipología colonial." *Boletín del Museo del Oro* 27 (1990): 120–26.

Londoño Laverde, Eduardo, and Clara Inés Casilimas. "El proceso contra el cacique de Ubaque en 1563." *Boletín del Museo del Oro* 49 (2001): 49–101.

López, Mercedes. *Tiempos para rezar y tiempos para trabajar: la cristianización de las comunidades muiscas coloniales durante el siglo XVI, 1550-1600.* Bogotá: ICANH, 2001.

López Medel, Tomás. *De los tres elementos: tratado sobre la naturaleza y el hombre del Nuevo Mundo.* Madrid: Alianza Editorial, 1990.

López Medel, Tomás. "Visita a Natagaima." In *Relaciones y visitas a los Andes*, edited by Hermes Tovar Pinzón, 4:405–18. Bogotá: Colcultura, Instituto de Cultura Hispánica, 1995.

López Medel, Tomás. "Visita de 1560." In *No hay caciques ni señores*, edited by Hermes Tovar Pinzón, 21–120. Barcelona: Sendai, 1988.

López Medel, Tomás. *Visita de la gobernación de Popayán: libro de tributos (1558-1559).* Edited by Berta Ares Queija. Madrid: CSIC, 1989.

López-Portillo, José-Juan. *"Another Jerusalem": Political Legitimacy and Courtly Government in the Kingdom of New Spain (1535-1568).* Leiden: Brill, 2017.

Lucena Salmoral, Manuel. "Leyes para esclavos: El ordenamiento jurídico sobre la condición, tratamiento, defensa y represión de los esclavos en las colonias de la América española." Fundación Ignacio Larramendi, 2000.

Lucena Salmoral, Manuel. *Nuevo Reino de Granada: Real Audiencia y presidentes. Presidentes de capa y espada (1605-1628)*, vol. 3, bk. 1. Historia extensa de Colombia 3. Bogotá: Ediciones Lerner, 1965.

Magaloni Kerpel, Diana Isabel. *The Colors of the New World: Artists, Materials, and the Creation of the Florentine Codex.* Los Angeles: Getty Research Institute, 2014.

Martínez, María Elena. *Genealogical Fictions: Limpieza de Sangre, Religion, and Gender in Colonial Mexico.* Stanford, CA: Stanford University Press, 2011.

Martínez, María Luisa. "Los intentos de pacificación de los indios pijao (Nuevo Reino de Granada) a fines del siglo XVI." *Revista de Indias* 49, no. 186 (1989): 355–77.

Masters, Adrian. *We, the King: Creating Royal Legislation in the Sixteenth-Century Spanish New World*. Cambridge: Cambridge University Press, 2023.

Matallana, Susana. "Yanaconas: indios conquistadores y colonizadores del Nuevo Reino de Granada, siglo XVI." *Fronteras de la Historia* 18, no. 2 (2013): 21-45.

Matthew, Laura, and Michel R. Oudijk. *Indian Conquistadors: Indigenous Allies in the Conquest of Mesoamerica*. Norman: University of Oklahoma Press, 2007.

Mauss, Marcel. *The Gift: The Form and Reason for Exchange in Archaic Societies*. London: Routledge, 1990.

Maya Restrepo, Luz Adriana. "Demografía histórica de la trata por Cartagena." In *Geografía humana de Colombia*, vol. 6, *Los Afrocolombianos*, edited by Luz Adriana Maya Restrepo, 9-52. Bogotá: Instituto Colombiano de Cultura Hispánica, 1998.

Mayer, Enrique. *The Articulated Peasant: Household Economies in the Andes*. Boulder, CO: Westview, 2002.

Mazín, Oscar. *Las representaciones del poder en las sociedades hispánicas*. Mexico City: El Colegio de México, 2012.

McEnroe, Sean F. "Sites of Diplomacy, Violence, and Refuge: Topography and Negotiation in the Mountains of New Spain." *Americas* 69, no. 2 (2012): 179-202.

Mejía Pavony, Germán. *La ciudad de los conquistadores: 1536-1604*. Bogotá: Editorial Pontificia Universidad Javeriana, 2012.

Melo, Jorge Orlando. "¿Cuánta tierra necesita un indio para sobrevivir?" *Gaceta* 12, no. 3 (1977): 28-32.

Melo, Jorge Orlando. *Historia de Colombia: el establecimiento de la dominación española*. Bogotá: Presidencia de la República, 1996.

Melville, Elinor G. K. *A Plague of Sheep: Environmental Consequences of the Conquest of Mexico*. Cambridge: Cambridge University Press, 1994.

Méndez, Cecilia. "De indio a serrano: nociones de raza y geografía en el Perú (siglos XVIII-XXI)." *Histórica* 35, no. 1 (2011): 53-102.

Méndez, Cecilia. "Incas Sí, Indios No: Notes on Peruvian Creole Nationalism and Its Contemporary Crisis." *Journal of Latin American Studies* 28, no. 1 (1996): 197-225.

Mignolo, Walter. *The Darker Side of the Renaissance: Literacy, Territoriality, and Colonization*. Ann Arbor: University of Michigan Press, 1995.

Millán de Benavides, Carmen. *Epítome de la conquista del Nuevo Reino de Granada: la cosmografía española del siglo XVI y el conocimiento por cuestionario*. Bogotá: Centro Editorial Javeriano, 2001.

Mills, Kenneth. *Idolatry and Its Enemies: Colonial Andean Religion and Extirpation, 1640-1750*. Princeton, NJ: Princeton University Press, 2018.

Montenegro, Giovanna. "Conquistadors and Indians 'Fail' at Gift Exchange: An Analysis of Nikolaus Federmann's Indianische Historia (Haguenau, 1557)." *MLN* 132, no. 2 (2017): 272-90.

Montoya Guzmán, Juan David. "La fabricación del enemigo: los indios pijaos en el Nuevo Reino de Granada, 1562-1611." *Trashumante. Revista Americana de Historia Social*, no. 19 (2022): 96-117.

Mumford, Jeremy. "The Taki Onqoy and the Andean Nation: Sources and Interpretations." *Latin American Research Review* 33, no. 1 (1998): 150-65.

Mumford, Jeremy. *Vertical Empire: The General Resettlement of Indians in the Colonial Andes.* Durham, NC: Duke University Press, 2012.

Mundy, Barbara. *The Death of Aztec Tenochtitlan, the Life of Mexico City.* Austin: University of Texas Press, 2015.

Mundy, Barbara. *The Mapping of New Spain: Indigenous Cartography and the Maps of the Relaciones Geográficas.* Chicago: University of Chicago Press, 2000.

Mundy, Barbara. "No Longer Home: The Smellscape of Mexico City, 1500–1600." *Ethnohistory* 68, no. 1 (2021): 77–101.

Múnera, Alfonso. *El fracaso de la nación: región, clase y raza en el Caribe colombiano (1717–1821).* Bogotá: Banco de la República, El Ancora Editores, 1998.

Muñoz-Arbeláez, Santiago. "Contested Customs: Reinventing Indigenous Authority in Sixteenth-Century Ubaque." *Renaissance Quarterly* 77, no. 4 (2024).

Muñoz-Arbeláez, Santiago. *Costumbres en disputa. Los muiscas y el Imperio español en Ubaque, siglo XVI.* Bogotá: Ediciones Uniandes, 2015.

Muñoz-Arbeláez, Santiago. "Medir y amojonar. La cartografía y la producción del espacio colonial en la provincia de Santa Marta, siglo XVIII." *Historia Crítica* 34 (2007): 208–31.

Muñoz-Arbeláez, Santiago. "Vagabundos urbanos. Las instrucciones para administrar indios, mestizos y mulatos en Santafé de Bogotá a fines del siglo XVI." *Anuario de historia regional y de las fronteras* 22, no. 1 (2017): 225–33.

Muñoz-Arbeláez, Santiago, Santiago Paredes Cisneros, and Marta Herrera Angel. "Geographies of the Name: Naming Practices among the Muisca and Páez in the Audiencias of Santafé and Quito, Sixteenth and Seventeenth Centuries." *Journal of Latin American Geography* 11, no. 2 (2012): 91–115.

Muro Orejón, Antonio. *Lecciones de historia del derecho hispano-indiano.* Mexico City: M. A. Porrúa, 1989.

Muro Orejón, Antonio. *Las leyes nuevas de 1542–1543.* Seville: Escuela de Estudios Hispano-Americanos de Sevilla, 1961.

Murra, John V. *Formaciones económicas y políticas del mundo andino.* Lima: Instituto de Estudios Peruanos, 1975.

Myers, Joan, Marc Simmons, and Donna Pierce. *Santiago: Saint of Two Worlds.* Albuquerque: University of New Mexico Press, 1991.

Nesvig, Martin. "Mendicant Defense of Indigenous Rights: Beyond Las Casas and Vitoria." Paper presented at the Rethinking Space in Latin American History, Yale University, 2014.

Netz, Reviel. *Barbed Wire: An Ecology of Modernity.* Middletown, CT: Wesleyan University Press, 2004.

Nieto Olarte, Mauricio. *Orden natural y orden social: ciencia y política en el Semanario del Nuevo Reyno de Granada.* Bogotá: Universidad de los Andes, 2009.

Oliveros, Diana. "Coyaimas y Natagaimas." In *Geografía humana de Colombia*, vol. 4, bk. 2, *Región Andina Central*, edited by Instituto Colombiano de Cultura Hispánica, 151–94. Bogotá: Instituto Colombiano de Cultura Hispánica, 1996.

Ordóñez de Ceballos, Pedro. *Viage del mundo.* Luis Sanchez, 1614.

Ortega Ricaurte, Enrique. *Los inconquistables. La guerra de los Pijaos, 1602–1603.* Bogotá: Archivo Nacional de Colombia, Ministerio de Educación Nacional, 1949.

Ortiz, Fernando. *Contrapunteo cubano del tabaco y el azúcar*. Barcelona: Linkgua Historia, 2019.

Osorio, Alejandra. "The Copy as Original: The Presence of the Absent Spanish Habsburg King and Colonial Hybridity." *Renaissance Studies* 34, no. 4 (2020): 704–21.

Osorio, Alejandra. *Inventing Lima: Baroque Modernity in Peru's South Sea Metropolis*. New York: Palgrave Macmillan, 2008.

Ospina Rey, Sergio. "Doctrina y trabajo para los indios desconsolados. El traslado de los indios de Cogua a Zipaquirá y a Nemocón (1599–1602)." In *Archivos y documentos: transcripciones documentales sobre la Nueva Granada en el período colonial*, edited by Marta Herrera Angel and Catalina Garzón Zapata, 35–68. Bogotá: Ediciones Uniandes, 2011.

Owensby, Brian. *Empire of Law and Indian Justice in Colonial Mexico*. Stanford, CA: Stanford University Press, 2008.

Padrón, Ricardo. *The Indies of the Setting Sun: How Early Modern Spain Mapped the Far East as the Transpacific West*. Chicago: University of Chicago Press, 2020.

Paepe, Paul de, and Marianne Cardale de Schrimpff. "Resultados de un estudio petrológico de cerámicas del periodo Herrera provenientes de la Sabana de Bogotá y sus implicaciones arqueológicas." *Boletín del Museo del Oro* 20 (1990): 98–119.

Pagden, Anthony. *The Fall of Natural Man: The American Indian and the Origins of Comparative Ethnology*. Cambridge: Cambridge University Press, 1986.

Paredes Cisneros, Santiago. "Lengua pijao como lengua franca en las gobernaciones de Popayán y Neiva, siglos XVI–XVII." *Fronteras de la Historia* 23, no. 1 (2018): 40–66.

Paredes Cisneros, Santiago. "Nombres de una expansión territorial. El proceso de configuración del territorio Páez en las gobernaciones de Popayán y Neiva durante el período colonial." Universidad de los Andes, 2014.

Parsons, James J., and William M. Denevan. "Pre-Columbian Ridged Fields." *Scientific American* 217, no. 1 (1967): 92–100.

Patiño Contreras, Alejandro. "Actividades domésticas en una unidad residencial prehispánica de la Sabana de Bogotá (Colombia)." *Revista de Arqueología del Área Intermedia* 5 (2003): 137–65.

Pearsall, Sarah. "'Having Many Wives' in Two American Rebellions: The Politics of Households and the Radically Conservative." *American Historical Review* 118, no. 4 (2013): 1001–28.

Pennock, Caroline Dodds. "Aztecs Abroad? Uncovering the Early Indigenous Atlantic." *American Historical Review* 125, no. 3 (2020): 787–814.

Pennock, Caroline Dodds. *On Savage Shores: How Indigenous Americans Discovered Europe*. New York: Alfred A. Knopf, 2023.

Pérez de Arteaga, Melchor. "Relación del Nuevo Reino." In *No hay caciques ni señores*, edited by Hermes Tovar Pinzón, 121–44. Barcelona: Sendai Ediciones, 1988.

Peterson, Jeanette Favrot, and Kevin Terraciano, eds. *The Florentine Codex: An Encyclopedia of the Nahua World in Sixteenth-Century Mexico*. Austin: University of Texas Press, 2019.

Phelan, John Leddy. *The Kingdom of Quito in the Seventeenth Century: Bureaucratic Politics in the Spanish Empire*. Madison: University of Wisconsin Press, 1967.

Pineda, Roberto. "Malocas de terror y jaguares españoles: aspectos de la resistencia indígena del Cauca ante la invasión española en el siglo." *Revista de Antropología* 3, no. 2
(1987): 83–114.

Pineda, Roberto. "El rescate de los Tamas: análisis de un caso de desamparo en el siglo
XVII." *Revista Colombiana de Antropología* 23 (1980): 329–63.

Plazas, Clemencia. *El humano-murciélago en el Área Intermedia Norte. Distribución, formas y
simbolismo.* Bogotá: Instituto Colombiano de Antropología e Historia, 2018.

Polo y La Borda, Adolfo. *Global Servants of the Spanish King: Mobility and Cosmopolitan-
ism in the Early Modern Spanish Empire.* Cambridge: Cambridge University Press,
2024.

Polo y La Borda, Adolfo. "Los orígenes del corrregidor del Cusco y el establecimiento
de la soberanía del Rey. Una perspectiva atlántica." In *Gobernar el virreinato del Perú,
s. XVI-XVII: praxis político-jurisdiccional, redes de poder y usos de la información oficial,*
305-31. Madrid: Sindéresis, 2022.

Poma de Ayala, Felipe Guamán. *Nueva coronica y buen gobierno.* 3 vols. Mexico City:
Fondo de Cultura Económica, 2005.

Portuondo, María M. "Cosmography at the Casa, Consejo, and Corte during the
Century of Discovery." In *Science in the Spanish and Portuguese Empires, 1500-1800,* edited by Daniela Bleichmar, 57-77. Stanford, CA: Stanford University Press, 2009.

Pratt, Mary Louise. *Imperial Eyes: Travel Writing and Transculturation.* London: Routledge, 2008.

Premo, Bianca. "Meticulous Imprecision: Calculating Age in Colonial Spanish American Law." *American Historical Review* 125, no. 2 (2020): 396-406.

Price, Richard. *Maroon Societies: Rebel Slave Communities in the Americas.* Baltimore: Johns
Hopkins University Press, 1996.

Proctor, Robert, and Londa L. Schiebinger. *Agnotology: The Making and Unmaking of Ignorance.* Stanford, CA: Stanford University Press, 2008.

Puente Luna, José Carlos de la. *Andean Cosmopolitans: Seeking Justice and Reward at the
Spanish Royal Court.* Austin: University of Texas Press, 2018.

Puente, José Carlos de la. "Choquecasa va a la Audiencia: cronistas, litigantes y el debate sobre la autoría del Manuscrito Quechua de Huarochirí." *Histórica,* no. 1 (2015):
139-58.

Puente Luna, José Carlos de la. "Of Widows, Furrows, and Seed: New Perspectives on
Land and the Colonial Andean Commons." *Hispanic American Historical Review* 101,
no. 3 (2021): 375-407.

Puerto Alegre, Gaspar de. "Relación del Nuevo Reino de Granada." In *No hay caciques ni
señores,* edited by Hermes Tovar Pinzón, 145-62. Barcelona: Sendai, 1988.

Pulido Rull, Ana. *Mapping Indigenous Land: Native Land Grants in Colonial New Spain.*
Norman: University of Oklahoma Press, 2020.

Quiroga Zuluaga, Marcela. "El proceso de reducciones entre los pueblos muiscas de
Santafé durante los siglos XVI y XVII." *Historia Crítica,* no. 52 (2014): 179-203.

Rama, Angel. *La ciudad letrada.* Santiago: Tajamar Editores, 2004.

Ramírez, María Clemencia. *Frontera fluida entre Andes, piedemonte y selva: el caso del Valle de
Sibundoy, siglos XVI-XVIII.* Bogotá: Instituto Colombiano de Cultura Hispánica, 1996.

Ramírez de Jara, María Clemencia, and María Lucía Sotomayor. "Subregionalización del Altiplano Cundiboyacense: reflexiones metodológicas." *Revista Colombiana de Antropología* 16 (1986): 174–201.

Ramos, Gabriela. "Política eclesiástica y extirpación de la idolatría: discursos y silencios en torno al Taqui Onqoy." *Revista Andina*, no. 19 (1992): 147–69.

Ramos, Gabriela, and Yanna Yannakakis. *Indigenous Intellectuals: Knowledge, Power, and Colonial Culture in Mexico and the Andes*. Durham, NC: Duke University Press, 2014.

Rappaport, Joanne. *Cumbe Reborn: An Andean Ethnography of History*. Chicago: University of Chicago Press, 1994.

Rappaport, Joanne. *The Disappearing Mestizo: Configuring Difference in the Colonial New Kingdom of Granada*. Durham, NC: Duke University Press, 2014.

Rappaport, Joanne. *The Politics of Memory: Native Historical Interpretation in the Colombian Andes*. Cambridge: Cambridge University Press, 1990.

Rappaport, Joanne. "¿Quién es mestizo? Descifrando la mezcla racial en el Nuevo Reino de Granada, siglos XVI y XVII." *Varia Historia* 25, no. 41 (2009): 43–60.

Rappaport, Joanne, and Thomas Cummins. *Beyond the Lettered City: Indigenous Literacies in the Andes*. Durham, NC: Duke University Press, 2012.

Recopilación de leyes de los reinos de las Indias. 4 vols. Madrid: Julián de Paredes, 1681.

Reichel-Dolmatoff, Gerardo. "The Agricultural Basis of the Sub-Andean Chiefdoms of Colombia." *Antropologica Suplemento* 2 (1961): 83–100.

Reichel-Dolmatoff, Gerardo. *Orfebrería y chamanismo: un estudio iconográfico del Museo del Oro*. Bogotá: Villegas Editores, 2005.

Reichel-Dolmatoff, Gerardo. "Templos Kogi. Introducción al simbolismo y a la astronomía del espacio sagrado." *Revista Colombiana de Antropología* 19 (1975): 199–245.

Reichel Dolmatoff, Gerardo. "Toponimia del Tolima y Huila." *Revista del Instituto Etnológico Nacional* 2 (1945): 105–34.

Reis, João José, and Flávio dos Santos Gomes. *Liberdade por um fio: história dos quilombos no Brasil*. São Paulo: Companhia das Letras, 1996.

"Relación de las cosas notables que hay en el distrito de esta Audiencia de el Nuevo Reyno de Granada." In *Relaciones y Visitas a los Andes*, edited by Hermes Tovar Pinzón, 3:483–501. Bogotá: Colcultura, Instituto de Cultura Hispánica, 1995.

Restall, Matthew. "A History of the New Philology and the New Philology in History." *Latin American Research Review* 38, no. 1 (2003): 113–34.

Restall, Matthew. "The New Conquest History." *History Compass* 10, no. 2 (2012): 151–60.

Restall, Matthew. *Seven Myths of the Spanish Conquest*. New York: Oxford University Press, 2003.

Restrepo, Luis Fernando. *Un Nuevo Reino imaginado: las Elegías de Varones Ilustres de Indias de Juan de Castellanos*. Bogotá: Instituto Colombiano de Cultura Hispanica, 1999.

Ricard, Robert. *The Spiritual Conquest of Mexico: An Essay on the Apostolate and the Evangelizing Methods of the Mendicant Orders in New Spain, 1523–1572*. Berkeley: University of California Press, 1966.

Rodríguez, Pablo. *Testamentos indígenas de Santafé de Bogotá, siglos XVI–XVII*. Bogotá: Alcaldía Mayor de Bogotá, Instituto Distrital Cultura y Turismo, Observatorio de Cultura Urbana, 2002.

Rodríguez Baquero, Luis Enrique. *Encomienda y vida diaria entre los indios de Muzo, 1550-1620*. Bogotá: Instituto Colombiano de Cultura Hispánica, 1995.

Rodriguez Gallo, Lorena. "Água e paisagem agrícola entre os grupos pré-hispânicos da Sabana de Bogotá—Colômbia." PhD thesis, Universidade de São Paulo, 2015.

Rodríguez Gallo, Lorena. "La construcción del paisaje agrícola prehispánico en los Andes colombianos: el caso de la Sabana de Bogotá." *SPAL—Revista de Prehistoria y Arqueología* 28, no. 1 (2019): 193-215.

Rodríguez Gallo, Lorena. "La ley se acata pero no se cumple: territorio y resistencia entre los muiscas durante la primera fase de la colonización." In *Estado, sociedad y conflicto en la historia colombiana*, edited by Lorena Rodríguez Gallo et al., 19-49. Bogotá: Universidad Manuela Beltrán, 2018.

Rodríguez Gallo, Lorena. "Permanencias y transformaciones: el territorio muisca en la Sabana de Bogotá en la segunda mitad del siglo XVI." *Anuario Colombiano de Historia Social y de la Cultura* 48, no. 2 (2021): 363-98.

Rojas, Ulises. *El cacique de Turmequé y su época*. Tunja: Imprenta Departamental, 1965.

Roller, Heather. *Amazonian Routes: Indigenous Mobility and Colonial Communities in Northern Brazil*. Stanford, CA: Stanford University Press, 2016.

Rostworowski, María. *Recursos naturales renovables y pesca, siglos XVI y XVII: curacas y sucesiones Costa norte*. Lima: IEP Ediciones, 2018.

Ruiz Ibañez, José Javier. *Hispanofilia. Los tiempos de la hegemonía española*. Madrid: Fondo de Cultura Económica, 2022.

Ruiz Ibañez, José Javier, ed. *Las Indias Occidentales: procesos de incorporación territorial a las Monarquías Ibéricas (siglos XVI a XVIII)*. Mexico City: El Colegio de México, 2013.

Ruiz Rivera, Julián. "Andrés Pérez de Pisa, contador-ordenador del Tribunal de Cuentas y alcalde mayor de Las Lajas en Mariquita, 1606-1650." *Boletín de Historia y Antigüedades* 870 (2020): 13-52.

Ruiz Rivera, Julián. *La plata de Mariquita en el siglo XVII: mita y producción*. Tunja: Ediciones Nuestra América, 1979.

Russo, Alessandra. *The Untranslatable Image: A Mestizo History of the Arts in New Spain, 1500-1600*. Austin: University of Texas Press, 2014.

Safford, Frank, and Marco Palacios. *Colombia: Fragmented Land, Divided Society*. New York: Oxford University Press, 2002.

Sahlins, Marshall David. *Stone Age Economics*. Routledge, 1972.

Saignes, Thierry, and C. Salazar-Soler. *Borrachera y memoria: la experiencia de lo sagrado en los Andes*. Lima: Instituto Francés de Estudios Andinos, 1993.

Saito, Akira, and Claudia Rosas Lauro, eds. *Reducciones: la concentración forzada de las poblaciones indígenas en el Virreinato del Perú*. Lima: Pontificia Universidad Católica del Perú, Fondo Editorial, 2017.

Salcedo, Jaime. *Urbanismo hispano-americano siglos XVI, XVII y XVIII: el modelo urbano aplicado a la América española, su génesis y su desarrollo teórico y práctico*. Bogotá: Pontificia Universidad Javeriana, 1996.

Salcedo, Jaime. "Un vestigio del cercado del señor de Bogotá en la traza de Santafé." *Ensayos. Historia y teoría del arte* 20 (2011): 155-90.

Salomon, Frank. *The Cord Keepers: Khipus and Cultural Life in a Peruvian Village*. Durham, NC: Duke University Press, 2004.

Salomon, Frank. "How an Andean 'Writing without Words' Works." *Current Anthropology* 42, no. 1 (2001): 1–27.

Salomon, Frank. *Native Lords of Quito in the Age of the Incas: The Political Economy of North-Andean Chiefdoms*. Cambridge: Cambridge University Press, 1986.

Salomon, Frank, and Stuart B. Schwartz. "New Peoples and New Kinds of People: Adaptation, Readjustment, and Ethnogenesis in South American Indigenous Societies (Colonial Era)." In *The Cambridge History of the Native Peoples of the Americas*, vol. 3, *South America*, pt. 2, edited by Frank Salomon and Stuart B. Schwartz, 443–501. Cambridge: Cambridge University Press, 2008.

Salomon, Frank, Jorge Urioste, and Francisco de Avila. *The Huarochirí Manuscript: A Testament of Ancient and Colonial Andean Religion*. Austin: University of Texas Press, 1991.

Sauer, Carl. *The Early Spanish Main*. Berkeley: University of California Press, 1966.

Schmidt-Nowara, Christopher. *The Conquest of History: Spanish Colonialism and National Histories in the Nineteenth Century*. Pittsburgh: University of Pittsburgh Press, 2006.

Schroeder, Susan. *The Conquest All Over Again: Nahuas and Zapotecs Thinking, Writing, and Painting Spanish Colonialism*. Portland: Sussex Academic Press, 2010.

Schwartz, Stuart. *Blood and Boundaries: The Limits of Religious and Racial Exclusion in Early Modern Latin America*. Waltham, MA: Brandeis University Press, 2020.

Schwartz, Stuart. *Implicit Understandings: Observing, Reporting, and Reflecting on the Encounters between Europeans and Other Peoples in the Early Modern Era*. Cambridge: Cambridge University Press, 1994.

Schwartz, Stuart. "Indian Labor and New World Plantations: European Demands and Indian Responses in Northeastern Brazil." *American Historical Review* 83, no. 1 (1978): 43–79.

Schwartz, Stuart. *Slaves, Peasants, and Rebels: Reconsidering Brazilian Slavery*. Urbana: University of Illinois Press, 1992.

Schwartz, Stuart. *Sovereignty and Society in Colonial Brazil: The High Court of Bahia and Its Judges, 1609-1751*. Berkeley: University of California Press, 1973.

Scott, James. *The Art of Not Being Governed: An Anarchist History of Upland Southeast Asia*. New Haven, CT: Yale University Press, 2009.

Scott, James. *The Moral Economy of the Peasant: Rebellion and Subsistence in Southeast Asia*. New Haven, CT: Yale University Press, 1976.

Sellers-García, Sylvia. *Distance and Documents at the Spanish Empire's Periphery*. Stanford, CA: Stanford University Press, 2016.

Serulnikov, Sergio. *Subverting Colonial Authority: Challenges to Spanish Rule in Eighteenth-Century Southern Andes*. Durham, NC: Duke University Press, 2003.

Sharp, William Frederick. *Slavery on the Spanish Frontier: The Colombian Chocó, 1680-1810*. Norman: University of Oklahoma Press, 1976.

Sidbury, James, and Jorge Cañizares-Esguerra. "Mapping Ethnogenesis in the Early Modern Atlantic." *William and Mary Quarterly* 68, no. 2 (2011): 181–208.

Silverblatt, Irene. *Modern Inquisitions: Peru and the Colonial Origins of the Civilized World.* Durham, NC: Duke University Press, 2004.

Simón, Pedro. *Primera parte de las noticias historiales de las conquistas de tierra firme, en las Indias Occidentales.* Cuenca: Domingo de la Iglesia, 1626.

Skopyk, Bradley. *Colonial Cataclysms: Climate, Landscape, and Memory in Mexico's Little Ice Age.* Tucson: University of Arizona Press, 2020.

Sluyter, Andrew. "Colonialism and Landscape in the Americas: Material/Conceptual Transformations and Continuing Consequences." *Annals of the Association of American Geographers* 91, no. 2 (2001): 410–28.

Solano, Francisco de. *Cedulario de tierras: compilación de legislación agraria colonial, 1497–1820.* Mexico City: Universidad Nacional Autónoma de México, 1991.

Solano, Francisco de. "Regimen de tierras y su composición de 1591." *Revista de la facultad de derecho de México* 26, no. 101 (1976): 649–70.

Solórzano y Pereira, Juan. *Política Indiana.* 6 vols. Antwerp: Henrico y Cornelio Verdussen, 1703.

Staden, Hans. *Hans Staden's True History: An Account of Cannibal Captivity in Brazil.* Edited and translated by Neil L. Whitehead and Michael Harbsmeier. Durham, NC: Duke University Press, 2008.

Stern, Steve. "Feudalism, Capitalism, and the World-System in the Perspective of Latin America and the Caribbean." *American Historical Review* 93, no. 4 (1988): 829–72.

Stern, Steve. *Peru's Indian Peoples and the Challenge of Spanish Conquest: Huamanga to 1640.* Madison: University of Wisconsin Press, 1993.

Stoler, Ann Laura. *Along the Archival Grain: Epistemic Anxieties and Colonial Common Sense.* Princeton, NJ: Princeton University Press, 2009.

Stone, Erin Woodruff. *Captives of Conquest: Slavery in the Early Modern Spanish Caribbean.* Philadelphia: University of Pennsylvania Press, 2021.

Sztutman, Renato. *O profeta e o principal: a ação política ameríndia e seus personagens.* São Paulo: FAPESP, 2012.

Tardieu, Jean-Pierre. *Cimarrones de Panamá: La forja de una identidad afroamericana en el siglo XVI.* Frankfurt: Vervuert Verlagsgesellschaft, 2009.

Taussig, Michael. *Shamanism, Colonialism, and the Wild Man: A Study in Terror and Healing.* Chicago: University of Chicago Press, 1986.

Taylor, Alan. *The Divided Ground: Indians, Settlers and the Northern Borderland of the American Revolution.* New York: Alfred Knopf, 2006.

TePaske, John, and Kendall W. Brown. *A New World of Gold and Silver.* Leiden: Brill, 2010.

Terraciano, Kevin. *The Mixtecs of Colonial Oaxaca: Ñudzahui History, Sixteenth through Eighteenth Centuries.* Stanford, CA: Stanford University Press, 2001.

Therrien, Monika. "Indígenas y mercaderes: agentes en la consolidación de facciones en la ciudad de Santafé." In *Los muiscas en los siglos XVI y XVII: miradas desde la arqueología, la antropología y la historia*, edited by Jorge Gamboa, 169–210. Bogotá: Ediciones Uniandes, 2008.

Thompson, E. P. *Customs in Common.* London: Merlin, 1991.

Thompson, E. P. *The Making of the English Working Class.* New York: Vintage, 1966.

Todorov, Tzvetan. *La conquista de América: el problema del otro*. Mexico City: Siglo XXI Editores, 1983.

Torres, James Vladimir. "Trade in a Changing World: Gold, Silver, and Commodity Flows in the Northern Andes 1780–1840." PhD diss, Georgetown University, 2021. Archived August 10, 2024, at Archive.org. https://web.archive.org /web/20240811003046/https://repository.library.georgetown.edu/bitstream/handle /10822/1064630/Torres_georgetown_0076D_15090.pdf.

Tovar Pinzón, Hermes. *La estación del miedo o la desolación dispersa: el Caribe colombiano en el siglo XVI*. Bogotá: Editorial Ariel, 1997.

Tovar Pinzón, Hermes. "Estado actual de los estudios de demografía histórica en Colombia." *Anuario Colombiano de Historia Social y de la Cultura* 5 (1970): 65–140.

Trouillot, Michel-Rolph. "The Anthropology of the State in the Age of Globalization: Close Encounters of the Deceptive Kind." *Current Anthropology* 42, no. 1 (2001): 125–38.

Trouillot, Michel-Rolph. *Silencing the Past: Power and the Production of History*. Boston: Beacon, 1995.

Tutino, John. *Making a New World: Founding Capitalism in the Bajío and Spanish North America*. Durham, NC: Duke University Press, 2011.

Uribe, Simón. *Frontier Road: Power, History, and the Everyday State in the Colombian Amazon*. Hoboken, NJ: Wiley, 2017.

Urton, Gary. *Inka History in Knots: Reading Khipus as Primary Sources*. Austin: University of Texas Press, 2017.

Valdez, Francisco. *Agricultura ancestral, camellones y albarradas. Contexto social, usos y retos del pasado y del presente*. Quito: Ediciones Abya-Yala, 2006.

Valencia Villa, Carlos Eduardo. *Alma en boca y huesos en costal: una aproximación a los contrastes socio-económicos de la esclavitud: Santafé, Mariquita y Mompox, 1610–1660*. Bogotá: ICANH, 2003.

Valenzuela, Jaime. "Del Biobío al Magdalena: para una historia conectada de experiencias militares y fronteras imperiales, Domingo de Erazo (1592–1617)." In *Trascendiendo fronteras. Circulaciones y espacialidades en torno al mundo americano*, edited by Ricardo Arias Trujillo and Fernando Purcell, 1–34. Bogotá: Ediciones Uniandes, 2020.

Van Deusen, Nancy E. "Why Indigenous Slavery Continued in Spanish America after the New Laws of 1542." *Americas* 80, no. 3 (2023): 395–432.

Vanegas, Claudia Marcela. "'Por la fuerza y contra su voluntad.' Producción indígena, abasto de mantas y mita de la leña en los Andes centrales neogranadinos, siglos XVI–XVII." Universidad Nacional Autónoma de México, 2016.

Vanegas, Claudia. "Los textiles indígenas en la época colonial. Tributo, comercio e intercambio de mantas de algodón en los Andes centrales neogranadinos, siglos XVI y XVII." *Historia y Sociedad*, no. 35 (2018): 33–60.

Vargas, Laura. *Del pincel al papel: fuentes para el estudio de la pintura en el Nuevo Reino de Granada (1552–1813)*. Bogotá: Instituto Colombiano de Antropología e Historia, 2012.

Vargas Machuca, Bernardo de. *The Indian Militia and Description of the Indies*. Edited by Kris Lane. Durham, NC: Duke University Press, 2008.

Vargas Machuca, Bernardo de. *Milicia y descripcion de las Indias*. Madrid: Pedro Madrigal, 1599.

Velasco Murillo, Dana. "Borderlands in the Silver Mines of New Spain, 1540–1660." In *The Oxford Handbook of Borderlands of the Iberian World*, edited by Danna Levin Rojo and Cynthia Radding, 371–95. New York: Oxford University Press, 2019.

Velasco Murillo, Dana. *Urban Indians in a Silver City: Zacatecas, Mexico, 1546–1810*. Stanford, CA: Stanford University Press, 2017.

Velásquez, Rafael, and Víctor Castillo. *Los Yareguíes: resistencia y exterminio*. Bogotá: Corporación Aury Sará Marrugo, 2022.

Vignolo, Paolo. *Cannibali, giganti e selvaggi: creature mostruose del Nuovo Mondo*. Milan: Bruno Mondadori, 2009.

Vilches, Elvira. "Business Tools and Outlooks: The Culture of Calculation in the Iberian Atlantic." *Journal for Early Modern Cultural Studies* 19, no. 2 (2019): 16–51.

Villamarín, Juan. "Encomenderos and Indians in the Formation of Society in the Sabana de Bogotá, Colombia, 1557 to 1740." Brandeis University, 1972.

Villamarín, Juan, and Judith Villamarín. "Kinship and Inheritance among the Sabana de Bogotá Chibcha at the Time of Spanish Conquest." *Ethnology* 14, no. 2 (1975): 173–79.

Viveiros de Castro, Eduardo. "Cosmological Deixis and Amerindian Perspectivism." *Journal of the Royal Anthropological Institute* 4, no. 3 (1998): 469–88.

Viveiros de Castro, Eduardo. *From the Enemy's Point of View: Humanity and Divinity in an Amazonian Society*. Chicago: University of Chicago Press, 1992.

Warsh, Molly. *American Baroque: Pearls and the Nature of Empire, 1492–1700*. Chapel Hill: University of North Carolina Press, 2018.

Weber, David. *Bárbaros: Spaniards and Their Savages in the Age of Enlightenment*. New Haven, CT: Yale University Press, 2005.

Weiner, Annette. *Inalienable Possessions: The Paradox of Keeping-while-Giving*. Berkeley: University of California Press, 1992.

West, Robert. *Colonial Placer Mining in Colombia*. Baton Rouge: Louisiana State University Press, 1952.

West, Robert. *The Pacific Lowlands of Colombia: A Negroid Area of the American Tropics*. Baton Rouge: Louisiana State University Press, 1957.

Wheat, David. *Atlantic Africa and the Spanish Caribbean, 1570–1640*. Chapel Hill: University of North Carolina Press, 2016.

White, Richard. *The Middle Ground: Indians, Empires, and Republics in the Great Lakes Region, 1650–1815*. Cambridge: Cambridge University Press, 1991.

Whitehead, Neil. *Dark Shamans: Kanaimà and the Poetics of Violent Death*. Durham, NC: Duke University Press, 2002.

Whitehead, Neil. "Native American Cultures along the Atlantic Littoral of South America, 1499–1650." *Proceedings of the British Academy* 81 (1993): 197–231.

Whitehead, Neil. "Native Peoples Confront Colonial Regimes in North Eastern South America." In *The Cambridge History of the Native Peoples of the Americas*, vol. 3, *South America*, edited by Frank Salomon and Stuart B. Schwartz, 382–442. Cambridge: Cambridge University Press, 2008.

Yannakakis, Yanna. "Allies or Servants? The Journey of Indian Conquistadors in the Lienzo of Analco." *Ethnohistory* 58, no. 4 (2011): 653–82.

Yannakakis, Yanna. "Costumbre: A Language of Negotiation in Eighteenth-Century Oaxaca." In *Negotiation within Domination: New Spain's Indian Pueblos Confront the Spanish State*, edited by Ethelia Ruiz Medrano and Susan Kellogg, 137–71. Boulder: University Press of Colorado, 2010.

Yannakakis, Yanna. *Since Time Immemorial: Native Custom and Law in Colonial Mexico.* Durham, NC: Duke University Press, 2023.

Yazdani, Kaveh, and Dilip Menon, eds. *Capitalisms: Towards a Global History.* Delhi: Oxford University Press, 2020.

Zalamea, Patricia. "The Drawings of the Cacique de Turmequé: Reclaiming Justice in a Colonial Context." *Miradas—Zeitschrift für Kunst- und Kulturgeschichte der Amérikas und der iberischen Halbinsel* 7 (2023): 64–78.

INDEX

Africa, 157; African descendants, 2, 218, 220, 225; African descendants as encomienda managers, 13; African descendants as interpreters, 13; and boga system, 6; and enslaved Africans, 13-16, 192-96, 225-26, 238-46; free Blacks, 240; and mantas, 97; and *negros de ley*, 238; petitions, 16, 57; as piezas or pieces, 238, 243; in port cities, 9. *See also* race; slavery

agriculture, 34, 64, 118, 198-200; agricultural terraces or raised beds, 64, 199, 201-3, 274n6, 274n8; and monocrop plantations, 203; polyculture farming, 202; seed crops, 118; and war, 230-32. *See also* cattle; foodstuff; trade

Aguirre, Lope de, 179, 180

Andean utopia. *See* utopia

Anserma, 97

anthropophagy: vs. cannibalism, 114-15, 135, 227, 247, 250; and Christianity, 132-40; ritual, 127; views on, 269-70n73

anticolonialism: coalitions, 227, 252; as a system, 110-17; project of, 2, 13, 17-18, 123-32, 140, 247; ritual of, 134. *See also* freedom; Pijao peoples

Antioquia, 97, 194

archives: on anthropophagy, 115-16, 137; archiving as royal mandate, 56-58; diversity of, 17; imperial, 84, 101, 110-11, 189; and Indigenous history, 248, 257n42; and methodology, 15, 17; and violence, 16. *See also* textual technologies

Argentina, 9, 97

Atahualpa, 22, 26, 31

Atahualpa, Alonso de, 145, 187

audiencia: and accounting, 196, 222, 236-39, 241-43, 245; y Cancillería Real, 52-53; de los Confines (or Guatemala and Nicaragua), 49, 60; Antonio González (president); and the governorship of Venezuela, 249; inspection to, 162-65, 173-75; as an institution, 51-58, 143, 206, 245; of Lima, 51, 164; and magistrates as cipas, 4, 57, 74-75; oidores, 74, 143; of Panamá, 51, 60, 190, 203, 205, 222, 227, 235; of Quito, 31, 130, 187, 229, 249; of Santo Domingo, 52, 159; visitas, 60, 67-75, 172-74, 219, 240; visitador Luis Enríquez, 92, 207, 211, 223-24; visitador Miguel de Ibarra, 92-93, 101, 206-11, 213, 216, 219-22. *See also* Audiencia of Santa Fe; institutions; justice; law; officials

Audiencia of Santa Fe: centrality of, 4-6; and chaos, 164-65; continuity, 60; and documents, 72-74; and evangelization, 171-73; inspections on, 173-75; jurisdiction of, 31, 107-8, 130, 144-48; magistrates of, 50, 58, 172; presidency of, 140, 223-24; *Relation of the Provisions and Royal Degrees of His Majesty Kept at the Audiencia of the New Kingdom of Granada*, 56-57; surveys for, 67-68

autonomy: loss of Indigenous, 2, 13, 105, 190, 196, 200, 221; of officials, 52. *See also* economic governance

Cocuy, 31, 42

Codazzi, Agustín, 249

coins. *See* currency. *See also* textual technologies

cold lands, 3–8, 24, 32–44, 119–20, 147, 173; classification of the region, 255n6; commercial networks with hot lands, 98; economies of, 195–96; laborers from, 17–18; people and, 249–51; visitas of the, 240; and wealth, 44. *See also* geography

Colombia, 1, 17, 82, 132, 137, 145, 203, 214, 251; Republic of, 249

colonialism: in Caribbean territories, 29; and cities, 43; and discourse, 24, 140; expansion of, 103, 136; and humanism, 50–51; and language of colonies, 256n28; and lettered republicans, 251; and markets, 97; modern, 11, 14, 19; Spanish, 8–14, 40, 66, 75, 111, 120–24, 140, 192–93, 240; and violence, 151. *See also* anticolonialism; audiencia; Catholicism

Comanche people, 130, 248

conducciones (labor drafts). *See* mining

conquest, 17, 23–24, 42–45, 52, 78; and archives, 248; and capitulaciones, 227; expeditions, 25–40, 44, 69, 104, 121, 179, 259n26; and gold, 104; methods of, 228; Native people as conquistadors, 27, 259n24; right of, 22, 171

Consejo Indio de las Indias or Indigenous Council of the Indies, 252. *See also* Council of the Indies

contraband trade, 9, 229–30, 238

copper, 217

Cortés, Hernán, 23, 26, 103, 227

Cosa, Juan de la, 29

cotton: fabric, 63, 85, 88, 247; idols of, 171; industry of, 3–4; raw, 90, 92, 98, 216; in Subachoque, 93–94; and trade, 34–35, 100–101. *See also* mantas; textiles

Council of the Indies, 9, 53, 60, 72, 159–62, 189; and expeditions, 31; and questionnaires, 55–56; standardization of the, 51; and wealth, 200. *See also* Consejo Indio de las Indias or Indigenous Council of the Indies; institutions

Covarrubias, Sebastián de, 5

Cundinamarca, 25, 31, 251

currency: coins, 198–99, 201, 217, 251; commutation, 101–2; lack of liquidity, 242; mantas as, 82, 90, 98–99; minted coins, 82, 109, 198–99, 217–18, 247; money, 35, 37, 86, 217–18, 243; real de a ocho or Spanish dollar, 104. *See also* mantas; taxes

Cuzco, 57, 64

decentralization, 3, 4, 10, 35–37, 64, 155, 245, 248; and economic space, 90; and mantas, 83, 85–86; peace and, 129

Díez de Armendáriz, Miguel, 53, 59

dispossession, 14, 196–99, 205–8, 213–14, 226, 247–50. *See also* enclosure; land; landscape

Drake, Francis, 230

Duitama, 86, 176

economic governance, 13, 193, 195, 201, 212–14, 245–49; arbitrios, 237; creation of imperial economy, 84–86, 97, 103–9, 193, 216–26; gift economy, 85, 95; Indigenous economy, 37, 69, 94; parasitic economy, 91, 95, 139, 221; pastoralist economy, 215; plantation economy, 9; tribute system, 5–15, 23, 39, 59, 76, 95–104, 166, 171–82. *See also* encomienda; mantas; trade

economic space: Andean, 9, 97, 99; in the New Kingdom, 9–10, 84, 90, 96–99

El Dorado, 26, 44, 179, 192

emeralds, 35, 83, 96, 191, 229; idols adorned with, 171; in Middle East, 10; specialized markets of, 86; Tunja, 32

empire: building of, 1, 2, 38, 44, 111, 140–59, 243–52; agents of the, 27; definition of, 4–15; Inca, 25; Indigenous, 10; legibility of, 71–75; morality of, 47–48; and writing, 55, 58

enclosure: of indigenous economies, 18, 195, 198–222, 226, 247, 250; as palisade, 63. *See also* dispossession; landscape

encomienda, 2, 42, 59, 69–72, 82–83, 133, 260n56; and colonialism, 120; vs. corregimiento, 190; decline of, 189, 213; definition of, 38–39; and distribution of Indigenous cacicazgos, 52–53; and encomenderos, 21–23, 45, 51–53, 61–62, 65, 91–104; Gonzalo García Zorro (encomendero), 95; and mantas, 89–92, 97–98; and Pijao peoples, 126; reforms, 199–200; and rituals, 38–39; and visits, 67–69. *See also* institutions; mantas; tribute

epidemics: chickenpox, 66; smallpox, 66, 232

capitalism, 201; in statistics, 72–73; villages for, 2, 15, 120, 216–20; as wretched people (*personae miserabilis*), 14, 23, 149, 166–68, 187, 243. *See also* race

Intermediate Area, 10, 255–56n6

institutions: cabildos, 40, 61, 202, 214; capitulaciones , 227–29; Casa de Contratación, 257n29; governorships, x, 5, 31, 51, 229; infrastructure of governance, 2, 12, 24, 76; rescate, 30; town councils, 30, 45, 51–52, 65, 198, 263n49; viceroyalties, 2–3, 9, 51, 217, 237, 249. *See also* audiencia; Catholicism; Council of the Indies

Isabella, Queen, 61

Jiménez de Quesada, Gonzalo, 22–23, 25–26, 28–32, 52, 227; La Grita, 28

justice: concept of, 11, 75–76, 110–11, 163, 205, 245–48; and caciques, 65; and colonialism, 14; divine, 48, 54; doctrine of restoration, 148; empire of "justice," 244; and encomiendas, 51–52; and freedom, 3, 105, 110; lawyers, 47, 55, 214; lawmaking, 24, 58, 155; litigations, 13, 24, 101, 111, 158, 213, 248; López Medel's imaginary trial, 48; monarchical, 16; petitioning system, 24, 51–55, 58, 143–48, 216; pre-Hispanic Indigenous, 65; procedures, 23–24, 45, 68. *See also* audiencia; law

kingdom: definition of, 1–2, 3–11, 13, 19, 248–49; failure of, 51, 73–75; foundation of, 24, 27; threat to the, 22; (un)making of, 10–15, 71–76, 212–13, 243, 245–52; and visual regimes, 17, 188

labor: and age, 70; alquiler general or general lease of, 209; forced, 68, 139, 166, 178; gendered, 71, 210; and geography, 195; jornaleros or day laborers, 200, 236, 239; mobile laborers, 222, 226, 235–36; and slavery, 13; system, 14, 92, 101, 103–5, 198–226, 246–50; wage, 18, 96, 193, 210, 217, 247; wages for taxes, 200–201, 237. *See also* economic governance; encomienda; mining; slavery

Lake Guatavita, 191–92

land: 1590 reforms, 199–213; agregaciones or aggregations, 200, 211; Castilla del oro, 30; composiciones de tierras or land title validation, 200, 204–8, 211–14, 222, 234, 275n23;

corregidor de naturales, 200, 208; ejidos or shared lands, 206; haciendas or individual estates, 98, 203, 206, 217, 222; realengos or royal grounds, 206–7; resguardos or communal lands, 201, 203, 206–8, 212–21, 234, 252; Tierra Firme or mainland, 25, 30; use of fences in, 214. *See also* dispossession; enclosure; landscape; maps

landscape: Christian, 65; and control, 12, 18; and fences, 64, 202, 214, 276n53; imperial, 58, 62–64, 75–76, 230; Indigenous, 26–27, 37, 41–42, 120, 131–34, 138, 146, 192–224; and republicans, 251–52; and space, 6, 23–24, 40, 66, 120; visibility, 43; war through, 230. *See also* geography; maps

language: Arawak, 38, 150; and evangelization, 15, 76, 155–56, 211–12, 276n48; Indigenous languages, 1, 13, 15, 69, 155–57, 245, 248; Latin, 12, 38; lengua general or lingua franca, 3, 132, 212, 235, 248; Nahuatl, 3, 10, 188; Nasa, 123, 128; Quechua, 3, 10, 57, 79, 188, 195, 248; Spanish, 56, 257n42; Spanish dictionary, 5; Spanish grammar, 49; Spanish pronunciation, 38. *See also* Carib linguistic family; Catholicism; Chibcha linguistic family; Muisca people; Pijao peoples

La Palma, 42, 240

Latin. *See* language

law: death penalty, 60, 183, 262n35; evangelic, 95; lawsuits, 23, 161, 195, 204, 213; legal governance or procedures, 23, 56, 68, 74, 141, 200; natural, 48, 59, 65, 139; Spanish, 29, 144–45, 162, 181, 188–89. *See also* justice; New Laws of 1542

Leyes nuevas de 1542. See New Laws of 1542

livestock, 92, 96, 198–99, 203–4, 210, 214–19; bulls, 197, 199; chicken, 92, 212, 217–18; cows, 15, 66, 199–200; furs, 63, 65, 96; hens, 66, 100; horses, 27, 39, 130, 199, 215, 218; and pastoralism, 199, 202, 213, 217; pigs, 66, 199–200, 203–4, 217; sheep, 15, 66, 100, 199–200, 217

López de Mesa, Luis, 249

López Medel, Tomás, 18, 24; arrival to Santa Fe, 58–62; *De los tres elementos* or *On the Three Elements*, 47–48, 76; descriptions, 36–37; and failure of the kingdom, 73–76, 89; and reducciones, 65; training, 49; and tributes, 82, 92, 102; and violence, 65, 169; as visitador, 67–73, 119, 147, 243

officials: accountants, 59, 84, 99, 172–73, 196, 234–42; alferez, 206; alguaciles or bailiffs, 155, 206; caciques, ix, 15, 34–38, 41, 45, 61–71, 81–91, 218; capa y espada magistrates, 228; corregidores, 54, 168–69, 208–16, 222, 276n36; escribanos or scribes, 15–16, 28, 55–58, 71, 84, 205, 252; lawyers, 47, 55, 214; lenguas or interpreters/translators, 15–21, 41, 69, 95, 125, 173, 247, 252; judges, 38, 69, 153, 174; notary publics, 55–58, 69, 252; Andrés Pérez de Pisa, 234–37; police squads, 69; protectores de indios, 49, 59, 168, 206; regidores, 206; Juan de Sologuren, 237–42; tax collectors, 15, 69, 235, 240; togados, 228; visitadores or inspectors, 60, 67–75, 91–102, 165–89, 194–95, 206–21, 240–46, 263n68. *See also* audiencia; institutions; Torre, Diego de la

Paipa, 73, 240
Pamplona, 42, 69, 97, 176, 240
Panama, 30, 260n54
paper: administration of, 55–58; flows of, 2, 16, 55, 58, 76, 105, 143; institutions and, 50–51; and justice, 2, 13; and titles, 200–201, 205, 207, 213–16; use of, 16, 58; and visits, 67–76; weapons, 13, 111. *See also* textual technologies
pax Hispanica, 26, 43
Pérez de Arteaga, Melchor, 30, 96
Pérez de Quesada, Hernán, 22–23, 44
Peru: access to, 241; communication with, 76; composiciones, 207; conquest of, 120, 172, 179; discussions on mestizo clerics, 157; Indigenous people from, 31; Lima, 2, 108, 237, 250; road to, 6, 26; and Philip II, 188–89; resettlement projects in, 61; spatial system, 10; and textiles, 79; viceroyalty of, 2–3, 9, 97, 130, 174, 217. *See also* Inca empire; peruleros
peruleros, 59–60, 67, 264n48
Philip II: and advice on good government, 2, 18, 103, 111, 143–45; ban on mestizos, 154–55, 157–74; bankruptcy, 236–37, 243; and Lake Guatavita, 191; and land titles, 206; and Lope de Aguirre, 179; and maps, 186; and mining, 191–94; and Orozco's accusations against Torre, 176; and questionnaires, 263n57. *See also* Torre, Diego de la
Philip III, 104, 228; reforms, 237

Philip IV, 242
Philip V, 249
Pijao peoples, 107–40, 224–43, 251; alliances with Paéz (Nasa) people, 125, 128–29; Amoyá, 129, 268n51; campaign against, 222; captive-taking, 127; coalition, 17–18, 125, 137, 164, 194, 224–43, 247–48; and gender, 131–32; history of the name, 113–14, 116, 118, 128–29, 252, 268n48; and isolation from Peru, 188; juntas, 129; and land, 2; language of, 118; lingua franca, 132; as a lowland group, 38; material culture, 109, 131; Bernardino de Mujica Guevara , 227; poetics of violence, 133–38; Ucoche's longhouse, 131. *See also* anthropophagy; anticolonialism; freedom
Pizarro, Francisco, 22–23, 25–26, 31, 40, 227
Popayán, x, 4–6, 108, 116, 241–43; according to historians, 82; general visit to, 58; governorship of, 14, 31, 67, 73–76, 125, 130–33, 231–32; and mantas, 93–97; and Pijao peoples, 229, 234; province of, 67–68; and salt, 36; sedition in, 123
Potosí, 9, 97, 99, 104, 193, 226, 228, 241–42
Prieto de Orellana, Juan, 165, 172, 176–77, 183–84, 189. *See also* audiencia

Quechua. *See* language
Quechua linguistic family, Ingas, 118
Quindío, 107, 119
Quintín Lame, Manuel, 252
Quito, 31, 40, 57, 120, 187, 232, 241, 249; bishopric of, 5; and communications, 6, 76, 108; as imperial center, 2; map of, 170; and Popayán, 67; textile production in, 9, 97

race: Alonso de Silva (case of), 145, 150–51, 157; early modern notions of, 11–15; Gonzalo García Zorro (case of), 158–59; and libres de todos los colores or "free people of all colors," 220–21; Lorenzo Requero (case of), 218–20, 277n76; and mestizos, 12, 96, 110, 144–45, 151, 154–58, 174, 233; and morenos, 233, 240; and mulatos, 12, 209, 233, 236, 240; and pardos, 240; and zambos, 12. *See also* Africa; indio; Torre, Diego de la
reading, 54–55; and literacy, 32, 214, 264n13; practices, 214

rebellions: accusation on Diego de la Torre, 145, 163, 183–84, 187; encomenderos and, 39; in Inca domains, 117; information on, 71; Muisca, 22; in Peru in 1540s, 42; and peruleros, 60, 67; and Pijao peoples, 126, 128; possibilities of, 14–15; Saguanmachica and, 33; and slavery, 238; textual technologies and, 246

reducciones or resettlement plans, 61–62, 65–66, 169, 202

reducir, 12, 60, 245

Reyes, Rafael, 249–50

Rio de la Plata, 9, 248

ritual: anthropophagy, 127, 133, 137; borracheras as, 87, 94–95, 150, 156, 269n54; bureaucratic, 38; Indigenous, 42, 79, 94, 139, 172; imperial rule as, 54; languages, 149–50

Rodríguez Freyle, Juan, 33, 41

Royal decree, 55, 159–61, 206

Sahagún, Bernandino de, 188

Saldaña River, 114, 118, 121–28, 131–32, 135, 227; Cacataima people, 124, 129; Doima people, 124. *See also* Pijao peoples

salt, 3, 34–37, 86, 92–98, 105, 211, 221, 247; cakes, 28, 35, 37; ceramic vessels for, 35–36, 211; along the Magdalena River, 28–29; mines, 210. *See also* trade

Samper, José María, 249

Santa Fe de Bogotá, 2, 22, 38–42, 52–57, 105, 130, 223; Bogotá, 31–32, 41–45, 64, 86, 102, 146, 172, 197; elites, 250; jail, 47; as lettered city, 55; name changing, 251; painting of, 198–205; partidos, 62; Teusaquillo, 41; Diego de la Torre's map of, 169–70. *See also* Bogotá; Muyquyta

Santa María de la Antigua del Darién, 30

Santa Marta, 5, 28, 30–31, 73

Santiago de Cuba, city of, 61

Santo Domingo, city of, 61, 159

San Vicente de Páez, 123

Seville, 2, 6, 57, 145, 159, 163, 185, 187

Silver, 9, 23. *See also* Mariquita; mining

Simón, Pedro, 33

Sioux people, 130

slavery, African, 239; forced Indigenous labor, 68, 194–95, 205, 239, 244; freedom as absence of, 181; and governance, 257n39; Indigenous slavery, 29–30, 114, 133, 168, 232, 234; as a mili-

tary principle, 232; Muisca people and, 236; in the New Kingdom of Granada, 13

Sogamoso, 86, 176, 179

Spanish. *See* language

state: and archiving, 58; avoidance of (and statelessness), 8, 118; and early modern politics, 11–12, 19, 256–57n29, 257n30; in the Intermediate Area, 4, 255–56n6; nation-state, 249–51; neo-Inca, 115; people's experience of, 69; and topography, 6–8; and violence, 44

surveillance: and Christianity, 172, 211–12; and inspections, 71, 245; officials and, 23–24, 92; and quadrilinear towns, 60, 74, 194; routines of, 24; in Torre's drawing, 185. *See also* paper technologies; reducciones

taxes, 15, 70–72, 90, 201, 206, 222, 243; alcabalas, 206; almonedas or auctions, 98–99; quinto real or royal fifth, 91, 102, 168, 172, 235; requinto, 211–12, 218, 240, 279n42; reservados, 70; tasa or rate, 60, 82; tithes, 95, 201, 209, 212; tributo or tribute, 82, 87. *See also* mantas

Tenochtitlan, 26, 64, 66

textiles: asymmetric reciprocity, 88–89; boi, 79, 90; categories for natives according to clothing, 48; and dressing, 264n1; fabric as metaphor, 15, 19, 45, 96–97, 99, 104–5, 246, 252; as goods, 3–5, 9, 77–105, 144–53, 200, 221, 247–48; hammocks, 92; khipus, 79, 264n6; and language, 79, 89; and prestige, 33–34, 39; and quca, 64; tapestries, 79; vests, 233; wool, 88, 100, 217. *See also* mantas

textual technologies, 16, 72, 198, 200–201, 245–46, 249; account books, 17, 217–18, 235, 238–39; censuses, 70–71, 140, 200; instructions, 56, 147, 155–56, 181–82, 200, 209–18; inventories, 69; ledgers, 217–18; letters, 16, 53–62, 70–76, 102–14, 151, 176–200, 239; lists, 16, 59, 67–76, 89, 91, 98, 195, 240; memorials, 58, 165–66, 186; money as, 200; printing press in the New Kingdom of Granada, 55; questionnaires, 55, 67, 70, 87, 169; tables, 56, 71–74; templates, 55, 69, 71; textual strategies, 56; titles, 17, 200, 208. *See also* audiencia; currency; maps; paper; Torre, Diego de la

tierra caliente. *See* hot lands

tierra fría. *See* cold lands

www.ingramcontent.com/pod-product-compliance
Lightning Source LLC
Chambersburg PA
CBHW032344280326
41935CB00008B/439